For Ken

Language in Thinking

Selected Readings

Edited by Parveen Adams

Penguin Books

Penguin Books Ltd, Harmondsworth,
Middlesex, England
Penguin Books Inc., 7110 Ambassador Road,
Baltimore, Md 21207, USA
Penguin Books Australia Ltd,
Ringwood, Victoria, Australia

First published 1972
This selection copyright © Parveen Adams, 1972
Introduction and notes copyright © Parveen Adams, 1972

Made and printed in Great Britain by
Richard Clay (The Chaucer Press) Ltd, Bungay, Suffolk
Set in Monotype Times

Contents

Introduction

The way in which language relates to thinking has long been of interest to philosophers, linguists, anthropologists and psychologists. For these thinkers language was the essential instrument determining the content and perhaps even the structure of thought.

More recently, a major theory of child development has fundamentally reoriented our conceptualization of the relation between language and thinking. Language no longer serves as an explanatory principle. The structures of thought are seen to be derived from the child's actions. It is the child's activities that constitute thinking, and structures of thinking prefigure the skills which are utilized later in language learning. Language plays a supportive rather than a determining role in thinking.

This view does not stand uncontested today, however. A major contemporary linguist holds that the rules of language are part of the conceptual equipment that the learner brings to the language-learning task. Earlier learning is not seen to have contributed to the growth of this conceptual apparatus. Linguistic rules are innate. The contrast between this view and the developmental position outlined above is clear.[1]

The material in this book centres on the major issues outlined above. Different theoretical positions together with a small selection of relevant experimental work are presented in the middle sections of the book.

The articles in Part One are chosen with a view to dislodging from his position, any reader who is in the grip of the widespread tendency to unquestioningly regard all conceptual development as language-linked if not language-determined. The conceptual achievements of deaf children with partial language should raise

1. In note 15 of Chomsky's article in the present collection (see p. 354), it is admitted that language acquisition is not an instantaneous process. Though he might allow a series of pre-structures and structures, he would still be at variance with the epistemological position taken by the developmental theory mentioned above. This latter views language as part of a larger cognitive activity and not as an autonomous 'objective of knowledge'.

many questions about the kind of facilitation language provides. Some of these articles are not well known, and all merit reprinting. The interested reader is referred to a theoretical model of the influence of language on classification, Furth and Milgram (1965).

Part Two consists of two articles, each of which concentrates on a different aspect of language acquisition. The first is a study of the acquisition of relational terms by young children. What does a young child understand by the terms 'more' and 'less'? Certainly his behaviour differs strikingly from that of an adult asked to add more to a smaller or a larger pile of items. The word has no power of itself, to convey the adult meaning. Whatever factors affect the gradual acquisition of this meaning, they do not appear to be wholly linguistic. Language learning may itself be like learning other conceptual skills. Is language learning akin to learning without language?

The second article, however, hypothesizes an innate set of cognitive capacities specific to language. This work on the acquisition of the negative in Japanese children provides comparative data pertinent to the problem of linguistic universals.

An excellent example of recent developments in the study of language acquisition is to be found in Brown and Bellugi (1964).

Part Three presents three major theoretical positions on the relation between language and thought. The first holds that language structures thought. The second subscribes to a very nearly opposite view. The third acknowledges a pre-intellectual stage in speech development and a pre-linguistic stage in thought development, but these lines of development soon cross, 'whereupon thought becomes verbal and speech rational'. Since acceptance of one or other position directs the choice of future research work, it is important that the problem be correctly posed. A disproportionate part of this introduction is therefore devoted to the task of explication. I shall first roughly define the three positions and then introduce them in somewhat greater detail.

The first isolates lexical and syntactic aspects of language and endeavours to demonstrate that these aspects broadly determine the patterns of thought. For thinkers of this tradition, what is determined is a general manner of thinking, including the way space and time are construed. The foremost exponent of this approach is the anthropologist and linguist B. L. Whorf.

The second approach to language and thought considers how the mastering of non-linguistic cognitive skills affects the acquisition of language skills. If the child can classify groups of objects in various ways, before he can classify them through the manipulation of words corresponding to those objects, then cognitive growth cannot be accounted for in terms of prior linguistic development. This is the position taken by Piaget, a major theorist of cognitive growth. The Piagetian theory of intellectual development is highly complex, consisting of many intricately related parts. The reader is therefore well advised not to rely on the article in this volume, but also to refer to his other works.

The third approach to language and thought concerns itself with verbal thought – a merging of the lines of development of pre-linguistic thought and pre-intellectual speech. Verbal thought progresses through a number of stages. At first, the child has to pronounce words to understand them, but soon he moves toward the ability to 'think words'. Once he has the ability to detach meaning from explicit pronunciation, he has inner speech. Words in inner speech have special characteristics. Are these words indispensable to the formation of new thoughts? This area has been most interestingly explored by the Russian psychologist L. S. Vygotsky. His chapter on 'The Genetic Roots of Thought and Speech' (Vygotsky, 1962), which is not included in this volume, is recommended to those sympathetic to this approach.

To return now to the first approach, it is centrally concerned with the question of how language can affect the manner in which we construe the world. It may seem that if all languages refer to the same reality, and if one language can be translated into another, then speakers of all languages must construe the world in the same way. But how do we determine either the meaning of the term 'the same reality' or of the proposition that languages are fully translatable? The problems of translatability, currently debated in philosophical and linguistic circles, are far from simple. Equally complex is the problem of the relation between language and reality. The Englishman, unlike the Eskimo, lacks a variegated vocabulary to describe different kinds of snow. Yet these differences in quality of snow are not, therefore, invisible to the Englishman. The 'reality' remains unchanged.

But when Whorf compares languages as radically different as

SAE (Standard Average European) and Hopi, profound conceptual differences engendered by these languages are highlighted. Our time and space, the immovable coordinates of existence, are no longer recognizable in Hopi. English relies heavily on spatial metaphor, and time itself is an objectified configuration of points on a line. But Hopi does not share the past, present and future tenses with SAE, and Hopi thinking has no imaginary space. If this is so, then such thought may be located in real space. Thought becomes an instrument affecting actual events. The intensity of a thought adds to its power over some future event. Surely it is a different world where the position of a thought along an intensity dimension influences future events. Sports fans may clench their fists, tense themselves, jump up and down and scream vociferously. There is an element in this behaviour of more than moral support for the runners, boxers, etc. who are being 'carried along' by their supporters. But there is no underlying belief in this spectator's power to influence events and the implications of such belief will not manifest themselves in the behaviour of such spectators. Conceptually, the Hopi and the European are worlds apart.

We now consider the second approach. It is certainly true that the child learns about the world both through its own actions and through the use of language. But what is the relation between these two aspects of behaviour in the development of the child's thought?

It appears plausible to think of the child's actions as a manipulation of that part of the world presented to the child at any one time and to think of language as conferring on the child the ability to transcend the 'here and now'. But the mental representation of objects and situations does not necessarily require language. The pre-linguistic child can utilize deferred imitation and mental imagery to achieve representation. And this facility itself depends on the prior development of action schemas. The schema is a kind of motor equivalent of a concept or an underlying strategy covering a number of similar action sequences. (There are schemas of sucking, grasping, etc.)

There is some support for the hypothesis that these action schemas of Piaget's sensori-motor period contribute substantially to the child's conceptual development. Children deprived of situations conducive to the growth of action schemas may be expected to be backward on conceptual tasks. Blind children were found to be four years behind sighted children on tests which required the construction of a series from a set of given lengths (Hatwell, 1960). Most interestingly, deaf children are often surprisingly close to normal children on certain conceptual tasks. The fact that the blind children have a normal use of language while the deaf children have minimal 'language' argues against the importance of language as a major determinant of conceptual development of this kind.

It may be thought that language accounts for logical operations. Piaget distinguishes between 'concrete' logical operations and the operations of propositional logic. He argues that the concrete operations which initially constitute a class are operations which coordinate actions and that this is a step prior to the appearance of these operations on the verbal plane. Similarly, the combinatorial operations required for propositional logic are prefigured in the child's ability to produce all possible combinations of differently coloured discs presented to him.

If Piaget's account is essentially correct, then the claim that there are innate language schemas must be modified. There may be innate cognitive mechanisms which are set into operation by specific types of environmental stimulation. The question is whether there are innate schemas specifically for language or whether language acquisition draws on abilities which are common to a variety of cognitive activities. Piaget has attempted to trace the stages of the child's cognitive development and has concluded that the skills necessary for language are the immediate product of operations which have themselves only gradually been mastered, through a process involving the continuous adjustment of schemas in the child's interaction with his world.

The third approach is concerned with verbal thought. This key concept designates a union of thought and word. The nature of this union can be observed in the development of word meanings. There are two senses in which word meanings change. The first is illustrated by the example of the child who uses 'quah' for a duck in a pond, then for any liquid, a coin with an eagle on it, for coins and finally for round objects. The concept itself is fluid and is based on a 'chaining' of successive meanings. There is no stable association between word and meaning. Indeed, the meaning is constantly changing. The use of words is seen as an integral part of the development of conceptual thinking. The word directs the processes of attention, abstraction, and synthesis of elements. The word 'at first plays the role of means in forming a concept and later becomes its symbol'.

This distinction between the role of means and of symbol marks the second sense in which word meaning develops. A feature of the child's early performance is his inability to separate the vocal and the semantic aspects of the word. It is a common experience for children to be surprised that two different persons are called by the same name. Meaning, independent of reference, appears at a later stage of development. It is only when the child is about seven years of age that he has the ability 'to "think words" instead of pronouncing them'. It can now be seen how the structures of speech become the basic structures of thinking. Note that this is still verbal thinking.

Words are indispensable to the development of conceptual thinking. Does this imply, however, that there can be no thoughts without words? Vygotsky speaks of a plane of thought which has its own structure. The problem is the transition from that plane into speech. At the same time, Vygotsky's brilliant account of inner speech provides, in my view, a description of the genesis of thoughts. His most important contribution to the definition of inner speech lies in the distinction between the sense and the meaning of a word. The meaning is only the most stable part of the sense of a word. The sense encompasses all the psychological processes aroused by the word. It is much more fluid and protean than the meaning. In inner speech words are 'saturated with sense'. The sense of the word, varying in different contexts, is surely an essential ingredient in the production of solutions to problems. It provides the recombinations and adjustments necessary to such thinking.

Furthermore, if 'thought itself is engendered by motivation, i.e., by our desires and needs, our interests and emotions', it is very close indeed to the sense of the word in inner speech which encompasses all the psychological processes aroused by the word.

The articles in Part Four correspond roughly to the theoretical positions in Part Three.

1. There is a large literature on the Whorfian hypothesis. Of the work omitted from this collection, Hoijer (1954) is of special interest.

2. There are few experimental studies of language development within the Piagetian framework. Those who read French are referred to Sinclair-De-Zwart (1967) for details of investigations into the effects of verbal training on intellectual operations.

3. Vygotsky's own investigations were the starting-point for the study of concept formation by Olver and Hornsby.

Part Five is concerned with the claim that there are innate language schemas. Since the work of the linguist Chomsky is not explicitly concerned with the way in which the structures of language are related to the structure of thought, his views on language learning have been placed apart from the main collection of theories in Part Three. His approach is presented here as part of a controversy with Sinclair-De-Zwart whose article is an explicit attack on Chomsky's position.

References

BROWN, R. and BELLUGI, U. (1964), 'Three processes in the child's acquisition of syntax', in E. Lenneberg (ed.), *New Directions in the Study of Language*, MIT Press.

FURTH, H. and MILGRAM J. (1965), 'The influence of language on classification: a theoretical model applied to normal, retarded and deaf children', *Genetic Psychol. Monog.*, vol. 72, pp. 317–51.

HATWELL, Y. (1960), *Privation Sensorielle et Intelligence*, Paris: Presses Univer, France.

HOIJER, H. (1954), 'Language in culture', *American Anthropologist*, Memoir 79, pp. 1–279.

PIAGET, J. (1962), *Play, Dreams and Imitation in Childhood*, Norton & Co.

PIAGET, J. (1969), 'Language and intellectual operations', in H. Furth, (ed.), *Piaget and Knowledge*, Prentice-Hall.

SINCLAIR-DE-ZWART, H. (1967), *Acquisition du Language et Développement de la Pensée*, Paris: Dunod.

VYGOTSKY, L. S. (1962), *Thought and Language*, MIT Press.

Part One **Learning without Language**

This section deals with experiments comparing the performance of deaf and normal subjects on cognitive tasks. Oléron's deaf subjects (Reading 2) were inferior to normals on certain cognitive tasks. Furth, however, investigated the nature of the task (Reading 3), making distinctions that Oléron's earlier studies had ignored, and found that the deaf performed as well as normals on some tasks and not on others. The Lantz and Lenneberg study (Reading 4) investigates the age variable among others. Of course, learning language is itself a conceptual task – one which the Gardners' chimpanzee, Washoe, is tackling with an unexpected degree of success.

1 R. A. Gardner and B. T. Gardner

Teaching Sign Language to a Chimpanzee[1]

R. A. Gardner and B. T. Gardner, 'Teaching sign language to a chimpanzee', *Science*, 1969, vol. 165, no. 3894, pp. 664–72.

The extent to which another species might be able to use human language is a classical problem in comparative psychology. One approach to this problem is to consider the nature of language, the processes of learning, the neural mechanisms of learning and of language, and the genetic basis of these mechanisms, and then, while recognizing certain gaps in what is known about these factors, to attempt to arrive at an answer by dint of careful scholarship (see Lenneberg, 1967). An alternative approach is to try to teach a form of human language to an animal. We chose the latter alternative and, in June 1966, began training an infant female chimpanzee, named Washoe, to use the gestural language of the deaf. Within the first thirty-two months of training it became evident that we had been correct in at least one major aspect of method, the use of a gestural language. Additional aspects of method have evolved in the course of the project. These and some implications of our early results can now be described in a way that may be useful in other studies of communicative behavior. Accordingly, in this article we discuss the considerations

1. We acknowledge a great debt to the personnel of the Aeromedical Research Laboratory, Holloman Air Force Base, whose support and expert assistance effectively absorbed all of the many difficulties attendant upon the acquisition of a wild-caught chimpanzee. We are also grateful to Dr Frances L. Fitz-Gerald of the Yerkes Regional Primate Research Center for detailed advice on the care of an infant chimpanzee. Drs Emanual Berger of Reno, Nevada, and D. B. Olsen of the University of Nevada have served as medical consultants and we are grateful to them for giving so generously of their time and medical skills. The faculty of the Sarah Hamilton Fleischmann School of Home Economics, University of Nevada, has generously allowed us to use the facilities of their experimental nursery school on weekends and holidays.

which led us to use the chimpanzee as a subject and American Sign Language (the language used by the deaf in North America) as a medium of communication; describe the general methods of training as they were initially conceived and as they developed in the course of the project; and summarize those results that could be reported with some degree of confidence by the end of the first phase of the project.

Preliminary considerations
The chimpanzee as a subject

Some discussion of the chimpanzee as an experimental subject is in order because this species is relatively uncommon in the psychological laboratory. Whether or not the chimpanzee is the most intelligent animal after man can be disputed; the gorilla, the orangutan, and even the dolphin have their loyal partisans in this debate. Nevertheless, it is generally conceded that chimpanzees are highly intelligent, and that members of this species might be intelligent enough for our purposes. Of equal or greater importance is their sociability and their capacity for forming strong attachments to human beings. We want to emphasize this trait of sociability; it seems highly likely that it is essential for the development of language in human beings, and it was a primary consideration in our choice of a chimpanzee as a subject.

Affectionate as chimpanzees are, they are still wild animals, and this is a serious disadvantage. Most psychologists are accustomed to working with animals that have been chosen, and sometimes bred, for docility and adaptability to laboratory procedures. The difficulties presented by the wild nature of an experimental animal must not be underestimated. Chimpanzees are also very strong animals; a full-grown specimen is likely to weigh more than 120 pounds (fifty-five kilograms) and is estimated to be from three to five times as strong as a man, pound-for-pound. Coupled with the wildness, this great strength presents serious difficulties for a procedure that requires interaction at close quarters with a free-living animal. We have always had to reckon with the likelihood that at some point Washoe's physical maturity will make this procedure prohibitively dangerous.

A more serious disadvantage is that human speech sounds are unsuitable as a medium of communication for the chimpanzee.

The vocal apparatus of the chimpanzee is very different from that of man (Bryan, 1963). More important, the vocal behavior of the chimpanzee is very different from that of man. Chimpanzees do make many different sounds, but generally vocalization occurs in situations of high excitement and tends to be specific to the exciting situations. Undisturbed, chimpanzees are usually silent. Thus, it is unlikely that a chimpanzee could be trained to make refined use of its vocalizations. Moreover, the intensive work of Hayes and Hayes (1951) with the chimpanzee Viki indicates that a vocal language is not appropriate for this species. The Hayeses used modern, sophisticated, psychological methods and seem to have spared no effort to teach Viki to make speech sounds. Yet in six years Viki learned only four sounds that approximated English words.[2]

Use of the hands, however, is a prominent feature of chimpanzee behavior; manipulatory mechanical problems are their forte. More to the point, even caged, laboratory chimpanzees develop begging and similar gestures spontaneously (Yerkes, 1943), while individuals that have had extensive contact with human beings have displayed an even wider variety of communicative gestures (Hayes and Hayes, 1955; W. N. Kellogg and L. A. Kellogg, 1967; W. N. Kellogg, 1968). In our choice of sign language we were influenced more by the behavioral evidence that this medium of communication was appropriate to the species than by anatomical evidence of structural similarity between the hands of chimpanzees and of men. The Hayeses point out that human tools and mechanical devices are constructed to fit the human hand, yet chimpanzees have little difficulty in using these devices with great skill. Nevertheless, they seem unable to adapt their vocalizations to approximate human speech.

Psychologists who work extensively with the instrumental conditioning of animals become sensitive to the need to use responses that are suited to the species they wish to study. Lever-pressing in rats is not an arbitrary response invented by Skinner to confound the mentalists; it is a type of response commonly made by rats when they are first placed in a Skinner

2. K. J. Hayes, personal communication. Dr Hayes also informed us that Viki used a few additional sounds which, while not resembling English words, were used for specific requests.

box. The exquisite control of instrumental behavior by schedules of reward is achieved only if the original responses are well chosen. We chose a language based on gestures because we reasoned that gestures for the chimpanzee should be analogous to bar-pressing for rats, key-pecking for pigeons, and babbling for humans.

American Sign Language

Two systems of manual communication are used by the deaf. One system is the manual alphabet, or finger spelling, in which configurations of the hand correspond to letters of the alphabet. In this system the words of a spoken language, such as English, can be spelled out manually. The other system, sign language, consists of a set of manual configurations and gestures that correspond to particular words or concepts. Unlike finger spelling, which is the direct encoding of a spoken language, sign languages have their own rules of usage. Word-for-sign translation between a spoken language and a sign language yields results that are similar to those of word-for-word translation between two spoken languages: the translation is often passable, though awkward, but it can also be ambiguous or quite nonsensical. Also, there are national and regional variations in sign languages that are comparable to those of spoken languages.

We chose for this project the American Sign Language (ASL), which, with certain regional variations, is used by the deaf in North America. This particular sign language has recently been the subject of formal analysis (Stokoe, Casterline and Croneberg, 1965, McCall, 1969). The ASL can be compared to pictograph writing in which some symbols are quite arbitrary and some are quite representational or iconic, but all are arbitrary to some degree. For example, in ASL the sign for 'always' is made by holding the hand in a fist, index finger extended (the pointing hand), while rotating the arm at the elbow. This is clearly an arbitrary representation of the concept 'always'. The sign for 'flower', however, is highly iconic; it is made by holding the fingers of one hand extended, all five fingertips touching (the tapered hand), and touching the fingertips first to one nostril then to the other, as if sniffing a flower. While this is an iconic sign for 'flower', it is only one of a number of conventions by which the concept 'flower' could be iconically represented; it is thus arbitrary to some degree. Undoubtedly, many of the signs of ASL that seem quite arbitrary today once had an iconic origin that was lost through years of stylized usage. Thus, the signs of ASL are neither uniformly arbitrary nor uniformly iconic; rather the degree of abstraction varies from sign to sign over a wide range. This would seem to be a useful property of ASL for our research.

The literate deaf typically use a combination of ASL and finger spelling; for purposes of this project we have avoided the use of finger spelling as much as possible. A great range of expression is possible within the limits of ASL. We soon found that a good way to practice signing among ourselves was to render familiar songs and poetry into signs; as far as we can judge, there is no message that cannot be rendered faithfully (apart from the usual problems of translation from one language to another). Technical terms and proper names are a problem when first introduced, but within any community of signers it is easy to agree on a convention for any commonly used term. For example, among ourselves we do not finger-spell the words *psychologist* and *psychology*, but render them as 'think doctor' and 'think science'. Or, among users of ASL, 'California' can be finger-spelled but is commonly rendered as 'golden playland'. (Incidentally, the sign for 'gold' is made by plucking at the earlobe with thumb and forefinger, indicating an earring – another example of an iconic sign that is at the same time arbitrary and stylized.)

The fact that ASL is in current use by human beings is an additional advantage. The early linguistic environment of the deaf children of deaf parents is in some respects similar to the linguistic environment that we could provide for an experimental subject. This should permit some comparative evaluation of Washoe's eventual level of competence. For example, in discussing Washoe's early performance with deaf parents we have been told that many of her variants of standard signs are similar to the baby-talk variants commonly observed when human children sign.

Washoe

Having decided on a species and a medium of communication, our next concern was to obtain an experimental subject. It is altogether possible that there is some critical early age for the acquisition of this type of behavior. On the other hand, newborn chimpanzees tend to be quite helpless and vegetative. They are also considerably less hardy than older infants. Nevertheless, we reasoned that the dangers of starting too late were much greater than the dangers of starting too early, and we sought the youngest infant we could get. Newborn laboratory chimpanzees are very scarce, and we found that the youngest laboratory infant we could get would be about two years old at the time we planned to start the project. It seemed preferable to obtain a wild-caught infant. Wild-caught infants are usually at least eight to ten months old before they are available for research. This is because infants rarely reach the United States before they are five months old, and to this age must be added one or two months before final purchase and two or three months for quarantine and other medical services.

We named our chimpanzee Washoe for Washoe County, the home of the University of Nevada. Her exact age will never be known, but from her weight and dentition we estimated her age to be between eight and fourteen months at the end of June 1966, when she first arrived at our laboratory. (Her dentition has continued to agree with this initial estimate, but her weight has increased rather more than would be expected.) This is very young for a chimpanzee. The best available information indicates that infants are completely dependent until the age of two years and semi-dependent until the age of four; the first signs of sexual maturity (for example, menstruation, sexual swelling) begin to appear at about eight years, and full adult growth is reached between the ages of twelve and sixteen (Goodall, 1965; Riopelle and Rogers, 1965). As for the complete life-span, captive specimens have survived for well over forty years. Washoe was indeed very young when she arrived; she did not have her first canines or molars, her hand–eye coordination was rudimentary, she had only begun to crawl about, and she slept a great deal. Apart from making friends with her and adapting her to the daily routine, we could accomplish little during the first few months.

Laboratory conditions

At the outset we were quite sure that Washoe could learn to make various signs in order to obtain food, drink, and other things. For the project to be a success, we felt that something more must be developed. We wanted Washoe not only to ask for objects but to answer questions about them and also to ask us questions. We wanted to develop behavior that could be described as conversation. With this in mind, we attempted to provide Washoe with an environment that might be conducive to this sort of behavior. Confinement was to be minimal, about the same as that of human infants. Her human companions were to be friends and playmates as well as providers and protectors, and they were to introduce a great many games and activities that would be likely to result in maximum interaction with Washoe.

In practice, such an environment is readily achieved with a chimpanzee; bonds of warm affection have always been established between Washoe and her several human companions. We have enjoyed the interaction almost as much as Washoe has, within the limits of human endurance. A number of human companions have been enlisted to participate in the project and relieve each other at intervals, so that at least one person would be with Washoe during all her waking hours. At first we feared that such frequent changes would be disturbing, but Washoe seemed to adapt very well to this procedure. Apparently it is possible to provide an infant chimpanzee with affection on a shift basis.

All of Washoe's human companions have been required to master ASL and to use it extensively in her presence, in association with interesting activities and events and also in a general way, as one chatters at a human infant in the course of the day. The ASL has been used almost exclusively, although occasional finger spelling has been permitted. From time to time, of course, there are lapses into spoken English, as when medical personnel must examine Washoe. At one time, we considered an alternative procedure in which we would sign and speak English to Washoe simultaneously, thus giving her an additional source of informative cues. We rejected this procedure, reasoning that, if she should come to understand speech sooner or more easily than ASL, then she might not pay sufficient attention to our gestures.

Another alternative, that of speaking English among ourselves and signing to Washoe, was also rejected. We reasoned that this would make it seem that big chimps talk and only little chimps sign, which might give signing an undesirable social status.

The environment we are describing is not a silent one. The human beings can vocalize in many ways, laughing and making sounds of pleasure and displeasure. Whistles and drums are sounded in a variety of imitation games, and hands are clapped for attention. The rule is that all meaningful sounds, whether vocalized or not, must be sounds that a chimpanzee can imitate.

Training methods
Imitation

The imitativeness of apes is proverbial, and rightly so. Those who have worked closely with chimpanzees have frequently remarked on their readiness to engage in visually guided imitation. Consider the following typical comment of Yerkes (Yerkes and Learned, 1925):

Chim and Panzee would imitate many of my acts, but never have I heard them imitate a sound and rarely make a sound peculiarly their own in response to mine. As previously stated, their imitative tendency is as remarkable for its specialization and limitations as for its strength. It seems to be controlled chiefly by visual stimuli. Things which are seen tend to be imitated or reproduced. What is heard is not reproduced. Obviously an animal which lacks the tendency to reinstate auditory stimuli – in other words to imitate sounds – cannot reasonably be expected to talk. The human infant exhibits this tendency to a remarkable degree. So also does the parrot. If the imitative tendency of the parrot could be coupled with the quality of intelligence of the chimpanzee, the latter undoubtedly could speak.

In the course of their work with Viki, the Hayeses devised a game in which Viki would imitate various actions on hearing the command 'Do this' (Hayes and Hayes, 1952). Once established, this was an effective means of training Viki to perform actions that could be visually guided. The same method should be admirably suited to training a chimpanzee to use sign language; accordingly we have directed much effort toward establishing a version of the 'Do this' game with Washoe. Getting Washoe to imitate us was not difficult, for she did so quite spontaneously, but getting her to imitate on command has been another matter altogether. It was not until the sixteenth month of the project that we achieved any degree of control over Washoe's imitation of gestures. Eventually we got to a point where she would imitate a simple gesture, such as pulling at her ears, or a series of such gestures – first we make a gesture, then she imitates, then we make a second gesture, she imitates the second gesture, and so on – for the reward of being tickled. Up to this writing, however, imitation of this sort has not been an important method for introducing new signs into Washoe's vocabulary.

As a method of prompting, we have been able to use imitation extensively to increase the frequency and refine the form of signs. Washoe sometimes fails to use a new sign in an appropriate situation, or uses another, incorrect sign. At such times we can make the correct sign to Washoe, repeating the performance until she makes the sign herself. (With more stable signs, more indirect forms of prompting can be used – for example, pointing at or touching Washoe's hand or a part of her body that should be involved in the sign; making the sign for 'sign,' which is equivalent to saying 'Speak up'; or asking a question in signs, such as 'What do you want?' or 'What is it?') Again, with new signs, and often with old signs as well, Washoe can lapse into what we refer to as poor 'diction'. Of course, a great deal of slurring and a wide range of variants are permitted in ASL as in any spoken language. In any event, Washoe's diction has frequently been improved by the simple device of repeating, in exaggeratedly correct form, the sign she has just made, until she repeats it herself in more correct form. On the whole, she has responded quite well to prompting, but there are strict limits to its use with a wild animal – one that is probably quite spoiled, besides. Pressed too hard, Washoe can become completely diverted from her original object; she may ask for something entirely different, run away, go into a tantrum, or even bite her tutor.

Chimpanzees also imitate, after some delay, and this delayed imitation can be quite elaborate (see Hayes and Hayes, 1952). The following is a typical example of Washoe's delayed imitation. From the beginning of the project she was bathed regularly and according to a standard routine. Also, from her second month with us, she always had dolls to play with. One day, during the tenth month of the project, she bathed one of her dolls in the way we usually bathed her. She filled her little bathtub with water, dunked the doll in the tub, then took it out and dried it with a towel. She has repeated the entire performance, or parts of it, many times since, sometimes also soaping the doll.

This is a type of imitation that may be very important in the acquisition of language by human children, and many of our procedures with Washoe were devised to capitalize on it. Routine activities – feeding, dressing, bathing, and so on – have been highly ritualized, with appropriate signs figuring prominently in the rituals. Many games have been invented which can be accompanied by appropriate signs. Objects and activities have been named as often as possible, especially when Washoe seemed to be paying particular attention to them. New objects and new examples of familiar objects, including pictures, have been continually brought to her attention, together with the appropriate signs. She likes to ride in automobiles, and a ride in an automobile, including the preparations for a ride, provides a wealth of sights that can be accompanied by signs. A good destination for a ride is a home or the university nursery school, both well stocked with props for language lessons.

The general principle should be clear: Washoe has been exposed to a wide variety of activities and objects, together with their appropriate signs, in the hope that she would come to associate the signs with their referents and later make the signs herself. We have reason to believe that she has come to understand a large vocabulary of signs. This was expected, since a number of chimpanzees have acquired extensive understanding vocabularies of spoken words, and there is evidence that even dogs can acquire a sizable understanding vocabulary of spoken words (Warden and Warner, 1928). The understanding vocabulary that Washoe has acquired, however, consists of signs that a chimpanzee can imitate.

Some of Washoe's signs seem to have been originally acquired by delayed imitation. A good example is the sign for 'toothbrush'. A part of the daily routine has been to brush her teeth after every meal. When this routine was first introduced Washoe generally resisted it. She gradually came to submit with less and less fuss and after many months she would even help to sometimes brush her teeth herself. Usually, having finished her meal, Washoe would try to leave her high-chair: we would restrain her, signing 'first, toothbrushing, then you can go'. One day, in the tenth month of the project, Washoe was visiting the Gardner home and found her way into the bathroom. She climbed up on the counter, looked at our mug full of toothbrushes, and signed 'toothbrush'. At the time, we believed that Washoe understood this sign but we had not seen her use it. She had no reason to ask for the toothbrushes, because they were well within her reach, and it is most unlikely that she was asking to have her teeth brushed. This was our first observation, and one of the clearest examples, of behavior in which Washoe seemed to name an object or an event for no obvious motive other than communication.

Following this observation, the tooth-brushing routine at mealtime was altered. First, imitative prompting was introduced. Then as the sign became more reliable, her rinsing-mug and toothbrush were displayed prominently until she made the sign. By the fourteenth month she was making the 'toothbrush' sign at the end of meals with little or no prompting; in fact she has called for her toothbrush in a peremptory fashion when its appearance at the end of a meal was delayed. The 'toothbrush' sign is not merely a response cued by the end of a meal; Washoe retained her ability to name toothbrushes when they were shown to her at other times.

The sign for 'flower' may also have been acquired by delayed imitation. From her first summer with us, Washoe showed a great interest in flowers, and we took advantage of this by providing many flowers and pictures of flowers accompanied by the appropriate sign. Then one day in the fifteenth month she made the sign, spontaneously, while she and a companion were walking toward a flower garden. As in the case of 'toothbrush', we believed that she understood the sign at this time, but we had made no attempt to elicit it from her except by making it ourselves in appropriate situations. Again, after the first observation, we proceeded to elicit this sign as often as possible by a variety of methods, most frequently by showing her a flower and giving it to her if she made the sign for it. Eventually the sign became very reliable and could be elicited by a variety of flowers and pictures of flowers.

It is difficult to decide which signs were acquired by the method of delayed imitation. The first appearance of these signs is likely to be sudden and unexpected; it is possible that some inadvertent movement of Washoe's has been interpreted as meaningful by one of her devoted companions. If the first observer were kept from reporting the observation and from making any direct attempts to elicit the sign again, then it might be possible to obtain independent verification. Quite understandably, we have been more interested in raising the frequency of new signs than in evaluating any particular method of training.

Babbling

Because the Hayeses were attempting to teach Viki to speak English, they were interested in babbling, and during the first year of their project they were encouraged by the number and variety of spontaneous vocalizations that Viki made. But, in time, Viki's spontaneous vocalizations decreased further and further to the point where the Hayeses felt that there was almost no vocal babbling from which to shape spoken language. In planning this project we expected a great deal of manual 'babbling', but during the early months we observed very little behavior of this kind. In the course of the project, however, there has been a great increase in manual babbling. We have been particularly encouraged by the increase in movements that involve touching parts of the head and body, since these are important components of many signs. Also, more and more frequently, when Washoe has been unable to get something that she wants, she has burst into a flurry of random flourishes and arm-waving.

We have encouraged Washoe's babbling by our responsiveness; clapping, smiling, and repeating the gesture much as you might repeat 'goo goo' to a human infant. If the babbled gesture has resembled a sign in ASL, we have made the correct form of the sign and have attempted to engage in some appropriate activity. The sign for 'funny' was probably acquired in this way. It first appeared as a spontaneous babble that lent itself readily to a simple imitation game – first Washoe signed 'funny', then we did, then she did, and so on. We would laugh and smile during the interchanges that she initiated, and initiate the game ourselves when something funny happened. Eventually Washoe came to use the 'funny' sign spontaneously in roughly appropriate situations.

Closely related to babbling are some gestures that seem to have appeared independently of any deliberate training on our part, and that resemble signs so closely that we could incorporate them into Washoe's repertoire with little or no modification. Almost from the first she had a begging gesture – an extension of her open hand, palm up, toward one of us. She made this gesture in situations in which she wanted aid and in situations in which we were holding some object that she wanted. The ASL signs for 'give me' and 'come' are very similar to this, except that they involve a prominent beckoning movement. Gradually Washoe came to incorporate a beckoning wrist movement into her use of this sign. In Table 1 we refer to this sign as 'come-gimme'. As Washoe has come to use it, the sign is not simply a modification of the original begging gesture. For example, very commonly she reaches forward with one hand (palm up) while she gestures with the other hand (palm down) held near her head. (The result resembles a classic fencing posture.)

Another sign of this type is the sign for 'hurry,' which, so far, Washoe has always made by shaking her open hand vigorously at the wrist. This first appeared as an impatient flourish following some request that she had made in signs; for example, after making the 'open' sign before a door. The correct ASL for 'hurry' is very close, and we began to use it often, ourselves, in appropriate contexts. We believe that Washoe has come to use this sign in a meaningful way, because she has frequently used it when she, herself, is in a hurry – for example, when rushing to her nursery chair.

Instrumental conditioning

It seems intuitively unreasonable that the acquisition of language by human beings could be strictly a matter of reiterated instrumental conditioning – that a child acquires language after the fashion of a rat that is conditioned, first, to press a lever for food in the presence of a stimulus, then to turn a wheel in the presence of another stimulus, and so on until a large repertoire of discriminated responses is acquired. Nevertheless, the so-called 'trick vocabulary' of early childhood is probably acquired in this way, and this may be a critical stage in the acquisition of language by children. In any case, a minimal objective of this project was to

Table 1 Signs used reliably by Chimpanzee Washoe within Twenty-Two Months of the Beginning of Training. (The signs are listed in the order of their original appearance in her repertoire; see text for the criterion of reliability and for the method of assigning the date of original appearance.)

Signs	Description	Context
Come-gimme	Beckoning motion, with wrist or knuckles as pivot.	Sign made to person or animals, also for objects out of reach. Often combined: 'come tickle', 'gimme sweet', etc.
More	Fingertips are brought together, usually overhead. (Correct ASL form: tips of the tapered hand touch repeatedly.)	When asking for continuation or repetition of activities such as swinging or tickling, for second helpings of food, etc. Also used to ask for repetition of some performance, such as a somersault.
Up	Arm extends upward, and index finger may also point up.	Wants a lift to reach objects such as grapes on vine, or leaves; or wants to be placed on someone's shoulders; or wants to leave potty-chair.
Sweet	Index or index and second fingers touch tip of wagging tongue. (Correct ASL form: index and second fingers extended side by side.)	For dessert; used spontaneously at end of meal. Also, when asking for candy.
Open	Flat hands are placed side by side, palms down, then drawn apart while rotated to palms up.	At door of house, room, car, refrigerator, or cupboard; or containers such as jars; and on faucets.
Tickle	The index finger of one hand is drawn across the back of the other hand. (Related to ASL 'touch'.)	For tickling or for chasing games.
Go	Opposite of 'come-gimme'.	While walking hand-in-hand or riding on someone's shoulders. Washoe usually indicates the direction desired.
Out	Curved hand grasps tapered hand; then tapered hand is withdrawn upward.	When passing through doorways; until recently, used for both 'in' and 'out'. Also, when asking to be taken outdoors.
Hurry	Open hand is shaken at the wrist. (Correct ASL form: index and second fingers extended side by side.)	Often follows signs such as 'come-gimme', 'out', 'open', and 'go', particularly if there is a delay before Washoe obeyed. Also, used while watching her meal being prepared.
Hear-listen	Index finger touches ear.	For loud or strange sounds: bells, car horns, sonic booms, etc. Also, for asking someone to hold a watch to her ear.

Sign	Description	Context
Toothbrush	Index finger is used as brush, to rub front teeth.	When Washoe has finished her meal, or at other times when shown a toothbrush.
Drink	Thumb is extended from fisted hand and touches mouth.	For water, formula, soda pop, etc. For soda pop, often combined with 'sweet.'
Hurt	Extended index fingers are jabbed toward each other. Can be used to indicate location of pain.	To indicate cuts and bruises on herself or on others. Can be elicited by red stains on a person's skin or by tears in clothing.
Sorry	Fisted hand clasps and unclasps at shoulder. (Correct ASL form: fisted hand is rubbed over heart with circular motion.)	After biting someone, or when someone has been hurt in another way (not necessarily by Washoe). When told to apologize for mischief.
Funny	Tip of index finger presses nose, and Washoe snorts. (Correct ASL form: index and second fingers used; no snort.)	When soliciting interaction play, and during games. Occasionally, when being pursued after mischief.
Please	Open hand is drawn across chest. (Correct ASL form: fingertips used, and circular motion.)	When asking for objects and activities. Frequently combined 'Please go,' 'Out, please,' 'Please drink.'
Food-eat	Several fingers of one hand are placed in mouth. (Correct ASL form: fingertips of tapered hand touch mouth repeatedly.)	During meals and preparation of meals.
Flower	Tip of index finger touches one or both nostrils. (Correct ASL form: tips of tapered hand touch first one nostril, then the other.)	For flowers.
Cover-blanket	Draws one hand toward self over the back of the other.	At bedtime or naptime, and, on cold days, when Washoe wants to be taken out.
Dog	Repeated slapping on thigh.	For dogs and for barking.
You	Index finger points at a person's chest.	Indicates successive turns in games. Also used in response to questions such as 'Who tickle?' 'Who brush?'
Napkin-bib	Fingertips wipe the mouth region.	For bib, for washcloth, and for Kleenex.
In	Opposite of 'out'.	Wants to go indoors, or wants someone to join her outdoors.
Brush	The fisted hand rubs the back of the open hand several times. (Adapted from the ASL 'polish'.)	For hairbrush, and when asking for brushing.

Table 1– continued

Signs	Description	Context
Hat	Palm pats top of head.	For hats and caps.
I-me	Index finger points at, or touches, chest.	Indicates Washoe's turn, when she and a companion share food, drink, etc. Also used in phrases, such as 'I drink', and in reply to questions such as 'Who tickle?' (Washoe: 'you'); 'Who I tickle?' (Washoe: 'Me.')
Shoes	The fisted hands are held side by side and strike down on shoes or floor. (Correct ASL form: the sides of the fisted hands strike against each other.)	For shoes and boots.
Smell	Palm is held before nose and moved slightly upward several times.	For scented objects: tobacco, perfume, sage, etc.
Pants	Palms of the flat hands are drawn up against the body toward waist.	For diapers, rubber pants, trousers.
Clothes	Fingertips brush down the chest.	For Washoe's jacket, nightgown, and shirts; also for our clothing.
Cat	Thumb and index finger grasp cheek hair near side of mouth and are drawn outward (representing cat's whiskers).	For cats.
Key	Palm of one hand is repeatedly touched with the index finger of the other. (Correct ASL form; crooked index finger is rotated against palm.)	Used for keys and locks and to ask us to unlock a door.
Baby	One forearm is placed in the crook of the other, as if cradling a baby.	For dolls, including animal dolls such as a toy horse and duck.
Clean	The open palm of one hand is passed over the open palm of the other.	Used when Washoe is washing, or being washed, or when a companion is washing hands or some other object. Also used for 'soap'.

teach Washoe as many signs as possible by whatever procedures we could enlist. Thus, we have not hesitated to use conventional procedures of instrumental conditioning.

Anyone who becomes familiar with young chimpanzees soon learns about their passion for being tickled. There is no doubt that tickling is the most effective reward that we have used with Washoe. In the early months, when we would pause in our tickling, Washoe would indicate that she wanted more tickling by taking her hands and placing them against her ribs or around her neck. The meaning of these gestures is unmistakable, but since we were not studying our human ability to interpret her chimpanzee gestures, we decided to shape an arbitrary response that she could use to ask for more tickling. We noted that, when tickled, she tended to bring her arms together to cover the place being tickled. The result was a very crude approximation of the ASL sign for 'more' (see Table 1). Thus, we would stop tickling and then pull Washoe's arms away from her body. When we released her arms and threatened to resume tickling, she tended to bring her hands together again. If she brought them back together, we would tickle her again. From time to time we would stop tickling and wait for her to put her hands together by herself. At first, any approximation to the 'more' sign, however crude, was rewarded. Later, we required closer approximations and introduced imitative prompting. Soon, a very good version of the 'more' sign could be obtained, but it was quite specific to the tickling situation.

In the sixth month of the project we were able to get 'more' signs for a new game that consisted of pushing Washoe across the floor in a laundry basket. In this case we did not use the shaping procedure but, from the start, used imitative prompting to elicit the 'more' sign. Soon after the 'more' sign became spontaneous and reliable in the laundry-basket game, it began to appear as a request for more swinging (by the arms) – again, after first being elicited with imitative prompting. From this point on, Washoe transferred the 'more' sign to all activities, including feeding. The transfer was usually spontaneous, occurring when there was some pause in a desired activity or when some object was removed. Often we ourselves were not sure that Washoe wanted 'more' until she signed to us.

The sign for 'open' had a similar history. When Washoe wanted to get through a door, she tended to hold up both hands and pound on the door with her palms or her knuckles. This is the beginning position for the 'open' sign (see Table 1). By waiting for her to place her hands on the door and then lift them, and also by imitative prompting, we were able to shape a good approximation of the 'open' sign, and would reward this by opening the door. Originally she was trained to make this sign for three particular doors that she used every day. Washoe transferred this sign to all doors; then to containers such as the refrigerator, cupboards, drawers, briefcases, boxes, and jars; and eventually – an invention of Washoe's – she used it to ask us to turn on water faucets.

In the case of 'more' and 'open' we followed the conventional laboratory procedure of waiting for Washoe to make some response that could be shaped into the sign we wished her to acquire. We soon found that this was not necessary; Washoe could acquire signs that were first elicited by our holding her hands, forming them into the desired configuration, and then putting them through the desired movement. Since this procedure of guidance is usually much more practical than waiting for a spontaneous approximation to occur at a favorable moment, we have used it much more frequently.

Results
Vocabulary

In the early stages of the project we were able to keep fairly complete records of Washoe's daily signing behavior. But, as the amount of signing behavior and the number of signs to be monitored increased, our initial attempts to obtain exhaustive records became prohibitively cumbersome. During the sixteenth month we settled on the following procedure. When a new sign was introduced we waited until it had been reported by three different observers as having occurred in an appropriate context and spontaneously (that is, with no prompting other than a question such as 'What is it?' or 'What do you want?'). The sign was then added to a checklist in which its occurrence, form, context, and the kind of prompting required were recorded. Two such checklists were filled out each day, one for the first half of the day and one for the second half. For a criterion of acquisition we chose a reported frequency of at least one appropriate and spontaneous occurrence each day over a period of fifteen consecutive days.

In Table 1 we have listed thirty signs that met this criterion by the end of the twenty-second month of the project. In addition, we have listed four signs ('dog', 'smell', 'me', and 'clean') that we judged to be stable, despite the fact that they had not met the stringent criterion before the end of the twenty-second month. These additional signs had, nevertheless, been reported to occur appropriately and spontaneously on more than half of the days in a period of thirty consecutive days. An indication of the variety of signs that Washoe used in the course of a day is given by the following data: during the twenty-second month of the study, twenty-eight of the thirty-four signs listed were reported on at least twenty days, and the smallest number of different signs reported for a single day was twenty-three, with a median of twenty-nine.[3]

The order in which these signs first appeared in Washoe's repertoire is also given in Table 1. We considered the first appearance to be the date on which three different observers reported appropriate and spontaneous occurrences. By this criterion, four new signs first appeared during the first seven months, nine new signs during the next seven months, and twenty-one new signs during the next seven months. We chose the twenty-first month rather than the twenty-second month as the cutoff for this tabulation so that no signs would be included that do not appear in Table 1. Clearly, if Washoe's rate of acquisition continues to accelerate, we will have to assess her vocabulary on the basis of sampling procedures. We are now in the process of developing procedures that could be used to make periodic tests of Washoe's performance on samples of her repertoire. However, now that there is evidence that a chimpanzee can acquire a vocabulary of more than thirty signs, the exact number of signs in her current vocabulary is less significant than the order of magnitude – fifty, 100, 200 signs, or more – that might eventually be achieved.

3. The development of Washoe's vocabulary of signs is being recorded on motion-picture film. At the time of this writing, thirty of the thirty-four signs listed in Table 1 are on film.

Differentiation

In Table 1, column 1, we list English equivalents for each of Washoe's signs. It must be understood that this equivalence is only approximate, because equivalence between English and ASL, as between any two human languages, is only approximate and because Washoe's usage does differ from that of standard ASL. To some extent her usage is indicated in the column labeled 'Context' in Table 1, but the definition of any given sign must always depend upon her own vocabulary, and this has been continually changing. When she had very few signs for specific things, Washoe used the 'more' sign for a wide class of requests. Our only restriction was that we discouraged the use of 'more' for first requests. As she acquired signs for specific requests, her use of 'more' declined until, at the time of this writing, she was using this sign mainly to ask for repetition of some action that she could not name, such as a somersault. Perhaps the best English equivalent would be 'do it again'. Still it seemed preferable to list the English equivalent for the ASL sign rather than its current referent for Washoe, since further refinements in her usage may be achieved at a later date.

The differentiation of the signs for 'flower' and 'smell' provides a further illustration of usage depending upon size of vocabulary. As the 'flower' sign became more frequent, we noted that it occurred in several inappropriate contexts that all seemed to include odors; for example, Washoe would make the 'flower' sign when opening a tobacco pouch or when entering a kitchen filled with cooking odors. Taking our cue from this, we introduced the 'smell' sign by passive shaping and imitative prompting. Gradually Washoe came to make the appropriate distinction between 'flower' contexts and 'smell' contexts in her signing although 'flower' (in the single-nostril form) (see Table 1) has continued to occur as a common error in 'smell' contexts.

Transfer

In general, when introducing new signs we have used a very specific referent for the initial training – a particular door for 'open', a particular hat for 'hat'. Early in the project we were concerned about the possibility that signs might become inseparable from their first referents. So far, however, there has been no problem of this kind: Washoe has always been able to transfer her signs spontaneously to new members of each class of referents. We have already described the transfer of 'more' and 'open'. The sign for 'flower' is a particularly good example of transfer, because flowers occur in so many varieties indoors, outdoors, and in pictures, that Washoe uses the same sign for all. It is fortunate that she has responded well to pictures of objects. In the case of 'dog' and 'cat' this has proved to be important because live dogs and cats can be too exciting, and we have had to use pictures to elicit most of the 'dog' and 'cat' signs. It is noteworthy that Washoe has transferred the 'dog' signs to the sound of barking of an unknown dog.

The acquisition and transfer of the sign for 'key' illustrates a further point. A great many cupboards and doors in Washoe's quarters have been kept secure by small padlocks that can all be opened by the same simple key.

Because she was immature and awkward, Washoe had great difficulty in learning to use these keys and locks. Because we wanted her to improve her manual dexterity, we let her practice with these keys until she could open locks quite easily (then we had to hide the keys). Washoe soon transferred this skill to all manner of locks and keys, including ignition keys. At about the same time, we taught her the sign for 'key' using the original padlock keys as a referent. Washoe came to use this sign both to name keys that were presented to her and to ask for the key to various locks when no one was in sight. She readily transferred the sign to all varieties of keys and locks.

Now, if an animal can transfer a skill learned with a certain key and lock to a new type of key and lock, it should not be surprising that the same animal can learn to use an arbitrary response to name and ask for a certain key and then transfer that sign to new types of keys. Certainly, the relationship between the use of a key and the opening of locks is as arbitrary as the relationship between the sign for 'key' and its many referents. Viewed in this way, the general phenomenon of transfer of training and the specifically linguistic phenomenon of labeling become very similar, and the problems that these phenomena pose for modern learning theory should require similar solutions. We do not mean to imply that the problem of labeling is less complex than has generally been supposed; rather we are suggesting that the problem of transfer of training requires an equally sophisticated treatment.

Combinations

During the phase of the project covered by this article we made no deliberate attempts to elicit combinations or phrases, although we may have responded more readily to strings of two or more signs than to single signs. As far as we can judge, Washoe's early use of signs in strings was spontaneous. Almost as soon as she had eight or ten signs in her repertoire, she began to use them two and three at a time. As her repertoire increased, her tendency to produce strings of two or more signs also increased, to the point where this has become a common mode of signing for her. We, of course, usually signed to her in combinations, but if Washoe's use of combinations has been imitative, then it must be a generalized sort of imitation, since she has invented a number of combinations, such as 'gimme tickle' (before we had ever asked her to tickle us), and 'open food drink' (for the refrigerator – we have always called it the 'cold box').

Four signs – 'please', 'com-gime', 'hurry', and 'more' – used with one or more other signs, account for the largest share of Washoe's early combinations. In general, these four signs have functioned as emphasizers, as in 'please open hurry' and 'gimme drink please'.

Until recently, five additional signs – 'go', 'out', 'in', 'open', and 'hear-listen' – accounted for most of the remaining combinations. Typical examples of combinations using these four are, 'go in' or 'go out' (when at some distance from a door), 'go sweet' (for being carried to a raspberry bush), 'open flower' (to be let through the gate to a flower garden), 'open key' (for a locked door), 'listen eat' (at the sound of an alarm clock signaling mealtime), and 'listen dog' (at the sound of barking by an unseen dog). All but the first and last of these six examples were inventions of Washoe's. Combinations of this type tend to amplify the meaning of the single signs used. Sometimes, however, the function of these five signs has been about the same as that of the emphasizers, as in 'open out' (when standing in front of a door).

Toward the end of the period covered in this article we were able to introduce the pronouns 'I–me' and 'you,' so that combinations that resemble short sentences have begun to appear.

Concluding observations

From time to time we have been asked questions such as, 'Do you think that Washoe has language?' or 'At what point will you be able to say that Washoe has language?' We find it very difficult to respond to these questions because they are altogether foreign to the spirit of our research. They imply a distinction between one class of communicative behavior that can be called language and another class that cannot. This in turn implies a well-established theory that could provide the distinction. If our objectives had required such a theory, we would certainly not have been able to begin this project as early as we did.

In the first phase of the project we were able to verify the hypothesis that sign language is an appropriate medium of two-way communication for the chimpanzee. Washoe's intellectual immaturity, the continuing acceleration of her progress, the fact that her signs do not remain specific to their original referents but are transferred spontaneously to new referents, and the emergence of rudimentary combinations all suggest that significantly more can be accomplished by Washoe during the subsequent phases of this project. As we proceed, the problems of these subsequent phases will be chiefly concerned with the technical business of measurement. We are now developing a procedure for testing Washoe's ability to name objects. In this procedure, an object or a picture of an object is placed in a box with a window. An observer, who does not know what is in the box, asks Washoe what she sees through the window. At present, this method is limited to items that fit in the box; a more ingenious method will have to be devised for other items. In particular, the ability to combine and re-combine signs must be tested. Here, a great deal depends upon reaching a stage at which Washoe produces an extended series of signs in answer to questions. Our hope is that Washoe can be brought to the point where she describes events and situations to an observer who has no other source of information.

At an earlier time we would have been more cautious about

suggesting that a chimpanzee might be able to produce extended utterances to communicate information. We believe now that it is the writers – who would predict just what it is that no chimpanzee will ever do – who must proceed with caution. Washoe's accomplishments will probably be exceeded by another chimpanzee, because it is unlikely that the conditions of training have been optimal in this first attempt. Theories of language that depend upon the identification of aspects of language that are exclusively human must remain tentative until a considerably larger body of intensive research with other species becomes available.

Summary

We set ourselves the task of teaching an animal to use a form of human language. Highly intelligent and highly social, the chimpanzee is an obvious choice for such a study, yet it has not been possible to teach a member of this species more than a few spoken words. We reasoned that a spoken language, such as English, might be an inappropriate medium of communication for a chimpanzee. This led us to choose American Sign Language, the gestural system of communication used by the deaf in North America, for the project.

The youngest infant that we could obtain was a wild-born female, whom we named Washoe, and who was estimated to be between eight and fourteen months old when we began our program of training. The laboratory conditions, while not patterned after those of a human family (as in the studies of Kellogg and Kellogg and of Hayes and Hayes), involved a minimum of confinement and a maximum of social interaction with human companions. For all practical purposes, the only verbal communication was in ASL, and the chimpanzee was maximally exposed to the use of this language by human beings.

It was necessary to develop a rough-and-ready mixture of training methods. There was evidence that some of Washoe's early signs were acquired by delayed imitation of the signing behavior of her human companions, but very few if any, of her early signs were introduced by immediate imitation. Manual babbling was directly fostered and did increase in the course of the project. A number of signs were introduced by shaping and instrumental conditioning. A particularly effective and convenient method of shaping consisted of holding Washoe's hands, forming them into a configuration, and putting them through the movements of a sign.

We have listed more than thirty signs that Washoe acquired and could use spontaneously and appropriately by the end of the twenty-second month of the project. The signs acquired earliest were simple demands. Most of the later signs have been names for objects, which Washoe has used both as demands and as answers to questions. Washoe readily used noun signs to name pictures of objects as well as actual objects and has frequently called the attention of her companions to pictures and objects by naming them. Once acquired, the signs have not remained specific to the original referents but have been transferred spontaneously to a wide class of appropriate referents. At this writing, Washoe's rate of acquisition of new signs is still accelerating.

From the time she had eight or ten signs in her repertoire, Washoe began to use them in strings of two or more. During the period covered by this article we made no deliberate effort to elicit combinations other than by our own habitual use of strings of signs. Some of the combined forms that Washoe has used may have been imitative, but many have been inventions of her own. Only a small proportion of the possible combinations have, in fact, been observed. This is because most of Washoe's combinations include one of a limited group of signs that act as combiners. Among the signs that Washoe has recently acquired are the pronouns 'I-me' and 'you'. When these occur in combinations the result resembles a short sentence. In terms of the eventual level of communication that a chimpanzee might be able to attain, the most promising results have been spontaneous naming, spontaneous combinations and recombinations of signs.

References

BRYAN, A. L. (1963), *Current Anthropology*, vol. 4, no. 297.
GOODALL, J. (1965), in I. deVore (ed.), *Primate Behavior*, Holt, Rinehart & Winston.
HAYES, K. J., and HAYES, C. (1951), *Proc. Amer. Phil. Soc.*, vol. 95, p. 105.
HAYES, K. J., and HAYES, C. (1952), 'Imitation in a home-raised chimpanzee', *J. comp. physiol. Psychol.*, vol. 45, no. 450, pp. 450–59.

HAYES, K. J., and HAYES, C. (1955), in J. A. Gavan (ed.), *The Non-Human Primates and Human Evolution*, Wayne University Press.

KELLOGG, W. N., and KELLOGG, L. A. (1967), *The Ape and the Child*, Hofner.

KELLOGG, W. N. (1968), 'Communication and language in the home-raised chimpanzee', *Science*, vol. 162, no. 3849, p. 423.

LENNEBERG, E. H. (1967), *Biological Foundations of Language*, Wiley.

McCALL, E. A. (1969), thesis, University of Iowa.

RIOPELLE, A. J., and ROGERS, C. M. (1965), A. M. Schrier, B. W. Harlow, and F. Stollintz (eds.), *Behavior of Non-Human Primates*, Academic Press.

STOKOE, W. C., CASTERLINE, D., and CRONEBERG, C. G. (1965), *A Dictionary of American Sign Language*, Gaullaudet College Press.

WARDEN, C. J., and WARNER, L. H. (1928), *Quart. Rev. Biol.*, vol. 3, no. 1.

YERKES, R. M. (1943), *Chimpanzees*, Yale University Press.

YERKES, R. M., and LEARNED, B. W. (1925), *Chimpanzee Intelligence and Its Vocal Expression*, Williams & Wilkins.

2 P. Oléron

Conceptual Thinking of the Deaf[1]

P. Oléron, 'Conceptual thinking of the deaf', *American Annals of the Deaf*, 1953, vol. 98, pp. 304–10.

Studies by psychologists (Oléron, 1950), as well as observations by educators (Doctor, 1950), indicate that deaf people are inferior to those with normal hearing, particularly in the domain of abstract mental activities.[2] It is therefore natural to be especially interested in this domain.

Among those mental activities, conceptual thinking seems to deserve study first of all. On the one hand, speaking in terms of the study of logic, concepts are basic to such mental operations as judgment and reasoning; and on the other hand, they depend for their formation on other operations such as abstraction.

From an experimental point of view, a concept is essentially a principle of classification, this classification being an operation by which objects are grouped according to a certain likeness. This is an *abstract* principle; that is to say, it is detached from observed data or imposed on these data. Conceptual thinking can therefore be studied experimentally with the aid of classification tests, provided these classifications have two characteristics; firstly, the category must be chosen from among other possible ones, secondly, the subject must be able to use successively the various possible categories. (If these two conditions are lacking, the classification could be made merely on the basis of perception or of interest.)

Such tests are classic: the Weigl form-color test, the sorting tests of Goldstein and of Halstead, the Wisconsin card sorting test.

1. An adaptation of a paper presented to the Thirteenth International Congress of Psychology at Stockholm, Sweden, 19 July 1951.
2. The deaf subjects considered here are subjects affected with a severe hearing loss, dating from birth or early childhood, who consequently could not have learned to speak in the normal way.

Three experimenters have applied tests of this kind to deaf subjects.

1. Höfler (1927) gave the Weigl sorting test (1927) to deaf children of school age. Among other behavior characteristics of these subjects, he noted, even in the oldest and most intelligent, attachment to a single aspect, use, or color. Out of thirty subjects, only four shifted spontaneously from one sorting to another.

2. MacAndrew (1948) used as materials twenty-five objects differing in form and substance (five forms: squares, circles, triangles, rectangles, semicircles; five substances: cork, cardboard, leather, plain glass, frosted glass). His deaf subjects, selected as to intelligence, had an average age of eleven years, eleven months. The test consisted of executing successively the two possible kinds of sorting. For this, the experimenter used three degrees of 'social pressure'. In ten trials only four children out of twenty-four succeeded, in spite of a preliminary exercise on ten objects sorted according to form and color.

3. Oléron (1951) used as materials twenty-seven cards which could be sorted according to the object represented, the color, or the number of these objects, as well as several series of blocks used for preliminary training. The subjects, having an average age of fifteen years seven months, were also selected as to intelligence. The test formed a progressive series. When the subject did not change his sorting category, the experimenter pointed out his error and made him try again. In case of a second failure the experimenter helped the subject by beginning to sort according to the new category. Out of twenty-four subjects, only six succeeded in sorting without error according to the three possible categories; the proportion of hearing subjects of the same age and mental level being fifteen out of twenty-four.

The agreement of the results of these three experiments is noteworthy and clearly indicates that the deaf experience difficulty in the realm of conceptual thinking. How can this fact be explained?

The difficulty of shifting has been described by Goldstein (Goldstein and Scheerer, 1941) and forms a part of what he calls the 'concrete attitude'. This concrete attitude is to be defined as the attitude of subjects who perceive objects as things with individual differences and not as representatives of a category or class. One might be led to apply Goldstein's theory to the deaf. This theory has been established in the study of aphasics who, like the deaf, present anomalies in the use of language.

As a matter of fact, one does observe behavior in deaf subjects similar to the behavior described by Goldstein or by his students, as follows (Oléron, 1951):

1. Pluralist sorting: the subject takes into account simultaneously several aspects (for example size and shape).

2. Concern for spatial arrangements (alignments, creation of equal series, etc).

3. Quest for 'difference' achieved by arranging the objects in alternating order (for instance, big, little, medium sized, instead of grouping all the big pieces or all the little ones).

However, Goldstein's view could not be accepted unless no differences existed between 'concrete' behavior and the behavior of the deaf subjects. However, differences exist, as listed below:

1. Deaf subjects can benefit from the experimenter's help; they understand easily when the experimenter begins to perform the correct sorting and they continue this.

2. In the color sorting test, deaf subjects do not in the least manifest the concrete behavior described by Goldstein. Heider and Heider (1940) have shown that deaf children sort color exactly like normal children.

3. The behavior described above, which one might be led to call 'concrete' is manifested by normal as well as by deaf subjects. Höfler (1934) had observed that the behavior of the deaf approximates that of normal young children (they associate objects which they have experienced) but only seldom resembles that of the aphasic (grouping of objects by pairs; for example, nail-hammer, etc.).

4. Finally the deaf subjects do not present the glaring anomalies discussed by Goldstein under the heading of the 'concrete attitude', (for example in the block design test).

Goldstein's view, therefore, cannot be applied to the deaf without modification. The characteristic common to the aphasics and the deaf is the difficulty of shifting, but this must be due to causes other than the 'concrete attitude'.

MacAndrew (1948) has advanced another hypothesis. He believes that the difficulty of shifting experienced by deaf subjects is due to the rigidity of their mental structure. This rigidity would be the result of their isolation from their environment and would also be found, but to a lesser degree, in the blind. In fact it is striking to note how deaf subjects persevere in the same mode of sorting and begin it again even though the experimenter asks them to change it.

MacAndrew's hypothesis is noteworthy, but what prevents one from accepting it is the very great ease manifested by deaf subjects in accepting suggestions or help (cf. above) which is not compatible with the idea of rigidity. Besides, the mental processes suggested by MacAndrew to explain this rigidity are hypothetical.

A more satisfactory and more comprehensive explanation can be found. When a subject sorts objects, he first must see if they are green or red, big or little. Next, he must group these objects by taking into account a common characteristic such as color, size or shape. In other words, two sorts of conditions are necessary: perceptive conditions (the perceptible qualities of the objects must be recognized); and also conceptual conditions (the objects must be grouped according to their belonging to a common class).

A sorting test, such as those considered here, cannot be correctly and easily carried out unless the first, or perceptive, conditions are subordinated to the second, or conceptual, ones. In this case the perceived characteristics (green, red, etc.) serve as clues or index, but the grouping is made according to the concept (color). However, this subordination may be imperfect or lacking, as happens when the subject lends too much importance to the observed data and tends to consider them as independent entities. At this point, it becomes difficult for him to perform the test correctly, because he becomes lost in irrelevant details and does not take into exclusive consideration the common class.

Thus a whole series of levels can be set up. On the highest level, the conceptual level, one finds perfect subordination of observed elements to the concept. On the successively lower levels, the observed elements tend more and more toward independence.

According to this interpretation, deaf subjects differ from hearing subjects in that they have a tendency to give too much importance to the observed elements. They find it difficult to subordinate these elements to concepts, but tend rather to regard them as independent entities. Thus they are usually found to be on an infra-conceptual level.

The above interpretation is confirmed by the examination of their verbal behavior. In one of the experiments mentioned (Oléron, 1951), the subjects were asked, once the task was finished, to state the reasons for their sorting (questions and answers were in written form). The descriptive attitude predominates in the answers, which seldom attain a level of logical thinking, i.e. a level in which the reasons for the action are given. Some of the subjects can only describe the objects, or the action that they or the experimenter have made. Others express the principle of classification in concrete terms (for example: the color blue, not color in general). The best answers point out the similarity of the objects grouped together which still is an observed datum. The idea of a common class is hardly ever expressed in abstract form (out of twenty-four subjects, only two spoke of 'number').

How does the view outlined above explain the difficulty of shifting? In order to sort the objects successively in different ways, the subject must distinguish the various sorting categories one from the other. For example, he must distinguish color from shape and number. But the objects seen are wholes in which the various aspects are fused together and do not appear as separate aspects. One sees, for example, three green trees; one does not apprehend the number, then the color, then the object. Thus, when the subject remains on a level in which perception dominates, he perceives objects as wholes. He sees the various aspects simultaneously present, but he is not able to use them successively in distinct classifications. The result is the repetition of the same kind of sorting and the apparent rigidity of behavior.

Therefore, the mental processes of the deaf are characterized by an especial concern for observed data, which data guide them in accomplishing the tasks set before them. This attitude becomes an obstacle when they are confronted with tests demanding a certain level of abstract thinking.

Unlike Goldstein's 'concrete attitude', this does not constitute an abnormal state. Rather it indicates a stage of incomplete development, similar to an earlier stage found in normal children. It can also be called a lack of balance in which the observed aspects outweigh the conceptual ones. However, the balance can be restored and deaf subjects can attain the conceptual level. This is, however, more difficult for them than for normal subjects.

It is legitimate to believe that education exerts a favorable influence here. Höfler (1934), for example, found that the Weigl sorting test was executed better by those subjects who possessed a better use of oral language. It must be that a knowledge of abstract terms, and especially an ability to use them, facilitates the execution of these tasks. A certain correlation exists (with, however, some exceptions) between the degree of success in sorting and the ability to relate verbally the reasons for the action. Language permits a more complete domination of concepts over observed elements.

In summary, the behavior of the deaf in sorting tests presents the following characteristics:

1. Difficulty in shifting from one sorting principle to another.

2. Repetition of one type of sorting already used, thus giving the impression of rigidity.

3. Difficulty in explaining the sorting principle adopted.

Neither Goldstein's theory on the concrete attitude nor MacAndrews' on rigidity due to isolation seems to provide a satisfactory explanation.

The view proposed in this paper holds that the difficulties of the deaf come from their attachment to observed data and from the nonsubordination of these data to abstract conceptual conditions. This is the mark of a retarded development rather than of a real incapacity. Progress in the use of language and of abstract terms should contribute to the development of conceptual thinking.

References

DOCTOR, P. V. (1950), 'On teaching the abstract to the deaf', *Volta Rev.*, vol. 52, pp. 547–9.

GOLDSTEIN, K., and SCHEERER, M. (1941), 'Abstract and concrete behavior: an experimental study with special tests', *Psycho. Monog.*, no. 1.

HEIDER, F., and HEIDER, G. M. (1940), 'Studies in the psychology of the deaf, 1: A comparison of color sorting behavior of deaf and hearing children', *Psychol. Monog.*, vol. 52, no. 1, pp. 6–22.

HÖFLER, R. (1927), 'Über die Bedeutung der Abstraktion für die geistige Entwicklung des taubstumme Kindes', *Z. Kinderforsch.*, vol. 33, pp. 414–44.

HÖFLER, R. (1934), 'Vergleichende Intelligerözuntersuchung bei Hörenden und Tauben mit Stummen Tests', *Vasammungbencht der Deutchen Gesellschaft fur Sprack-und Stimmbeilkunde*, Leipzig.

MACANDREW, H. (1948), 'Rigidity and isolation: a study of the deaf and the blind', *J. abnorm. soc. Psychol.*, vol. 43, pp. 470–94.

OLÉRON, P. (1950), 'A study of the intelligence of the deaf', *American Annals of the Deaf*, vol. 45, pp. 779–95.

OLÉRON, P. (1951), 'Pensée conceptuelle et language. Performances comparées de sourds-muets et d'entendants dans des epicures de classements multiples', *Année Psychologique*, vol. 41, pp. 89–120.

WEIGL, E. (1927), 'Zur Psychologie sogenannter Abstraktions prozesse', *Z. Psychologie*, vol. 103, pp. 1–45.

3 H. G. Furth

The Influence of Language on the Development of Concept Formation in Deaf Children[1]

H. G. Furth, 'The influence of language on the development of concept formation in deaf children', *Journal of Abnormal and Social Psychology*, 1961, volume 63, pp. 386–9.

Attempts to appraise the contribution of language[2] in the development of thinking are made difficult by the fact that ordinarily language and thinking develop together. However, children born with profound deafness, or afflicted with it at a very early age, do not learn ordinary language as the usual by-product of living; through them we may study the influence of language deficiency on the development of cognitive functions and clarify the role of language in cognition. There appears to be wide agreement that the average deaf person is inferior to hearing persons in all activities requiring thinking in abstract terms (Levine, 1950), Ewing and Stanton (1943), Templin (1950), Myklebust and Brutten (1953), and Oléron (1953) among others have held that the 'conceptual retardation' of deaf people is intrinsically related to their lack of language experience.

The purpose of this study is to demonstrate that the capacity of deaf people to deal with conceptual tasks may not in fact be generally retarded or impaired. Cognitive capacity, it is proposed, develops naturally with living, whether or not spoken language is part of the child's experience, and the role of language is restricted and extrinsic: e.g., familiarity with certain words may increase the efficiency with which the solution of certain problems may be reached. It follows that deaf children should not differ from hear-

1. This report is based on a Ph.D. dissertation submitted to the University of Portland, and part of this paper was read at the APA convention, Chicago, 1960. This investigation was supported by a fellowship, M F 9902, from the National Institutes of Health, United States Public Health Service.
2. The meaning of language in this article is restricted to the ordinary spoken language of a society.

ing children in their performance on conceptual learning tasks where it can be assumed that specific language experience does not favor the hearing child. However, on conceptual tasks where one has reason to assume that specific language familiarity gives the hearing child an advantage, deaf children should be inferior to hearing children.

Following a lead of Levy and Cuddy (1956), three concept learning tasks, differing in relation to the language repertoire of the two samples, were chosen to measure the basic cognitive potential of the children and establish norms for various age groups. The tasks were nonverbal and consisted of the operational attainment of a concept or a principle according to which a subject's choice could be consistently correct. For the first two tasks the correct principle or concept could be assumed to be as familiar or unfamiliar to the deaf as to the hearing children. The idea of 'same', involved in the first task, is so primitive that workers with deaf children report that there is no deaf child in school who does not have at least some gesture for this idea. On the basis of Levy and Ridderheim's (1958) study, partially replicated here, it seems that hearing children before the age of twelve do not have the concept of 'symmetry' readily available and, therefore, also should have no advantage over the deaf children on the symmetry task.

The concept of 'opposition', however, should be quite familiar to hearing children beyond six years old, as a study of Kreezer and Dallenbach (1929) showed. Our language employs many dimensions in terms of opposites: hot–cold, good–bad, long–short. As a rule a child learns the words denoting extremes before he learns the words characterizing the dimension as such. In such linguistic contexts a child becomes naturally acquainted with the concept of opposition and when he has reached the age of six can readily grasp the meaning of the word 'opposite'. In distinction from the hearing child, the deaf child, without the benefit of this specific language experience, finds it relatively difficult to learn the concept of 'opposite' for one dimension and then generalize the concept to other dimensions. Teachers of the deaf report that their pupils are being 'taught' the meaning of 'opposite' when they are in the intermediate grades or about fourteen years old.

Method
Subjects

All pupils aged seven to twelve years from the three schools for the deaf located in one state, with an additional forty-four subjects from a neighboring state, made up the deaf sample. Excluded were those few who did not have an early hearing loss of at least fifty decibels in the better ear. There were thirty subjects in each of the six age groups. Since the majority of the deaf sample consisted of practically all deaf children of the desired age living in the state at one time, it can be reasonably assumed that a relatively unbiased and representative sample of deaf children was achieved. The hearing sample consisted of 180 subjects randomly selected from five different grade schools and classified into six age groups, seven to twelve years, of thirty subjects each. The hearing sample had an equal number of boys and girls; however, the deaf sample at ages seven, nine and twelve showed a slight imbalance in favor of boys.

The procedure of matching the hearing and deaf group only on age and sex and permitting other possibly pertinent variables to vary randomly was judged superior to an attempted control of IQ, institutional education, etc. With regard to IQ in particular, it is known that tests, standardized on a hearing sample and based on an average experiential and educational background, are of questionable value with deaf children. The deaf group had a somewhat lower overall socioeconomic rating than the particular hearing sample used in this study. In the light of the reported relationship between the intelligence of children and parental occupation (Terman and Merrill, 1937), the somewhat uneven socioeconomic distribution in the two samples would bias the results, if at all, against the deaf and, therefore, against the main hypothesis.

Tasks

The three tasks employed in the study were these:

Sameness task. This task consisted of a series of forty different pairs of round tin covers with two simple figures drawn on each cover. The two figures on one of the covers were identical, on the other the two were different. Under the cover with the identical figures a checker was placed indicating to the child the correct choice. The criterion for success was ten consecutive correct choices. The trials were terminated after the criterion was reached, or with the first error after trial thirty. A modified stimulus presentation apparatus was used on this and the following task.

Symmetry task. Forty different pairs of 7 × 9 inch cards were prepared for this task and simple figures were drawn in heavy black ink on a white background. On one card of each pair the figure to be rewarded was a symmetrical one, while on the other it was asymmetrical. The procedure and criterion were the same as those used with the 'sameness' task.

Opposition task. This task was in two parts:

1. Opposition Acquisition. From a set of eight wooden discs ranging in diameter from 0·5 inch to 2·25 inches and hidden from the subject's view, four were selected in a fixed order and randomly thrown on the table in front of the child. The experimenter either pointed to the largest or to the smallest disc. If the experimenter picked the largest, the subject's task was to discover that he had to pick the smallest; if the experimenter picked the smallest, the subject had to pick the largest. Subjects were given a maximum of thirty-six trials. The criterion was six consecutive correct choices.

2. Opposition Transfer. One uncorrected trial was given only to those subjects who succeeded on Opposition Acquisition, on each of the following six Transfer dimensions: Volume, Length, Number, Brightness, Position, and Texture. While the experimenter pointed to the stimulus on one extreme of the continuum of four or five stimuli, the child showed transfer of concept by pointing to the opposite extreme.

The performance of the two groups was compared in terms of the proportion of subjects reaching the criterion. Other methods of measuring performance yielded similar trends and are not reported here except in the case of Opposition Acquisition. For Opposition Transfer the total number of nontransferred responses was used for computational purposes.

Results

The results for the three Acquisition tasks are presented in Table 1. The chi squares are based on the actual number of passing and failing subjects, a total of thirty for each age group and 180 for each entire sample.

The comparative results for the sameness and symmetry tasks were fairly similar. The hearing group showed no superiority over the deaf; on the contrary, there was a tendency for the younger deaf children to surpass the hearing children of comparable age. Also, the overall comparisons for all ages combined on the symmetry task was significantly in favor of the deaf group.

Both groups showed a significant change of proportional success with age: on the sameness task the chi square ($df = 5$) for the hearing group was $18 \cdot 27$ ($p < 0 \cdot 01$) and for the deaf group $13 \cdot 75$ ($p < 0 \cdot 02$); on the symmetry task the respective values were $23 \cdot 04$ and $29 \cdot 00$ ($p < 0 \cdot 01$). While this change was consistently in a positive direction for the hearing children, the eleven-year-old deaf group reversed the trend for the deaf sample: the chi square, comparing the successes of the eleven- and ten-year-old deaf children for the sameness task was $5 \cdot 42$ ($p < 0 \cdot 05$) and for the symmetry task $4 \cdot 27$ ($p < 0 \cdot 02$).

Table 1 Number of Successful Hearing and Deaf Subjects on Concept Tasks in Each Age Group
(30 subjects in each age group)

	Sameness			Symmetry			Opposition Acquisition		
Age	Hearing	Deaf	x^2	Hearing	Deaf	x^2	Hearing	Deaf	x^2
7	4	7	0·44	6	4	0·12	29	14	16·09**
8	6	16	5·81*	4	11	3·20	26	19	3·20
9	12	16	0·60	8	19	6·73**	28	23	2·09
10	11	20	4·27*	12	21	4·31*	30	28	0·31
11	13	11	0·07	14	11	0·27	30	28	0·31
12	22	15	2·54	21	19	0·08	30	27	1·40
Total	68	85	2·91	65	85	4·13*	173	139	26·18**

* $p = 0 \cdot 05$.
** $p = 0 \cdot 01$.

Hearing children were significantly superior to deaf children on the opposition acquisition task, as indicated by the chi square testing for overall differences. The consistency of this superiority at each age level is more clearly revealed in Table 2. The median number of errors for the combined samples was $3 \cdot 05$. Analysing these data for improvement of performance with age, the chi square values of 27·67 for the hearing group and 14·17 for the deaf group were found to be significant at the 0·01 and 0·02 levels, respectively ($df = 5$).

Table 2 Number of Subjects Making Less than Median Errors on Opposition Acquisition

Age	Hearing	Deaf	Chi square
7	8	0·5	5·79*
8	9	3	3·75
9	16	7	5·71*
10	17	8·5	4·93*
11	19·5	9	7·37**
12	25	10	15·43**
Total	94·5	38	36·79**

* $p = 0·05$.
** $p = 0·01$.

Table 3 Mean Nontransferred Responses of Deaf and Hearing Subjects on Opposition Transfer in Each Age Group

	Hearing		Deaf	
Age	N	Mean responses	N	Mean responses
7	29	2·00	14	2·78
8	26	1·54	19	2·80
9	28	1·25	23	2·17
10	30	0·73	28	1·61
11	30	0·60	28	1·78
12	30	0·57	27	1·48
Total	173	1·10	139	2·00

Table 3 provides the relevant data for the transfer test. As the nontransferred responses were fairly normally distributed they were subjected to an analysis of variance. For this purpose thirty-four hearing subjects were randomly eliminated so that the N of corresponding cells for each age group was equal. The analysis yielded an F of 24·02 for the hearing–deafness variable, an F of 9·42 for the age variable, and an F of 4·50 for the interaction. The significant ($p < 0.01$) interaction and differences obtained between the two samples at each age level indicated that the hearing children were superior, the degree of superiority varying with age.

Discussion

The facilitative influence of language was highlighted in the present study when one considers that the same deaf children who demonstrated their equality on the sameness and symmetry tasks were consistently below the same hearing children on the opposition task. On the two former problems, the deaf children in the lower age range were actually superior, perhaps because of their less sophisticated approach to the problem situation. Insofar as the problem required the attainment of one simple concept, the hearing child's greater store of available categories may have been distracting.

Regarding the developmental trend in the hearing group, the findings on the symmetry task are in excellent agreement with the results of Levy and Ridderheim (1958) on an entirely different sample. The drop in the relative performance of the eleven- and twelve-year-old deaf group is somewhat puzzling, if it is not a sampling artifact.

Successful performance on these concept learning tasks, it should be understood, is related to, but in no way identified with, the knowledge of the concept or of the word. Although both deaf and hearing children at the youngest age level knew the word or the concept of 'sameness', only few of them succeeded on the sameness task. At the other extreme, neither deaf nor hearing seven-year-old children were familiar with the word 'symmetry', yet a few seven-year-old children succeeded on that particular task.

Summary

Contrary to widely accepted conclusions that deaf people are inferior in conceptual thinking and the theories proposed to link conceptual inferiority and language retardation, the present study suggested that the influence of language on concept formation is extrinsic and specific. According to this view, language experience may increase the efficiency of concept formation in a certain situation, but is not a necessary prerequisite for the development of the basic capacity to abstract and generalize.

To test this assumption, 180 deaf and 180 hearing subjects, thirty subjects for each age group from seven to twelve years, were given three nonverbal concept learning tasks differing with respect to the relevance of the language experience of the two samples. With regard to the sameness and symmetry task, the groups were assumed to be equivalent in relevant language experience. In contrast, concerning Opposition Acquisition and Transfer, specific language experience was assumed to give hearing children an advantage over the deaf. Accordingly, it was predicted that the hearing subjects would not be superior to the deaf subjects in their performance on the sameness and symmetry tasks, yet would be superior on Opposition Acquisition and Transfer problems. The results confirmed the experimental predictions and gave support to the proposed theory.

References

EWING, A. S. G., and STANTON, D. A. G. (1943), 'A study of children with defective hearing', *Teach. Deaf.*

KREEZER, G., and DALLENBACH, K. M. (1929), 'Learning relation of opposition', *Amer. J. Psycol.*, vol. 41, pp. 432–41.

LEVINE, E. (1950), 'Psychological testing of the deaf', in *Rehabilitation of the Deaf and the Hard of Hearing*, Federal Security Agency, Office of Vocational Rehabilitation, Washington.

LEVY, N. M., and CUDDY, J. M. (1956), 'Concept learning in the educationally retarded child of normal intelligence', *J. consult. Psychol.*, vol. 20, pp. 445–8.

LEVY, N. M., and RIDDERHEIM, D. S. (1958), 'A developmental study of the concept of symmetry', paper read at Eastern Psychological Association, Philadelphia.

MYKLEBUST, H. R., and BRUTTEN, M. (1953), 'A study of the visual perception of deaf children', *Acta oto-laryngol*, Stockholm supplement, no. 105.

OLÉRON, P. (1953), 'Conceptual thinking of the deaf', *Amer. Ann. Deaf*, vol. 98, pp. 304–10.

TEMPLIN, M. C. (1950), *The Development of Reasoning in Children with Normal and Defective Hearing*, University of Minnesota Press.

TERMAN, L. M., and MERRILL, M.A. (1937), *Measuring Intelligence*, Houghton Mifflin.

4 De Lee Lantz and E. H. Lenneberg

Verbal Communication and Colour Memory[1]

De Lee Lantz and E. H. Lenneberg, 'Verbal communication and color memory in the deaf and hearing', *Child Development* (1966), volume 37, pp. 765–79.

In a recent study by Lantz and Steffire (1964), a language variable (Communication Accuracy) was found to be related to performance on a cognitive task (memory). The accuracy with which colors could be remembered was significantly correlated with the accuracy with which they could be communicated in the language. Given the results of this study, which used adults with normal language skills as subjects, another question suggested itself: How would people who have a very limited language system perform on the same task? If they are able to do equally well, we cannot make the statement that a well-developed language system is necessarily related to this kind of cognitive performance. There may be more than one way this performance can be mediated. If they are not able to do as well on the memory task, we have additional support for the hypothesis that language is helpful in at least certain kinds of cognitive behavior. The task was therefore repeated in the present study with young deaf children and control group of hearing children.

A further question concerns the generality of the Lantz and Steffire findings. Will Communication Accuracy predict memory

1. The project described in this paper was supported by the National Science Foundation, Grant GS300, and by the Center for Cognitive Studies, Harvard University. We are very grateful to the following institutions, their superintendents and staffs, for their cooperation and participation in the study: E. B. Boatner, American School for the Deaf, West Hartford, Connecticut; W. H. Bragner, Beverly School for the Deaf, Beverly Massachusetts; F. I. Phillips, Kendall School for the Deaf, Washington, D.C.; C. D. O'Connor, Lexington School for the Deaf, New York City; G. Detmold, Gallaudet College, Washington, D.C.; J. W. McGrath, Belmont Public Schools, Belmont, Massachusetts; and D. Ogden, Old Dominion College, Norfolk, Virginia. W. Banks, F. Rhodes, and F. Thomas provided assistance in the data collection.

performance for groups who perhaps use language differently from normal speakers? That is, if Communication Accuracy differs in such groups, is memory still related to it in the way it was for the Lantz and Stefflre subjects (Ss)? To provide information on this point, deaf adults and a hearing-adult control group were also studied, which gave us four groups to compare, each differing on the dimensions of age and hearing.

Not all comparisons between deaf and hearing subjects allow clearcut inferences about the specific role that language plays in given tasks. In order to understand the role of language it is necessary to demonstrate in a general way that some aspect of language is related to a given psychological phenomenon (Lenneberg, 1953; Lenneberg and Roberts, 1956). In this study we begin with a cognitive task – a memory test – which has been shown to be highly correlated with a measurable language variable – Communication Accuracy – and is not just assumed to be related to language.

Method
Subjects

Four groups of Ss were tested: six-year-old hearing children, six-year-old deaf children, deaf college students, and hearing college students.

Deaf children. A totally language-free sample could not be obtained since deaf children are frequently given some language tutoring at an early age. It would have been impossible to find a sizable number of children old enough to be able to grasp the task instructions who had no language training. But the language experience and skills possessed by a six-year-old deaf child are very meager compared to those of six-year-old hearing children who have been exposed to oral language all their lives.

Thirty children (eighteen girls and twelve boys) from four residential schools for the deaf in four different states were used as subjects. Only children with congenital peripheral deafness and no other handicaps (for example, brain damage) were included in the study. The criterion for degree of deafness was a loss of at least 75 db averaged over the three critical speech frequencies (500, 1000, and 2000 cps) in the better ear. The average loss was 87 db. or profound deafness, with a range from 75 to 102 db, and a modal loss of 92 db. The average age was six years, four months. IQ scores were obtained from the schools. The Leiter International Performance Scale had been used in most instances, but the WISC, the Merill-Palmer, and the Hiskey's Nebraska Test of Learning Aptitude in Young Deaf Children had been used with some children. IQ scores ranged from eighty-two to 133. The average IQ score (109) is not very meaningful in view of the different tests used, the probable differences in administration, and the general unreliability of IQ scores for children of this age. However, it does indicate that the average level of intellectual functioning is probably quite within the 'average' range.

Hearing children. Forty-five first graders (twenty-three girls and twenty-two boys) in a public school were used in the study. The average age was six years, five months at the time of testing. The IQ scores on the Stanford Binet, which all the children had been given the year before, ranged from ninety-one to 138 with an average of 113. Again, caution should be used in interpreting these figures.

Deaf and hearing adults. Thirty-eight undergraduates (twenty-one men and seventeen women) at a college for the deaf comprised the adult deaf sample. The average hearing loss was 84 db. in the critical speech frequencies. All *S*s had been deaf from birth or became deaf within the first eighteen months of life.

The hearing adults (fifteen men and fifteen women) were also college undergraduates. They were all native English speakers without specialized training with color.

Stimulus materials

The colors used were part of the Farnsworth-Munsell 100 Hue Test. This is a circular array of low-saturation colors, perceptually equidistant steps apart, varying only in hue and having nearly constant saturation and brightness (Farnsworth, 1949). The colors are set in black plastic caps. Figs. 1 and 2 show the inside and outside of the apparatus for presenting the colors, described in detail in Lantz and Stefflre (1964). The twenty chips on the inner circle are the 'test colors', since they are the ones on which *S*s are tested in the memory task. The forty-three colors on the outer circle – referred to here as 'comparison colors' – include duplicates of the twenty test colors.

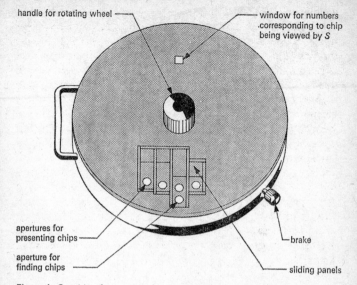

handle for rotating wheel

window for numbers corresponding to chip being viewed by *S*

apertures for presenting chips

aperture for finding chips

brake

sliding panels

Figure 1 Outside of apparatus for presenting color chips

Procedure

For three groups – hearing children, deaf adults, and hearing adults – both the language measure (Communication Accuracy) and the cognitive measure (recognition scores) were determined as described by Lantz and Stefflre (1964). For the deaf children, only the recognition task could be administered, since they lacked the skills necessary for the Communication Accuracy task (which is why this group was originally chosen). Fifteen of the thirty deaf six-year-olds were able to name some of the colors so that *E* could understand them. This information was collected.

Color ordering and sorting. Some control for level of perceptual acuity was wanted so that differences in recognition could not be ascribed to differences in ability to discriminate the Farnsworth-Munsell colors. The Farnsworth-Munsell 100 Hue Test of Color Discrimination (1949) was administered in its originally designed form to eighteen deaf adults and ten hearing adults. The first color of the series (chip no. 1) and a middle color chip (no. 43) were

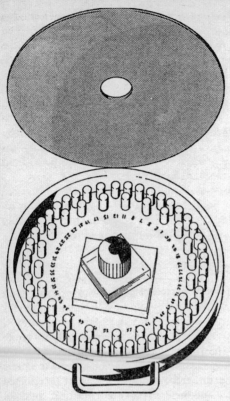

Figure 2 Apparatus with lid open to show test and comparison colors

placed about a foot apart from one another on the table, and the twenty-two colors in between were mixed up and put in front of S. The S's task was to line up the colors between the two end ones so that they formed an orderly series in terms of hue from one end to the other. The S was instructed to work quickly for he would be stopped at the end of ninety seconds. All Ss finished within this time. When the first half had been done, chip nos. forty-five and eighty-five were placed on the table, and the colors in between were given to S with the same instructions.

Pilot testing revealed that this ordering task was extremely difficult to convey to six-year-olds. Therefore, a sorting test using 21 Farnsworth-Munsell colors (every fourth color) was devised for both hearing and deaf children. The S's task was to sort the twenty-one colors into groups that he thought belonged together. Since this is a circular array with equal intervals between colors, breaking points between groups of colors are completely arbitrary. This makes it a category-formation test, as well as a perceptual test, on which the two groups of children could be compared. Any number of groups was acceptable, as was any number of colors within a group. Perceptual errors occurred when color chips put in one group were not sequentially numbered, or in other words, when hues were out of place.

Since verbal instructions could not be given to the 6-year-old deaf Ss, two nonverbal demonstration tasks were used for all children, hearing as well as deaf. Thirty deaf children and twenty hearing children were used in this phase of the experiment.

Recognition. After the sorting (or ordering) task, the same Ss were given the recognition task. This was the nonverbal memory task to be related to the linguistic variable, Communication Accuracy. Two test colors were presented simultaneously for five seconds through openings in the lid of the test apparatus. Following a five-second interval during which no colors were in view, S was asked to find each of the two colors among the forty-three comparison colors which could be viewed one at a time through another opening in the apparatus. The S rotated the color disk himself. This was repeated ten times, or until all twenty test colors had been shown. Pairings were random from S to S. For the hearing and deaf adults, instructions were given verbally or in writing.

Again, since verbal or written instructions could not be given to the deaf children, both the hearing and the deaf six-year-old Ss were given a series of demonstration tasks which contained the idea of picking out from a group of colors some color they had just been shown. After S successfully completed the demonstration tasks, the experimental task itself was introduced.

Recognition error scores were obtained by recording the difference between the code number of the comparison chip selected by S and the code number of the test chip which had been presented. The total score for a color was the sum of these individual scores divided by the sample N. This yielded a mean error score for each of the twenty test colors which could be compared to the mean error score for Communication Accuracy for that chip. This arithmetic procedure was possible because Farnsworth-Munsell code numbers correspond to hue steps which are equidistant.

Communication Accuracy. The language variable used in this study was Communication Accuracy, or how accurately a color description communicates to someone else. Measurement of Communication Accuracy required two sets of Ss: one group (encoders) who named colors and another group (decoders) who received only the names and tried to find the colors to which the names originally referred. Fifteen hearing children, ten deaf adults, and ten hearing adults acted as encoders, and another ten Ss in each group acted as decoders. Neither encoders nor decoders were used in the recognition task.

The general procedure for encoding was to show each S the twenty test colors one at a time in the test apparatus. Ss were asked to name the color, 'using the word or words you would use to name it to a friend so that he or she could pick it out.' They were asked to do it as quickly as they could but to take time to be satisfied with their answer. The entire range of colors was shown to S before he began naming. For the adult deaf Ss, instructions were written out.

As the next step in determining Communication Accuracy, the names given by the encoders were read to the decoders. On a table in front of a decoding S were the forty-three comparison colors. The E instructed S: 'After I say a name, look at the colors in front of you, and point to the one that seems to be the color to which that name refers.' When S chose a color, E wrote down the Farnsworth-Munsell color code number.

Decoding responses could be expressed in error terms by noting the difference between the code number of the chip to which the encoder originally gave a name and the code number of the chip selected by the decoder when he was read that name. The error scores were then averaged across Ss, giving each test color a mean error score. That is, each of the twenty test colors was scored on how accurately it could be communicated from S to S within each of the three groups for whom Communication Accuracy measures were obtained. (The procedure for measuring Communication Accuracy is given in detail in Lantz and Steffire, 1964.)

Results and discussion
Group differences in recognition and communication accuracy scores

Table 1 gives recognition and communication accuracy mean error scores and standard deviations. If possession of language skills is related to memory, we would expect the subject group with the greatest language facility to perform the best on recognition, and vice versa. As expected, hearing adults did best on the task, and deaf children did least well. The order obtained on recognition for the two groups in between is consistent with the order obtained on Communication Accuracy.

Table 1 Means and Standard Deviations of Recognition and Communication Accuracy Error Scores for All Groups

Group	Recognition error score		Communication Accuracy error score	
	Mean	*S D*	*Mean*	*S D*
Deaf children	3·37	0·36		
Hearing children	2·87	0·42	2·33	0·83
Deaf adults	2·13	0·54	2·25	0·58
Hearing adults	2·00	0·40	2·06	0·52

A two-way analysis of variance for the effects of age and hearing on recognition was performed. The effect of age was significant beyond the 0·001 level ($F = 73 \cdot 56$), and the effect of hearing status was significant beyond the 0·05 level ($F = 5 \cdot 06$). There was no interaction ($F = 2 \cdot 91$). Then t tests of the differences of the recognition means for each group were made between all six possible pairings of the four groups of Ss. All ts were significant at the 0·001 level (one-tailed test), except the t for hearing and deaf adults which was not significant. Figure 3 illustrates relations among the recognition curves. (Color chip no. 17 is a yellow-green, 41 a blue-green, 55 a blue, and 79 a red-purple, with gradations in between in this circular array of colors.) Communication Accuracy scores do not differ significantly from one another when compared in terms of parametric statistics; there are, however, differences between the Communication Accuracy curves obtained from the deaf and from the hearing adults in terms of the spectral location of the peaks.

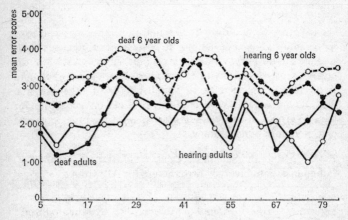

Farnsworth – Munsell stimulus continuum

Figure 3 Recognition error scores for all groups

None of the recognition differences between the deaf and hearing can be explained on the basis of differences in perceptual discrimination. The percentage of deaf and hearing children who made no errors on the sorting task was practically identical (53 per cent of the deaf, 54·5 per cent of the hearing). Likewise, there was little difference in the percentage of each group making only one error (10 per cent of the deaf and 13·6 per cent of the hearing). Almost twice as many hearing as deaf children made multiple errors, but this was counterbalanced by the fact that, while none of the hearing children failed to do the last demonstration task and move on to the experimental task, five of the deaf children could not do the task. Since the mean recognition error of these five Ss (3·37) did not differ from the mean error of the other deaf Ss, they were included in the analysis of the recognition data.

The average discrimination score for the deaf adults was 3·27, or less than one error per S (one error, the transposition of two adjacent color caps, receives a score of 4 (Farnsworth, 1949)). On the other hand, the average score for the hearing adults was six, or $1\frac{1}{2}$ errors per S. While the difference between the scores of the two groups is not statistically significant, certainly it is large enough in favor of the deaf to demonstrate that any differences in their use of color cannot be accounted for by poorer discrimination.

If we view the children's sorting task as a category-formation test in addition to a perceptual discrimination test, we again find no difference between the deaf and hearing. The two groups differed little on the average number of categories into which they sorted the twenty-one colors, (5·6 for the deaf, 5·7 for the hearing), the average size of the group they formed (4·1 and 3·9 colors per group), or the size of group most frequently formed (4 and 3 colors). The ranges, too, were quite similar.

Relations between communication accuracy and recognition

Of greater interest than the mean performance differences among the groups is the consistency with which Communication Accuracy scores predict recognition scores. The product-moment correlation coefficient between Communication Accuracy and recognition were 0·53 ($p < 0·01$, one-tailed test) for the hearing children, 0·44 ($p < 0·025$) for the deaf adults, and 0·67 ($p < 0·005$) for the hearing adults. Figures 4, 5, and 6 illustrate the relation between the two variables.

The size of these correlations bears mentioning. Earlier studies (Brown and Lenneberg, 1954; Lantz and Steffle, 1964) demonstrated that the correlation between language measures and recognition increases as the difficulty of the recognition task increases. Rather than use a more difficult task (more colors than two and a longer interval than five seconds), which may have led to larger correlations, a relatively simple task was chosen for this study to assure that the six-year-old children could grasp the requirements.

The *patterning* of Communication Accuracy scores across the stimulus continuum is not the same for deaf and hearing adults (see Figs. 5 and 6) even though the means are similar. A rank-

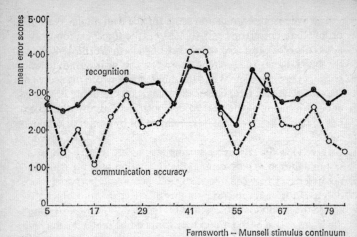

Figure 4 Relations between Communication Accuracy and recognition scores for hearing six year olds

order correlation between Communication Accuracy scores for these two groups was only 0·23 (not significant). The two groups are using the aspect of language under study in different ways, yet the correlation between the language variable and recognition holds in each group. This attests to the generality of the predictive ability of Communication Accuracy.

On the other hand, the patterning of the scores of the hearing children is similar to that of the hearing adults (see Figs. 4 and 6). The rank-order correlation between them was 0·47 ($p < 0·05$). This is of importance because it indicates that hearing six-year-old children are already using this aspect of language in much the same way as hearing adults, whereas deaf adults have developed a different pattern altogether.

The same phenomenon holds for recognition as well. Examination of Fig. 3 discloses that the recognition scores of deaf six-year-olds and deaf adults vary in much the same way, although the average error of the adults is lower. The recognition variations of deaf children and deaf adults have a rank-order correlation of 0·73 ($p < 0·001$). The same thing is true for hearing six-year-olds and hearing adults, although to a lesser extent (the rank-order

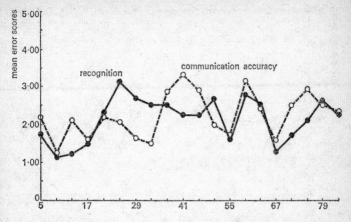

Figure 5 Relations between Communication Accuracy and recognition scores for deaf adults

correlation between their scores is 0·47 ($p < 0·05$)). As with Communication Accuracy, the hearing seem to develop from childhood to adulthood, along a single path, becoming increasingly better with age, but keeping the same patterning. The deaf, to an even more striking degree, do the same thing but along a different path, as further examination of Fig. 3 suggests. The divergence of the paths for deaf and hearing is also statistically indicated by nonsignificant rank-order correlations between recognition scores of 0·26 for deaf and hearing children and 0·37 for deaf and hearing adults.

The fact that six-year-old deaf children have already established a patterning of recognition very similar to the patterning for the adult deaf, whose recognition can be predicted by Communication Accuracy, raises a crucial point regarding the developmental role played by language in this skill. Two interpretations immediately present themselves: Either the children were not as deficient in their use of language as we thought – and therefore the high correlation is because the children are already using Communication Accuracy in the same way as the adults – or language is something that develops later and follows the lines already laid down by other cognitive skills.

De Lee Lantz and E. H. Lenneberg 69

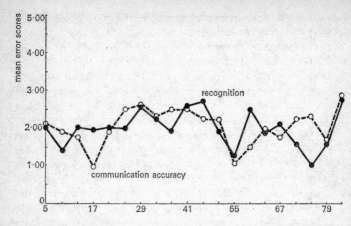

Figure 6 Relations between Communication Accuracy and recognition scores for hearing adults

It is easy to demonstrate that neither of these alternatives is correct. Both of them would necessarily lead to the prediction that Communication Accuracy scores of the deaf adults would correlate positively with recognition scores of the deaf children. However, the rank-order correlation for these variables is only 0·1, making it clear that neither are the six year olds using language in the way the adults are, nor does this aspect of language develop by molding itself to the contours of previously established recognition performance. (The recognition scores of the hearing children, however, does correlate significantly with Communication Accuracy scores of hearing adults. That rank-order correlation was 0·40 ($p < 0.05$). Since the children's own Communication Accuracy scores correlated 0·53 with their recognition scores, and since differences due to age are present, we would expect to find a correlation somewhere below 0·53 but still significant if they share a common language usage.)

A third interpretation seems more likely to explain why the recognition scores of deaf children and deaf adults correlate strongly (0·73), while the adults' Communication Accuracy correlates (0·44) only with adult recognition but not with the children's recognition. Even though children and adults behave in very much the same way on recognition, the children's scores do not coincide completely with the adult scores. In other words, there is some aspect in the recognition behavior of the adult that we cannot predict from the children's scores, indicating that some influence affects the adults that is not affecting the children. Our data suggest that this additional influence is due to the language variable, Communication Accuracy. Apparently, sometime before the age of six, the deaf establish a characteristic pattern of memory (relative facilitation for recognizing some and inhibition for other colors). To a significant extent, this pattern remains in effect in adulthood, but now, with the acquisition of language, a new mnemonic vehicle has become available. Our variable Communication Accuracy may be regarded as a characterization of this vehicle.

Could it be that the varying recognition scores along the color continuum are simply a reflection of random sampling variation? This possibility is definitely ruled out by the repeatability of the patterns of recognition. Correlations between sets of recognition scores found in three different studies (Burnham and Clark, 1955; Lantz and Stefflre, 1964; and the present study) range from 0·60 to 0·68. Thus the color recognition of hearing adults is always facilitated for certain colors in our array and at a disadvantage for others. The patterning of errors along this continuum is very stable. The hearing children were found to have the same patterning of recognition errors, that is, were facilitated in the same areas of the color spectrum as the adults, even though their recognition skill is not yet as good. The fact that deaf children and deaf adults are also alike in their recognition patterning but both differ from the hearing makes it unlikely that we are dealing with any spurious phenomenon.

Our findings pose a further problem about which we can only speculate. Why does the divergence in language occur between the deaf and hearing, as indicated by the low correlation between Communication Accuracy for deaf and hearing adults? Probably the divergence has its origins in the very early verbal and social influence upon the hearing children as against the relative isolation of the deaf. But exactly what is influencing the deaf and leading to their common characteristic performance is an intriguing question that is unanswerable on the basis of our data. The difference in Communication Accuracy between the deaf and hearing adults is particularly interesting because, after all, both groups use English. The incongruence between the performances indicates that Communication Accuracy reflects not only the semantic properties of a natural language but also the particular use that a group of speakers makes of the language. The deaf when communicating to each other or to themselves apparently make a different use of English than the hearing population.

Comparisons of deaf and hearing children

In spite of the very strong overall trend for the deaf children to do worse on recognition than the hearing children, they did slightly better than the hearing children on four color chips out of the total of twenty. These four inconsistencies could be due simply to chance fluctuations. However, if even one of them represents a true superiority, it demonstrates something that is usually overlooked. It may be true that language does, as Luria (1959) states, free us from control by environmental stimuli. However, along with the much discussed advantages of this goes the disadvantage of misjudging the environment when our language for that particular aspect is ineffective, that is, when codability is poor. In that case, language habits may actually hinder a person – may exert a 'pull' on memory in the wrong direction. (A demonstration of this is reported in Lantz and Stefflre, 1964, in a section on influence of judgments of typical colors on memory.) Deaf children, being free from this pull, may then do better than the hearing children at recognizing some of these poorly coded colors, even though, on the whole, their memory is handicapped by lack of a language system.

These speculations are, of course, merely suggested, not demonstrated, by the data. Consistent with this reasoning is the fact that two of the four colors the deaf remembered better were colors which received the poorest Communications Accuracy scores from the hearing children. The largest discrepancy from the trend and, therefore, presumably the least likely to be due to chance, occurred at the color which, for the hearing children, received the worst Communication Accuracy score.

Smaller correlations between language measures and recognition have been found in adults as the recognition task was made easier. Brown and Lenneberg (1954) and Lantz and Stefflre (1964) conjectured that when the task is simple and the time interval small, visual memory can be relied on, and the necessity to store a verbal label is not so great. Reasoning from this, and from the idea that language increases the amount of information a person can store, we expected that the deaf children would probably do much better at making their first recognition choice than at making their second recognition choice of the pair of test colors presented simultaneously. Since the interval between presentation of the two colors and recognition is only five seconds, visual memory alone might be an effective aid in picking out one color but would break down on the second color, both because more time had elapsed and because the additional color may place too great a burden on storage. Hearing children, however, storing verbal descriptions rather than relying on visual memory alone, would not be expected to show as great a discrepancy between their first and second recognition choices. Two colors would not place as much of a burden on their more efficient storage system.

To test this, a recognition score was obtained for the first and second recognition choices separately, and t tests of the differences were done. For the deaf children, the mean recognition error score was 4·35 for the first color and 5·41 for the second color. (In order to see the differences more clearly, no cut-off point was used in calculating these recognition errors. For the calculation of the means given in Table 1, a cut-off point of ± 5 hue steps was used, making those means lower in comparison with the ones given here.) This difference in accuracy between the first and second choices was significant beyond the 0·001 level. Since any given pairing of colors was not repeated, but randomized from S to S, there is little likelihood that the colors chosen second were, as a group, inherently more difficult. No significant difference was found for the hearing children, whose mean scores were 3·52 for the first color choice and 3·94 for the second. (No differences were found for either adult group.) This is consistent with our view that utilization of verbal descriptions in memory is a more efficient system that can handle two colors about as easily as one, whereas the efficiency of purely visual memory rapidly falls off as more information must be stored over longer periods of time.

Much of the work on the language-thought hypothesis has been based on the belief that possession of a verbal label (especially possession of a commonly agreed-upon label) underlies the ability to perform various cognitive tasks more effectively. The fact that some of the deaf children in this study possessed the same names for the colors as the hearing children, but were far inferior to them on ability to remember the colors, makes it clear that the mere possession of a verbal label does not necessarily affect cognitive behavior. Apparently the hearing children used their verbal descriptions in some kind of intrapersonal communication system – that is, communicated to themselves across time – and the deaf children did not make this kind of use of their verbal descriptions.

In spite of good color-discrimination abilities, a completely nonverbal test, high motivation, and much experience with the kind of task used (exposure to the John Tracy Clinic Correspondence Course which introduces color matching at the age of two), the deaf children still did worse than the hearing children on the recognition task. None of these factors can explain the results.

The complex interrelations between recognition and communication accuracy point up the necessity of having not only information about cognition but also about a language variable before conclusions can be drawn about the role of language in cognitive abilities of the deaf. The results are consistent with the idea that a more adequately developed language system than the deaf children possessed is necessary to do well on the kind of memory task used here. Deaf adults are able to do well on the memory task not because language plays no part in the task (as might have been concluded if no language variable had been measured) but because they had adequately developed and utilized the pertinent aspect of language. The fact that they develop this aspect of language, as well as recognition, differently from hearing Ss raises some important unanswered questions, but it does allow an answer to one of our initial questions. Communication Accuracy, no matter how it is patterned by a group, continues to predict recognition, which strengthens the belief that this is indeed a variable of general influence and interest.

References

BROWN, B. W., and LENNEBERG, E. H. (1954), 'A study in language and cognition', *J. abnorm. soc. Psychol.*, vol. 49, pp. 454–82.

BURNHAM, R. W., and CLARK, J. R. (1955), 'A test of hue memory', *J. appl. Psychol.*, vol. 39, pp. 164–72.

FARNSWORTH, D. (1949), *The Farnsworth-Munsell 100 Hue Test for the Examination of Color Discrimination: Manual.* Munsell Color Co, Baltimore.

LANTZ, DE LEE, and STEFFLRE, V. (1964), 'Language and cognition revisited', *J. abnorm. soc. Psychol.*, vol. 69, pp. 472–81.

LENNEBERG, E. H. (1953), 'Cognition in ethnolinguistics', *Language*, vol. 29, pp. 463–71.

LENNEBERG, E. H., and ROBERTS, J. M. (1956), 'The language of experiment: a study in methodology', *Int. J. Amer. Linguist.*, vol. 22, suppl. (mem. 13).

LURIA, A. B. (1959), 'The directive function of speech in development and dissolution', *Word*, vol. 15, pp. 341–64.

Part Two Learning Language

There are few experimenters to date who have explicitly considered language development in relation to cognitive development. Donaldson and Wales (Reading 5) have attempted to do this for some relational terms. The McNeills (Reading 6) studied the development of the negative in one Japanese child. Negation is syntactically simple, but has several distinct lexical forms in Japanese. These forms indicate different dimensions of meaning, and the McNeills demonstrated that these dimensions of meaning were successively acquired, with the general word for denial appearing last.

5 M. Donaldson and R. Wales

On the Acquisition of Some Relational Terms[1]

Abridged from M. Donaldson and R. Wales, 'On the acquisition of some relational terms', in J. R. Hayes, (ed.) *Cognition and the Development of Language*, 1970, Wiley, pp. 235–67.

McNeill, in a recent review of work on the development of language (in press), remarks that, while much attention has been given to the question of how language influences thought (the problem of 'language and cognition'), little or nothing has been done so far about the converse problem of 'cognition and language'. That is, there has been little attempt to account for the fundamental features of language acquisition in terms of a general theory of cognitive development. McNeill doubts whether at the moment we are in a position to carry this enterprise far, and his doubt seems well-founded. Donaldson (1966) has, however, already argued that, even in the present state of knowledge, we ought always to try to relate what is said about language acquisition to other aspects of cognitive development instead of considering it in isolation. This chapter has been prepared with this in mind.

The chapter, as the title indicates, is concerned primarily (and exclusively in so far as it contributes empirical findings) with the acquisition of *some* relational terms – indeed, with a limited, though possibly a very important, set. But given the objective just stated, it is obviously advisable to undertake some preliminary consideration of relational terms in general and of what may be involved in the acquisition of the ability to make relational judgements and statements.

1. George Balfour, Robin Campbell, John Taylor and Brian Young have been our colleagues since the project started in 1966. Eve Clark was responsible for the collection of much of the spontaneous speech recorded in the first year. Julian Dakin helped with some analysis of the speech data. We are indebted to all of these, and to David McNeill, Bernard Meltzer, John Marshall, and James Peter Thorne, who read and commented on an earlier draft of the manuscript.

It can reasonably be maintained that most of language is composed of relational terms. This was the position reached by Peirce, for instance, as he developed his relational logic. Peirce (1933) appears to allow that 'indexical words' such as proper nouns or demonstratives are strictly nonrelational, and he seems to be prepared to admit this of words referring to certain attributes which can be described as one-place predicates. But otherwise, for him words are, in essence, relational. This claim is more obviously incontrovertible in the case of some words than of others – more evidently true of 'lover', for instance, than of 'tree'. All common nouns might be held to be relational in that they are class names, though some of them, like 'lover', have a further relational property which others, like 'tree', do not possess.

This raises a question central to the present discussion. Within the class of relational terms, many different subdivisions have been proposed – and used for various purposes. For instance, distinctions can be drawn in terms of number of predicate places. Then the relation may be classified as reflexive or irreflexive, symmetrical or asymmetrical, transitive or intransitive, and so on. Peirce himself indulges on occasion in much more complicated and obscure classificatory exercises, but at present there is no need to be concerned with these. The question that has to be asked is: what distinctions are significant for questions of development? Are there some relational terms that are acquired very early? If so, what are their general features? How do they differ from those acquired later? And how can we relate these features to what we know – or may be led by available evidence to postulate – about the general nature of developing cognitive processes?

It is widely accepted that the earliest one-word utterances of children are holophrastic, which is, of course, to say that the single word somehow functions as a whole statement – although the word 'statement' suggests a degree of conceptual articulation that is presumably quite lacking. McNeill (in press) remarks of this earliest period: 'Except for those occasions when children's speech is purely expressive, it is invariably predicative. Children cry, or comment, and sometimes both. But they never utter mere labels'. It may be hard to prove this last claim. But the predicative nature of two-word utterances, when these begin to appear, is, on the other hand, very clear. What is quite commonly lacking, indeed, is explicit statement of the subject. The following samples of the speech of a child of twenty-seven months, quoted by McNeill from data collected by Brown and Bellugi, illustrate this:

up dere; in ere; read dat; hit hammer; hurt . . .;
no down there; get broom; put suitcase.

In each of these utterances a preposition or a transitive verb occurs. The child seems to be expressing relations in space (and usually in proximate space: *up dere, in ere, down there*); or else to be describing actions directly concerning physical objects. Now it is known that by this age the child has a considerable ability to manage spatial relations on the level of action – to make detours, to look for objects behind or under other objects, and so on. He also, and by the same token, has a rich repertoire of types of action available for the manipulation of physical objects ('schemas of actions', as Piaget would call them). And he appears to have developed some conception of a world of enduring objects. We have only to suppose him firstly capable of relating action to objects perceived (which involves, of course, differentiating the two) and secondly capable of relating one perceived spatial position to another, in order to provide him with cognitive capacities that are at least consistent with the production of utterances of the above kind. That is to say, no major discrepancy seems to be revealed here between his known linguistic cognitive skills and his linguistic utterances. One relational term included in the above list is, perhaps, not quite covered in this way, however – and that is the negative in *no down there*. There is also another utterance, not so far quoted but drawn from the same source, that seems to contain in it the germ of a relational cognition of a new kind: the phrase *Yep, it fit.* The context in which this was uttered is not made clear (except that the statement was an answer to the question *Does that one fit?*), and it is obviously important to know what the context was. But if the child is really engaged in a consideration of whether 'X fits Y', then he is involved in a kind of relational activity that goes beyond the linking of action schemas and physical objects.

It should also be observed that, although in the beginning

physical actions and physical objects dominate the linguistic scene, nevertheless, at an early age, words which refer to attributes of objects rather than to objects themselves (or which would certainly do so in the adult language) begin to appear. Thus, phrases like *green coat* and *wet sock* are reported. These, if they are to be regarded as predicative, can be classed as one-place predicates. A more complicated – and particularly interesting – situation arises because of the early occurrence of phrases like *big boat* and *more milk*. Both *big* and *more*, as they occur in the adult language, could logically be considered as two-place predicates, though they may not take this overt form. Whether the reference is made explicit or not, X 'has more' or 'is big' by reference to some standard of comparison.

The making of comparative judgements seems to be pervasive in thinking, yet the acquisition of the ability to comprehend and produce terms that are relational in this last sense – namely, in that they imply comparison across space or across time – has, until now, been the object of very little direct inquiry, in spite of the fact that they have figured in crucial ways in much cognitive research. However, the explicit study of such terms has been a focal topic in the research project that has yielded the data to be reviewed and discussed later in this chapter.

In the context of such a study, it would help greatly if a full formal linguistic analysis of comparative constructions were available. It would help if we had such an analysis even for English alone, and would help still more if an analysis of wider application had been proposed. However, given the great diversity of the linguistic constructions through which comparative judgements may be expressed, it seems hardly surprising that attempts to encompass them within the scope of a (possibly universalizable) set of syntactic rules have not yet met with universal success! At present, there is not even any reasonable consensus about what such an analysis would require to account for (see Jespersen, 1924; Smith, 1961; Lees, 1961; Chomsky, 1965). It has usually been considered that an attempt should be made to include such forms as *more* and *less* (both as separate comparatives and as one way of forming a comparative in English by conjunction with other adjectives); comparatives of the *X-er* variety; the relation of comparatives with superlatives; the forms *too-X* and *X-enough*;

the equative construction *as . . . as*; and possibly such sentences as *John is tall*, on the argument that, in their deep structure, these are implicitly comparative and so should be assigned an analysis which reads (roughly!) *John is taller than average*. Arguably, however, certain verbs (such as *exceed*), and expressions like *to the right of*, might also need to be included; and the words *same* and *different* can hardly be ignored.

In reporting our findings, we shall be concerned with this last pair of terms, and with *more* and *less* in their use as separate comparative forms. We shall also be considering a number of spatial comparative adjectives such as *tall* and *short*, and *high* and *low*; and in connection with this last group, we shall be concerned not only with the *X-er* comparative forms but also with superlatives, with *too-X* and *X-enough* and with the equative construction. Linking all these studies is a common theme to which it will be necessary to return frequently – the fundamental import-ance of the distinction between the different (positive and negative) poles of the contrasted terms.

In the case of the spatial adjectives, we shall be in a position to report the children's performance on a number of different tasks. It will become clear that we have been led by our research to regard this as a matter of considerable methodological importance in a study of this kind.

Logically dominating the use of relational terms that involve comparison is a question that seems to have a good claim to a position of central importance in the operation of cognitive pro-cesses: 'Is X the same as Y in some specified respect or respects – or is it not?' The way in which this question is answered opens or closes certain further possible paths of inquiry. Clearly, if X is asserted to be the same as Y with respect, say, to quantity (X and Y supposedly being sets of discrete entities), then it is possible to seek further specification by asking some such ques-tion as 'What is the number that each set contains?' However, it is when X is asserted to be not the same as Y that the search for more precise specification makes it appropriate to go on to questions involving further comparative terms. For instance, in the present example, the question 'Does X contain more elements than Y or less elements than Y?' may then be asked. It is perhaps advisable to remark at this point that the question of the relations between *same* and *different* will be treated more fully at later points in this chapter; and that this will involve consideration of the possibility that *sameness* may be derivable from complex conjunctions of difference. Furthermore, it should be noted that nothing which has been said is meant to imply that the terms *not the same* and *different* function in strictly equivalent ways within the language.

The question of sameness may or may not be limited to the consideration of certain specified attributes, depending on one's purpose; and accordingly, the word *same* is used in a variety of different ways. An attempt will now be made to indicate the complexity of the situation.

First, there is the sense of *same* in which the reference is to full identity – the identity of one enduring object. This notion has traditionally perplexed philosophers, and it is easy enough to get into considerable entanglements of thought over it, as both Locke and Hume, for instance, discovered. The problem, of course, is that in the case of one entity, when we are led to ask if it is the same (one), we are normally making a temporal comparison – and across time objects change. So how can they change and still remain the same? This, as Vlastos (1965, p. 15) suggests, is one of the reasons why Plato considered the Forms to be more real – or 'cognitively reliable' – than their sensible instances, since the latter, by being F at one time and not-F at another, are 'logical monstrosities, systematically violating the principle of noncontradiction' (Vlastos, 1965). However, if we were to allow this kind of consideration to lead us to deny enduring identity, we would be brought to what Penelhum (1967) calls 'the extreme language-destroying consequence that no predicates which cannot be simultaneously ascribed to one subject can be ascribed to a subject at two different times.' So it seems best to simply adopt the opinion, apparently reached by most children of eighteen months, that we live in a universe in which objects do endure, though they may change, and consider that it makes sense to ask 'Is this the same pen that I had here yesterday – or is it a different one?' Notice that we are in much greater difficulty if we want an answer to a question such as 'Is this the same idea that I had here yesterday – or is it a different one?' Problems of the latter kind have, of course, also received a great deal of attention from philosophers, and various attempts have been made to define identity in a way that extends beyond consideration of the primitive identity of concrete objects. (See, for instance, the discussion in Reichenbach (1947) of Russell's proposed definition.) For present purposes, however, these arguments are not of great relevance. What is important is to consider the further complexities that attend the word *same*, even when only concrete objects and their physical properties are in question.

1. We commonly speak of two (or more) objects as being *the same* when they are alike with respect to all observable attributes. (By virtue of the very fact that at least two objects are specified, this statement may be held to exclude from 'observable attributes' likeness in respect of locus in space-time.)

2. We use the word *same* with reference to two (or more) objects when they are alike with respect to at least one observable attribute, but different with respect to at least one other.

3. We say that two concrete entities are *the same* in some respect that is not directly observable.

Under this third heading many possibilities of subdivision arise. Recognition of the respect of sameness may involve the combined consideration of attributes, each of which, taken separately, is observably different – as seems to occur in Piaget's conservation tasks, for instance. Or the judgement of sameness may depend on previous perception of an attribute which is not actually observable at the time the judgement is made. This can be illustrated by reference to a test devised for use in the Edinburgh Cognition Project. The material is six cards, three of which are blank on both sides, while three are blank on one side and have pictures of aeroplanes on the other. If the cards are first inspected on both sides and then arrayed with six blank sides showing, it is appropriate to judge that the cards are still *the same* with respect to the number of aeroplanes on them. So the test, though not devised primarily for this purpose, allows number conservation – or 'maintained sameness of number' – to be assessed in a situation in which the critical change is perceptual disappearance rather than shift in configuration. In all cases of this last kind, of course, the sameness, not being directly perceptible, must be inferred.

It is perhaps reasonable now to conclude (even without pushing on to a consideration of, say, analogies, where the same relation holds between the terms of two different pairs) that the achieving of mastery of the relational terms *same* and *different* looks like a task of very considerable complexity. 'Sameness' and 'difference' must always be judged with respect to certain criteria, and the criteria shift – both with our purposes and (in a different way) across time in a changing universe.

The Edinburgh Cognition Project is a study (currently in progress) of the development of cognitive and linguistic skills in children between the ages of three-and-a-half and five. The experimental group consists of fifteen subjects who come daily for two-and-a-half hours to a nursery school specially set up for the purposes of the research. In social background, the children represent the middle range of the population. They come neither from culturally deprived homes nor from homes that are especially intellectually stimulating. Examples of parental occupations are plasterer, miner, and laboratory technician. When the work began about a year ago (at which time the children were around three-and-a-half years old) the children were given a set of fifteen pretests that had previously been prepared and pilot-tested. Some of the tests were inspired by tasks used by Piaget to assess the change from pre-operational to concrete operational thinking; others were specifically devised for use in the project. The objective was to sample a wide range of skills that there was reason to think were likely to be of fundamental importance for later cognitive development. Also, the aim was to construct the tests in such a way that children of three-and-a-half would be able to make some attempt at tackling them, while most children, as they attained the age of five, would still have some difficulty with them. Analysis of these tests, after they had been constructed on the above general principles, showed that all (except perhaps one which was a test of imagery) involved, as an important feature, some judgement of sameness or difference. Findings from six of these tests will be reported here. First, however, it may be well to mention that, after a period of approximately six months of systematic training (which is just ending), the same tests will be administered again. The general aim of the research, as will by now be plain, is to assess the effects

of this experimental intervention (which has been much more pro-
longed than that in most 'training studies' of a controlled kind)
on the capacity to perform these tasks. For present purposes,
however, it will be possible to refer only to a very limited part of
the data from the pretests and to some evidence obtained from the
spontaneous speech of these children, samples of which are recorded daily in the nursery [. . .]

What follows is the editor's summary of a test of classification:

There were two major sets of stimuli. The first consisted of four
kinds of objects (three exemplars of each) and four colours – form
and colour were coincident, e.g. all three toothbrushes were blue,
all three egg-cups were red, etc. The second set had four objects
and three colours – form and colour were *not* coincident, e.g. of
three toothbrushes, one was white, one red and one yellow. Note
that an item from the first set was either similar in all respects or
different in all respects from any other item in the set, and that
an item from the second set was either different in all respects, or
the same in at least one respect and different in at least one
respect from any other item in the set.

The child is presented with a stimulus object and one set of
objects, and instructed to choose an object either 'the same in
some way' or 'different in some way' from the stimulus object.

When presented with a choice from the first set, children tend
to choose objects similar in *all* respects, *regardless* of the instruction, i.e. the children choose an object 'the same in some
way', without making a distinction between *Give me one that is
the same in some way* and *Give me one that is different in some way*.

Interestingly, when presented with a choice from the second
set, the child is almost always correct, i.e. in response to either
instruction, he chooses an object that simultaneously satisfies
both instructions. He chooses the object which is similar in at
least one way and different in at least one way. As before, the
child is really choosing objects 'the same in some way'. This
interpretation is supported by the absence of choices from the set
of objects different in all ways, when the instruction is to pick
out an object 'different in some way'.]

Tests were devised to assess the children's comprehension of
the terms 'more' and 'less'. The results obtained when this was

administered as a pretest are reported in full in Donaldson and Balfour (1968). Here, a considerably abbreviated account will be given.

The first study had the following characteristics:

1. Discrete units were used. There was no investigation of continuous quantities.

2. There were always two sets involved in the comparison.

3. Both static and changing situations were used.

4. The sets were sometimes initially equal to one another and sometimes unequal.

5. The subject was sometimes asked to effect a change himself and sometimes merely to observe and judge it. Sometimes he observed the change as it actually took place, and sometimes only the outcome of the change.

6. When change was effected by the experimenter, only one set was altered.

7. The direction of change sometimes accorded with the final state of the sets relative to one another and sometimes did not.

In a second supplementary study, carried out approximately six months later, subjects were asked to deal with only one set and to effect a change (in this case, a decrease) in its quantity.

In the main study, eight different stimulus situations, involving the variables described above, were used. On the first occasion, the children were asked questions about each of these situations, all of the questions involving the term *more*. On the second occasion a day or two later, questions of the same form, but now using *less*, were put to them.

The material used consisted of two cardboard apple trees, with six hooks in corresponding positions on each; and twelve red apples which could be hung on the trees. The trees could swivel, when this was desired, so that the child could not see the apples being hung on them. When the sets of apples were made equal by E, the spatial distributions always corresponded. For each stimulus situation there were a number of trials involving different numbers of apples. The numbers used to make up a set on a given tree ranged from one to five and the differences between sets ranged from one to four.

The following descriptions illustrate the kinds of procedure used.

1. S was asked to judge a situation of static equality presented by E. S did not see the apples being put on the trees. When they were swivelled round for him to observe, he was asked: *Does one tree have more (less) apples on it than the other?* If he answered *Yes* he was asked *Which tree has more (less) apples?* If he answered *No* he was asked *Is there the same number of apples on each tree?*

2. S was shown a situation of initial inequality, prepared, as before, out of his sight. He was told: *Now make it so that there are more apples on this tree* (lesser number) *than on this tree –* or else . . . *so that there are less apples on this tree* (greater number). . . . When S had finished he was asked: *Does one tree have more (less) apples than the other?* If he said *Yes* he was then asked: *Which tree has more (less) apples?*

Other tasks involved, for example, the presentation of situations of static inequality with a simple request for comparative judgement; the presentation of initial equality with a request to the child to *make it so that there are more (less) apples on this tree than on this one*; the presentation of initial inequality with subsequent addition by E, while S watched, of one or more apples to the lesser set (or, alternatively, subtraction by E of one or more apples from the greater set) followed by the usual request for comparative judgement. In this last case, the direction of change did not accord with the final state of the sets; that is, the tree to which more apples had been added still always had less apples than the other tree after the addition had been made – and similarly for the operation of subtraction.

The supplementary study was simpler in conception and design. Only one tree was used and there were only two stimulus situations: (1) four apples on the tree, two on the table; and (2) three apples on the tree, three on the table.

Each of these was presented twice, the order of presentation being (1), (2), (1), (2). The child was asked in each case: *Make it so that there are less apples on the tree.*

This additional test was given for two main reasons.

1. To see if there had been change in the typical response patterns over the interval of six months.

2. To check on the possibility that the responses to *less* questions on the first occasion had been influenced by the fact that they had been preceded (though, it will be recalled, not on the same day) by questions involving *more*.

The complex data obtained from these two studies cannot readily be presented in summary form. However, there are two main findings that are relevant to the present discussion. In all the differing situations that were used on the first test, the great majority of the responses gave no indication that the children were making any distinction between *less* and *more*. Only one child answered *less* questions with a high degree of success throughout. The remainder of the children (that is, thirteen, since one child gave so few responses that he cannot be included) responded to these questions just as they did to the corresponding questions containing *more*; and their responses were typically of kinds that constituted correct response to *more* and, consequently, incorrect response to *less*.

The position may be illustrated by giving a detailed analysis of responses to the stimulus situation in which S had to pass judgement on a situation of static inequality presented to him by E. In this situation, a few children completed as many as seven trials with *more* and six trials with *less*. But other children would not continue for so long. The total number of responses available is 69 for *more* and 55 for *less*. The results are presented in Table 1.

On forty trials, then, the child, having judged that one set contained less apples than the other, proceeded to choose, as the one that had less, the one that in fact had more. The fifteen correct choices of the tree with *less* were contributed by five children, of whom only one was correct on all presentations attempted. Two additional children were correct in more than half the responses they made.

It was a marked feature of the results that in the 'active' tasks (that is, those in which the children themselves were asked to effect a change), children very rarely removed apples from the trees, but almost always added, whether the request was to *make*

Table 1

	Yes	No (subsequently changed to Yes)	Same	Total
Does one have more ?	65	3	1	69
Does one have less ?	55	0	0	55

	Correct choice	Incorrect choice	No choice	Total
Which one has more ?	63	5	1	69
Which one has less ?	15	40	0	55

it more or to *make it less*. But in the stimulus situation described above, in which the child was asked to *make it so that there are more apples* on the tree that initially had less (and vice versa), even the instruction containing *more* proved very difficult, and only three children carried it out without error. If there is a tendency for the children to take *more* as meaning 'larger present quantity', then the phrase *make it so that there are more . . .* may well be expected to prove difficult for them to interpret. Many children made alterations which differed in type from one trial to the next (they might add to one tree, or to both, and end up with equal or unequal sets) and there was, in general, much inconsistency. However, the task gave further confirmation to the view that *less* was generally regarded as equivalent to *more*. One child made this explicit. Asked to make three less than two, he said: *But it is less on that tree*.

The results of the supplementary study indicated that, for many of the children, the interpretation of *less* as meaning *more* still persisted. Fourteen subjects were tested, one of the group being at this time in hospital. One of the fourteen responded to the initial instruction by saying: *How can I?*, and then made no further response to urgings by E that he should try. At one point he said *Take them off, you mean?* but then made no move to do so. However, he readily added apples when E finally tried replacing *less* in the instruction by *more*. Clearly, for this child *less* and *more* were no longer synonymous, but the opposition of the two did not seem to be effectively established as a relation between language and action.

From the thirteen remaining children, fifty-two responses were obtained. The distribution of these is shown in Table 2. The third column reports the frequency with which the response of removing apples and then putting some back on again occurred.

Table 2

Instruction	Response by			
	Addition	Subtraction	Addition followed by subtraction	Subtraction followed by addition
Make it less	41	6	1	4

The one child who had consistently differentiated *less* and *more* on the original pretest accounts for three of the six subtraction responses. Three children contributed the four cases of 'subtraction plus addition'. It may be worth observing that two of these made remarks which referred explicitly to *trying to make it less*, while indicating that they thought they had failed.

There is, then, in this second test, slightly more evidence of perplexity over *less* than was provided by the first test (where signs of perplexity were almost wholly lacking). But the general pattern with respect to that feature of the results that we are at present considering remains substantially unchanged.

The second finding to be considered here concerns the responses to the situation in which the two sets are initially equal and the child is asked: *Does one tree have more (less) apples on it than the other?* In this case, three subjects denied on every trial that one had more and likewise denied on every trial that one had less, responding, as might have been anticipated, by a simple *no* or shake of the head or by some such assertion as *They're the same*. However, a further six children gave evidence of denial of inequality, if responses such as *both of them, both the trees, that one does an' that one, they two ones, each tree,* and *these two have* are accepted as a form of denial. Of the six children who made assertions of the above kind, two, at one point or another, spontaneously asserted that the sets of apples were *both the same* or *both the same number*, and all answered *Yes* to the question *Is there the same number of apples on each tree?* However, it should be noted that three of these children gave answers of this kind only in response to the question *Does one tree have more . . .?*, whereas in answer to *less . . .?* they simply chose one of the trees. The other three responded to *less . . .?* in the same way as they did to *more . . .?* using, once again, such expressions as *on each tree* and *both the trees*.

The evidence that has been presented so far indicates that, in the case of two pairs of antonyms, the children studied manifested in their responses a failure to differentiate between the two opposing members of the pair, showing in each case, a strong tendency to interpret both members in a way that would be correct for one of them in the adult language. In other words, the expected oppositions did not seem to be established.

The two pairs of antonyms may logically be related to one another in a way that has already been briefly indicated. Judgements of 'more' and 'less' already imply a judgement of difference. To use the terminology of the calculus of relations (Tarski, 1965), the relation 'more than' and the relation 'less than' are both included in the relation of diversity.

Further observations may be made about the logical properties of the relations. To take the most obvious, 'same' is symmetrical, reflexive and transitive. 'Different' is also symmetrical, but it is irreflexive and intransitive.

'More' and 'less', on the other hand, are each symmetrical, irreflexive and transitive. That is, considered logically as relations, they resemble one another more closely than do 'same' and 'different'.

Yet indifferentiation of the antonyms occurs in both cases. It is probably necessary, then, to turn, in the search for an interpretation of the findings, to a consideration of the highly complex functioning of relational terms in the language. Although *same/different* and *more/less* are certainly antonyms, they are by no means straightforwardly opposite to one another, even for adults. If we took only the above formal properties into account, then it would seem that, at least for *more* and *less* where these properties coincide, this ought to be the case. But it is sufficient to reflect that you can *put more in* to a glass, whereas you cannot (in the same sense) *take less out* for it to become evident that this is not so. In effect, *more* is ambiguous. It may be used in a simply additive sense as well as in a strictly comparative sense. It should be noted that ambiguity of this kind is not confined to *more*. This will be further discussed later.

In the attempt to interpret the findings, it may be best to begin by discussing what seem likely to be, ontogenetically, the most primitive contexts of the words we are considering.

More seems to be that one of the four that is normally produced soonest. Brown and Bellugi (1964) report, among the earliest noun phrases noted in the speech of their subjects, *more coffee* and *more nut*. It seems very probable that *more* is first comprehended – and produced – by children with reference to a context where one entity is changing – say, when the child wants food in addition to what he has already been given – and that judgement of one entity or set as having *more than* another is an appreciably later event. Notice that the word *less*, if heard by the child in the context that is here being postulated as the earliest for *more*, might well carry some such meaning as *more, but not so much more*. One adult might say to another, *That's too much. Give him less*. But there is no way of determining, on available evidence, whether this might have any connection with the findings reported here. However, a point that is in some ways similar may be made with respect to *different* and *same*. In everyday speech, sentences such as *Give me a different one* can – and commonly do – mean *Give me another one that is of the same kind*. In other words, the emphasis here is on difference in identity combined with some sort of similarity – and in this case, the phrase *a different one* is very close in meaning to the phrase *another one*. Now, while the word *different* does not seem to occur commonly in the early utterances of children, *other* is perhaps less rare. A child of seventeen months, fetching the second of a pair of slippers, was observed to remark *other one* as she did so; and she then proceeded to fetch a pair of shoes, place them beside the slippers and again say *other one*.

It is possible, then, that *different* is first comprehended as implying a denial of object identity along with the presence of some sort of similarity; and that when the children in our group respond to the instruction *different in some way* in sets II and IV by preferring P(a,b) to D(a,b), they are in fact interpreting the instruction in this way. [Here a,b = specific items within a stimulus set, D = *different*, with respect to all observable attributes, P = *same*, with respect to at least one observable attribute and *different*, with respect to at least one.] It is worth noting that the set of eleven objects from which they have to choose (the standard constituting, of course, the twelfth of the 4 by 3 matrix) contains six objects that satisfy the relation D(a,b) against five that satisfy the relation P(a,b). The preference for P(a,b) reported in Table 1 is therefore very marked.

It may, on the other hand, be that *different* and *same* are being treated as synonyms – which is what seems to happen in the case of *more* and *less*, as will shortly be discussed.

Before going on to this, however, it seems appropriate to make some reference to evidence concerning *same* and *different* as they occurred in the spontaneous speech of our subjects in the nursery over a period of eleven months from February to December 1967 – that is, from roughly three-and-a-half to four-and-a-half years of age.

In the first place, utterances containing the word *same* are appreciably more frequent than those containing *different*. *Different* is recorded only five times.

1. *I've been to a different one, not the same as that*. Here the child is denying that a picture represents a beach he has visited. The two beaches are not identical (not 'one and the same') though obviously similar in many respects.

A second child uses *different* in the same sense and context three days later:

2. *A different seaside*.

3. *They're all the same, but they're different*. Here the child is speaking of books, and it again seems possible that *different* carries the meaning 'not identical' or 'different individuals'. But this is less likely. Neil might be saying that though they are all alike in belonging to the class of books, they are different with respect to observable attributes such as size.

4. Neil: *What color, Maureen?*

Maureen: *Yellow. There's different colors on mine*.

Here, beads are under discussion and, plainly, comparison of attributes is involved.

5. *I'm going to mend the car, because it's a different car.* The function of *because* here is obscure, but 'different individual' is once more clearly implied. So this seems to be the sense carried by *different* in three out of the five recorded instances.

The word *same* occurs in sixteen utterances (excluding (1) and (3) above, where it occurs along with *different*). These may involve comparisons of objects or of actions, though the former are more common. In general, two objects are compared with respect to some attribute; that is, *same* is not used to mean 'same individual'. Examples are given below.

1. *I've got the same color*, referring to beads which two of the children are playing with.
2. *You've got the same as Alan.*
3. *We've all got the same* (with reference to color of straws).
4. *I want one the same* (with reference to a toy car).
5. *His looks the same size.*
6. *And if you turn the pages, you'll get the same thing again.*
7. *The airplanes are going the same way.*
8. *I can do the same as you.*
Most of the utterances are well-formed, but two are not;
9. *Got whiskers, a rabbit, same's mine.*
10. *This slide's the same like the slide when I go to Grannie's.*

The general conclusion is that the children show a greater tendency to use *same* than to use *different* where comparison of the properties of objects or actions is at issue. However, at this point a further consideration seems relevant. It has already been remarked that relations expressing a precise kind and direction of difference are included logically within the general relation of diversity. So then it may be that when the children recognize – and want to speak about – differences in attributes, there is a tendency for them to move directly to the greater degree of specificity – to say, for instance, *mine's bigger than yours* (a very common type of statement in their spontaneous conversations) rather than to make the more general statement, *mine's different from yours.*

This, in turn, suggests some further reflections. It seems reasonable – and in accordance with available data – to suppose that it is easier to predicate one attribute of one object than to predicate one attribute of two (or more) objects at once. Children typically make utterances like *that's a blue flower* (Brown and Bellugi, 1964) before offering plural versions of the same kind of construction. And often, at a somewhat later stage, they will say *that one's green and that one's green* instead of *they are green*, or *both are green*. Now, it is known that children dealing with the Stanford-Binet (Form L-M) question on pictorial similarities and differences at age 5 will sometimes make statements like *that one is the same and that one is the same* – presumably by analogy with *that one's green and that one's green*. Statements like *that one is the same and that one is the same* are, of course, not well-formed, and suggest a failure to comprehend the relational nature of *same*. Yet they might possibly be an important step in the direction of the correct utterance *they are the same* – and the ultimate correct comprehension of what this implies. (This is obviously suggestive when seen in the light of the arguments of Lyons (1963) about locatives).

Consider, however, the case of observed difference in attributes. *That one's green and that one's blue* cannot yield, by quite the same direct analogy, *that one's different and that one's different* – and hence the ultimate assertion *they are different* may have to be arrived at by an alternative route.

Another way to express a similar notion is to remark that when two things are 'the same', there is, after all, at least some one attribute which they share and which may facilitate the plural form that unites them in one predicate. But when 'they are different' – what is 'this thing' that they are . . . ?

The evidence concerning *less* and *more* must now be further considered. A first obvious suggestion is that children rarely hear the word *less* in ordinary conversation. (Both *less* and *more* are among the first 500 words in the Thorndike and Lorge (1944) frequency counts, but this does not dispose of the question of whether, in everyday interchange between children and adults, the frequency differs significantly.)

However, if the explanation of the responses to *less* was merely that the children had rarely heard the term, they might reasonably be expected to show perplexity when given instructions containing it – or, at any rate, to interpret it in a diversity of ways. What we have to account for is that they so regularly, and with so little sign of hesitation, interpret it as a synonym for *more*, sometimes making this interpretation very explicit, as in the case of the child who, asked to make a set of three less than one of two, replied: *But it is less*. What happened was that the children responded as if they knew the word *less* and knew that it referred to quantity, but as if it remained for them undifferentiated from *more*, with *more* as the consistently dominant interpretation for the undifferentiated pair. When perplexity did appear (though even then it was rare), it was in the supplementary test, given six months after the original one – and so it presumably represents developmental advance by comparison with the earlier untroubled state.

An attempt to handle these issues more precisely is made in Donaldson and Balfour (1968).

In the records of the children's spontaneous speech during the first eleven months, there were only six utterances in which *more* occurred. No use of *less* was recorded. Only two of the uses of *more* were unambiguously comparative in the full sense. Both were produced by the same child (the child, incidentally, who successfully differentiated *less* from *more* in the formal task) and both referred to a number of beads:

I've got more on than the other boy.
We've got more beads than you have.

The other utterances involved requests for *more bricks*, and references to *getting some more tea* or to adding *some more* pieces to a figure that was being constructed.

There was one isolated use of *most*: *I've got the most* (wooden shapes). *I've got most of them. You can have some.*

We now go on to a discussion of the studies of the spatial comparative adjectives.

Reference has been made at an earlier point in this paper to the current lack of any formal linguistic analysis of comparative constructions, to the extreme diversity of these and to the problem of giving an account of them that will reveal the nature of their underlying relatedness. Study of the data that we are about to report has brought us increasingly to a belief in the value of a semantically-based approach to this problem. The nature of this approach can only be sketched here, but it has as an essential feature an emphasis on recognition of the importance of contextual reference. This is meant to imply that comparative constructions can only be interpreted with reference to some attribute of a given context. Thus, even *John is tall*, if interpreted as *John is taller than average*, is likely to make different sense to different people if the context of 'taller than average' is *not* supplied; for example it will probably be interpreted differently by Gulliver, a Lilliputian, an adult pygmy, and a four-year-old child. If this point is accepted as even arguable, then this implies that at least this set of constructions can only be analyzed correctly by taking into account aspects of the possible referential contexts. This is not, of course, to say that it is necessary to commit the analysis to some limited theory of reference, but rather that an analysis, in dealing, for instance, with *John is taller than average*, would have to take into account the possibility of handling *tall* semantically (for instance, as Bierwisch (1967) does); of handling a semantic (or pragmatic) specification of *than average* in this context; and also of handling the implication, carried linguistically, of the nature of the normative comparison being expressed. The point of the phrase 'nature of the comparison' is that there is a distinction to be drawn between two different kinds of comparison, and the distinction is one that may prove to be of considerable significance for the study of ontogenesis. Expressions like *taller* are what we might call *descriptively comparative*; but there are other comparative constructions, notably *too-X* and *X-enough*, that may more appropriately be called *functionally comparative*. The following sets of sentences illustrate this distinction and some of its implications for the admissibility of utterances. (Asterisks mark inadmissible sentences.)

  1. John is taller than the wall.
  2. John is not taller than the wall.
  3. John is shorter than the wall.
  4. John is not shorter than the wall.
  5. John is tall enough to see over the wall.
  6. John is not tall enough to see over the wall.
*7. John is short enough to see over the wall.
*8. John is not short enough to see over the wall.

    *9. John is too tall to see over the wall.
  *10. John is not too tall to see over the wall.
   11. John is too short to see over the wall.
   12. John is not too short to see over the wall.

If John's problem were not seeing over the wall but walking under a bar (a certain distance above the ground), then the permissible set would be:

   13. John is taller than the bar.
   14. John is not taller than the bar.
   15. John is shorter than the bar.
   16. John is not shorter than the bar.
  *17. John is tall enough to walk under the bar.
  *18. John is not tall enough to walk under the bar.
   19. John is short enough to walk under the bar.
   20. John is not short enough to walk under the bar.
   21. John is too tall to walk under the bar.
   22. John is not too tall to walk under the bar.
  *23. John is too short to walk under the bar.
  *24. John is not too short to walk under the bar.

The appropriateness of the comparatives here is closely linked to the prepositions. Notice the further interesting point that the inadmissible cases above, namely (7) and (8), (9) and (10), (17) and (18), and (23) and (24) are all inadmissible in the negative when inadmissible in the affirmative. On the other hand, if the verb rather than the comparative adjective is negated, the admissibility changes (cf. *John is short enough not to see over the wall*). These facts suggest that there are interesting semantic interconnections between comparison and negation.

It is important to observe at this point that *too-X* and *X-enough* are not always so clearly or completely asymmetric in admissibility as they are here. It depends on the functional properties of the situation. In the above illustrations, the functional comparatives are a way of marking in sentences the satisfaction (or otherwise) of some criterion of adequacy, where adequacy is bounded on one side only. But in certain circumstances – notably where 'exact fit' is in question – adequacy is bounded on both sides (cf. the hierarchy of n-state comparisons) and the relations between functional comparatives are thereby altered. This illustrates what has already been said about the importance of referential context.

The complexity of the situation we are considering may be illustrated in a number of additional ways. First, while polar antonyms are in general implicitly comparative, the positive (but not the negative) pole may be ambiguous in much the same way as *more* is ambiguous. Certainly all the unidimensional adjectives are thus ambiguous in English, and also a few multidimensional ones such as *great* and – similarly in Latin – *maximus*. This can be seen through their occurrence in measure phrases. *Policemen are six feet tall* merely means *are tall* as determined by the arbitrary constant of being six feet or more in height. They cannot be six feet short. Thus in this example the negative pole is strictly inadmissible. However, even in cases in which the use of the negative pole is not impossible – for example, *How shallow is the lake?* – it seems intuitively obvious that a speaker would normally tend to ask *How deep is the lake?* unless there were some contextual constraint. That is, the positive pole is the preferred term in most circumstances.

A further illustration of the complexity of interconnections that has to be recognized is provided by consideration of the equative form *as . . . as*. If we say that (a) *X is not as big as Y*, we would generally take (a) to mean (b) *X is smaller than Y*; and not take it as an ambiguous utterance with (c) *X is bigger than Y* as an alternative reading. This asymmetry can be shown to be general with reference to functional contexts. If we are talking about something of size X with respect to the possibility of its fitting (exactly) into a given hold of size Y, we might say *X is as big as Y*. This would mean that *X is not too big to fit Y*; *X is not too small to fit Y*; *X is big enough to fit Y*; and *X is small enough to fit Y*. If, however, *X is not as big as Y* (with reference to the same functional context), this would mean *X is too small to fit Y*, and *X is not big enough to fit Y*. (It would *not* mean *X is too big to fit Y* or *X is not small enough to fit Y*). If we now pursue these alternatives, together with the negation of such related expressions as *X is big*, *X is bigger than Y*, and the like, it soon becomes clear that the comparatives and equatives are essentially asymmetric in their interaction with negative forms.

Note now that the equative *X is as . . . as Y* can be logically defined (cf. Quine, 1953) as the conjunction of the negation of the contradictory comparatives. To use Quine's example:

Consider a theory of bodies compared in point of length. The values of the bound variables are physical objects, and the only predicate is L where Lxy means *x is longer than y*. Now where $\sim Lxy$. $\sim Lyx$, anything that can be truly said of x within this theory holds equally for y and vice-versa. Hence it is convenient to treat $\sim Lxy$. $\sim Lyx$ as $x = y$. Such identification amounts to reconstruing the values of our variables as universals, namely, lengths, instead of physical objects (p. 117).

Such universals 'may be regarded as entering here merely as a manner of speaking – through the metaphorical use of the identity sign for what is really not identity but sameness *of length*' (p. 118) [italics supplied]. This particular illustration might point to the source of some of the difficulty, indicated earlier, that arises over *same/different*. Later we shall also indicate that the strong and necessary use of a sameness relation is a logical consequence of the conjoining of the negation of contradictory comparatives only when there is reference to a given physical system. That the use of *same* does not always hold as a strong *same* relation in the language is pointed out by the fact that we have expressions like *exactly the same, just as . . . as*, and the like.

The need to take account of the interrelations of comparison, negation and particular referential contexts, and to look at the use of comparatives in terms of the semantic function involved, should now be clear. We think it important to stress that our awareness of these issues developed as a direct outcome of our attempts to make sense of the child's acquisition and use of comparatives of this complex sort.[2]

2. A related issue is the role of *and* and *but* but in conjoining comparative statements. Take for illustration a situation (used in the Edinburgh Cognition Project) in which a subject has to press a key when he sees a card that related to the standard, X, in a way described by such a conjoining. Consider the following:

  25. as tall as X and as wide as X
  26. as tall as X and wider than X
  27. as tall as X and not as wide as X
*28. as tall as X but as wide as X
  29. as tall as X but as wide as Y
  30. as tall as X but not as wide as X
  31. as tall as X but wider than X

A detailed discussion of relevant syntactic and semantic issues will be found in Campbell and Wales (1969); and these and other related problems will be considered with special reference to onto-genesis in future work of Wales and Campbell. Meanwhile, on the basis of this preliminary survey of the issues and of what needs to be incorporated in any analysis that will be interesting from a performance point of view, we would suggest the following hierarchy of complexity of comparisons that may be expressed in the language:

1. *One-state comparison.* This is exemplified by the use of 'more' in its additive sense. While this is perhaps not strictly compara-tive, it might be claimed that it would be unintelligible without a prior general context of comparative judgements.

2. *Two-state comparison.* The defining feature here is that there is comparison between an object and a standard (implicit or explicit), but the comparative judgement requires only a yes/no decision and the standard is not definite. Superlatives (in which the comparison is between a member and the rest of the class) and all adjectives that are implicitly comparative are included here. So also are the functional comparatives *too-X* and *X-enough*, given a context in which exactness of fit is not at issue.

3. *Three-state comparison.* Here the standard is definite and the comparative judgement involves explicit reference to one of two possible directions of departure from it, the directions being those marked by the polarities of the antonymous stems. All explicit descriptive comparatives, such as *more . . . than* and *X-er than*, fall into this category.

4. *Four-state comparison.* In this case there are functional con-texts requiring not only a yes/no comparison, but also comparison of exactness of fit (or lack of it) with respect to a given standard, such as *just . . . enough* (and the like), and also *just the same as*.

Notice in the last three the issue of definiteness, and notice also, in general terms, that *enough* marks an inequality towards a

---

These clearly provide still further evidence of the interconnection between comparison, negation, and reference. (They also indicate the value of the traditional notion that *but* serves not only for conjoining statements but also for denying that statements are in certain respects consistent with each other.)

norm, whereas the others mark inequalities away from a norm. Definiteness is seen to be important by consideration of the ambiguity of reference of *a bigger one*, whereas *the bigger one* is unambiguous.

[Four studies of comparatives are described. The following is the editor's summary of the first study:

Do children respond differentially to the positive and negative poles of adjective pairs, e.g. thickest: thinnest, longest: shortest. Various different sets of objects (four at a time) were used, e.g. four rectangles of decreasing height and increasing width. The child would be presented with a set and asked a series of questions involving comparatives and superlatives, e.g. *Point to the longest one, Give me the shortest one*, etc.

The superlative was understood correctly when the positive pole + *est* was used; but the negative pole − *est*, though it elicited a majority of correct choices, often led to the choice of the object immediately adjacent to the chosen positive pole. The superiority of performance on positive poles was not so marked for comparatives.

The conclusions drawn from the remaining studies of comparatives are given below.]

There are a number of conclusions that may already be clear from the above results on the comparatives: first, the children do operate in terms of the polarities assumed in most theoretical discussions; second, even before they are used in a well-formed fashion, comparatives are differentiated from superlatives, though they are sometimes used as equivalent expressions; and third, the use and appropriateness of the comparative expressions can only be fully understood in terms of the referential contexts of their use. This latter point is very clear from the 'spontaneous' use of comparatives recorded in the nursery – of which, in the first eleven months, there were 160 utterances (therefore they cannot be analysed here). It is very striking, however, that it is relatively easy to classify the uses in terms of the situations in which they occurred, for instance asking for things, modeling, and talking about things the children can see. Perhaps the most interesting point here is that the uses of 'true' comparatives are often in (roughly) 'competitive discourse' situations, such as the following (Neil is playing with a car):

NEIL   I've got a little black one.

MAUREEN   I've got a little black one in my house.

NEIL   I've got a bigger one than you ... up to my ceiling.

MAUREEN   So've I.

If comparatives are used typically to *justify* certain comparative judgements, then this is precisely the kind of discourse situation in which they could be expected to occur in an appropriate form.

Finally, it seems as though the stem polar adjectives (such as *big*, *more*, and *tall*) are ontogenetically prior to any other comparative constructions. Perhaps the order of acquisition subsequently proceeds: superlatives, *too-x* (used descriptively), and 'true' comparatives (*more than x-er*, etc), followed by *too-x* and *x-enough* used as functional comparatives. Of course, inferences and claims about the order of acquisition of structures can only be safely made from longitudinal data. This we hope to analyze in due course.

Concluding comments

Such studies are better understood as posing than as resolving problems. As a matter of fact, given the present state of developmental psycholinguistics, we would be uneasy if this were other than the case.

An immediate conclusion that may be drawn is that children's failure to respond appropriately in tasks in which they are instructed to perform in accord with such talk as *same as*, *different from*, *more than*, *Is there more here or more here?* and the like, may be as attributable to the structure of the child's language as to other aspects of his cognitive apparatus. Much more work needs to be done before results from such studies become, in any systematic fashion, fully interpretable. To show that similar results may be found when the 'same' tasks are presented 'non-verbally' merely begs the question unless it can be clearly demonstrated that the apparent convergence of the language performance and other cognitive performance misleadingly reflects two quite unrelated systems of competence. We hold that the simplest interpretation is that the apparent convergence reflects an interaction of the two systems of competence – in a noncircular fashion – because of the apparent need in considering both systems independently, to take account of referential aspects of the situation the child is immediately confronted with, together with what look like the same formal relations some of the time. Having said that is not to have said very much, except, however, that in this instance, data instead of pure conjecture have helped us to say it. What is now needed is an attempt to develop alternative formalizations that might be appropriate and also to show, through further observation and experiment, what usefulness there may be in trying to map certain cognitive relations in ways that are consistent with linguistic relations or vice-versa. On the cognitive side some valuable suggestions already exist through the work of Piaget (as in Beth and Piaget, 1966), though alternative formalizations may be required, and, anyway, evaluative criteria need to be developed to assess their appropriateness. On the language side we are strongly hinting that what psycholinguistics needs are criteria of *context appropriateness* for *utterances* constrained by the linguistic criteria for *grammaticality/acceptability* of *sentences*. That we are not being too unrealistic in expressing these desires is shown, on the one hand, by the increased interest in the possibility that deep structure categories are semantically derived (for example, Lyons, 1968; Fillmore, 1968); and on the other, by the current interest in the possibility that *speech acts*, in Austin's sense, must be expressed in the deep structure analyses of sentences (for example, Boyd and Thorne, 1969). It is presumably quite possible that these two approaches will converge. They certainly both seem to be motivated by some of the same problems that have concerned us in this chapter when we have talked of the need to consider the referential-semantic aspects of the comparative constructions, and the need to consider the functional appropriateness of the utterances. Both approaches also seem to be involved in a shift to the hazy border-line between linguistic competence and performance. One of the reasons for our use of a fully overt performance approach is the belief that only through the study of the same kind of linguistic relation in different performance settings will a sufficiently reliable consensus of data enable us to formulate a theoretically interesting description of competence. Presumably, in fact, linguists have to start from performance in the first place in the description of competence; for example, in the partitioning of some acceptable utterances from others that are not acceptable, and the like. If this is so, then it might be a misleading methodological move to attempt to discuss what is the appropriate grammatical description of the child's language before at least a reasonably coherent rule-of-thumb interpretation of the child's performance is available. Traditional and contemporary linguistic, philosophical, or psychological theories, or our own intuitions, may serve as sources of hypotheses as to what to look for in such an interpretation. The need for a variety of ways of looking at the child's language is well illustrated by our own study in which, if we had attempted to view the child's *competence* solely on the ground of any one of our tests, or solely on the 'spontaneous' utterances in the nursery, we would almost certainly have been led to serious distortions in our understanding of what sorts of structure were involved. As it is, a fairly coherent picture is starting to emerge. We will not rehash findings and conclusions already formulated in the body of the chapter since, among other things, this is merely the summary of a continuing study. It would be foolhardy to try to draw the conclusion that we have shown necessary relatedness between the linguistic and cognitive structures of the child, but our results suggest that it would be equally foolhardy to reject the possibility without much more careful study and much richer theories.

References

BETH, E. W., and PIAGET, J. (1966), *Mathematical Epistemology and Psychology*, Reidel.

BIERWISCH, M. (1967), 'Some semantic universals of German adjectivals', *Found. Language*, vol. 3, pp. 1–36.

BOYD, J., and THORNE, J. P. (1969), 'The semantics of modal verbs', *J. Linguistics*, vol. 5, pp. 57–74.

BROWN, R., and BELLUGI, U. (1964), 'Three processes in the child's acquisition of syntax', *Harvard educ. Rev.*, vol. 34, p. 151.

CAMPBELL, R. N., and WALES, R. J. (1969), 'Comparative structures in English', *J. Linguistics*, vol. 5, pp. 215–51.

CHOMSKY, N. (1965), *Aspects of the Theory of Syntax*, MIT Press.

DONALDSON, M. (1966), 'Comment on a paper by D. McNeill', in J. Lyons and R. J. Wales (eds.), *Psycholinguistics Papers*, Edinburgh University Press.

DONALDSON, M., and BALFOUR, G. (1968), 'Less is more: a study of language comprehension in children', *Brit. J. Psychol.*, vol. 59, pp. 461–71.

FILLMORE, C. (1968), 'The case for case', in E. Bach and R. Harms (eds.), *Universals in Linguistic Theory*, Holt, Rinehart & Winston.

JESPERSEN, O. (1924), *The Philosophy of Grammar*, Allen & Unwin.

LEES, R. B. (1961), 'Grammatical analysis of the English comparative construction', *Word*, vol. 17, pp. 171–85.

LYONS, J. (1963), *Structural Semantics*, Blackwell.

LYONS, J. (1968), *Introduction to Theoretical Linguistics*, Cambridge University Press.

MACNEILL, D. (in press), 'The development of language', in P. A. Mussen (ed.), *Carmichael's Manual of Child Psychology*.

PEIRCE, C. S. (1933), *Collected Papers*, vol. 3, C. Hartshorne and P. Weiss (eds.), Harvard University Press.

PENELHUM, T. (1967), 'Personal identity', in P. Edwards (ed.), *Encyclopedia of Philosophy*, vol. 6, Macmillan

QUINE, W. VAN O. (1953), *From a Logical Point of View*, Harvard University Press.

REICHENBACH, H. (1947), *Elements of Symbolic Logic*, Free Press.

SMITH, C. S. (1961), 'A class of complex modifiers in English', *Language*, vol. 41, pp. 37–58.

THORNDIKE, E. L., and LORGE, I. (1944), *The Teacher's Word Book of 30,000 Words*, Teacher's College, Columbia University.

VLASTOS, G. (1965), 'Degrees of reality in Plato', in R. Bambrough (ed.), *New Essays on Plato and Aristotle*, Routledge & Kegan Paul.

6 D. McNeill and N. B. McNeill

What Does a Child Mean When He Says 'No'?[1]

D. McNeill and N. B. McNeill, 'What does a child mean when he says
"no"?' *Proceedings of the Conference on Language and Language Behavior*,
1968, edited by E. M. Zale.

The emergence of negation in English is a portrait of a child's
resolution of complexity. Very roughly, negation in English
requires two transformations – one to remove an underlying
negative element from where it is located in the deep structure of
a sentence, and the other to introduce an auxiliary verb (*do* or
can) to support this element in the surface structure (Klima,
1964). This sketch omits most significant matters, but it reveals
an important part of what a child must acquire in order to negate
in the English manner.

One hypothesis about language acquisition is that it rests on a
set of specific cognitive capacities. These may be innate and may
be described by the so-called theory of grammar, or linguistic
theory (Chomsky, 1965; Katz, 1966; McNeill, in press). The
suggestion is that the universal form of language reflects children's
capacity for language – language has the form described by the
theory of grammar because of the innate capacities of children
to acquire language. Children's capacities everywhere in the
world impose the same features on language, which, therefore,
appear as linguistic universals.

An advantage of this view is that it accounts for the existence
of linguistic abstractions, features in adult grammar that are
never included in the overt forms of speech. Such features, of
course, cannot be presented to children; yet, they exist as a part
of adult linguistic knowledge. On the capacity hypothesis, such

1. This report is a slightly revised version of the paper presented by the
major author, David McNeill, at the Conference on Language and Language
Behavior. It is based on research supported by a contract with the Office of
Education, US Department of Health, Education & Welfare, under
provisions of P. L. 83–531, Cooperative Research, and Title VI, P. L. 85–
864, as amended.

abstractions are held to be linguistic universal, deriving from children's capacity for language, and they are *made* abstract through the acquisition of transformations.

An example of a linguistic abstraction, never presented as an overt form of speech, is the location of NEG at the beginning of the deep structure of English sentences. On the capacity hypothesis, this abstraction is *possible* because the location of NEG on the boundary of a sentence reflects an aspect of children's capacity for language. The principle would be, roughly, that every proposition can be denied by attaching to it a minus sign.

In this light, it is interesting that Bellugi (1964) finds the earliest negative sentences from children to be NEG + S and S + NEG – i.e., sentences in which a negative element (usually *no* or *not*) is placed outside an otherwise affirmative sentence. Examples are *no drop mitten*, and *wear mitten no*. This form of negation persists until a child shows independent evidence of having the two transformations mentioned above, at which time it completely disappears – having now presumably become abstract (McNeill, 1966). The same is true of the primitive negation of children learning Russian (Slobin, 1966) and French (our records).

The syntax of negation in Japanese

We mention these findings with children exposed to English and other languages in order to compare them to the development of negation in Japanese. Syntactically, negation in Japanese is rather simple. Except for order, the relevant part of the deep structure is identical to the deep structure of English sentences:

In Japanese, however, there are *no* order-changing transformations involved in carrying the negative aspect of this structure to the surface. The surface structure of a negative Japanese sentence is also *NP NP V NEG*. On the capacity hypothesis, therefore, the development of negation in Japanese should be likewise simple. Indeed, on the capacity hypothesis, Japanese children should not be *able* to make syntactic errors.

We thus take it to be consistent with the English findings and the capacity hypothesis that neither of the two children we have been following has *ever* uttered a grammatically-deviant negative. Their negative sentences are identical to some of the negatives that Bellugi described, i.e., S + NEG, and this is entirely correct in Japanese.

Syntactically, the development of negation thus poses no problem in Japanese. The language does not require more from children than is already available in their general capacity for negation. In Japanese, the problem is of a different sort.

The semantics of negation in Japanese

Although syntactically simple, negation in Japanese is *semantically* complex. In contrast to English, for example, the language provides several distinct forms; it is here that one can gain some insight into the process of development.

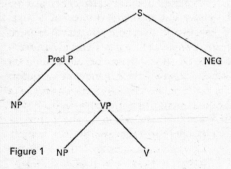

Figure 1

There are four common forms of negation in Japanese: *nai* (aux.), *nai* (adj.), *iya*, and *iiya*. *Nai* (aux.) is the form introduced into the phrase-marker given above. It is attached both to verbs, as indicated, and to adjectives. *Nai* (adj.), like all adjectives in Japanese, has verbal force, so that one can say, for example, *peace-nai*, meaning *there is no peace*. *Iya* stands alone, and means, roughly, *I do not want*. *Iiya* also stands alone and means that what was just said is wrong *and* something else is right. There are other forms than these four, but they are restricted to special situations – formal speech, for example.

These four forms – *nai* (aux.), *nai* (adj.), *iya*, and *iiya* – embody three dimensions of meaning. *Nai* (adj.) is used in such sentences as 'there's not an apple here', said after someone has asked about a place where there is no apple. The use of *nai* (adj.), therefore, depends on the *non-existence of objects and events*.

Nai (aux.) is used in such a sentence as 'that's not an apple', said after someone else, pointing to a pear, said, 'that's an apple'. The use of *nai* (aux.), therefore, depends on the *falsity of statements*.

Iya is used in such sentences as 'no, I don't want an apple'. *Iya* by itself conveys the idea of 'I don't want', and its use, therefore, depends on *internal desire*, or the lack of it.

Iiya is used in such sentences as 'No, I didn't have an apple, I had a pear.' Contrastive stress can convey this idea in English: 'No, I didn't have an *apple*, I had a *pear*.' The import of *iiya* is that one alternative (already mentioned or somehow in mind) is false and another is true. We will call this type of negation *entailment*, since, in this case, the negation of one statement entails the truth of another.

The four kinds of negative in Japanese thus involve three dimensions, or contrasts: *Entailment–Non-entailment*, *External–Internal*, and *Existence–Truth* (the last to be understood as indicating the *condition* of negation – the *existence*, or lack of it, of some *thing*, versus the *truth*, or lack of it, of some *sentence*).

One can organize the dimensions of negation into a cube (Fig.2), always a mark of progress in this area, and locate the four negative terms in Japanese at the appropriate corners.

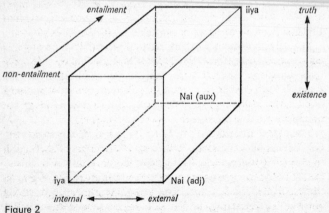

Figure 2

Alternatively, one can define the terms of negation in Japanese by means of feature matrices:

	Nai (adj.)	Nai (aux.)	Iya	Iiya
Existence	+	−	+	−
Entailment	−	−	−	+
External	+	+	−	+

According to these matrices, *iya* and *iiya* are diametrically-opposite kinds of negation, and the two kinds of *nai* are identical, except that one depends on the non-existence of objects and the other on the falsity of sentences. Both implications accord with native intuition.

The matrices also help explain what always strikes English speakers as a bit of oriental exotica when they first learn how Japanese affirm or deny negative questions. If someone asks, in English, 'Is there no pear?' and you wish to give an affirmative answer, the correct response is 'no, there is no pear', or some idiomatic variant. In Japanese, however, it is the reverse. If one wishes to give an affirmative answer, the reply should be, 'Yes, there is no pear'. A similar reversal exists for denial. In English it is 'yes, there is a pear', but in Japanese it is 'no, there is a pear'.

The difference is that 'yes' and 'no' in Japanese are (−Existence), whereas 'yes' and 'no' in English are (+Existence). Thus, the Japanese 'yes' refers to the truth-value of the sentence, whereas the English 'yes' refers to the existence of the pear. Similarly for 'no' in the two languages: in Japanese it signifies a false statement, whereas, in English it signifies non-existence.

The cube indicates that there are four other negatives possible but not used in Japanese. One, for example, would be a negative that denies the *truth of statements* on the grounds of *internal desire*, but which does *not entail* a true alternative. It would be a negative for existentialists: What you don't desire is false, but nothing in particular is thereby true. This is despair.

These three dimensions can be found in English negation also, but English is ambiguous with respect to them. The English 'no' is (+Existence) when discussing the physical environment, but it becomes (−Existence) in other contexts: for example, 'three plus two is six', '*no*'. And when one says, 'No, anything but *that*!', presumably the left side of the cube is evoked. But

English does not have separate terms sorted out in the analytic Japanese manner. When a child says, for example, *no dirty* in English, he is at least four-ways, and possibly eight-ways ambiguous.

Japanese, since it distinguishes among words along the three dimensions of negation, makes it possible to trace the order in which the dimensions emerge. We have looked for patterns of confusion – which negatives replace others – and from these patterns have attempted to infer the sequence of development. In effect, we have asked, how is the cube built up? Or, equivalently, in what order are the rows of the feature matrix added?

The development of negation in Japanese

We have worked with tape-recordings of the speech of two Japanese children. Both children are girls and both live in Tokyo. To date, there is some seven months' accumulation of speech. One of these children presents very little data, and what she does present so far eludes our understanding. The other child, whom we call Izanami, will be described here.

At twenty-seven months, the youngest age at which we have recordings, three of the four negative forms occur. These are *nai* (adj.), *nai* (aux.), and *iya*. *Iya* is always used alone. *Nai* (adj.) is used alone and after nouns, and both are correct syntactic contexts in Japanese. *Nai* (aux.) is used with just one verb – *shira-nai* – meaning 'I don't know'.

Of the two forms abundantly present at twenty-seven months, *nai* (adj.) is always used when called for, as far as this can be judged from context. That is, whenever non-existence is referred to, Izanami uses *nai* (adj.). *Iya*, however, is often replaced by *nai* (adj.). For instance, if Izanami's mother said, 'Let's give you some', Izanami would sometimes apparently reply, 'There's no giving', instead of 'I don't want'. *Nai* (adj.) intruded thus into as many as 40 per cent of the contexts appropriate for *iya*. *Iya*, on the other hand, never intruded into contexts appropriate to *nai* (adj.).

This pattern of confusion would arise if Izanami did not yet know *any* of the dimensions involved in negation, but reacted instead only to non-existence. Then *nai* (adj.) would be used whenever called for, and *iya* (being in her vocabulary) would oscillate with *nai* (adj.) in contexts calling for an expression of personal desire, but not involving non-existence. Let us assume then that Izanami began with the registration of simple non-existence as the occasion for negation. In effect, she began with the *nai*.(adj) *termini* of each of the three dimensions, but did not yet have the dimensions themselves. She built from *Existence*, *Non-entailment*, and *External*. We have called this *Stage 1*.

About two months later, two things happened to *iya*. First, it began to appear in contexts calling for *nai* (aux.). For example, if Izanami's mother said (falsely), 'This is an apple', pointing to a pear, Izanami would reply with *iya*, apparently meaning 'I don't want it'. This is only apparently odd. We will return to it shortly. The second development with *iya* is that it began to appear in contexts calling for *iiya*.

The last intrusion, *iya* in place of *iiya*, is totally inexplicable on the feature analysis. These terms share no features – they are at opposite corners of the cube – and so should never be confused, so long as at least one dimension has been acquired. Moreover, *iya* has been present in Izanami's vocabulary since the beginning, but it appears in contexts calling for *iiya* only now, after two months. We are fairly certain, therefore, that the intrusion is the result of a new development.

Let us suppose that it is not *iya* but really *iiya* that appears in contexts calling for *iya*. Vowel-vowel sequences are common in Japanese, but Izanami has none at this time. Since *iya* and *iiya* can be distinguished only through a difference in vowel length, it is at least possible that Izanami intends to say *iiya*, even though she actually says *iya*. In support of this interpretation is one further fact. From the beginning, *nai* (adj.) has appeared in context-calling for *iiya*, but the intrusion *ends* at this same time – again, indicating that Izanami has acquired *iiya*. If we accept the interpretation that Izanami says *iya* when she intends to say *iiya*, we can conclude that Izanami has added the *Existence–Truth*, or the *Entailment–Non-entailment* dimensions, or both.

Of the two, the evidence favors *Existence–Truth*. Recall that contexts calling for *nai* (aux.) begin taking *iya* about this time. Instead of saying, 'It's not an apple', Izanami apparently says, 'I don't want an apple'. However, if it is really *iiya* appearing in place of *nai* (aux.) – so that she is saying, 'It's not an apple (but something else)' – we then know that Izanami has acquired the *Existence–Truth* contrast only. It could not have been *Entailment–Non-entailment* because *iiya* and *nai* (aux.) are distinct on this feature – one being *Entailment*, the other being *Non-entailment*. They could not be confused, if this dimension has been acquired. However, they are alike on *Existence–Truth*, both being marked for *Truth*, and so *could* be confused if Izanami had acquired this dimension alone.

Thus, the first dimension to emerge is *Existence–Truth*, and its appearance marks *stage 2*, at which time Izanami's knowledge of negation presumably is as follows:

	Nai (adj.)	Nai (aux.)	Iya	Iiya
1. No contrasts				
2. Existence	+	−	+	−

Stage 3 took place two months later. The replacement of *iya* by *nai* (adj.), which had been present from the beginning, stops altogether. Izanami no longer apparently says, 'There isn't an apple,' when she should say, 'I don't want an apple'. The new development must signify acquisition of the *External–Internal* dimension, as well as the virtually certain appearance of *iya* (as opposed to the truncated *iiya*). No other possibility exists, given our semantic analysis, since *External–Internal* is the only dimension on which *iya* and *nai* (adj.) contrast. There is no problem here of distinguishing *iya* and *iiya*, of course, since the observation involves the pronunciation (or lack of it) of *nai*. For the same reason, no assumptions are made about the meaning of *iya* when Izanami uses it, but only about the existence of *iya*-contexts.

Thus, Izanami has two dimensions by stage 3, and *iiya* and *nai* (aux.) are synonyms:

	Nai (adj.)	Nai (aux.)	Iya	Iiya
1. No contrasts				
2. Existence	+	−	+	−
3. External	+	+	−	+

About a month later, Izanami apparently acquired the *Entailment–Non-entailment* dimension. The evidence is that she distinguished *nai* (aux.) from *iiya*, and so eliminated the remaining confusion: (*i*)*iya* no longer appeared in *nai* (aux.) contexts. Thus, Izanami developed the entire system of negation in Japanese in some five months' time.

At the moment that Entailment–Non-entailment emerged, an interesting further development occurred. A new word, *chigau*, appeared, and did so in considerable numbers. It had been completely absent from Izanami's speech before this time.

Chigau is not a negative. It is variously translated as 'different', 'wrong', or 'disagree' – and so is different from such words as 'no', 'not', or 'no–but'. Syntactically, it is a verb.

However, Izanami uses *chigau* in none of the senses just given. For her, *chigau* is an omnibus negative, used in completely diverse contexts. It appears in situations calling for *iiya* and *iya* – even though *iiya* and *iya* share no features of negation at all – and possibly appears also in contexts appropriate to *nai* (adj.) and *nai* (aux.), although we have not observed this. If we assume that Izanami's use of *chigau* has not yet demolished the system of negation just developed – as, indeed, it apparently has not, since she continues to use the four terms of negation as well – we must conclude that *chigau* has negative import but is marked on none of the dimensions of negation. Thus, it appears in contexts calling for Truth as well as Existence, External as well as Internal, and Entailment as well as Non-entailment. In fact, Izanami's use of *chigau* resembles most closely the use of *un-uh* in English: 'Do you want some?' 'Un-uh'; 'Did you have a pear?' 'Un-uh, I had an apple'; 'Springfield is the capital of Massachusetts.' 'Un-uh'; 'Does she have a wart on her nose?' 'Un-uh'. *Un-uh*, too, represents omnibus negation.

How are we to account for the sudden appearance of an omnibus negative? It seems most plausible to suppose that Izanami's use of *chigau* reflects the *concept* of negation, as opposed to the particular forms of denial (*iya*, *nai* (adj.), etc.), or the particular dimensions of negation. As such, *chigau* adds the idea of general denial, as an abstract possibility, and so liberates negation from the semantic constraints represented in the three contrasts of *Truth–Existence*, *External–Internal* and *Entailment–Non-entailment*.

However, the interesting fact is not so much that Izanami eventually developed a form of omnibus negation, but that she did so *after* having developed the various special forms of negation. For Izanami's parents use *chigau* in the omnibus sense, too. *Chigau*, as a kind of featureless denial, has been presented to Izanami as a model throughout the five-month period we have studied (and doubtlessly before), yet Izanami resisted developing *chigau* precisely until she had acquired the last of the three contrasts of negation. On this evidence, generic negation is not primitive, as often claimed. It is, instead, a late development, constructed from, and possibly summarizing, the three features of negation discussed above. It is these features that are preliminary. If anything in Izanami's history of negation reflects some aspect of children's capacity for negation, it is the features of negation and not the general concept of denial.

We can summarize our findings, and answer the question, 'What does a child mean when he says "no"?', by setting down the following five points:

1. At first, Izanami had no features of negation at all. At this point 'no' meant something did not exist, and nothing more. Subsequent development consisted of forming contrasts with the ends of the dimensions represented in *nai* (adj.); that is, with Existence, External, and Non-entailment.

2. The first such contrast to emerge was between *Existence* and *Truth*. In addition to marking the existence and non-existence of events and objects, Izanami came to mark the correctness and incorrectness of statements. By stage 2, 'no' had come to mean false, as well as not here, creating an order of development that appears to be quite natural. Izanami judged relations about language only after she had judged other relations about the external world.

3. The next contrast to emerge was between *External* and *Internal*. Besides registering the non-existence of events, Izanami began to mark her desires concerning events. By stage 3, 'no' meant disapproval or rejection, as well as false and not here. Another direction of development, therefore, was from outside to inside, and this, too, seems to be in a natural order. Note that Izanami had the idea of linguistically registering the truth of statements before she had the idea of linguistically registering her inner states in relation to outer ones.

4. The last contrast to emerge was *Entailment–Non-entailment*. With this dimension, 'no' also came to mean 'no but', which requires an ability to organize statements into mutually exclusive pairs. Because *Entailment–Non-entailment* requires a child to hold in mind two propositions at once, it would naturally follow either of the other two contrasts, both of which involve judgements about single propositions or events.

5. The last step was the formation of an abstract concept of negation – the equivalent of *un-uh*. If *chigau* is a construction, its appearance last is also natural.

It is possible that these same steps, insofar as they follow a natural order, are also taken by English-speaking children. As pointed out above, the three dimensions of Japanese negation are used in English as well. Hopefully, future work will discover some way to investigate this possibility.

References

BELLUGI, U. (1964), *The Emergence of Inflections and Negation Systems in the Speech of Two Children*, paper presented at the New England Psychological Association.

CHOMSKY, N. (1965), *Aspects of the Theory of Syntax*, MIT Press.

KATZ, J. J. (1966), *The Philosophy of Language*, Harper & Row.

KLIMA, E. S. (1964), 'Negation in English', in J. A. Fodor and J. J. Katz (eds), *The Structure of Language*, Prentice-Hall.

MCNEILL, D. (1966), 'Developmental psycholinguistics' in *The Genesis of Language: A Psycholinguistic Approach*, MIT Press.

MCNEILL, D. (in press), 'On theories of language acquisition', in *Verbal Behavior Theory and its Relation to Theory*, Prentice-Hall.

SLOBIN, D. I. (1966), 'The acquisition of Russian as a native language', in F. Smith and G. A. Miller (eds) *The Genesis of Language: A Psycholinguistic Approach*, MIT Press.

Part Three
Cognitive Dimensions of Language: Conceptual Studies

Three theoretical positions on the relation between language and cognition are represented here. Whorf's principle of 'linguistic relativity' (Reading 7) has long been of interest, in spite of many problems of interpretation and lack of substantial experimental evidence. Piaget's emphasis on a general cognitive framework for language, is based on a large body of theoretical and empirical work (Reading 10). Vygotsky's article (Reading 11) is built around the concept of 'verbal thought' – language and thought to a large degree inseparable in the growing child. This article is an excerpt from a book originally published in 1934: it remains of major importance.

7 B. Whorf

The Relation of Habitual Thought and Behaviour to Language

B. Whorf, 'The relation of habitual thought and behaviour to language',
in L. Spier (ed.), *Lanugage, Culture, and Personality: Essays in Memory of Edward Sapir*, 1941, University of Utah Press.

Human beings do not live in the objective world alone, nor alone in the world of social activity as ordinarily understood, but are very much at the mercy of the particular language which has become the medium of expression for their society. It is quite an illusion to imagine that one adjusts to reality essentially without the use of language and that language is merely an incidental means of solving specific problems of communication or reflection. The fact of the matter is that the 'real world' is to a large extent unconsciously built up on the language habits of the group. . . . We see and hear and otherwise experience very largely as we do because the language habits of our community predispose certain choices of interpretation. (Edward Sapir)

There will probably be general assent to the proposition that an accepted pattern of using words is often prior to certain lines of thinking and forms of behavior, but he who assents often sees in such a statement nothing more than a platitudinous recognition of the hypnotic power of philosophical and learned terminology on the one hand or of catchwords, slogans, and rallying cries on the other. To see only thus far is to miss the point of one of the important interconnections which Sapir saw between language, culture, and psychology, and succinctly expressed in the introductory quotation. It is not so much in these special uses of language as in its constant ways of arranging data and its most ordinary everyday analysis of phenomena that we need to recognize the influence it has on other activities, cultural and personal.

The name of the situation as affecting behavior
I came in touch with an aspect of this problem before I had studied under Dr Sapir, and in a field usually considered remote from

linguistics. It was in the course of my professional work for a fire insurance company, in which I undertook the task of analysing many hundreds of reports of circumstances surrounding the start of fires, and in some cases, of explosions. My analysis was directed toward purely physical conditions, such as defective wiring, presence or lack of air spaces between metal flues and woodwork, etc., and the results were presented in these terms. Indeed it was undertaken with no thought that any other significances would or could be revealed. But in due course it became evident that not only a physical situation *qua* physics, but the meaning of that situation to people, was sometimes a factor, through the behavior of the people, in the start of the fire. And this factor of meaning was clearest when it was a *linguistic meaning*, residing in the name or the linguistic description commonly applied to the situation. Thus, around a storage of what are called 'gasoline drums', behavior will tend to a certain type, that is, great care will be exercised; while around a storage of what are called 'empty gasoline drums', it will tend to be different – careless, with little repression of smoking or of tossing cigarette stubs about. Yet the 'empty' drums are perhaps the more dangerous, since they contain explosive vapor. Physically the situation is hazardous, but the linguistic analysis according to regular analogy must employ the word 'empty', which inevitably suggests lack of hazard. The word 'empty' is used in two linguistic patterns:

1. As a virtual synonym for 'null and void, negative, inert'.

2. Applied in analysis of physical situations without regard to, e.g., vapor, liquid vestiges, or stray rubbish, in the container.

The situation is named in one pattern (2) and the name is then 'acted out' or 'lived up to' in another (1), this being a general formula for the linguistic conditioning of behavior into hazardous forms.

In a wood distillation plant the metal stills were insulated with a composition prepared from limestone and called at the plant 'spun limestone'. No attempt was made to protect this covering from excessive heat or the contact of flame. After a period of use, the fire below one of the stills spread to the 'limestone', which to everyone's great surprise burned vigorously. Exposure to acetic acid fumes from the stills had converted part of the limestone (calcium carbonate) to calcium acetate. This when heated in a fire decomposes, forming inflammable acetone. Behavior that tolerated fire close to the covering was induced by use of the name 'limestone', which because it ends in '-stone' implies non-combustibility.

A huge iron kettle of boiling varnish was observed to be over-heated, nearing the temperature at which it would ignite. The operator moved it off the fire and ran it on its wheels to a distance, but did not cover it. In a minute or so the varnish ignited. Here the linguistic influence is more complex; it is due to the meta-phorical objectifying (of which more later) of 'cause' as contact or the spatial juxtaposition of 'things' – to analysing the situation as 'on' versus 'off' the fire. In reality, the stage when the external fire was the main factor had passed; the overheating was now an internal process of convection in the varnish from the intensely heated kettle, and still continued when 'off' the fire.

An electric glow heater on the wall was little used, and for one workman had the meaning of a convenient coathanger. At night a watchman entered and snapped a switch, which action he verbalized as 'turning on the light'. No light appeared, and this result he verbalized as 'light is burned out'. He could not see the glow of the heater because of the old coat hung on it. Soon the heater ignited the coat, which set fire to the building.

A tannery discharged waste water containing animal matter into an outdoor settling basin partly roofed with wood and partly open. This situation is one that ordinarily would be verbalized as 'pool of water'. A workman had occasion to light a blowtorch near by, and threw his match into the water. But the decomposing waste matter was evolving gas under the wood cover, so that the setup was the reverse of 'watery'. An instant flare of flame ignited the woodwork, and the fire quickly spread into the adjoining building.

A drying room for hides was arranged with a blower at one end to make a current of air along the room and thence outdoors through a vent at the other end. Fire started at a hot bearing on the blower, which blew the flames directly into the hides and fanned them along the room, destroying the entire stock. This hazardous setup followed naturally from the term 'blower' with its linguistic equivalence to 'that which blows', implying that its function necessarily is to 'blow'. Also its function is verbalized as 'blowing air for drying', overlooking that it can blow other things, e.g., flames and sparks. In reality, a blower simply makes a current of air and can exhaust as well as blow. It should have been installed at the vent end to *draw* the air over the hides, then through the hazard (its own casing and bearings), and thence outdoors.

Beside a coal-fired melting pot for lead reclaiming was dumped a pile of 'scrap lead' – a misleading verbalization for it consisted of the lead sheets of old radio condensers, which still had paraffin paper between them. Soon the paraffin blazed up and fired the roof, half of which was burned off.

Such examples, which could be greatly multiplied, will suffice to show how the cue to a certain line of behavior is often given by the analogies of the linguistic formula in which the situation is spoken of, and by which to some degree it is analysed, classified, and allotted its place in that world which is 'to a large extent unconsciously built up on the language habits of the group.' And we always assume that the linguistic analysis made by our group reflects reality better than it does.

Grammatical patterns as interpretations of experience

The linguistic material in the above examples is limited to single words, phrases, and patterns of limited range. One cannot study the behavioral compulsiveness of such material without suspecting a much more far-reaching compulsion from large-scale patterning of grammatical categories, such as plurality, gender and similar classifications (animate, inanimate, etc.), tenses, voices, and other verb forms, classifications of the type of 'parts of speech', and the matter of whether a given experience is denoted by a unit morpheme, an inflected word, or a syntactical combination. A category such as number (singular *v.* plural) is an attempted interpretation of a whole large order of experience, virtually of the world or of nature; it attempts to say how experience is to be segmented, what experience is to be called 'one' and what 'several'. But the difficulty of appraising such a far-reaching influence is great because of its background character, because of the difficulty of standing aside from our own language, which is a habit and a cultural *non est disputandum*, and scrutinizing it objectively. And if we take a very dissimilar language, this language becomes a part of nature, and we even do to it what we have already done to nature. We tend to think in our own language in order to examine the exotic language. Or we find the task of unraveling the purely morphological intricacies so gigantic that it seems to absorb all else. Yet the problem, though difficult, is feasible; and the best approach is through an exotic language, for in its study we are at long last pushed willy-nilly out of our ruts. Then we find that the exotic language is a mirror held up to our own.

In my study of the Hopi language, what I now see as an opportunity to work on this problem, was first thrust upon me before I was clearly aware of the problem. The seemingly endless task of describing the morphology did finally end. Yet it was evident, especially in the light of Sapir's lectures on Navaho, that the description of the *language* was far from complete. I knew, for example, the morphological formation of plurals, but not how to use plurals. It was evident that the category of plural in Hopi was not the same thing as in English, French, or German. Certain things that were plural in these languages were singular in Hopi. The phase of investigation which now began consumed nearly two more years.

The work began to assume the character of a comparison between Hopi and western European languages. It also became evident that even the grammar of Hopi bore a relation to Hopi culture, and the grammar of European tongues to our own 'Western' or 'European' culture. And it appeared that the interrelation brought in those large subsummations of experience by language, such as our own terms 'time', 'space', 'substance', and 'matter'. Since, with respect to the traits compared, there is little difference between English, French, German, or other European languages with the *possible* (but doubtful) exception of Balto-Slavic and non-Indo-European, I have lumped these languages into one group called SAE, or 'Standard Average European'.

That portion of the whole investigation here to be reported may be summed up in two questions: firstly, are our own concepts of 'time', 'space', and 'matter' given in substantially the same form by experience to all men, or are they in part conditioned by the structure of particular languages? Secondly, are there traceable affinities between (1) cultural and behavioral norms and (2) large-scale linguistic patterns? (I should be the last to pretend that there is anything so definite as 'a correlation' between culture and language, and especially between ethnological rubrics such as 'agricultural, hunting', etc., and linguistic ones like 'inflected', 'synthetic', or 'isolating'.[1]) When I began the study, the problem was by no means so clearly formulated, and I had little notion that the answers would turn out as they did.

Plurality and numeration in SAE and Hopi

In our language, that is SAE, plurality and cardinal numbers are applied in two ways: to real plurals and imaginary plurals. Or more exactly if less tersely: perceptible spatial aggregates and metaphorical aggregates. We say 'ten men' and also 'ten days'. Ten men either are or could be objectively perceived as ten, ten in one group perception[2] – ten men on a street corner, for instance. But 'ten days' cannot be objectively experienced. We experience only one day, today; the other nine (or even all ten) are something conjured up from memory or imagination. If 'ten days' be regarded as a group it must be as an 'imaginary,' mentally constructed group. Whence comes this mental pattern? Just as in the case of the fire-causing errors, from the fact that our language confuses the two different situations, has but one pattern for both. When we speak of 'ten steps forward, ten strokes on a bell,' or any similarly described cyclic sequence, 'times' of any sort, we are doing the same thing as with 'days'. *Cyclicity* brings the response of imaginary plurals. But a likeness of cyclicity to aggregates is not unmistakably given by experience prior to

1. We have plenty of evidence that this is not the case. Consider only the Hopi and the Ute, with languages that on the overt morphological and lexical level are as similar as, say, English and German. The idea of 'correlation' between language and culture, in the generally accepted sense of correlation, is certainly a mistaken one.

2. As we say, 'ten at the *same time*,' showing that in our language and thought we restate the fact of group perception in terms of a concept 'time', the large linguistic component of which will appear in the course of this paper.

language, or it would be found in all languages, and it is not.

Our *awareness* of time and cyclicity does contain something immediate and subjective – the basic sense of 'becoming later and later'. But, in the habitual thought of us SAE people, this is covered under something quite different, which though mental should not be called subjective. I call it *objectified*, or imaginary, because it is patterned on the *outer* world. It is this that reflects our linguistic usage. Our tongue makes no distinction between numbers counted on discrete entities and numbers that are simply 'counting itself'. Habitual thought then asumes that in the latter the numbers are just as much counted on 'something' as in the former. This is objectification. Concepts of time lose contact with the subjective experience of 'becoming later' and are objectified as counted *quantities*, especially as lengths, made up of units as a length can be visibly marked off into inches. A 'length of time' is envisioned as a row of similar units, like a row of bottles.

In Hopi there is a different linguistic situation. Plurals and cardinals are used only for entities that form or can form an objective group. There are no imaginary plurals, but instead ordinals used with singulars. Such an expression as 'ten days' is not used. The equivalent statement is an operational one that reaches one day by a suitable count. 'They stayed ten days' becomes 'they stayed until the eleventh day' or 'they left after the tenth day.' 'Ten days is greater than nine days' becomes 'the tenth day is later than the ninth'. Our 'length of time' is not regarded as a length but as a relation between two events in lateness. Instead of our linguistically promoted objectification of that datum of consciousness we call 'time', the Hopi language has not laid down any pattern that would cloak the subjective 'becoming later' that is the essence of time.

Nouns of physical quantity in SAE and Hopi

We have two kinds of nouns denoting physical things: individual nouns, and mass nouns, e.g., 'water, milk, wood, granite, sand, flour, meat'. Individual nouns denote bodies with definite outlines: 'a tree, a stick, a man, a hill'. Mass nouns denote homogeneous continua without implied boundaries. The distinction is marked by linguistic form; e.g., mass nouns lack plurals,[3] in English drop articles, and in French take the partitive article *du*, *de la*, *des*. The distinction is more widespread in language than in the observable appearance of things. Rather few natural occurrences present themselves as unbounded extents; 'air' of course, and often 'water, rain, snow, sand, rock, dirt, grass'. We do not encounter 'butter, meat, cloth, iron, glass', or most 'materials' in such kind of manifestation, but in bodies small or large with definite outlines. The distinction is somewhat forced upon our description of events by an unavoidable pattern in language. It is so inconvenient in a great many cases that we need some way of individualizing the mass noun by further linguistic devices. This is partly done by names of body-types: 'stick of wood, piece of cloth, pane of glass, cake of soap'; also, and even more, by introducing names of containers though their contents be the real issue: 'glass of water, cup of coffee, dish of food, bag of flour, bottle of beer'. These very common container formulas, in which 'of' has an obvious, visually perceptible meaning ('contents'), influence our feeling about the less obvious type-body formulas: 'stick of wood, lump of dough', etc. The formulas are very similar: individual noun plus a similar relator (English 'of'). In the obvious case this relator denotes contents. In the inobvious one it 'suggests' contents. Hence the 'lumps, chunks, blocks, pieces', etc., seem to contain something, a 'stuff', 'substance', or 'matter' that answers to the 'water', 'coffee', or 'flour' in the container formulas. So with SAE people the philosophic 'substance' and 'matter' are also the naïve idea; they are instantly acceptable, 'common sense'. It is so through linguistic habit. Our language patterns often require us to name a physical thing by a binomial that splits the reference into a formless item plus a form.

Hopi is again different. It has a formally distinguished class of nouns. But this class contains no formal subclass of mass nouns.

3. It is no exception to this rule of lacking a plural that a mass noun may sometimes coincide in lexeme with an individual noun that of course has a plural; e.g., 'stone' (no pl.) with 'a stone' (pl. 'stones'). The plural form denoting varieties, e.g., 'wines' is of course a different sort of thing from the true plural; it is a curious outgrowth from the SAE mass nouns, leading to still another sort of imaginary aggregates, which will have to be omitted from this paper.

All nouns have an individual sense and both singular and plural forms. Nouns translating most nearly our mass nouns still refer to vague bodies or vaguely bounded extents. They imply indefiniteness, but not lack, of outline and size. In specific statements, 'water' means one certain mass or quantity of water, not what we call 'the substance water'. Generality of statement is conveyed through the verb or predicator, not the noun. Since nouns are individual already, they are not individualized by either typebodies or names of containers, if there is no special need to emphasize shape or container. The noun itself implies a suitable type-body or container. One says, not 'a glass of water' but *kə·yi* 'a water,' not 'a pool of water' but *pa·hə*,[4] not 'a dish of cornflour' but *ŋəmni* 'a (quantity of) cornflour', not 'a piece of meat' but *sikʷi* 'a meat'. The language has neither need for nor analogies on which to build the concept of existence as a duality of formless item and form. It deals with formlessness through other symbols than nouns.

Phases of cycles in SAE and Hopi

Such terms as 'summer, winter, September, morning, noon, sunset' are with us nouns, and have little formal linguistic difference from other nouns. They can be subjects or objects, and we say 'at sunset' or 'in winter' just as we say 'at a corner' or 'in an orchard'.[5] They are pluralized and numerated like nouns of physical objects, as we have seen. Our thought about the referents of such words hence becomes objectified. Without objectification, it would be a subjective experience of real time, i.e., of the consciousness of 'becoming later and later' – simply a cyclic phase similar to an earlier phase in that ever-later-becoming duration. Only by imagination can such a cyclic phase be set beside another and another in the manner of a spatial (i.e., visually per-

4. Hopi has two words for water quantities; *kə·yi* and *pa·hə*. The difference is something like that between 'stone' and 'rock' in English, *pa·hə* implying greater size and 'wildness'; flowing water, whether or not outdoors or in nature; is *pa·hə*; so is 'moisture'. But, unlike 'stone' and 'rock', the difference is essential, not pertaining to a connotative margin, and the two can hardly ever be interchanged.

5. To be sure, there are a few minor differences from other nouns, in English for instance in the use of the articles.

ceived) configuration. But such is the power of linguistic analogy that we do so objectify cyclic phasing. We do it even by saying 'a phase' and 'phases' instead of, e.g., 'phasing'. And the pattern of individual and mass nouns, with the resulting binomial formula of formless item plus form, is so general that it is implicit for all nouns, and hence our very generalized formless items like 'substance, matter', by which we can fill out the binomial for an enormously wide range of nouns. But even these are not quite generalized enough to take in our phase nouns. So for the phase nouns we have made a formless item, 'time'. We have made it by using 'a time', i.e. an occasion or a phase, in the pattern of a mass noun, just as from 'a summer' we make 'summer' in the pattern of a mass noun. Thus with our binomial formula we can say and think 'a moment of time, a second of time, a year of time'. Let me again point out that the pattern is simply that of 'a bottle of milk' or 'a piece of cheese'. Thus we are assisted to imagine that 'a summer' actually contains or consists of such-and-such a quantity of 'time'.

In Hopi however all phase terms, like 'summer, morning', etc., are not nouns but a kind of adverb, to use the nearest SAE analogy. They are a formal part of speech by themselves, distinct from nouns, verbs, and even other Hopi 'adverbs'. Such a word is not a case form or a locative pattern, like 'des Abends' or 'in the morning'. It contains no morpheme like one of 'in the house' or 'at the tree'.[6] It means 'when it is morning' or 'while morning-phase is occurring'. These 'temporals' are not used as subjects or objects, or at all like nouns. One does not say 'it's a hot summer' or 'summer is hot'; summer is not hot, summer is only *when* conditions are hot, *when* heat occurs. One does not say '*this* summer', but 'summer now' or 'summer recently'. There is no objectification, as a region, an extent, a quantity, of the subjective duration-feeling. Nothing is suggested about time except the perpetual 'getting later' of it. And so there is no basis here for a formless item answering to our 'time'.

6. 'Year' and certain combinations of 'year' with name of season, rarely season names alone, can occur with a locative morpheme 'at', but this is exceptional. It appears like historical detritus of an earlier different patterning, or the effect of English analogy, or both.

Temporal forms of verbs in SAE and Hopi

The three-tense system of SAE verbs colors all our thinking about time. This system is amalgamated with that larger scheme of objectification of the subjective experience of duration already noted in other patterns – in the binomial formula applicable to nouns in general, in temporal nouns, in plurality and numeration. This objectification enables us in imagination to 'stand time units in a row'. Imagination of time as like a row harmonizes with a system of THREE tenses; whereas a system of TWO, an earlier and a later, would seem to correspond better to the feeling of duration as it is experienced. For if we inspect consciousness we find no past, present, future, but a unity embracing complexity. *Everything* is in consciousness, and everything in consciousness IS, and is together. There is in it a sensuous and a nonsensuous. We may call the sensuous – what we are seeing, hearing, touching – the *present* while in the nonsensuous the vast image-world of memory is being labeled the *past* and another realm of belief, intuition, and uncertainty the *future*; yet sensation, memory, foresight, all are in consciousness together – one is not 'yet to be' nor another 'once but no more'. Where real time comes in is that all this in consciousness is 'getting later', changing certain relations in an irreversible manner. In this 'latering' or 'durating' there seems to me to be a paramount contrast between the newest, latest instant at the focus of attention and the rest – the earlier. Languages by the score get along well with two tenselike forms answering to this paramount relation of 'later' to 'earlier'. We can of course *construct and contemplate in thought* a system of past, present, future, in the objectified configuration of points on a line. This is what our general objectification tendency leads us to do and our tense system confirms.

In English the present tense seems the one least in harmony with the paramount temporal relation. It is as if pressed into various and not wholly congruous duties. One duty is to stand as objectified middle term between objectified past and objectified future, in narration, discussion, argument, logic, philosophy. Another is to denote inclusion in the sensuous field: 'I *see* him.' Another is for nomic, i.e. customarily or generally valid, statements: 'We *see* with our eyes.' These varied uses introduce confusions of thought, of which for the most part we are unaware.

Hopi, as we might expect, is different here too. Verbs have no 'tenses' like ours, but have validity-forms ('assertions'), aspects, and clause-linkage forms (modes), that yield even greater precision of speech. The validity-forms denote that the speaker (not the subject) reports the situation (answering to our past and present) or that he expects it (answering to our future)[7] or that he makes a nomic statement (answering to our nomic present). The aspects denote different degrees of duration and different kinds of tendency 'during duration'. As yet we have noted nothing to indicate whether an event is sooner or later than another when both are reported. But need for this does not arise until we have two verbs: i.e. two clauses. In that case the 'modes' denote relations between the clauses, including relations of later to earlier and of simultaneity. Then there are many detached words that express similar relations, supplementing the modes and aspects. The duties of our three-tense system and its tripartite linear objectified 'time' are distributed among various verb categories, all different from our tenses; and there is no more basis for an objectified time in Hopi verbs than in other Hopi patterns; although this does not in the least hinder the verb forms and other patterns from being closely adjusted to the pertinent realities of actual situations.

Duration, intensity and tendency in SAE and Hopi

To fit discourse to manifold actual situations, all languages need to express durations, intensities, and tendencies. It is characteristic of SAE and perhaps of many other language types to express them metaphorically. The metaphors are those of spatial extension, i.e. of size, number (plurality), position, shape, and motion. We express duration by 'long, short, great, much, quick, slow',

7. The expective and reportive assertions contrast according to the 'paramount relation'. The expective expresses anticipation existing *earlier* than objective fact, and coinciding with objective fact *later* than the status quo of the speaker, this status quo, including all the subsummation of the past therein, being expressed by the reportive. Our notion 'future' seems to represent at once the earlier (anticipation) and the later (afterwards, what will be), as Hopi shows. This paradox may hint of how elusive the mystery of real time is, and how artificially it is expressed by a linear relation of past–present–future.

etc.; intensity by 'large, great, much, heavy, light, high, low, sharp, faint', etc.; tendency by 'more, increase, grow, turn, get, approach, go, come, rise, fall, stop, smooth, even, rapid, slow'; and so on through an almost inexhaustible list of metaphors that we hardly recognize as such, since they are virtually the only linguistic media available. The nonmetaphorical terms in this field, like 'early, late, soon, lasting, intense, very, tending', are a mere handful, quite inadequate to the needs.

It is clear how this condition 'fits in'. It is part of our whole scheme of *objectifying* – imaginatively spatializing qualities and potentials that are quite nonspatial (so far as any spatially perceptive senses can tell us). Noun-meaning (with us) proceeds from physical bodies to referents of far other sort. Since physical bodies and their outlines in *perceived space* are denoted by size and shape terms and reckoned by cardinal numbers and plurals, these patterns of denotation and reckoning extend to the symbols of nonspatial meanings, and so suggest an *imaginary space*. Physical shapes 'move, stop, rise, sink, approach', etc., in perceived space; why not these other referents in their imaginary space? This has gone so far that we can hardly refer to the simplest nonspatial situation without constant resort to physical metaphors. I 'grasp' the 'thread' of another's arguments, but if its 'level' is 'over my head' my attention may 'wander' and 'lose touch' with the 'drift' of it, so that when he 'comes' to his 'point' we differ 'widely', our 'views' being indeed so 'far apart' that the 'things' he says 'appear' 'much' too arbitrary, or even 'a lot' of nonsense!

The absence of such metaphor from Hopi speech is striking. Use of space terms when there is no space involved is *not there* – as if on it had been laid the taboo teetotal! The reason is clear when we know that Hopi has abundant conjugational and lexical means of expressing duration, intensity, and tendency directly as such, and that major grammatical patterns do not, as with us, provide analogies for an imaginary space. The many verb 'aspects' express duration and tendency of manifestations, while some of the 'voices' express intensity, tendency, and duration of causes or forces producing manifestations. Then a special part of speech, the 'tensors', a huge class of words, denotes only intensity, tendency, duration, and sequence. The function of the tensors is to express intensities, 'strengths', and how they continue or vary, their rate of change; so that the broad concept of intensity, when considered as necessarily always varying and/or continuing, includes also tendency and duration. Tensors convey distinctions of degree, rate, constancy, repetition, increase and decrease of intensity, immediate sequence, interruption or sequence after an interval, etc., also *qualities* of strengths, such as we should express metaphorically as smooth, even, hard, rough. A striking feature is their lack of resemblance to the terms of real space and movement that to us 'mean the same'. There is not even more than a trace of apparent derivation from space terms.[8] So, while Hopi in its nouns seems highly concrete, here in the tensors it becomes abstract almost beyond our power to follow.

Habitual thought in SAE and Hopi

The comparison now to be made between the habitual thought worlds of SAE and Hopi speakers is of course incomplete. It is possible only to touch upon certain dominant contrasts that appear to stem from the linguistic differences already noted. By 'habitual thought' and 'thought world' I mean more than simply language, i.e. than the linguistic patterns themselves. I include all the analogical and suggestive value of the patterns (e.g., our 'imaginary space' and its distant implications), and all the give-and-take between language and the culture as a whole, wherein is a vast amount that is not linguistic but yet shows the shaping influence of language. In brief, this 'thought world' is the microcosm that each man carries about within himself, by which he measures and understands what he can of the macrocosm.

The SAE microcosm has analysed reality largely in terms of what it calls 'things' (bodies and quasibodies) plus modes of

8. One such trace is that the tensor 'long in duration', while quite different from the adjective 'long' of space, seems to contain the same root as the adjective 'large' of space. Another is that 'somewhere' of space used with certain tensors means 'at some indefinite time.' Possibly however this is not the case and it is only the tensor that gives the time element, so that 'somewhere' still refers to space and that under these conditions indefinite space means simply general applicability, regardless of either time or space. Another trace is that in the temporal (cycle word) 'afternoon' the element meaning 'after' is derived from the verb 'to separate'. There are other such traces, but they are few and exceptional, and obviously not like our own spatial metaphorizing.

extensional but formless existence that it calls 'substances' or 'matter'. It tends to see existence through a binomial formula that expresses any existent as a spatial form plus a spatial formless continuum related to the form, as contents is related to the outlines of its container. Nonspatial existents are imaginatively spatialized and charged with similar implications of form and continuum.

The Hopi microcosm seems to have analysed reality largely in terms of *events* (or better 'eventing'), referred to in two ways, objective and subjective. Objectively, and only if perceptible physical experience, events are expressed mainly as outlines, colors, movements, and other perceptive reports. Subjectively, for both the physical and nonphysical, events are considered the expression of invisible intensity factors, on which depend their stability and persistence, or their fugitiveness and proclivities. It implies that existents do not 'become later and later' all in the same way; but some do so by growing like plants, some by diffusing and vanishing, some by a procession of metamorphoses, some by enduring in one shape till affected by violent forces. In the nature of each existent able to manifest as a definite whole is the power of its own mode of duration: its growth, decline, stability, cyclicity, or creativeness. Everything is thus already 'prepared' for the way it now manifests by earlier phases, and what it will be later, partly has been, and partly is in act of being so 'prepared'. An emphasis and importance rests on this preparing or being prepared aspect of the world that may to the Hopi correspond to that 'quality of reality' that 'matter' or 'stuff' has for us.

Habitual behavior features of Hopi culture

Our behavior, and that of Hopi, can be seen to be coordinated in many ways to the linguistically conditioned microcosm. As in my fire casebook, people act about situations in ways which are like the ways they talk about them. A characteristic of Hopi behavior is the emphasis on preparation. This includes announcing and getting ready for events well beforehand, elaborate precautions to insure persistence of desired conditions, and stress on goodwill as the preparer of right results. Consider the analogies of the day-counting pattern alone. Time is mainly reckoned 'by day' (*taʟk*, *-tala*) or 'by night' (*tok*), which words are not nouns but tensors, the first formed on a root 'light, day,' the second on a root 'sleep'. The count is by *ordinals*. This is not the pattern of counting a number of different men or things, even though they appear successively, for, even then, they *could* gather into an assemblage. It is the pattern of counting successive reappearances of the *same* man or thing, incapable of forming an assemblage. The analogy is not to behave about day-cyclicity as to several men ('several days'), which is what *we* tend to do, but to behave as to the successive visits of the *same man*. One does not alter several men by working upon just one, but one can prepare and so alter the later visits of the same man by working to affect the visit he is making now. This is the way the Hopi deal with the future – by working within a present situation which is expected to carry impresses, both obvious and occult, forward into the future event of interest. One might say that Hopi society understands our proverb 'Well begun is half done,' but not our 'Tomorrow is another day.' This may explain much in Hopi character.

This Hopi preparing behavior may be roughly divided into announcing, outer preparing, inner preparing, covert participation, and to persistence. Announcing, or preparative publicity, is an important function in the hands of a special official, the Crier Chief. Outer preparing is preparation involving much visible activity, not all necessarily directly useful within our understanding. It includes ordinary practicing, rehearsing, getting ready, introductory formalities, preparing of special food, etc. (all of these to a degree that may seem overelaborate to us), intensive sustained muscular activity like running, racing, dancing, which is thought to increase the intensity of development of events (such as growth of crops), mimetic and other magic, preparations based on esoteric theory involving perhaps occult instruments like prayer sticks, prayer feathers, and prayer meal, and finally the great cyclic ceremonies and dances, which have the significance of preparing rain and crops. From one of the verbs meaning 'prepare' is derived the noun for 'harvest' or 'crop': *na'twani* 'the prepared' or the 'in preparation'.[9]

9. The Hopi verbs of preparing naturally do not correspond neatly to our 'prepare'; so that *na'twani* could also be rendered 'the practiced-upon, the tried-for,' and otherwise.

Inner preparing is use of prayer and meditation, and at lesser intensity good wishes and good will, to further desired results. Hopi attitudes stress the power of desire and thought. With their 'microcosm' it is utterly natural that they should. Desire and thought are the earliest, and therefore the most important, most critical and crucial, stage of preparing. Moreover, to the Hopi, one's desires and thoughts influence not only his own actions, but all nature as well. This too is wholly natural. Consciousness itself is aware of work, of the feel of effort and energy, in desire and thinking. Experience more basic than language tells us that, if energy is expended, effects are produced. *We* tend to believe that our bodies can stop up this energy, prevent it from affecting other things until we will our *bodies* to overt action. But this may be so only because we have our own linguistic basis for a theory that formless items like 'matter' are things in themselves, malleable only by similar things, by more matter, and hence insulated from the powers of life and thought. It is no more unnatural to think that thought contacts everything and pervades the universe than to think, as we all do, that light kindled outdoors does this. And it is not unnatural to suppose that thought, like any other force, leaves everywhere traces of effect. Now, when *we* think of a certain actual rosebush, we do not suppose that our thought goes to that actual bush, and engages with it, like a searchlight turned upon it. What then do we suppose our consciousness in dealing with when we are thinking of that rosebush? Probably we think it is dealing with a 'mental image' which is not the rosebush but a mental surrogate of it. But why should it be *natural* to think that our thought deals with a surrogate and not with the real rosebush? Quite possibly because we are dimly aware that we carry about with us a whole imaginary space, full of mental surrogates. To us, mental surrogates are old familiar fare. Along with the images of imaginary space, which we perhaps secretly know to be only imaginary, we tuck the thought-of actually existing rosebush, which may be quite another story, perhaps just because we have that very convenient 'place for it'. The Hopi thought-world has no imaginary space. The corollary to this is that it may not locate thought dealing with real space anywhere but in real space, nor insulate real space from the effects of thought. A Hopi would naturally suppose that his thought (or he himself) traffics with the actual rosebush – or more likely, corn plant – that he is thinking about. The thought then should leave some trace of itself with the plant in the field. If it is a good thought, one about health and growth, it is good for the plant; if a bad thought, the reverse.

The Hopi emphasize the intensity-factor of thought. Thought to be most effective should be vivid in consciousness, definite, steady, sustained, charged with strongly felt good intentions. They render the idea in English as 'concentrating, holding it in your heart, putting your mind on it, earnestly hoping.' Thought power is the force behind ceremonies, prayer sticks, ritual smoking, etc. The prayer pipe is regarded as an aid to 'concentrating' (so said my informant). Its name, *na'twanpi*, means 'instrument of preparing'.

Covert participation is mental collaboration from people who do not take part in the actual affair, be it a job of work, hunt, race, or ceremony, but direct their thought and good will toward the affair's success. Announcements often seek to enlist the support of such mental helpers as well as of overt participants, and contain exhortations to the people to aid with their active good will.[10] A similarity to our concepts of a sympathetic audience or the cheering section at a football game should not obscure the fact that it is primarily the power of directed thought, and not merely sympathy or encouragement, that is expected of covert participants. In fact these latter get in their deadliest work before, not during, the game! A corollary to the power of thought is the power of wrong thought for evil; hence one purpose of covert participation is to obtain the mass force of many good wishers to offset the harmful thought of ill wishers. Such attitudes greatly favor cooperation and community spirit. Not that the Hopi community is not full of rivalries and colliding interests. Against the tendency to social disintegration in such a small, isolated group, the theory of 'preparing' by the power of thought, logically leading to the great power of the combined, intensified,

10. See, e.g., Beaglehole (1937), especially the reference to the announcement of a rabbit hunt, and the description of the activities in connection with the cleaning of Toreva Spring – announcing, various preparing activities, and finally, preparing the continuity of the good results already obtained and the continued flow of the spring.

and harmonized thought of the whole community, must help vastly towards the rather remarkable degree of cooperation that, in spite of much private bickering, the Hopi village displays in all the important cultural activities.

Hopi 'preparing' activities again show a result of their linguistic thought background in an emphasis on persistence and constant insistent repetition. A sense of the cumulative value of innumerable small momenta is dulled by an objectified, spatialized view of time like ours, enhanced by a way of thinking close to the subjective awareness of duration, of the ceaseless 'latering' of events. To us, for whom time is a motion on a space, unvarying repetition seems to scatter its force along a row of units of that space, and to be wasted. To the Hopi, for whom time is not a motion but a 'getting later' of everything that has ever been done, unvarying repetition is not wasted but accumulated. It is storing up an invisible change that holds over into later events.[11] As we have seen, it is as if the return of the day were felt as the return of the same person, a little older but with all the impresses of yesterday, not as 'another day', i.e. like an entirely different person. This principle joined with that of thought-power and with traits of general Pueblo culture is expressed in the theory of the Hopi ceremonial dance for furthering rain and crops, as well as in its short, piston-like tread, repeated thousands of times, hour after hour.

Some impresses of linguistic habit in Western civilization

It is harder to do justice in few words to the linguistically conditioned features of our own culture than in the case of the Hopi, because of both vast scope and difficulty of objectivity – because

11. This notion of storing up power, which seems implied by much Hopi behavior, has an analog in physics: acceleration. It might be said that the linguistic background of Hopi thought equips it to recognize naturally that force manifests not as motion or velocity, but as accumulation or acceleration. Our linguistic background tends to hinder in us this same recognition, for having legitimately conceived force to be that which produces change, we then think of change by our linguistic metaphorical analog, motion, instead of by a pure motionless changingness concept, i.e. accumulation or acceleration. Hence it comes to our naïve feeling as a shock to find from physical experiments that it is not possible to define force by motion, that motion and speed, as also 'being at rest', are wholly relative, and that force can be measured only by acceleration.

of our deeply ingrained familiarity with the attitudes to be analysed. I wish merely to sketch certain characteristics adjusted to our linguistic binomialism of form plus formless item or 'substance', to our metaphoricalness, our imaginary space, and our objectified time. These, as we have seen, are linguistic.

From the form-plus-substance dichotomy the philosophical views most traditionally characteristic of the 'Western world' have derived huge support. Here belong materialism, psychophysical parallelism, physics – at least in its traditional Newtonian form – and dualistic views of the universe in general. Indeed here belongs almost everything that is 'hard, practical common sense'. Monistic, holistic, and relativistic views of reality appeal to philosophers and some scientists, but they are badly handicapped in appealing to the 'common sense' of the Western average man – not because nature herself refutes them (if she did, philosophers could have discovered this much), but because they must be talked about in what amounts to a new language. 'Common sense', as its name shows, and 'practicality' as its name does not show, are largely matters of talking so that one is readily understood. It is sometimes stated that Newtonian space, time, and matter are sensed by everyone intuitively, whereupon relativity is cited as showing how mathematical analysis can prove intuition wrong. This, besides being unfair to intuition, is an attempt to answer the first offhand question put at the outset of this paper, to answer which this research was undertaken. Presentation of the findings now nears its end, and I think the answer is clear. The offhand answer, laying the blame upon intuition for our slowness in discovering mysteries of the cosmos, such as relativity, is the wrong one. The right answer is: Newtonian space, time, and matter are no intuitions. They are recepts from culture and language. That is where Newton got them.

Our objectified view of time is, however, favorable to historicity and to everything connected with the keeping of records, while the Hopi view is unfavorable thereto. The latter is too subtle, complex, and ever-developing, supplying no ready-made answer to the question of when 'one' event ends and 'another' begins. When it is implicit that everything that ever happened still is, but is in a necessarily different form from what memory or record reports, there is less incentive to study the past. As for the present, the incentive would be not to record it but to treat it as 'preparing.' But OUR objectified time puts before imagination something like a ribbon or scroll marked off into equal blank spaces, suggesting that each be filled with an entry. Writing has no doubt helped toward our linguistic treatment of time, even as the linguistic treatment has guided the uses of writing. Through this give-and-take between language and the whole culture we get, for instance:

1. Records, diaries, bookkeeping, accounting, mathematics stimulated by accounting.

2. Interest in exact sequence, dating, calendars, chronology, clocks, time wages, time graphs, time as used in physics.

3. Annals, histories, the historical attitude, interest in the past, archaeology, attitudes of introjection toward past periods, e.g., classicism, romanticism.

Just as we conceive our objectified time as extending in the future in the same way that it extends in the past, so we set down our estimates of the future in the same shape as our records of the past, producing programs, schedules, budgets. The formal equality of the spacelike units by which we measure and conceive time leads us to consider the 'formless item' or 'substance' of time to be homogeneous and in ratio to the number of units. Hence our pro-rata allocation of value to time, lending itself to the building up of a commercial structure based on time-pro-rata values: time wages (time work constantly supersedes piece work), rent, credit interest, depreciation charges, and insurance premiums. No doubt this vast system, once built, would continue to run under any sort of linguistic treatment of time; but that it should have been built at all, reaching the magnitude and particular form it has in the Western world, is a fact decidedly in consonance with the patterns of the SAE languages. Whether such a civilization as ours would be possible with widely different linguistic handling of time is a large question – in our civilization, our linguistic patterns and the fitting of our behavior to the temporal order are what they are, and they are in accord. We are of course stimulated to use calendars, clocks, and watches, and to try to measure time ever more precisely; this aids science, and science in turn, following these well-worn cultural grooves, gives back to culture an ever-growing store of applications, habits, and values, with which culture again directs science. But what lies outside this spiral? Science is beginning to find that there is something in the cosmos that is not in accord with the concepts we have formed in mounting the spiral. It is trying to frame a *new language* by which to adjust itself to a wider universe.

It is clear how the emphasis on 'saving time' which goes with all the above and is very obvious objectification of time, leads to a high valuation of 'speed', which shows itself a great deal in our behavior.

Still another behavioral effect is that the character of monotony and regularity possessed by our image of time as an evenly scaled limitless tape measure persuades us to behave as if that monotony were more true of events than it really is. That is, it helps to routinize us. We tend to select and favor whatever bears out this view, to 'play up to' the routine aspects of existence. One phase of this is behavior evincing a false sense of security or an assumption that all will always go smoothly, and a lack of foreseeing and protecting ourselves against hazards. Our technique of harnessing energy does well in routine performance, and it is along routine lines that we chiefly strive to improve it – we are, for example, relatively uninterested in stopping the energy from causing accidents, fires, and explosions, which it is doing constantly and on a wide scale. Such indifference to the unexpectedness of life would be disastrous to a society as small, isolated, and precariously poised as the Hopi society is, or rather once was.

Thus our linguistically determined thought world not only collaborates with our cultural idols and ideals, but engages even our unconscious personal reactions in its patterns and gives them certain typical characters. One such character, as we have seen, is *carelessness*, as in reckless driving or throwing cigarette stubs into waste paper. Another of different sort is *gesturing* when we talk. Very many of the gestures made by English-speaking people at least, and probably by all SAE speakers, serve to illustrate, by a movement in space, not a real spatial reference but one of the nonspatial references that our language handles by metaphors of imaginary space. That is, we are more apt to make a grasping gesture when we speak of grasping an elusive idea than when we speak of grasping a doorknob. The gesture seeks to make a metaphorical and hence somewhat unclear reference more clear. But, if a language refers to nonspatials without implying a spatial analogy, the reference is not made any clearer by gesture. The Hopi gesture very little, perhaps not at all in the sense we understand as gesture.

It would seem as if kinesthesia, or the sensing of muscular movement, though arising before language, should be made more highly conscious by linguistic use of imaginary space and metaphorical images of motion. Kinesthesia is marked in two facets of European culture: art and sport. European sculpture, an art in which Europe excels, is strongly kinesthetic, conveying great sense to the body's motions; European painting likewise. The dance in our culture expresses delight in motion rather than symbolism or ceremonial, and our music is greatly influenced by our dance forms. Our sports are strongly imbued with this element of the 'poetry of motion'. Hopi races and games seem to emphasize rather the virtues of endurance and sustained intensity. Hopi dancing is highly symbolic and is performed with great intensity and earnestness, but not much movement or swing.

Synesthesia, or suggestion by certain sense receptions of characters belonging to another sense, as of light and color by sounds and vice versa, should be made more conscious by a linguistic metaphorical system that refers to nonspatial experiences by terms for spatial ones, though undoubtedly it arises from a deeper source. Probably in the first instance metaphor arises from synesthesia and not the reverse; yet metaphor need not become firmly rooted in linguistic pattern, as Hopi shows. Nonspatial experience has one well-organized sense, *hearing* – for smell and taste are but little organized. Nonspatial consciousness is a realm chiefly of thought, feeling, and *sound*. Spatial consciousness is a realm of light, color, sight, and touch, and presents shapes and dimensions. Our metaphorical system, by naming nonspatial experiences after spatial ones, imputes to sounds, smells, tastes, emotions, and thoughts qualities like the colors, luminosities, shapes, angles, textures, and motions of spatial experience. And to some extent the reverse transference occurs; for, after much talking about tones as high, low, sharp, dull, heavy, brilliant, slow, the talker finds it easy to think of some factors in spatial experience as like factors of tone. Thus we speak of 'tones' of color, a gray 'monotone', a 'loud' necktie, a 'taste' in dress: all spatial metaphor in reverse. Now European art is distinctive in the way it seeks deliberately to play with synesthesia. Music tries to suggest scenes, color, movement, geometric design; painting and sculpture are often consciously guided by the analogies of music's rhythm; colors are conjoined with feeling for the analogy to concords and discords. The European theater and opera seek a synthesis of many arts. It may be that in this way our metaphorical language that is in some sense a confusion of thought is producing, through art, a result of far-reaching value – a deeper esthetic sense leading toward a more direct apprehension of underlying unity behind the phenomena so variously reported by our sense channels.

Historical implications

How does such a network of language, culture, and behavior come about historically? Which was first: the language patterns or the cultural norms? In the main they have grown up together, constantly influencing each other. But in this partnership the nature of the language is the factor that limits free plasticity and rigidifies channels of development in the more autocratic way. This is so because a language is a system, not just an assemblage of norms. Large systematic outlines can change to something really new only very slowly, while many other cultural innovations are made with comparative quickness. Language thus represents the mass mind; it is affected by inventions and innovations, but affected little and slowly, whereas *to* inventors and innovators it legislates with the decree immediate.

The growth of the SAE language-culture complex dates from ancient times. Much of its metaphorical reference to the non-spatial by the spatial was already fixed in the ancient tongues, and more especially in Latin. It is indeed a marked trait of Latin. If we compare, say Hebrew, we find that, while Hebrew has some allusion to not-space as space, Latin has more. Latin terms for non-spatials, like *educo, religio, principia, comprehendo*, are usually metaphorized physical references: lead out, tying back, etc. This is not true of all languages – it is quite untrue of Hopi. The fact that in Latin the direction of development happened to be from spatial to nonspatial (partly because of secondary stimulation to abstract thinking when the intellectually crude Romans encountered Greek culture) and that later tongues were strongly stimulated to mimic Latin, seems a likely reason for a belief, which still lingers on among linguists, that this is the natural direction of semantic change in all languages, and for the persistent notion in Western learned circles (in strong contrast to Eastern ones) that objective experience is prior to subjective. Philosophies make out a weighty case for the reverse, and certainly the direction of development is sometimes the reverse. Thus the Hopi word for 'heart' can be shown to be a late formation within Hopi from a root meaning think or remember. Or consider what has happened to the word 'radio' in such a sentence as 'he bought a new radio', as compared to its prior meaning 'science of wireless telephony'.

In the Middle Ages the patterns already formed in Latin began to interweave with the increased mechanical invention, industry, trade, and scholastic and scientific thought. The need for measurement in industry and trade, the stores and bulks of 'stuffs' in various containers, the type-bodies in which various goods were handled, standardizing of measure and weight units, invention of clocks and measurement of 'time', keeping of records, accounts, chronicles, histories, growth of mathematics and the partnership of mathematics and science, all cooperated to bring our thought and language world into its present form.

In Hopi history, could we read it, we should find a different type of language and a different set of cultural and environmental influences working together. A peaceful agricultural society isolated by geographic features and nomad enemies in a land of scanty rainfall, arid agriculture that could be made successful only by the utmost perseverance (hence the value of persistence and repetition), necessity for collaboration (hence emphasis on the psychology of teamwork and on mental factors in general), corn and rain as primary criteria of value, need of extensive *preparations* and precautions to assure crops in the poor soil and precarious climate, keen realization of dependence upon nature favoring prayer and a religious attitude toward the forces of nature, especially prayer and religion directed toward the ever-needed blessing, rain – these things interacted with Hopi linguistic patterns to mold them, to be molded again by them, and so little by little to shape the Hopi world-outlook.

To sum up the matter, our first question asked in the beginning (p. 127) is answered thus: Concepts of 'time' and 'matter' are not given in substantially the same form by experience to all men but depend upon the nature of the language or languages through the use of which they have been developed. They do not depend so much upon any *one* system (e.g., tense, or nouns) within the grammar as upon the ways of analysing and reporting experience which have become fixed in the language as integrated 'fashions of speaking' and which cut across the typical grammatical classifications, so that such a 'fashion' may include lexical, morphological, syntactic, and otherwise systemically diverse means coordinated in a certain frame of consistency. Our own 'time' differs markedly from Hopi 'duration'. It is conceived as like a space of strictly limited dimensions, or sometimes as like a motion upon such a space, and employed as an intellectual tool accordingly. Hopi 'duration' seems to be inconceivable in terms of space or motion, being the mode in which life differs from form, and consciousness *in toto* from the spatial elements of consciousness. Certain ideas born of our own time-concept, such as that of absolute simultaneity, would be either very difficult to express or impossible and devoid of meaning under the Hopi conception, and would be replaced by operational concepts. Our 'matter' is the physical subtype of 'substance' or 'stuff', which is conceived as the formless extensional item that must be joined with form before there can be real existence. In Hopi there seems to be nothing corresponding to it; there are no formless extensional items; existence may or may not have form, but what it also has, with or without form, is intensity and duration, these being non-extensional and at bottom the same.

But what about our concept of 'space', which was also included in our first question? There is no such striking difference between Hopi and SAE about space as about time, and probably the apprehension of space is given in substantially the same form by experience irrespective of language. The experiments of the Gestalt psychologists with visual perception appear to establish this as a fact. But the *concept* of space will vary somewhat with language, because, as an intellectual tool,[12] it is so closely linked with the concomitant employment of other intellectual tools, of the order of 'time' and 'matter', which are linguistically conditioned. We see things with our eyes in the same space forms as the Hopi, but our idea of space has also the property of acting as a surrogate of nonspatial relationships like time, intensity, tendency, and as a void to be filled with imagined formless items, one of which may even be called 'space'. Space as sensed by the Hopi would not be connected mentally with such surrogates, but would be comparatively 'pure', unmixed with extraneous notions.

As for our second question on page 128: There are connections but not correlations or diagnostic correspondences between cultural norms and linguistic patterns. Although it would be impossible to infer the existence of Crier Chiefs from the lack of tenses in Hopi, or vice versa, there is a relation between a language and the rest of the culture of the society which uses it. There are cases where the 'fashions of speaking' are closely integrated with the whole general culture, whether or not this be universally true, and there are connections within this integration, between the kind of linguistic analyses employed and various behavioral reactions and also the shapes taken by various cultural developments. Thus the importance of Crier Chiefs does have a connection, not with tenselessness itself, but with a system of thought in which categories different from our tenses are natural. These connections are to be found not so much by focusing attention on the typical rubrics of linguistic, ethnographic, or sociological description as by examining the culture and the language (always and only when the two have been together historically for a considerable time) as a whole in which concatenations that run across these departmental lines may be expected to exist, and, if they do exist, eventually to be discoverable by study.

Reference

BEAGLEHOLE, E. (1937), *Notes on Hopi Economic Life*, Publications in Anthropology, no. 15, Yale University.

12. Here belong 'Newtonian' and 'Euclidean' space, etc.

8 B. Malinowski

Supplement to 'The Meaning of Meaning'

B. Malinowski, section 2 of the supplement to C. K. Ogden and
I. A. Richards, *The Meaning of Meaning*, 1927, Routledge & Kegan Paul.

This general statement of the linguistic difficulties which beset
an ethnographer in his field-work, must be illustrated by a
concrete example. Imagine yourself suddenly transported on to a
coral atoll in the Pacific, sitting in a circle of natives and listening
to their conversation. Let us assume further that there is an
ideal interpreter at hand, who, as far as possible, can convey the
meaning of each utterance, word for word, so that the listener is
in possession of all the linguistic data available. Would that make
you understand the conversation or even a single utterance?
Certainly not.

Let us have a look at such a text, an actual utterance taken down
from a conversation of natives in the Trobriand Islands, N.E.
New Guinea. In analysing it, we shall see quite plainly how helpless one is in attempting to open up the meaning of a statement
by mere linguistic means; and we shall also be able to realize
what sort of additional knowledge, besides verbal equivalence, is
necessary in order to make the utterance significant.

I adduce a statement in native, giving under each word its
nearest English equivalent:

tasakaulo	*kaymatana*	*yakida*
We run	front-wood	ourselves

tawoulo	*ovanu*	*tasivila*	*tagine*
we paddle	in place	we turn	we see

soda		*isakaulo*	*ka'u'uya*
companion ours		he runs	rear-wood

oluvieki	*similaveta*	*Pilolu*
behind	their sea-arm	Pilolu

The verbatim English translation of this utterance sounds at first like a riddle or a meaningless jumble of words; certainly not like a significant, unambiguous statement. Now if the listener, whom we suppose acquainted with the language, but unacquainted with the culture of the natives, were to understand even the general trend of this statement, he would have first to be informed about the situation in which these words were spoken. He would need to have them placed in their proper setting of native culture. In this case, the utterance refers to an episode in an overseas trading expedition of these natives, in which several canoes take part in a competitive spirit. This last-mentioned feature explains also the emotional nature of the utterance: it is not a mere statement of fact, but a boast, a piece of self-glorification, extremely characteristic of the Trobrianders' culture in general and of their ceremonial barter in particular.

Only after a preliminary instruction is it possible to gain some idea of such technical terms of boasting and emulation as *kaymatana* (front-wood) and *ka'u'uya* (rear-wood). The metaphorical use of *wood* for *canoe* would lead us into another field of language psychology, but for the present it is enough to emphasize that 'front' or 'leading canoe' and 'rear canoe' are important terms for a people whose attention is so highly occupied with competitive activities for their own sake. To the meaning of such words is added a specific emotional tinge, comprehensible only against the background of their tribal psychology in ceremonial life, commerce and enterprise.

Again, the sentence where the leading sailors are described as looking back and perceiving their companions lagging behind on the sea-arm of Pilolu, would require a special discussion of the geographical feeling of the natives, of their use of imagery as a linguistic instrument and of a special use of the possessive pronoun (*their* sea-arm Pilolu).

All this shows the wide and complex considerations into which we are led by an attempt to give an adequate analysis of meaning. Instead of translating, of inserting simply an English word for a native one, we are faced by a long and not altogether simple process of describing wide fields of custom, of social psychology and of tribal organization which correspond to one term or another. We see that linguistic analysis inevitably leads us into the study of all the subjects covered by ethnographic field-work.

Of course the above given comments on the specific terms (front-wood, rear-wood, their sea-arm Pilolu) are necessarily short and sketchy. But I have on purpose chosen an utterance which corresponds to a set of customs, already described quite fully.[1] The reader of that description will be able to understand thoroughly the adduced text, as well as appreciate the present argument.

Besides the difficulties encountered in the translation of single words, difficulties which lead directly into descriptive ethnography, there are others, associated with more exclusively linguistic problems, which however can be solved only on the basis of psychological analysis. Thus it has been suggested that the characteristically Oceanic distinction of inclusive and exclusive pronouns requires a deeper explanation than any which would confine itself to merely grammatical relations.[2] Again, the puzzling manner in which some of the obviously correlated sentences are joined in our text by a mere juxtaposition would require much more than a simple reference, if all its importance and significance had to be brought out. Those two features are well known and have been often discussed, though according to my ideas not quite exhaustively.

There are, however, certain peculiarities of primitive languages, almost entirely neglected by grammarians, yet opening up very interesting questions of savage psychology. I shall illustrate this by a point, lying on the borderland between grammar and lexicography and well exemplified in the utterance quoted.

In the highly developed Indo-European languages, a sharp distinction can be drawn between the grammatical and lexical function of words. The meaning of a root of a word can be isolated from the modification of meaning due to accidence or some other grammatical means of determination. Thus in the word *run* we distinguish between the meaning of the root – rapid personal displacement – and the modification as to time, tense, definiteness, etc., expressed by the grammatical form, in which the word is found in a given context. But in native languages the distinction is by no means so clear and the functions of grammar and

1. See Malinowski (1922) – an account of native enterprise and adventure in the archipelagoes of Melanesian New Guinea.

2. See the important Presidential Address by Rivers (1922).

radical meaning respectively are often confused in a remarkable manner.

In the Melanesian languages there exist certain grammatical instruments, used in the flection of verbs, which express somewhat vaguely relations of time, definiteness and sequence. The most obvious and easy thing to do for a European who wishes to use roughly such a language for practical purposes, is to find out what is the nearest approach to those Melanesian forms in our languages and then to use the savage form in the European manner. In the Trobriand language, for instance, from which we have taken our above example, there is an adverbial particle *boge*, which, put before a modified verb, gives it, in a somewhat vague manner, the meaning either of a past or of a definite happening. The verb is moreover modified by a change in the prefixed personal pronoun. Thus the root *ma* (come, move hither) if used with the prefixed pronoun of the third singular *i* – has the form *ima* and means (roughly), *he comes*. With the modified pronoun *ay* – or, more emphatical, *lay* – it means (roughly) *he came* or *he has come*. The expression *boge ayna* or *boge layma* can be approximately translated by *he has already come*, the participle *boge* making it more definite.

But this equivalence is only approximate, suitable for some practical purposes, such as trading with the natives, missionary preaching and translation of Christian literature into native languages. This last cannot, in my opinion, be carried out with any degree of accuracy. In the grammars and interpretations of Melanesian languages, almost all of which have been written by missionaries for practical purposes, the grammatical modifications of verbs have been simply set down as equivalent to Indo-European tenses. When I first began to use the Trobriand language in my field-work, I was quite unaware that there might be some snares in taking savage grammar at its face value and followed the missionary way of using native inflection.

I had soon to learn, however, that this was not correct and I learnt it by means of a practical mistake, which interfered slightly with my field-work and forced me to grasp native flection at the cost of my personal comfort. At one time I was engaged in making observations on a very interesting transaction which took place in a lagoon village of the Trobriands between the coastal fishermen and the inland gardeners.[3] I had to follow some important preparations in the village and yet I did not want to miss the arrival of the canoes on the beach. I was busy registering and photographing the proceedings among the huts, when word went round, 'they have come already' – *boge laymayse*. I left my work in the village unfinished to rush some quarter of a mile to the shore, in order to find, to my disappointment and mortification, the canoes far away, punting slowly along towards the beach! Thus I came some ten minutes too soon, just enough to make me lose my opportunities in the village!

It required some time and a much better general grasp of the language before I came to understand the nature of my mistake and the proper use of words and forms to express the subtleties of temporal sequence. Thus the root *ma* which means *come, move hither*, does not contain the meaning, covered by our word *arrive*. Nor does any grammatical determination give it the special and temporal definition, which we express by, 'they have come, they have arrived.' The form *boge laymayse*, which I heard on that memorable morning in the lagoon village, means to a native 'they have already been moving hither' and not 'they have already come here.'

In order to achieve the spatial and temporal definition which we obtain by using the past definite tense, the natives have recourse to certain concrete and specific expressions. Thus in the case quoted, the villagers, in order to convey the fact that the canoes had arrived, would have used the word *to anchor, to moor*. 'They have already moored their canoes', *boge aykotasi*, would have meant, what I assumed they had expressed by *boge laymayse*. That is, in this case the natives use a different root instead of a mere grammatical modification.

Returning to our text, we have another telling example of the characteristic under discussion. The quaint expression 'we paddle in place' can only be properly understood by realizing that the word *paddle* has here the function, not of describing what the crew are doing, but of indicating their immediate proximity to the village of their destination. Exactly as in the previous example the past tense of the word to come ('they have come') which we would have used in our language to convey the fact of arrival,

3. It was a ceremony of the *Wasi*, a form of exchange of vegetable food for fish. See Malinowski (1922, plate 26).

has another meaning in native and has to be replaced by another root which expresses the idea; so here the native root *wa, to move thither*, could not have been used in (approximately) past definite tense to convey the meaning of 'arrive there', but a special root expressing the concrete act of paddling is used to mark the spatial and temporal relations of the leading canoe to the others. The origin of this imagery is obvious. Whenever the natives arrive near the shore of one of the overseas villages, they have to fold the sail and to use the paddles, since there the water is deep, even quite close to the shore, and punting impossible. So 'to paddle' means 'to arrive at the overseas village.' It may be added that in this expression 'we paddle in place', the two remaining words *in* and *place* would have to be retranslated in a free English interpretation by *near the village*.

With the help of such an analysis as the one just given, this or any other savage utterance can be made comprehensible. In this case we may sum up our results and embody them in a free commentary or paraphrase of the statement:

A number of natives sit together. One of them, who has just come back from an overseas expedition, gives an account of the sailing and boasts about the superiority of his canoe. He tells his audience how, in crossing the sea-arm of Pilolu (between the Trobriands and the Amphletts), his canoe sailed ahead of all others. When nearing their destination, the leading sailors looked back and saw their comrades far behind, still on the sea-arm of Pilolu.

Put in these terms, the utterance can at least be understood broadly, though for an exact appreciation of the shades and details of meaning a full knowledge of the native customs and psychology, as well as of the general structure of their language, is indispensable.[4]

4. All I have said in this section is only an illustration on a concrete example of the general principles so brilliantly set forth by Ogden and Richards in chapters 1, 3 and 4 of their work. What I have tried to make clear by analysis of a primitive linguistic text is that language is essentially rooted in the reality of the culture, the tribal life and customs of a people, and that it cannot be explained without constant reference to these broader contexts of verbal utterance. The theories embodied in Ogden and Richards' diagram of chapter 1, in their treatment of the 'sign-situation' (chapter 3) and in their analysis of perception (chapter 4) cover and generalize all the details of my example.

References

MALINOWSKI, B. (1922), *Argonauts of the Western Pacific*.
RIVERS, W. H. (1922), 'Presidential Address', *J. Royal anthrop. Inst.*,
vol. 52, p. 21.

9 E. H. Lenneberg

Cognition in Ethnolinguistics[1]

E. Lenneberg, 'Cognition in ethnolinguistics', *Language*, 1953, vol. 29,
  pp. 463–71.

The republication of B. L. Whorf's articles on what Trager calls
meta-linguistics has aroused a new interest in this country in the
problem of the relationship that a particular language may have to
its speakers' cognitive processes. Does the structure of a given
language affect the thoughts (or thought potential), the memory,
the perception, the learning ability of those who speak that
language? These questions have often been asked and many
attempts have been made to answer them.[2] The present paper is an
attempt to lay bare the logical structure of this type of investigation.

Critical retrospect
A basic assumption

Underlying all of Whorf's theoretical work is the fundamental
assumption that the individual's conception of the world (including perception, abstraction, rationalization, categorization) is
intimately related to the nature of his native language.[3] Through-

1. This paper was stimulated by research carried on under the auspices of
the Values Study in the Laboratory of Social Relation, Harvard University,
and the Communications Project at the Center for International Studies,
Massachusetts Institute of Technology. I wish to express my thanks to both
institutions. I am also greatly indebted to H. Hoijer for inviting me to
participate in the Conference on Ethnolinguistics, held in Chicago during
March 1953, where the discussion of some of the problems raised in this
paper helped to clarify my thoughts. Finally I gratefully acknowledge the
many helpful suggestions made to me by N. Chomsky, who read two earlier
versions of this article.
   2. Bibliographies of the voluminous literature may be found in the following works: Goldstein (1948); Kainz (1941/43); Miller (1952); Morris,
(1946); Olmsted (1950); Pronko (1946).
   3. Whorf is not alone in making this assumption, cf. Lee (1944); Lévy-
Bruhl (1910); Weisgerber (1929). The last of these is a representative of what
Basilius (1952) has called Neo-Humboldtian ethnolinguistics; the entire
movement is based on the assumption discussed here.

out his work Whorf illustrates this idea with examples from American Indian languages, showing how they differ from English. However, a demonstration that certain languages differ from each other suggests but does not prove that the speakers of these languages differ from each other as a group in their psychological potentialities. To prove this, it would be necessary to show first that certain aspects of language have a direct influence on or connection with a given psychological mechanism, or at least that speakers of different languages differ along certain psychological parameters. In addition to comparative data Whorf adduces occasionally a different type of evidence. An example is his analysis of many hundreds of reports of circumstances surrounding the start of fires, for instance the empty-gas-drum case (Whorf, 1941a). An explosion had been caused by an individual who had carelessly flung a burning cigarette stub into a gas drum which this person in his insurance report called *empty*. Whorf argues that the individual's carelessness was caused by the fact that the word *empty* has two different meanings in English: first null and void, negative, inert, and second a space which may contain nothing but a vapor, liquid vestiges, or stray rubbish. The English language forced the individual to call the gas drum *empty*, and think of it in terms of that word. Since this word could mean null and void, Whorf argues that the presence of explosive vapors and inflammable liquid vestiges could be disregarded by the speaker, who then behaved towards the drum as if it were absolutely empty. I cannot accept this as evidence for the assumption that behavior is influenced by language. Clearly, English is capable of distinguishing between a drum filled with an explosive vapor, one that contains only air, and one which is void of any matter. This very sentence is my evidence. The person who caused the fire could have replaced the word *empty* by *filled with explosive vapor*. His failing to do so (as well as his careless behavior) points to a lack of experience with explosive vapors, perhaps complete ignorance of their existence. The linguistic – or rather stylistic – fact of the occurrence of the word *empty* in the individual's insurance report would indeed be interesting if Whorf could have shown at the same time that this man had had plenty of contact with and knowledge of the explosive vapors which form in emptied gas drums. This Whorf did not try to do. In short, the basic assumption that language affects non-linguistic behavior derives from an inspection of linguistic facts. Therefore nothing is added to such an hypothesis by referring back to the same or similar linguistic facts.

Translation

1. Translation, while useful for the formulation of working hypotheses of the most exploratory nature, is in itself an inadequate way towards the finding of objective facts. Obvious as this may seem, it is necessary to spell out in detail the shortcomings of the translation method in ethnolinguistics.

2. I illustrate my point with another example taken from Whorf (1941b). After posing the question: 'What do different languages do . . . with the flowing face of nature . . .?', Whorf answers:

Here we find differences in segmentation and selection of basic terms. We might isolate something in nature by saying, 'It is a dripping spring.' Apache erects the statement on a verb *ga*: 'be white (including clear, uncolored, and so on)'. With the prefix *no-*, the meaning of downward motion enters: 'whiteness moves downward'. Then *to*, meaning both 'water' and 'spring' is prefixed. The result corresponds to our 'dripping spring', but synthetically it is: 'as water, or springs, whiteness moves downward'. How utterly unlike our way of thinking! [NB!] The same verb, *ga*, with a prefix that means 'a place manifests the condition' becomes *gohlga*: 'the place is white, clear; a clearing, a plain'. These examples show that some languages have means of expression . . . in which the separate terms are not as separate as in English but flow together into plastic synthetic creations.

Whorf analyses the Apachean statement by giving the English equivalent for the general meaning of each Apachean element, and then compares the resulting sequence of meanings to the phrase, 'it is a dripping spring'. The sequence of meanings (i.e. the glosses) and the English phrase are not, however, quite comparable. Whorf does not give the general meaning of the English morphemes. If he had, something like this would have resulted:

It, any object or organism which is not an adult human being; *is*, particle which denotes that what follows is a predicate of what precedes; *a*, particle which denotes that what follows is to be understood generically, not specifically; *drip(p)*, process in which any liquid falls in small natural segments; *-ing*, particle which denotes that the preceding process has not come to an end; *spring*, something that is not static (eruption of water, device to make mattresses elastic, and so on).

To abstract a general meaning of a morpheme or lexeme may occasionally be of some methodological use; but we must not confuse such an abstraction with an isolable segment of an utterance. General meanings lack reality, so to speak. It makes no sense to equate the global meaning of an utterance with the sequence of abstracted, general meanings of the morphemes that occur in that utterance. To translate the Apachean statement *it is a dripping spring* appears no less reasonable than to translate it as *water or springs, whiteness moves downward at a place* (or, *the place is white, clear; a clearing; a plain* – which, I gather from Whorf, is the synthesis of the elements); for what we translate are equivalent verbal responses to particular stimulus situations, and the Apachean response to the natural phenomenon in question corresponds to our response *it is a dripping spring*. This type of linguistic evidence, therefore, stands or falls with our philosophy of translation. It might be objected here that Whorf's evidence is not the translation itself but the fact that the Apachean's verbal response to this natural phenomenon is the same as his verbal response to a different phenomenon, namely one to which we respond *the place is white, clear*, etc. and that the Apachean therefore makes a single response to stimuli to which we make distinct responses. This objection, while touching upon an important problem, does not justify the translation method. For what we really want to know is how the Apachean structure of syntactic categories differs from the English one. Translation cannot answer this problem. Through it – and that is its value – we merely know that the problem is not a spurious one.

3. A further objection to translation as a sufficient method in this type of research is that it actually vitiates the attempt to demonstrate cognitive difference as evidenced in two or more languages. For, if a language were actually an aspect of a particular psychological make-up or state of mind (or more precisely, an aspect of a cognitive process, which is not to be confused with the thought

content), then, in the process of translation, we would be substituting the psychological elements characteristic of one make-up for those of another, so that we would finally compare two sets of elements of one and the same psychological structure.

4. There is a metaphorical element in language *per se*. The literal meaning of many metaphors, especially the most frequent ones, never penetrates consciousness, e.g. *everybody, in the face of, beforehand, breakfast, inside, already*. The translation method, however, distorts the significance of such forms of speech and often induces investigators to draw rather ludicrous conclusions. To illustrate the mentality of certain African tribes, Cassirer (1923) writes[4]: 'The languages of the Sudan usually express the circumstance that a subject is in process of action by means of a locution which really means (NB!) that the subject is *inside* that action. But since, moreover, this *inside* is usually expressed very concretely, phrases result such as *I am on the inside of walking, I am the belly of walking*, for "I am in the process of walking".'

5. The process of taking stock of general meanings, which underlies translations, engenders the belief that languages can convey no more and no less than the general meanings of morphemes. It seems more fruitful to assume[5] that much more is cognized than is expressed by individual morphemes. Morphemes and their meaning are regarded more appropriately as mnemotechnical pegs of a whole situation which is brought into consciousness by the statement as a whole. The general meaning of morphemes is probably of lesser importance in cognition than the *sum of associations* bound up with the complete utterance, or with even individual morphemes or groups of morphemes.

6. When the translation involves a juxtaposition of totally different cultures (say Chukchee and English) we are not only faced with a semantic problem. No matter what precautions we take in glossing a word, almost no correspondences can be established between many denotata. For instance, the cultural and physical contexts of Chukchee utterances are, with a few exceptions, incomparable with the contexts within which English is spoken. Chukchee

4. Cassirer's source is Westermann's *Sudansprachen*.
5. This assertion and the following are based on evidence from experimental psychology. See Humphrey (1951); Miller (1952).

weapons, food, manners, standards of any sort, landscape, fauna, and flora are mostly unfamiliar to English-speaking cultures. Thus, practically no common frame of reference, no basis for a segmental, one-by-one comparison exists between these two languages. Translation here can be only a very rough approximation of what has been said and intended originally.

Ad-hoc theories

It is a commonplace in scientific methodology to avoid etiological theories which are incapable of satisfying more than one single and specific occurrence of events; yet by necessity working hypotheses often have to be of this nature. We see a picture fall off a wall directly after hearing a dog bark in the neighborhood. As a working hypothesis the two events might be causally related. Upon verification of the hypothesis we note, however, that in general barking is not followed by things dropping to the ground, nor is the falling of pictures from the wall usually preceded by barking or similar noises. We are unable in this instance to formulate a theory because the working hypothesis cannot be generalized. Turning to ethnolinguistic literature we find an abundance of working hypotheses where it is difficult to see how they might contribute to a universally valid and useful theory of language (such that language is related to non-linguistic behavior), because the facts underlying such working hypotheses cannot be generalized so as to fit more than a single language.[6] I am not saying that such hypotheses are right or wrong; many have been proposed to experts on specific cultures, by scientists of undisputed merit. I am merely pointing to the difficulty, if not impossibility, of deducing from these hypotheses, if they are sound, general and verifiable laws. A common means of validating hypotheses has been barred from the beginning in these cases, namely cross-cultural verification. This, however, does not exclude the possibility that the investigators may have intra-cultural evidence for each individual hypothesis proposed.

6. Most of Whorf's and Lee's working hypotheses are of this nature. Hoijer (1951), and the tentative connections between various linguistic features and nonlinguistic behavior mentioned by Lévy-Strauss (1951), also fall into this category of working hypotheses.

Towards a methodology
Codification and cognition

1. A basic maxim in linguistics is that anything can be expressed in any language.[7] There may be differences in the ease and facility for the expression of certain things among various languages but at present we do not know whether this difference in ease is attributable to the properties of a given language *qua* vehicle of communication[8] or to the cultural development of the speakers. In fact, this is one of the problems to be solved in ethnolinguistics. Now, if we believe as we do, that we *can* say anything we wish in any language, then it would seem as if the content or subject matter of utterances does not characterize or, indeed, give us any clear information on the communicative properties of a language. Thus we are led to the somewhat banal conclusion that the only pertinent linguistic data in this type of research is the *how* of communication and not the *what*. This *how* I call the codification; the *what* I call the messages. Codification can be studied in three phases:

(a) The process of encoding.

(b) The code.

(c) The process of decoding. (Carroll, 1951.)

The study of the code results, for instance, in statements about the structure of phonemes, morphemes, and syntactic categories; about acoustic characteristics of speech sounds; about the frequency distributions and the transitional probabilities of given segments; about the efficiency of the code within stated contexts. In these instances meaning can be excluded entirely from our research, at least theoretically, and we have therefore an assurance that we are not actually studying aspects of codification. Unfortunately, however, it is not always easy to decide whether a

7. cf. Sapir (1949). It is assumed here that any vocabulary can be expanded.

8. The use of the term *vehicle of communication* does not mean that I deny (or even take a position toward) the epistemological contention that language and knowledge are indistinguishable. I am merely referring to the communicative capacities of language.

phenomenon is pertinent to codification or not. Many assertions about language which derive from semantic observations or, at any rate, which include elements of meaning, nevertheless seem to be relevant to codification. Most obvious in this connection is the fact that a language always selects for codification highly specific aspects from the physical and social environment. This raises two questions: How can we describe objectively the aspects that are being selected out of a great number of other possible aspects? Why are these aspects selected and not others? There can be little doubt that these considerations, though clearly of a semantic character, have a bearing on the problem of codification. Hence, the distinction between codification and messages is not the same as between syntactics and semantics or between form and meaning. All those observations about meaning are relevant to codification which refer to an aspect of speech behavior which is forced upon the individual speaker by the rules of his language and where infringement of the rules would result in defective communication. For instance, an individual reporting about a given event is forced to stipulate very definite conditions, aspects, and relationships if he wants to be understood.[9] However, he is free to report on the event in the first place, and also to elaborate on circumstances of the event which are not included in the compulsory stipulations. Whatever information is optional in his communication is message.

2. Once we have clearly isolated data on codification, such data may be related hypothetically to nonlinguistic behavior. If the researcher is interested in cognition,[10] as I am, he will investigate relations that obtain between codification and such behavior as is indicative of memory, recognition, learning, problem solving, concept formation, and perception, hoping to show that certain peculiarities in these processes can be explained by – and only by – knowledge of the speakers' peculiarities of codification.[11]

9. These conditions, aspects, and relationships are primarily but not exclusively expressed by grammatical categories.
10. For a modern definition of this term see Leeper (1951).
11. What I am proposing to do here is not in principle different from what Whorf (for instance) occasionally suggested. The difference between Whorf and me is rather in our respective attempts to substantiate our hypotheses.

The intra-cultural approach

1. Ethnolinguistic research based on cross-cultural comparison must endeavor to isolate data, both on codification and on cognition, that are general enough to have comparable equivalents in at least two different languages and cultures; otherwise comparison would be meaningless. It is not infrequent, however, that a working hypothesis relates a certain cognitive datum to some phenomenon pertinent to codification which appears to be unique, lacking entirely a parallel in any other language. There is a simple way of studying this situation; I call it the intra-cultural approach, because it reduces cross-cultural comparison to a desirable but not indispensable expansion of investigations. This method is so easy to manipulate that many investigators may perhaps come to use it even where the cross-cultural approach is applicable directly.

2. I begin with a practical demonstration of the method. Problem: Languages differ in their systems of classifying the ten million odd colors which every normal individual can discriminate (cf. Evans, 1948). Under laboratory conditions the power of color discrimination is probably the same for all human beings, irrespective of their language background. But we do not know whether the habitual grouping of colors, according to certain labels provided by every language, might not affect some other cognitive processes involving color stimuli. To be more specific, in English obviously not all colors are named with equal ease and unambiguity. Do English-speaking people therefore recognize easily-named (i.e. highly codeable) colors with greater facility than colors not so easily named?[12]

The first step toward solution of this problem is to ascertain the linguistic facts.[13] A representative sample of English speakers is

12. This is a specific question within a problem that has been posed by many other investigators. Sapir said: 'Language is a . . . self-contained, creative symbolic organization, which not only refers to experience largely acquired without its help, but actually defines experience for us by reason of its formal completeness and because of our unconscious projection of its implicit expectations into the field of experience.' (Conceptual categories in primitive languages, quoted by Lee (1949)). Sapir makes the same point in 'The status of linguistics as a science' (1949).

13. The following is an outline of research in progress carried on by Roger Brown of Harvard University and myself. The details of the project will be published as soon as the data are fully assembled.

drawn and a number of colors are prepared that have comparable perceptual properties. Then the notion 'codeable' is investigated and defined operationally, so that we can divide the physical color stimuli by means of one or a combination of a few simple criteria, into two groups: one consisting of 'highly codeable' and one of 'less codeable' colors. I must omit here the details of this procedure and also the reasoning that underlies the individual steps leading to the development of such a criterion. Let me simply state that *unanimity in response* proves to be a useful criterion (among others) in this connection. Some colors are consistently given the same name by every speaker; others are given a variety of names, sometimes as many names as there are subjects. Regarding the speakers now as a group giving a linguistic response to each color, we may say that some colors have the property of eliciting a homogeneous response from English-speakers, whereas other colors elicit a heterogeneous response. This is to say that linguistic communication in English is more efficient when some colors are referred to than when others are.[14] There are cogent reasons to assume that the distinction made here between the colors is a purely linguistic one, and that there are no physical properties in the colors or physiological ones in the eye which would elucidate the difference in response made by English-speakers to these colors.[15]

The next step is to determine whether there is a difference in ease of recognition by English-speakers between the colors constituting one group and those constituting the other. The two groups, I repeat, are perfectly balanced in physical and perceptual properties; the only difference is that the colors in one group have

14. If there is no well defined name for a color, it is reasonable to assume that linguistic communication about it is poor.

15. Again space does not permit me to cite all the evidence in support of this assertion. The interested reader may inspect the colors used; they are produced by the Munsell Color Co., a scientific research organization. Most of them are published in the two volumes of the *Munsell Book of Colors* (Baltimore, 1921 and 1942). Codeable colors have the notation $2 \cdot 5$ PB/7/6, 5 PB/4/10, 10 P/3/10, 5 RP/6/10, 5 YR/3/4, 3 GY/7$\cdot$5/11$\cdot$2, 7$\cdot$5 GY/3/4, $2 \cdot 5$ G/5/8, 5 Y/8/12, 7$\cdot$5 G/8/4, $2 \cdot 5$ R/7/8. Non-codeable colors have the notation 10 BG/6/6, 8$\cdot$5 B/3/6$\cdot$8, 10 PB/5/10, 2$\cdot$5 R/5/10, 8 RP/3$\cdot$4/12$\cdot$1, 7$\cdot$5 R/8/4, 2$\cdot$5 Y/7/10, 7$\cdot$5 Y/6/8, 7$\cdot$5 YR/5/8, 5 P/8/4, 5 BG/3/6. Colorimetric and psycho-physical data on these colors are published in *Journal of the Optical Society of America*, vol. 30, pp. 573–645.

well-defined names in English, whereas the colors in the other do not.[16] If we now use, in random order, colors belonging to either group, say ten from each, in a standard recognition test,[17] we can easily discover whether English speakers do better when they have to recognize colors which are highly codeable in their language than when they recognize less codeable colors. In the actual performance of the experiment[18] this appears to be the case. Statistically, codeable colors are recognized significantly more often than less codeable ones, and thus there is good evidence that the particular linguistic fact, codeability, affects the cognitive process, recognition.

3. Suppose now that the entire color research were repeated in a different culture where a different language is spoken. If our predictions about recognition, based on previously determined facts of codification (which vary of course from language to language), should not be borne out in this other language, the argument advanced in the first experiment would be seriously weakened. Conversely, if the results should be confirmed, this would fortify the argument. In either case, however, *validation* of the basic hypothesis is independent of cross-cultural comparison. The cross-cultural comparison merely adds or subtracts weight. It is very important to realize that the validation itself is the result of intra-cultural correlation of two sets of recognition behavior on the one hand (in the described context we may say 'good' and 'bad' behavior) with two sets of English speech behavior on the other hand (efficient and not so efficient linguistic communication). It appears that recognition behavior is inefficient where speech behavior is inefficient.

4. Not only is the validity of this experiment independent of cross-

16. Codeability of colors does not seem to be linked to cultural importance or preference for these colors. The reader may convince himself of this by trying to name all the colors in his environment. He will notice that colors for which he has a 'good' name occur much less frequently than colors which are difficult to label unambiguously.

17. Such tests are described in Koffka (1935).

18. The test colors were exposed four at a time, for two seconds. After a waiting period of thirty seconds, subjects had to find the test colors on a color chart of 120 colors. All colors were identified by numbers. The subjects used in this experiment were not required to use any color name whatever.

cultural comparison; but if cross-cultural comparison is desired, the method dispenses with the necessity for translation, or the exact equation of linguistic data between one language and another. For what will be compared are *correlations of speech behavior with recognition behavior*, not linguistic forms. Superficially it may look as if the translation method were implicitly the same as the intra-cultural method, for both methods seem to be concerned with the meaning of certain linguistic forms which are being compared. However, the intra-cultural method resembles the translation method only in its very elementary and primary step: both methods recognize the existence of a problem on the grounds of intuitive knowledge of the meaning of forms. The translation method defines meanings by trying to equate forms of a language foreign to the investigator to forms of his native language (where meanings are said to be known). The intra-cultural method need not rely on this haphazard procedure; instead, it objectifies the intuited meanings of forms by carefully relating them to stimuli of the environment. Thus it is possible (at least in some instances) to specify meaning by referral to the physical properties of those stimuli.

5. Stated in general terms, the intra-cultural approach consists of the following. Some aspect of codification is described in order to correlate it with non-linguistic behavior. A frame of reference is established in terms of which both the speech behavior and the non-linguistic behavior can be described or specified; a particularly convenient frame of reference is the physical environment within which both types of behavior take place. In the experiment described, the frame of reference was provided by the stimuli sensed as colors. The speech events (color terms) and the behavioral events (recognition) were related to these stimuli. The specifications of the physical properties of the stimuli served as a metalanguage, so to speak, for the description of both types of events.

The fundamental principle of the intra-cultural method is that the physical stimuli, whatever they may be, can be classified on the grounds of linguistic criteria so that the constituents of each class are all characterized by the particular way in which they are codified. It is necessary that the codification criterion should be the *only* criterion by which the stimuli can be grouped in this way.

If now the non-linguistic behavior in response to the stimuli thus classified varies systematically in accordance with the class to which the individual stimulus has been assigned, we may attribute such regular variation in non-linguistic behavior to the regular variation in the speech correlates.

References

BASILIUS, H. (1952), 'Neo-Humboldian ethnolinguistics', *Word*, vol. 8, pp. 95–105.

CARROLL, J. B. (1951), Report and Recommendation of the Inter-Disciplinary Summer Seminar in Psychology and Linguistics, vol. 8.

CASSIRER, E. (1923), *Philosophie de symbolischen Formen: Die Sprache*, Berlin.

EVANS, R. M. (1948), *An Introduction to Color*, Wiley.

GOLDSTEIN, K. (1948), *Language and Language Disturbances*.

HOIJER, H. (1951), 'Cultural implications of some Navaho linguistic categories', *Language*, vol. 27, pp. 111–20.

HUMPHREY, G. (1951), *Thinking: An Introduction to Experimental Psychology*, chs. 4 and 8, Wiley.

KAINZ, F. (1941/63), *Psychologie der Sprache*.

KOFFKA, K. (1935), *Principles of Gestalt Psychology*, Harcourt, Brace & World.

LEE, D. L. (1944), 'Linguistic reflection of Wintu thought', IJAL, no. 10, pp. 181–7.

LEE, I. J. (1949), *The Language of Wisdom and Folly*, Institute of General Semantics.

LEEPER, R. (1951), 'Cognitive processes', in S. S. Stevens (ed.), *Handbook of Experimental Psychology*, pp. 730–57.

LÉVY-BRUHL, L. (1910), *Les Fonctions Mentales dans les Societies Inferieurs*, ch. 4.

LÉVY-STRAUSS (1951), 'Language and the analysis of social laws', *Amer. Anthrop.*, no. 53, pp. 155–63.

MILLER, G. A. (1952), *Language and Communication*, McGraw-Hill.

MORRIS, C. (1946), *Signs, Language and Behavior*, Braziller.

OLMSTED, D. L. (1950), *Ethnolinguistics So Far*, ScIL occasional papers, no. 2.

PRONKO, N. H. (1946), 'Language and psycholinguistics: a review', *Psych. Bull.*, no. 43, pp. 189–239.

SAPIR, E. (1949), *Selected Writings of Edward Sapir*, University of California Press.

WEISGERBER, L. (1929), 'Adjektivistische und verbale Auffassung der Gesichtsempfindungen', *Worter und Sachen*, no. 12, pp. 197–226.

WESTERMANN, D. (19—), *Sudansprachen*.

WHORF, B. L. (1941a), 'The relation of habitual thought and behavior to language', *Language, Culture and Personality*, pp. 75–93, Menasha, Wisconsin.

WHORF, B. L. (1941b), 'Languages and Logic', *Technology Rev.*, vol. 43.

10 J. Piaget

Language and Thought from the Genetic Point of View

J. Piaget, 'Language and thought from the genetic point of view',[1] in D. Elkind (ed.), *Psychological Studies* 1967, Random House.

The following pages contain some of my personal views concerning the role of language in the formation of intelligence generally and of logical operations in particular. My remarks concerning the relationship between language and thought will be grouped according to three age periods:

1. The age period during which language is first acquired.

2. The age period during which emerge concrete logical operations (certain operations common to the logic of classes and of relations and applied, from seven to eleven years of age, to manipulable things).

3. The period during which formal or interpropositional operations are acquired (propositional logic is achieved between the ages of twelve and fifteen).

Thought and the symbolic function

When a child of two to three years in possession of elementary verbal expressions is compared with a baby of eight to ten months whose intelligence is still sensorimotor in nature, i.e., whose intellectual instruments consist of only percepts and movements, it seems at first glance that language has profoundly changed this initial intelligence of action by adding thinking to it. Thanks to language, the child has become capable of evoking absent situations and of liberating himself from the frontiers of immediate space and time, i.e., from the limits of the perceptual field, whereas sensorimotor intelligence is almost entirely confined within these frontiers. Also, thanks to language, objects and events are no longer experienced only in their perceptual imme-

1. Originally published in *Acta Psychologica*, 1954, vol. 10, pp. 88–98.

diacy; they are experienced within a conceptual and rational framework which enriches the understanding of them. In short, if the child's behavior prior to language is compared with his behavior after the inception of language, it is tempting to conclude, with Watson (1919) and many others, that language is the source of thought.

A closer examination, however, of the changes which occur in intelligence when language is acquired shows that language alone is not responsible for these transformations. The two essential innovations which we have just mentioned can be considered as the beginning of representation and of representative schematization (concepts, etc.), by contrast with sensorimotor schematization, which is concerned with actions themselves or with perceptual forms. There are sources other than language capable of explaining certain representations and certain representative schematizations. Language is necessarily interpersonal and is composed of a system of *signs* ('arbitrary' or conventional signifiers). But besides language, the small child, who is less socialized than he is after the age of seven to eight years and much less so than the adult, needs another system of signifiers which are more individual and more 'motivated'. These are the *symbols* which are most commonly found in the symbolic or imaginative play of the young child. Symbolic play appears at about the same time as language but independently of it and is of considerable significance in the young child's thinking. It is a source of personal cognitive and affective representations and of equally personal representative schematizations. For example, the first symbolic play observed in one of my children consisted of his pretending to sleep. In order to go to sleep he always held a corner of his pillowcase in his hand and put the thumb of the same hand into his mouth. One morning, sitting wide awake on his mother's bed, Laurent noticed a corner of the sheet and it reminded him of the corner of his pillowcase. He grabbed the corner of the sheet firmly in his hand, put his thumb in his mouth, closed his eyes, and while still sitting, smiled broadly. Here we have an example of a representation independent of language but attached to a ludic[2] symbol, which consists of appropriate gestures imitating those which ordinarily accompany

2. A ludic symbol is one related to or derived from play activity.

a predetermined action. Action thus represented is not related to the present or the actual; it refers to an evoked context or situation, which is the hallmark of 'representation'.

Symbolic play is not the only form of personal symbolism. Another form emerges during the same period and also plays an important role in the genesis of representation. This is 'deferred imitation' or imitation that occurs for the first time in the absence of the model to which it corresponds. For example, one of my daughters, while entertaining a small friend, was surprised to see him become angry, then cry and bang his feet. She did not react in his presence, but after his departure she imitated the scene without any sign of anger on her part.

Thirdly, all mental imagery can be classed among personal symbols. We know now that the image is neither an element of thought itself nor a direct continuation of perception. It is a symbol of the object which is not yet manifested at the level of sensorimotor intelligence (otherwise the solution of many practical problems would be much easier). The image can be conceived as an internalized imitation. The sonorous image is merely the internal imitation of its correspondent and the visual image is the product of an imitation of an object or of a person, either by the whole body or by ocular movements in the case of a small figure.

The three types of personal symbols we have cited (we might add dream symbols, but this would involve too long a discussion) are derived from (motor) imitation. This then is one of the possible links between sensorimotor behavior and representative behavior. It is independent of language, even though it aids in the acquisition of language.

We can say, therefore, that a symbolic function exists which is broader than language and encompasses both the system of verbal signs and that of symbols in the strict sense. It can thus be argued that the source of thought is to be sought in the symbolic function. But it can just as legitimately be maintained that the symbolic function itself is explained by the formation of representations. In fact, the essence of the symbolic function lies in the differentiation of the signifiers (signs and symbols) from the signified (objects or events that are schematic or conceptualized). In the sensorimotor realm, systems of signification already exist, since all perception and all cognitive adaptation consist of conferring significations (forms, ends and means, etc.). But the only signifier known to sensorimotor behavior is the *index* (as opposed to signs and symbols) or the *signal* (conditioned behavior).[3] Now the index and the signal are signifiers that are relatively undifferentiated from what they signify. They are actually merely parts or aspects of what is signified and not representations permitting their evocation. They lead to what is signified in the way that a part leads to the whole or the means to the ends and not as a sign or a symbol which permits the evocation (through thought) of an absent object or event. The symbolic function, on the other hand, consists of differentiating the signifiers from what is signified so that the former can permit the evocation of the representation of the latter. To ask whether the symbolic function engenders thought or thought permits the formation of symbolic function is as vain as to try to determine whether the river orients its banks or the banks orient the river.

As language is only a particular form of the symbolic function and as the individual symbol is certainly simpler than the collective sign, it is permissible to conclude that thought precedes language and that language confines itself to profoundly transforming thought by helping it to attain its forms of equilibrium by means of a more advanced schematization and a more mobile abstraction.

Language and the 'concrete' logical operations

But is language the only source of certain particular forms of thought, such as logical thought? The thesis of numerous logicians (the Vienna circle, Anglo-Saxon logical empiricists, etc.) is well known concerning the linguistic nature of logic conceived as a syntax and general semantics. But here again genetic psychology allows us to place in proper perspective certain theses which are exclusively derived from the examination of adult thought.

3. A footprint, for example, is an index of the animal who made it. A signal, on the other hand, is a stimulus which occurs with the object but is not causally related to it. The bell associated with food presentation in classical conditioning is a good example of a neutral stimulus which comes to be a signal [Ed].

The first lesson to be learned from the study of the formation of logical operations in the child is that they are not constructed all at once but rather are elaborated in two successive stages. The propositional operations (propositional logic) with their particular groupings, such as those of the lattice and the group of four transformations (identity, inversion, reciprocity, and correlativity), do not appear until around eleven to twelve years of age and do not become systematically organized until between twelve and fifteen. By contrast, as of age seven or eight, systems of logical operations do not yet bear on propositions as such but on the classes and relations of objects themselves; and they are organized apropos of the real or imagined manipulation of these objects. This first set of operations, which we shall call 'concrete operations', involves only the additive and multiplicative operations upon classes and relations which result in classifications, seriations, correspondences, etc. These operations do not cover the logic of classes and relations in its entirety but only the elementary 'groupings', such as the semilattices and imperfect logical groups.

The problem of the relationship between language and thought can thus be posed in terms of these concrete operations. Is language the only source of the classifications, seriations, etc., which characterize the form of thought linked to these operations, or, on the contrary, are the latter relatively independent of language? Here is a highly simplified example. All birds (class A) are animals (class B), but all animals are not birds, because there are nonbird animals (class A'). The problem, then, is whether the operations $A + A' = B$ and $A = B - A'$ derive from language alone, which allows for the grouping of objects into classes, A, A', and B, or whether these operations have roots that lie deeper than language. An analogous problem can be posed with respect to the seriation: $A < B < C < \ldots$ etc.

Now the study of the development of operations in the child permits one to make a highly instructive observation. This is that the operations which make possible the combination or the dissociation of classes or relations are actions prior to their becoming operations of thought. Before he can combine or dissociate relatively universal and abstract classes, such as the classes of birds or of animals, the child can already classify collections of objects in the same perceptual field; he can combine or dissociate them manually before he can do so linguistically. By the same token, before he can seriate objects evoked by means of language alone (as, for example, in Burt's 1913 test: 'Edith is blonder than Susan and darker than Lily; who is the darkest of the three?'), the child can construct a series if, for example, he is given a set of rulers graduated as to length. The operations $+$, $-$, etc., are thus coordinations among actions before they are transposed into verbal form, so that language cannot account for their formation. Language indefinitely extends the power of these operations and confers on them a mobility and a universality which they would not have otherwise, but it is by no means the source of such coordinations.

We are at present conducting research in collaboration with Miss Inhelder and Miss Affolter in order to determine which of the mechanisms proper to the concrete operations subsist in the thinking of deaf-mutes. It appears that the fundamental operations inherent in classification and seriation are more widely represented here than is generally believed. No doubt it could be rejoined that the deaf-mute has a language of gestures and that the young child who constructs classifications and seriations in action has also acquired spoken language which can then be transformed into these manipulations.

It suffices, however, to look at the sensorimotor intelligence which exists prior to the acquisition of language in order to find in the infant's elementary practical coordinations the functional equivalents of the operations of combination and dissociation. If a twelve-to-twenty-four-month-old baby sees a watch placed under a blanket and then, when he looks for it, finds instead a beret or a hat (under which the watch has been hidden), he immediately lifts up the beret and expects to find the watch.[4]

4. This is a somewhat confused and confusing example. A more clearcut illustration is as follows:

obs. 64 At 1;7 (20) Jacqueline watches me when I put a coin in my hand and then put my hand under a coverlet. I withdraw my hand closed; Jacqueline opens it, then searches under the coverlet until she finds the object (Piaget, 1954).

In this example the transitivity relation is clear: the coin was in the hand; the hand was under the coverlet; therefore the coin is under the coverlet. Ed.

Thus he understands, in action, a sort of transitivity of relations which might be explained verbally as follows: 'The watch was under the hat; the hat was under the blanket; therefore the watch is under the blanket.' Such transitivity of actions constitutes the functional equivalent of what, on the representational plane, will be the transitivity of serial relations or topological nestings and even the inclusions of classes. Language makes these structures more universal and mobile than the sensorimotor coordinations, but where do the constitutive operations of representational nestings derive from if their roots do not reach down to the sensorimotor coordinations themselves? A large number of comparable examples demonstrates that these coordinations comprise, in actions, combinations and dissociations functionally comparable to the future operations of thought.

Language and propositional logic

While it is comprehensible that the concrete operations of classes and relations stem from acts of combination and dissociation, it may be argued that the propositional operations (i.e. those which characterize propositional logic) are, by contrast, an authentic product of language itself. In effect, the implications, disjunctions, incompatibilities, etc., which characterize propositional logic only appear at about eleven to twelve years. At this level reasoning becomes hypothetico-deductive; it is liberated from its concrete attachments and comes to rest on the universal and abstract plane for which only verbal thought appears to furnish the necessary generative conditions.

We certainly do not deny the considerable role language plays in the formation of such operations. But the question is not simply whether language is a necessary condition for the formation of formal operations. To that proposition we naturally concede. The question is also whether language is sufficient in and of itself to give rise to these operations *ex nihilo* or whether, on the contrary, its role is limited to allowing the fulfillment of structuring which originates from the systems of concrete operations and, therefore, from the wellsprings of action itself.

In order to grasp the psychology of operations peculiar to propositional logic, one should not address himself to the logistic axiomatization of propositions or to a simple enumeration of their isolable operations. The fundamental psychological reality which characterizes such operations is the integrated grouping which unites them in the same system and defines their algebraic utilization (the 'calculus' of propositions).

While the formal grouping is complex, it is nonetheless undissociably bound to the concrete operational structures found in middle childhood. This formal grouping consists, first of all, of a 'lattice', in the algebraic sense of the term.

The psychological problem in the formation of propositional operations consists of determining how the subject passes from elementary concrete structures (classifications, seriations, double entry matrices, etc.) to the structure of the lattice. The answer to this question is simple. What distinguishes a lattice from a simple classification (such as zoological classifications, for example) is the intervention of combinatory operations. Thus the sixteen binary operations which can be constructed with two propositions p and q result from one combination. The four basic associations $(p \cdot q)$, $(p \cdot \bar{q})$, $(\bar{p} \cdot q)$, $(\bar{p} \cdot \bar{q})$ are isomorphic to what would be produced by a simple multiplication of classes $(P + \bar{P}) \times \times (Q + \bar{Q}) = PQ + P\bar{Q} + \bar{P}Q + \bar{P}\bar{Q}$, hence to an operation already accessible to subjects of seven to eight years. But the innovation peculiar to the propositional operations is that these four basic associations, which we shall call 1, 2, 3 and 4, give rise to sixteen combinations: 1, 2, 3, 4, 12, 13, 14, 23, 24, 34, 123, 124, 134, 234, 1234, and 0.

The question, then, is to ascertain whether language makes such combinatory operations possible or whether the operations evolve independently of language. Genetic facts leave no doubt as to the reply. Inhelder's (Inhelder and Piaget, 1958) experiments on experimental reasoning and the induction of physical laws by adolescents, as well as the preceding research by Inhelder and the writer (Piaget and Inhelder, 1951) on the development of combinatory operations show that these operations are constituted at about eleven to twelve years in all fields at once and not only on the verbal plane. For example, if subjects are asked to combine three or four different-colored discs according to all the combinations possible, up to eleven to twelve years the combinations remain incomplete and are constructed unsystematically, whereas from then on the subject manages to construct a complete and methodical system. It would be difficult to maintain that this system is a product of the evolution of language. On the contrary, the acquisition of combinatory operations permits the subject to complete his verbal classifications and to make these correspond to the abstract relationships inherent in the propositional operations.

Another aspect of the formal grouping of propositional operations is the 'group' of the following four commutative transformations: for each propositional operation – e.g., the implication (p, q) – there is a corresponding inverse $N(p, \bar{q})$, a reciprocal $R(q, p)$ and a correlative $C(\bar{p}, q)$. Together with the identical transformation I, we have: $CN = R$; $CR = N$; $RN = C$; and $RNC = I$.

Of these four transformations the two principal ones are inversion or negation N and reciprocity R. The correlative C is none other than the reciprocal of the inverse ($RN = C$) or, which amounts to the same thing, the inverse of the reciprocal ($NR = C$). The question then is, once again, whether language brings about this coordination of transformations by inversion and by reciprocity or whether the transformations exist prior to their verbal expression and language is limited to facilitating their use and coordination.

Here, once again, the examination of genetic facts furnishes a reply which is oriented much more in the direction of an interaction between linguistic mechanisms and the subjacent operational mechanisms than in the direction of linguistic determinism.

Inversion and reciprocity are rooted in soil which antedates their symbolic function and which is, properly speaking, sensorimotor in nature. Inversion or negation is none other than an elaborated form of processes which are found at all levels of development. The baby already knows how to use an object as a means to attain a goal, as well as how to get rid of it as an obstacle in order to reach a new goal. The origins of this transformation by inversion or negation can be seen in the mechanisms of neural inhibition – for example, withdrawing the hand and arm after having stretched them out in a certain direction, etc. Reciprocity also extends to perceptual and motor symmetries, which are just as precocious as the preceding mechanisms.

While the parallel history of the diverse forms of inversion and reciprocity can be followed throughout the course of mental development, their coordination, i.e., their integration into a single system which implicates them both, is effected only at the level of propositional operations with the advent of the INRC 'group' just described. It would be difficult to maintain that this coordination was due to language alone. This coordination is due to the construction of the grouping which participates both in the 'lattice' and the 'group' and engenders the propositional operations; it is not due to the verbal expression of these operations. In other words, this coordination is at the source of the operations and does not constitute their end product.

In the three domains we have just covered in broad outline, we have noted that language is not enough to explain thought, because the structures that characterize thought have their roots in action and in sensorimotor mechanisms that are deeper than linguistics. It is also evident that the more the structures of thought are refined, the more language is necessary for the achievement of this elaboration. Language is thus a necessary but not a sufficient condition for the construction of logical operations. It is necessary because within the system of symbolic expression which constitutes language the operations would remain at the stage of successive actions without ever being integrated into simultaneous systems or simultaneously encompassing a set of interdependent transformations. Without language the operations would remain personal and would consequently not be regulated by interpersonal exchange and cooperation. It is in this dual sense of symbolic condensation and social regulation that language is indispensable to the elaboration of thought. Thus language and thought are linked in a genetic circle where each necessarily leans on the other in interdependent formation and continuous reciprocal action. In the last analysis, both depend on intelligence itself, which antedates language and is independent of it.

References

INHELDER, B., and PIAGET, J. (1958), *The Growth of Logical Thinking from Childhood to Adolescence*, Routledge & Kegan Paul.

PIAGET, J., and INHELDER, B. (1951), *La Genèse de L'idée de Hasard chez L'enfant*, PUF, Paris.

WATSON, J. B. (1919), *Psychology from the Standpoint of a Behaviourist*, Lippincott.

11 L. S. Vygotsky

Thought and Word

'Thought and word', in L. S. Vygotsky, *Thought and Language*, 1962, MIT Press, pp. 114–53.

I have forgotten the word I intended to say, and my thought, unembodied returns to the realm of shadows.

O. Mandelstam

I

We began our study with an attempt to discover the relation between thought and speech at the earliest stages of phylogenetic and ontogenetic development. We found no specific interdependence between the genetic roots of thought and of word. It became plain that the inner relationship we were looking for was not a prerequisite for, but rather a product of, the historical development of human consciousness.

In animals, even in anthropoids whose speech is phonetically like human speech and whose intellect is akin to man's, speech and thinking are not interrelated. A prelinguistic period in thought and a preintellectual period in speech undoubtedly exist also in the development of the child. Thought and word are not connected by a primary bond. A connection originates, changes, and grows in the course of the evolution of thinking and speech.

It would be wrong, however, to regard thought and speech as two unrelated processes, either parallel or crossing at certain points and mechanically influencing each other. The absence of a primary bond does not mean that a connection between them can be formed only in a mechanical way. The futility of most of the earlier investigations was largely due to the assumption that thought and word were isolated, independent elements, and verbal thought the fruit of their external union.

The method of analysis based on this conception was bound to fail. It sought to explain the properties of verbal thought by breaking it up into its component elements, thought and word, neither of which, taken separately, possesses the properties of the whole. This method is not true analysis helpful in solving concrete problems. It leads, rather, to generalization. We compared it to the analysis of water into hydrogen and oxygen – which can result only in findings applicable to all water existing in nature, from the Pacific Ocean to a raindrop. Similarly, the statement that verbal thought is composed of intellectual processes and speech functions proper applies to all verbal thought and all its manifestations and explains none of the specific problems facing the student of verbal thought.

We tried a new approach to the subject and replaced analysis into elements by analysis into *units*, each of which retains in simple form all the properties of the whole. We found this unit of verbal thought in *word meaning*.

The meaning of a word represents such a close amalgam of thought and language that it is hard to tell whether it is a phenomenon of speech or a phenomenon of thought. A word without meaning is an empty sound; meaning, therefore, is a criterion of 'word', its indispensable component. It would seem, then, that it may be regarded as a phenomenon of speech. But from the point of view of psychology, the meaning of every word is a generalization or a concept. And since generalizations and concepts are undeniably acts of thought, we may regard meaning as a phenomenon of thinking. It does not follow, however, that meaning formally belongs in two different spheres of psychic life. Word meaning is a phenomenon of thought only in so far as thought is embodied in speech, and of speech only in so far as speech is connected with thought and illumined by it. It is a phenomenon of verbal thought, or meaningful speech – a union of word and thought.

Our experimental investigations fully confirm this basic thesis. They not only proved that concrete study of the development of verbal thought is made possible by the use of word meaning as the analytical unit but they also led to a further thesis, which we consider the major result of our study and which issues directly from the first: the thesis that word meanings develop. This insight must replace the postulate of the immutability of word meanings.

From the point of view of the old schools of psychology, the bond between word and meaning is an associative bond, established through the repeated simultaneous perception of a certain sound and a certain object. A word calls to mind its content as the overcoat of a friend reminds us of that friend, or a house of its inhabitants. The association between word and meaning may grow stronger or weaker, be enriched by linkage with other objects of a similar kind, spread over a wider field, or become more limited, i.e. it may undergo quantitative and external changes, but it cannot change its psychological nature. To do that, it would have to cease being an association. From that point of view, any development in word meanings is inexplicable and impossible – an implication which handicapped linguistics as well as psychology. Once having committed itself to the association theory, semantics persisted in treating word meaning as an association between a word's sound and its content. All words, from the most concrete to the most abstract, appeared to be formed in the same manner in regard to meaning, and to contain nothing peculiar to speech as such; a word made us think of its meaning just as any object might remind us of another. It is hardly surprising that semantics did not even pose the larger question of the development of word meanings. Development was reduced to changes in the associative connections between single words and single objects. A word might denote at first one object and then become associated with another, just as an overcoat, having changed owners, might remind us first of one person and later of another. Linguistics did not realize that in the historical evolution of language the very structure of meaning and its psychological nature also change. From primitive generalizations, verbal thought rises to the most abstract concepts. It is not merely the content of a word that changes, but the way in which reality is generalized and reflected in a word.

Equally inadequate is the association theory in explaining the development of word meanings in childhood. Here, too, it can account only for the purely external, quantitative changes in the bonds uniting word and meaning, for their enrichment and strengthening, but not for the fundamental structural and psychological changes that can and do occur in the development of language in children.

Oddly enough, the fact that associationism in general had been abandoned for some time did not seem to affect the interpretation of word and meaning. The Würzburg school, whose main object was to prove the impossibility of reducing thinking to a mere play of associations and to demonstrate the existence of specific laws governing the flow of thought, did not revise the association theory of word and meaning, or even recognize the need for such a revision. It freed thought from the fetters of sensation and imagery and from the laws of association, and turned it into a purely spiritual act. By so doing, it went back to the prescientific concepts of St Augustine and Descartes and finally reached extreme subjective idealism. The psychology of thought was moving toward the ideas of Plato. Speech, at the same time, was left at the mercy of association. Even after the work of the Würzburg school, the connection between a word and its meaning was still considered a simple associative bond. The word was seen as the external concomitant of thought, its attire only, having no influence on its inner life. Thought and speech had never been as widely separated as during the Würzburg period. The overthrow of the association theory in the field of thought actually increased its sway in the field of speech.

The work of other psychologists further reinforced this trend. Selz continued to investigate thought without considering its relation to speech and came to the conclusion that man's productive thinking and the mental operations of chimpanzees were identical in nature – so completely did he ignore the influence of words on thought.

Even Ach, who made a special study of word meaning and who tried to overcome associationism in his theory of concepts, did not go beyond assuming the presence of 'determining tendencies' operative, along with associations, in the process of concept formation. Hence, the conclusions he reached did not change the old understanding of word meaning. By identifying concept with meaning, he did not allow for development and changes in concepts. Once established, the meaning of a word was set forever; its development was completed. The same principles were taught by the very psychologists Ach attacked. To both sides, the starting point was also the end of the development of a concept; the disagreement concerned only the way in which the formation of word meanings began.

In Gestalt psychology, the situation was not very different. This school was more consistent than others in trying to surmount the general principle of associationism. Not satisfied with a partial solution of the problem, it tried to liberate thinking *and* speech from the rule of association and to put both under the laws of structure formation. Surprisingly, even this most progressive of modern psychological schools made no progress in the theory of thought and speech.

For one thing, it retained the complete separation of these two functions. In the light of Gestalt psychology, the relationship between thought and word appears as a simple analogy, a reduction of both to a common structural denominator. The formation of the first meaningful words of a child is seen as similar to the intellectual operations of chimpanzees in Köhler's experiments. Words enter into the structure of things and acquire a certain functional meaning, in much the same way as the stick, to the chimpanzee, becomes part of the structure of obtaining the fruit and acquires the functional meaning of tool. The connection between word and meaning is no longer regarded as a matter of simple association but as a matter of structure. That seems like a step forward. But if we look more closely at the new approach, it is easy to see that the step forward is an illusion and that we are still standing in the same place. The principle of structure is applied to all relations between things in the same sweeping, undifferentiated way as the principle of association was before it. It remains impossible to deal with the specific relations between word and meaning. They are from the outset accepted as identical in principle with any and all other relations between things. All cats are as gray in the dusk of Gestalt psychology as in the earlier fogs of universal associationism.

While Ach sought to overcome associationism with the 'determining tendency', Gestalt psychology combated it with the principle of structure – retaining, however, the two fundamental errors of the older theory: the assumption of the identical nature of all connections and the assumption that word meanings do not change. The old and the new psychology both assume that the development of a word's meaning is finished as soon as it emerges. The new trends in psychology brought progress in all branches except in the study of thought and speech. Here the new principles resemble the old ones like twins.

If Gestalt psychology is at a standstill in the field of speech, it has made a big step backward in the field of thought. The Würzburg school at least recognized that thought had laws of its own. Gestalt psychology denies their existence. By reducing to a common structural denominator the perceptions of domestic fowl, the mental operations of chimpanzees, the first meaningful words of the child, and the conceptual thinking of the adult, it obliterates every distinction between the most elementary perception and the highest forms of thought.

This critical survey may be summed up as follows: all the psychological schools and trends overlook the cardinal point that every thought is a generalization, and they all study word and meaning without any reference to development. As long as these two conditions persist in the successive trends, there cannot be much difference in the treatment of the problem.

II

The discovery that word meanings evolve leads the study of thought and speech out of a blind alley. Word meanings are dynamic rather than static formations. They change as the child develops; they change also with the various ways in which thought functions.

If word meanings change in their inner nature, then the relation of thought to word also changes. To understand the dynamics of that relationship, we must supplement the genetic approach to our main study by functional analysis and examine the role of word meaning in the process of thought.

Let us consider the process of verbal thinking from the first dim stirring of a thought to its formulation. What we want to show now is not how meanings develop over long periods of time but the way they function in the live process of verbal thought. On the basis of such a functional analysis, we shall be able to show also that each stage in the development of word meaning has its own particular relationship between thought and speech. Since functional problems are most readily solved by examining the highest form of a given activity, we shall, for a while, put aside the problem of development and consider the relations between thought and word in the mature mind.

The leading idea in the following discussion can be reduced to this formula: The relation of thought to word is not a thing but a process, a continual movement back and forth from thought to word and from word to thought. In that process the relation of thought to word undergoes changes which themselves may be regarded as development in the functional sense. Thought is not merely expressed in words; it comes into existence through them Every thought tends to connect something with something else, to establish a relationship between things. Every thought moves, grows and develops, fulfills a function, solves a problem. This flow of thought occurs as an inner movement through a series of planes. An analysis of the interaction of thought and word must begin with an investigation of the different phases and planes a thought traverses before it is embodied in words.

The first thing such a study reveals is the need to distinguish between two planes of speech. Both the inner, meaningful, semantic aspect of speech and the external, phonetic aspect, though forming a true unity, have their own laws of movement. The unity of speech is a complex, not a homogeneous, unity. A number of facts in the linguistic development of the child indicate independent movement in the phonetic and the semantic spheres. We shall point out two of the most important of these facts.

In mastering external speech, the child starts from one word, then connects two or three words; a little later, he advances from simple sentences to more complicated ones, and finally to coherent speech made up of series of such sentences; in other words, he proceeds from a part to the whole. In regard to meaning, on the other hand, the first word of the child is a whole sentence. Semantically, the child starts from the whole, from a meaningful complex, and only later begins to master the separate semantic units, the meanings of words, and to divide his formerly undifferentiated thought into those units. The external and the semantic aspects of speech develop in opposite directions – one from the particular to the whole, from word to sentence, and the other from the whole to the particular, from sentence to word.

This in itself suffices to show how important it is to distinguish between the vocal and the semantic aspects of speech. Since they move in reverse directions, their development does not coincide, but that does not mean that they are independent of each other. On the contrary, their difference is the first stage of a close union. In fact, our example reveals their inner relatedness as clearly as it does their distinction. A child's thought, precisely because it is born as a dim, amorphous whole, must find expression in a single word. As his thought becomes more differentiated, the child is less apt to express it in single words but constructs a composite whole. Conversely, progress in speech to the differentiated whole of a sentence helps the child's thoughts to progress from a homogeneous whole to well-defined parts. Thought and word are not cut from one pattern. In a sense, there are more differences than likenesses between them. The structure of speech does not simply mirror the structure of thought; that is why words cannot be put on by thought like a ready-made garment. Thought undergoes many changes as it turns into speech. It does not merely find expression in speech; it finds its reality and form. The semantic and the phonetic developmental processes are essentially one, precisely because of their reverse directions.

The second, equally important fact emerges at a later period of development. Piaget (1923) demonstrated that the child uses subordinate clauses with *because*, *although*, etc., long before he grasps the structures of meaning corresponding to these syntactic forms. Grammar precedes logic. Here, too, as in our previous example, the discrepancy does not exclude union but is, in fact, necessary for union.

In adults the divergence between the semantic and the phonetic aspects of speech is even more striking. Modern, psychologically oriented linguistics is familiar with this phenomenon, especially in regard to grammatical and psychological subject and predicate. For example, in the sentence 'The clock fell', emphasis and meaning may change in different situations. Suppose I notice that the clock has stopped and ask how this happened. The answer is, 'The clock fell'. Grammatical and psychological subject coincide: 'The clock' is the first idea in my consciousness; 'fell' is what is said about the clock. But if I hear a crash in the next room and inquire what happened, and get the same answer, subject and predicate are psychologically reversed. I knew something had fallen – that is what we are talking about. 'The clock' completes the idea. The sentence could be changed to: 'What has fallen is the clock'; then the grammatical and the psychological subject would coincide. In the prologue to his play *Duke Ernst von Schwaben*, Uhland says: 'Grim scenes will pass before you.' Psychologically, 'will pass' is the subject. The spectator knows he will see events unfold; the additional idea, the predicate, is 'grim scenes'. Uhland meant, 'What will pass before your eyes is a tragedy.' Any part of a sentence may become the psychological predicate, the carrier of topical emphasis; on the other hand, entirely different meanings may lie hidden behind one grammatical structure. Accord between syntactical and psychological organization is not as prevalent as we tend to assume – rather, it is a requirement that is seldom met. Not only subject and predicate, but grammatical gender, number, case, tense, degree, etc., have their psychological doubles. A spontaneous utterance, wrong from the point of view of grammar, may have charm and aesthetic value. Absolute correctness is achieved only beyond natural language, in mathematics. Our daily speech continually fluctuates between the ideals of mathematical and of imaginative harmony.

We shall illustrate the interdependence of the semantic and the grammatical aspects of language by citing two examples which show that changes in formal structure can entail far-reaching changes in meaning.[1]

In translating the fable *La Cigale et la Fourmi*, Krylov substituted a dragonfly for La Fontaine's grasshopper. In French *grasshopper* is feminine and therefore well suited to symbolize a lighthearted, carefree attitude. The nuance would be lost in a literal translation, since in Russian *grasshopper* is masculine. When he settled for *dragonfly*, which is feminine in Russian, Krylov disregarded the literal meaning in favor of the grammatical form required to render La Fontaine's thought.

Tjutchev did the same in his translation of Heine's poem about a fir and a palm. In German *fir* is masculine and *palm* feminine, and the poem suggests the love of a man for a woman. In Russian, both trees are feminine. To retain the implication, Tjutchev replaced the fir by a masculine cedar. Lermontov, in his more

1. Vygotsky's examples lose some of their impact in English because English grammar does not distinguish between genders. Some explanations have been added to make the point [Ed].

literal translation of the same poem, deprived it of these poetic overtones and gave it an essentially different meaning, more abstract and generalized. One grammatical detail may, on occasion, change the whole purport of what is said.

Behind words, there is the independent grammar of thought, the syntax of word meanings. The simplest utterance, far from reflecting a constant, rigid correspondence between sound and meaning, is really a process. Verbal expressions cannot emerge fully formed but must develop gradually. This complex process of transition from meaning to sound must itself be developed and perfected. The child must learn to distinguish between semantics and phonetics and understand the nature of the difference. At first he uses verbal forms and meanings without being conscious of them as separate. The word, to the child, is an integral part of the object it denotes. Such a conception seems to be characteristic of primitive linguistic consciousness. We all know the old story about the rustic who said he wasn't surprised that savants with all their instruments could figure out the size of stars and their course – what baffled him was how they found out their names. Simple experiments show that preschool children 'explain' the names of objects by their attributes. According to them, an animal is called 'cow' because it has horns, 'calf' because its horns are still small, 'dog' because it is small and has no horns; an object is called 'car' because it is not an animal. When asked whether one could interchange the names of objects, for instance call a cow 'ink', and ink 'cow', children will answer no, 'because ink is used for writing, and the cow gives milk'. An exchange of names would mean an exchange of characteristic features, so inseparable is the connection between them in the child's mind. In one experiment, the children were told that in a game a dog would be called 'cow'. Here is a typical sample of questions and answers:

'Does a cow have horns?'
'Yes.'
'But don't you remember that the cow is really a dog? Come now, does a dog have horns?'
'Sure, if it is a cow, if it's called cow, it has horns. That kind of dog has got to have little horns.'

We can see how difficult it is for children to separate the name of an object from its attributes, which cling to the name when it is transferred like possessions following their owner.

The fusion of the two planes of speech, semantic and vocal, begins to break down as the child grows older, and the distance between them gradually increases. Each stage in the development of word meanings has its own specific interrelation of the two planes. A child's ability to communicate through language is directly related to the differentiation of word meanings in his speech and consciousness.

To understand this, we must remember a basic characteristic of the structure of word meanings. In the semantic structure of a word, we distinguish between referent and meaning; correspondingly, we distinguish a word's nominative from its significative function. When we compare these structural and functional relations at the earliest, middle, and advanced stages of development, we find the following genetic regularity: in the beginning, only the nominative function exists; and semantically, only the objective reference; signification independent of naming, and meaning independent of reference, appear later and develop along the paths we have attempted to trace and describe.

Only when this development is completed does the child become fully able to formulate his own thought and to understand the speech of others. Until then, his usage of words coincides with that of adults in its objective reference but not in its meaning.

III

We must probe still deeper and explore the plane of inner speech lying beyond the semantic plane. We shall discuss here some of the data of the special investigation we have made of it. The relationship of thought and word cannot be understood in all its complexity without a clear understanding of the psychological nature of inner speech. Yet, of all the problems connected with thought and language, this is perhaps the most complicated, beset as it is with terminological and other misunderstandings.

The term *inner speech*, or *endophasy*, has been applied to various phenomena, and authors argue about different things that they call by the same name. Originally, inner speech seems to have been understood as verbal memory. An example would be the silent recital of a poem known by heart. In that case, inner speech differs from vocal speech only as the idea or image of an object differs from the real object. It was in this sense that inner speech was understood by the French authors who tried to find out how words were reproduced in memory – whether as auditory, visual, motor, or synthetic images. We shall see that word memory is indeed one of the constituent elements of inner speech but not all of it.

In a second interpretation, inner speech is seen as truncated external speech – as 'speech minus sound' (Mueller) or 'sub-vocal speech' (Watson). Bekhterev defined it as a speech reflex inhibited in its motor part. Such an explanation is by no means sufficient. Silent 'pronouncing' of words is not equivalent to the total process of inner speech.

The third definition is, on the contrary, too broad. To Goldstein (1927, 1932), the term covers everything that precedes the motor act of speaking, including Wundt's 'motives of speech' and the indefinable, nonsensory and nonmotor specific speech experience – i.e., the whole interior aspect of any speech activity. It is hard to accept the equation of inner speech with an inarticulate inner experience in which the separate identifiable structural planes are dissolved without trace. This central experience is common to all linguistic activity, and for this reason alone Goldstein's interpretation does not fit that specific, unique function that alone deserves the name of inner speech. Logically developed, Goldstein's view must lead to the thesis that inner speech is not speech at all but rather an intellectual and affective-volitional activity since it includes the motives of speech and the thought that is expressed in words.

To get a true picture of inner speech, one must start from the assumption that it is a specific formation, with its own laws and complex relations to the other forms of speech activity. Before we can study its relation to thought, on the one hand, and to speech, on the other, we must determine its special characteristics and function.

Inner speech is speech for oneself; external speech is for others. It would indeed be surprising if such a basic difference in function did not affect the structure of the two kinds of speech. Absence of vocalization *per se* is only a consequence of the specific nature of inner speech, which is neither an antecedent of external speech nor its reproduction in memory but is, in a sense, the opposite of external speech. The latter is the turning of thought into words, its materialization and objectification. With inner speech, the process is reversed: speech turns into inward thought. Consequently, their structures must differ.

The area of inner speech is one of the most difficult to investigate. It remained almost inaccessible to experiments until ways were found to apply the genetic method of experimentation. Piaget was the first to pay attention to the child's egocentric speech and to see its theoretical significance, but he remained blind to the most important trait of egocentric speech – its genetic connection with inner speech – and this warped his interpretation of its function and structure. We made that relationship the central problem of our study and thus were able to investigate the nature of inner speech with unusual completeness. A number of considerations and observations led us to conclude that egocentric speech is a stage of development preceding inner speech. Both fulfill intellectual functions; their structures are similar; egocentric speech disappears at school age, when inner speech begins to develop. From all this we infer that one changes into the other.

If this transformation does take place, then egocentric speech provides the key to the study of inner speech. One advantage of approaching inner speech through egocentric speech is its accessibility to experimentation and observation. It is still vocalized, audible speech, i.e., external in its mode of expression, but at the same time inner speech in function and structure. To study an internal process it is necessary to externalize it experimentally, by connecting it with some outer activity; only then is objective functional analysis possible. Egocentric speech is, in fact, a natural experiment of this type.

This method has another great advantage: since egocentric speech can be studied at the time when some of its characteristics are waning and new ones forming, we are able to judge which traits are essential to inner speech and which are only temporary, and thus to determine the goal of this movement from egocentric to inner speech – i.e., the nature of inner speech.

Before we go on to the results obtained by this method, we shall briefly discuss the nature of egocentric speech, stressing the differences between our theory and Piaget's. Piaget contends that the child's egocentric speech is a direct expression of the egocentrism of his thought, which in turn is a compromise between the primary autism of his thinking and its gradual socialization. As the child grows older, autism recedes and socialization progresses, leading to the waning of egocentrism in his thinking and speech.

In Piaget's conception, the child in his egocentric speech does not adapt himself to the thinking of adults. His thought remains entirely egocentric; this makes his talk incomprehensible to others. Egocentric speech has no function in the child's realistic thinking or activity – it merely accompanies them. And since it is an expression of egocentric thought, it disappears together with the child's egocentrism. From its climax at the beginning of the child's development, egocentric speech drops to zero on the threshold of school age. Its history is one of involution rather than evolution. It has no future.

In our conception, egocentric speech is a phenomenon of the transition from interpsychic to intrapsychic functioning, i.e., from the social, collective activity of the child to his more individualized activity – a pattern of development common to all the higher psychological functions. Speech for oneself originates through differentiation from speech for others. Since the main course of the child's development is one of gradual individualization, this tendency is reflected in the function and structure of his speech.

Our experimental results indicate that the function of egocentric speech is similar to that of inner speech: It does not merely accompany the child's activity; it serves mental orientation, conscious understanding; it helps in overcoming difficulties; it is speech for oneself, intimately and usefully connected with the child's thinking. Its fate is very different from that described by Piaget. Egocentric speech develops along a rising, not a declining, curve; it goes through an evolution, not an involution. In the end, it becomes inner speech.

Our hypothesis has several advantages over Piaget's: It explains the function and development of egocentric speech and, in particular, its sudden increase when the child faces difficulties which demand consciousness and reflection – a fact uncovered by our experiments and which Piaget's theory cannot explain. But the greatest advantage of our theory is that it supplies a satisfying answer to a paradoxical situation described by Piaget himself. To Piaget, the quantitative drop in egocentric speech as the child grows older means the withering of that form of speech. If that were so, its structural peculiarities might also be expected to decline; it is hard to believe that the process would affect only its quantity, and not its inner structure. The child's thought becomes infinitely less egocentric between the ages of three and seven. If the characteristics of egocentric speech that make it incomprehensible to others are indeed rooted in egocentrism, they should become less apparent as that form of speech becomes less frequent; egocentric speech should approach social speech and become more and more intelligible. Yet what are the facts? Is the talk of a three year old harder to follow than that of a seven year old? Our investigation established that the traits of egocentric speech which make for inscrutability are at their lowest point at three and at their peak at seven. They develop in a reverse direction to the frequency of egocentric speech. While the latter keeps falling and reaches zero at school age, the structural characteristics become more and more pronounced.

This throws a new light on the quantitative decrease in egocentric speech, which is the cornerstone of Piaget's thesis.

What does this decrease mean? The structural peculiarities of speech for oneself and its differentiation from external speech increase with age. What is it then that diminishes? Only one of its aspects: vocalization. Does this mean that egocentric speech as a whole is dying out? We believe that it does not, for how then could we explain the growth of the functional and structural traits of egocentric speech? On the other hand, their growth is perfectly compatible with the decrease of vocalization – indeed, clarifies its meaning. Its rapid dwindling and the equally rapid growth of the other characteristics are contradictory in appearance only.

To explain this, let us start from an undeniable, experimentally established fact. The structural and functional qualities of egocentric speech become more marked as the child develops. At three, the difference between egocentric and social speech equals zero; at seven, we have speech that in structure and function is totally unlike social speech. A differentiation of the two speech functions has taken place. This is a fact – and facts are notoriously hard to refute.

Once we accept this, everything else falls into place. If the developing structural and functional peculiarities of egocentric speech progressively isolate it from external speech, then its vocal aspect must fade away; and this is exactly what happens between three and seven years. With the progressive isolation of speech for oneself, its vocalization becomes unnecessary and meaningless and, because of its growing structural peculiarities, also impossible. Speech for oneself cannot find expression in external speech. The more independent and autonomous egocentric speech becomes, the poorer it grows in its external manifestations. In the end it separates itself entirely from speech for others, ceases to be vocalized, and thus appears to die out.

But this is only an illusion. To interpret the sinking coefficient of egocentric speech as a sign that this kind of speech is dying out is like saying that the child stops counting when he ceases to use his fingers and starts adding in his head. In reality, behind the symptoms of dissolution lies a progressive development, the birth of a new speech form.

The decreasing vocalization of egocentric speech denotes a developing abstraction from sound, the child's new faculty to 'think words' instead of pronouncing them. This is the positive meaning of the sinking coefficient of egocentric speech. The downward curve indicates development toward inner speech.

We can see that all the known facts about the functional, structural, and genetic characteristics of egocentric speech point to one thing: It develops in the direction of inner speech. Its developmental history can be understood only as a gradual unfolding of the traits of inner speech.

We believe that this corroborates our hypothesis about the origin and nature of egocentric speech. To turn our hypothesis into a certainty, we must devise an experiment capable of showing which of the two interpretations is correct. What are the data for this critical experiment?

Let us restate the theories between which we must decide. Piaget believes that egocentric speech stems from the insufficient socialization of speech and that its only development is decrease and eventual death. Its culmination lies in the past. Inner speech is something new brought in from the outside along with socialization. We believe that egocentric speech stems from the insufficient individualization of primary social speech. Its culmination lies in the future. It develops into inner speech.

To obtain evidence for one or the other view, we must place the child alternately in experimental situations encouraging social speech and in situations discouraging it, and see how these changes affect egocentric speech. We consider this an *experimentum crucis* for the following reasons.

If the child's egocentric talk results from the egocentrism of his thinking and its insufficient socialization, then any weakening of the social elements in the experimental setup, any factor contributing to the child's isolation from the group, must lead to a sudden increase in egocentric speech. But if the latter results from an insufficient differentiation of speech for oneself from speech for others, then the same changes must cause it to decrease.

We took as the starting point of our experiment three of Piaget's own observations:

1. Egocentric speech occurs only in the presence of other children engaged in the same activity, and not when the child is alone; i.e., it is a collective monologue.

2. The child is under the illusion that his egocentric talk, directed to nobody, is understood by those who surround him.

3. Egocentric speech has the character of external speech: It is not inaudible or whispered.

These are certainly not chance peculiarities. From the child's own point of view, egocentric speech is not yet separated from social speech. It occurs under the subjective and objective conditions of social speech and may be considered a correlate of the insufficient isolation of the child's individual consciousness from the social whole.

In our first series of experiments (Vygotsky and Luria, 1929), we tried to destroy the illusion of being understood. After measuring the child's coefficient of egocentric speech in a situation similar to that of Piaget's experiments, we put him into a new situation: either with deaf-mute children or with children speaking a foreign language. In all other respects the set-up remained the same. The coefficient of egocentric speech dropped to zero in the majority of cases, and in the rest to one-eighth of the previous figure, on the average. This proves that the illusion of being understood is not a mere epiphenomenon of egocentric speech but is functionally connected with it. Our results must seem paradoxical from the point of view of Piaget's theory: The weaker the child's contact is with the group – the less the social situation forces him to adjust his thoughts to others and to use social speech – the more freely should the egocentrism of his thinking and speech manifest itself. But from the point of view of our hypothesis, the meaning of these findings is clear: Egocentric speech, springing from the lack of differentiation of speech for oneself from speech for others, disappears when the feeling of being understood, essential for social speech, is absent.

In the second series of experiments, the variable factor was the possibility of collective monologue. Having measured the child's coefficient of egocentric speech in a situation permitting collective monologue, we put him into a situation excluding it – in a group of children who were strangers to him, or by himself at a separate table in a corner of the room; or he worked quite alone, even the experimenter leaving the room. The results of this series agreed with the first results. The exclusion of the group monologue caused a drop in the coefficient of egocentric speech, though not such a striking one as in the first case – seldom to zero and, on the average, to one-sixth of the original figure. The different methods of precluding collective monologue were not equally effective in reducing the coefficient of egocentric speech. The trend, however, was obvious in all the variations of the experiment. The exclusion of the collective factor, instead of giving full freedom to egocentric speech, depressed it. Our hypothesis was once more confirmed.

In the third series of experiments, the variable factor was the vocal quality of egocentric speech. Just outside the laboratory where the experiment was in progress, an orchestra played so loudly, or so much noise was made, that it drowned out not only the voices of others but the child's own; in a variant of the experiment, the child was expressly forbidden to talk loudly and allowed to talk only in whispers. Once again the coefficient of egocentric speech went down, the relation to the original figure being 5:1. Again the different methods were not equally effective, but the basic trend was invariably present.

The purpose of all three series of experiments was to eliminate those characteristics of egocentric speech which bring it close to social speech. We found that this always led to the dwindling of egocentric speech. It is logical, then, to assume that egocentric speech is a form developing out of social speech and not yet separated from it in its manifestation, though already distinct in function and structure.

The disagreement between us and Piaget on this point will be made quite clear by the following example: I am sitting at my desk talking to a person who is behind me and whom I cannot see; he leaves the room without my noticing it, and I continue to talk, under the illusion that he listens and understands. Outwardly, I am talking with myself and for myself, but psychologically my speech is social. From the point of view of Piaget's theory, the opposite happens in the case of the child: His egocentric talk is for and with himself; it only has the appearance of social speech, just as my speech gave the false impression of being egocentric. From our point of view, the whole situation is much more complicated than that. Subjectively, the child's egocentric speech already has its own peculiar function – to that extent, it is independent from social speech; yet its independence is not complete because it is not felt as inner speech and is not distinguished by the child from speech for others. Objectively, also, it is different from social speech but again not entirely, because it functions only within social situations. Both subjectively and objectively, egocentric speech represents a transition from speech for others to speech for oneself. It already has the function of inner speech but remains similar to social speech in its expression.

The investigation of egocentric speech has paved the way to the understanding of inner speech, which we shall examine next.

IV

Our experiments convinced us that inner speech must be regarded, not as speech minus sound, but as an entirely separate speech function. Its main distinguishing trait is its peculiar syntax.

Compared with external speech, inner speech appears disconnected and incomplete.

This is not a new observation. All the students of inner speech, even those who approached it from the behavioristic standpoint, noted this trait. The method of genetic analysis permits us to go beyond a mere description of it. We applied this method and found that as egocentric speech develops it shows a tendency toward an altogether specific form of abbreviation: namely, omitting the subject of a sentence and all words connected with it, while preserving the predicate. This tendency toward predication appears in all our experiments with such regularity that we must assume it to be the basic syntactic form of inner speech.

It may help us to understand this tendency if we recall certain situations in which external speech shows a similar structure. Pure predication occurs in external speech in two cases: either as an answer or when the subject of the sentence is known beforehand to all concerned. The answer to 'Would you like a cup of tea?' is never 'No, I don't want a cup of tea,' but a simple 'No.' Obviously, such a sentence is possible only because its subject is tacitly understood by both parties. To 'Has your brother read this book?' no one ever replies, 'Yes, my brother has read this book.' The answer is a short 'Yes,' or 'Yes, he has.' Now let us imagine that several people are waiting for a bus. No one will say, on seeing the bus approach, 'The bus for which we are waiting is coming.' The sentence is likely to be an abbreviated 'Coming,' or some such expression, because the subject is plain from the situation. Quite frequently, shortened sentences cause confusion. The listener may relate the sentence to a subject foremost in his own mind, not the one meant by the speaker. If the thoughts of two people coincide, perfect understanding can be achieved through the use of mere predicates, but if they are thinking about different things they are bound to misunderstand each other.

Very good examples of the condensation of external speech and its reduction to predicates are found in the novels of Tolstoy, who quite often dealt with the psychology of understanding: 'No one heard clearly what he said, but Kitty understood him. She understood because her mind incessantly watched for his needs' (*Anna Karenina*, pt 5, ch. 18). We might say that her thoughts, following the thoughts of the dying man, contained the subject to which his word, understood by no one else, referred. But perhaps the most striking example is the declaration of love between Kitty and Levin by means of initial letters:

'I have long wished to ask you something.'

'Please do.'

'This,' he said, and wrote the initial letters: *W y a : i c n b, d y m t o n.* These letters meant: 'When you answered: it can not be, did you mean then or never?' It seemed impossible that she would be able to understand the complicated sentence.

'I understand', she said, blushing.

'What word is that?' he asked, pointing to the *n* which stood for 'never'.

'The word is "never"', she said, 'but that is not true.' He quickly erased what he had written, handed her the chalk, and rose. She wrote: *I c n a o t.*

His face brightened suddenly: he had understood. It meant: 'I could not answer otherwise then.'

She wrote the initial letters: *s t y m f a f w h.* This meant: 'So that you might forget and forgive what happened.'

He seized the chalk with tense, trembling fingers, broke it, and wrote the initial letters of the following: 'I have nothing to forget and forgive. I never ceased loving you.'

'I understand', she whispered. He sat down and wrote a long sentence. She understood it all and, without asking him whether she was right, took the chalk and answered at once. For a long time he could not make out what she had written, and he kept looking up into her eyes. His mind was dazed with happiness. He was quite unable to fill in the words she had meant; but in her lovely, radiantly happy eyes he read all that he needed to know. And he wrote down three letters. Before he had finished writing, she was already reading under his hand, and she finished the sentence herself and wrote the answer, 'yes.' Everything had been said in their conversation: that she loved him, and would tell her father and mother that he would call in the morning. (*Anna Karenina*, pt. 4, ch. 13.)

This example has an extraordinary psychological interest because, like the whole episode between Kitty and Levin, it was taken by Tolstoy from his own life. In just this way, Tolstoy told his future wife of his love for her. These examples show clearly that when the thoughts of the speakers are the same the role of speech is reduced to a minimum. Tolstoy points out elsewhere that between people who live in close psychological contact, such communication by means of abbreviated speech is the rule rather than the exception.

Now Levin was used to expressing his thought fully without troubling to put it into exact words: He knew that his wife, in such moments filled with love, as this one, would understand what he wanted to say from a mere hint, and she did. (*Anna Karenina*, pt. 6, ch. 3.)

A simplified syntax, condensation, and a greatly reduced number of words characterize the tendency to predication which appears in external speech when the partners know what is going on. In complete contrast to this kind of understanding are the comical mix-ups resulting from people's thoughts going in different directions. The confusion to which this may lead is well rendered in this little poem:

Before the judge who's deaf two deaf men bow.
One deaf man cries: 'He led away my cow.'
'Beg pardon,' says the other in reply,
'That meadow was my father's land in days gone by.'
The judge decides: 'For you to fight each other is a shame.
Nor one nor t'other, but the girl's to blame.'

Kitty's conversation with Levin and the judgement of the deaf are extreme cases, the two poles, in fact, of external speech. One exemplifies the mutual understanding that can be achieved through utterly abbreviated speech when the subject is the same in two minds; the other, the total misunderstanding, even with full speech, when people's thoughts wander in different directions. It is not only the deaf who cannot understand one another but any two people who give a different meaning to the same word or who hold divergent views. As Tolstoy noted, those who are accustomed to solitary, independent thinking do not easily grasp another's thought and are very partial to their own; but people in close contact apprehend one another's complicated meanings by 'laconic and clear' communication in the fewest words.

V

Having examined abbreviation in external speech, we can now return enriched to the same phenomenon in inner speech, where it is not an exception but the rule. It will be instructive to compare abbreviation in oral, inner, and written speech. Communication in writing relies on the formal meanings of words and requires a much greater number of words than oral speech to convey the same idea. It is addressed to an absent person who rarely has in mind the same subject as the writer. Therefore it must be fully deployed; syntactic differentiation is at a maximum; and expressions are used that would seem unnatural in conversation. Griboedov's 'He talks like writing' refers to the droll effect of elaborate constructions in daily speech.

The multifunctional nature of language, which has recently attracted the close attention of linguists, had already been pointed out by Humboldt in relation to poetry and prose – two forms very different in function and also in the means they use. Poetry, according to Humboldt, is inseparable from music, while prose depends entirely on language and is dominated by thought. Consequently, each has its own diction, grammar, and syntax. This is a conception of primary importance, although neither Humboldt nor those who further developed his thought fully realized its implications. They distinguished only between poetry and prose, and within the latter between the exchange of ideas and ordinary conversation, i.e. the mere exchange of news or conventional chatter. There are other important functional distinctions in speech. One of them is the distinction between dialogue and monologue. Written and inner speech represent the monologue; oral speech, in most cases, the dialogue.

Dialogue always presupposes in the partners sufficient knowledge of the subject to permit abbreviated speech and, under certain conditions, purely predicative sentences. It also presupposes that each person can see his partners, their facial expressions and gestures, and hear the tone of their voices. We have already discussed abbreviation and shall consider here only its auditory aspect, using a classical example from Dostoevski's *The Diary of a Writer* to show how much intonation helps the subtly differentiated understanding of a word's meaning.

Dostoevski relates a conversation of drunks which entirely consisted of one unprintable word:

One Sunday night I happened to walk for some fifteen paces next to a group of six drunken young workmen, and I suddenly realized that all thoughts, feelings and even a whole chain of reasoning could be expressed by that one noun, which is moreover extremely short. One young fellow said it harshly and forcefully, to express his utter contempt for whatever it was they had all been talking about. Another answered with the same noun but in a quite different tone and sense – doubting that the negative attitude of the first one was warranted. A third suddenly became incensed against the first and roughly intruded on the conversation, excitedly shouting the same noun, this time as a curse and obscenity. Here the second fellow interfered again, angry at the third, the aggressor, and restraining him, in the sense of 'Now why do you have to butt in, we were discussing things quietly and here you come and start swearing.' And he told this whole thought in one word, the same venerable word, except that he also raised his hand and put it on the third fellow's shoulder. All at once a fourth, the youngest of the group, who had kept silent till then, probably having suddenly found a solution to the original difficulty which had started the argument, raised his hand in a transport of joy and shouted . . . 'Eureka, do you think? I have it? No, not eureka and not I have it'; he repeated the same unprintable noun, one word, merely one word, but with ecstasy, in a shriek of delight – which was apparently too strong, because the sixth and the oldest, a glum-looking fellow, did not like it and cut the infantile joy of the other one short, addressing him in a sullen, exhortative bass and repeating . . . yes, still the same noun, forbidden in the presence of ladies but which this time clearly meant 'What are you yelling yourself hoarse for?' So, without uttering a single other word, they repeated that one beloved word six times in a row, one after another, and understood one another completely. (*The Diary of a Writer*, for 1873.)

Inflection reveals the psychological context within which a word is to be understood. In Dostoevski's story, it was contemptuous negation in one case, doubt in another, anger in the third. When the context is as clear as in this example, it really becomes possible to convey all thoughts, feelings, and even a whole chain of reasoning by one word.

In written speech, as tone of voice and knowledge of subject are excluded, we are obliged to use many more words, and to use them more exactly. Written speech is the most elaborate form of speech.

Some linguists consider dialogue the natural form of oral speech, the one in which language fully reveals its nature, and monologue to a great extent artificial. Psychological investigation leaves no doubt that monologue is indeed the higher, more complicated form, and of later historical development. At present, however, we are interested in comparing them only in regard to the tendency toward abbreviation.

The speed of oral speech is unfavorable to a complicated process of formulation – it does not leave time for deliberation and choice. Dialogue implies immediate unpremeditated utterance. It consists of replies, repartee; it is a chain of reactions. Monologue, by comparison, is a complex formation; the linguistic elaboration can be attended to leisurely and consciously.

In written speech, lacking situational and expressive supports, communication must be achieved only through words and their combinations; this requires the speech activity to take complicated forms – hence the use of first drafts. The evolution from the draft to the final copy reflects our mental process. Planning has an important part in written speech, even when we do not actually write out a draft. Usually we say to ourselves what we are going to write; this is also a draft, though in thought only. This mental draft is inner speech. Since inner speech functions as a draft not only in written but also in oral speech, we shall now compare both these forms with inner speech in respect to the tendency toward abbreviation and predication.

This tendency, never found in written speech and only sometimes in oral speech, arises in inner speech always. Predication is the natural form of inner speech; psychologically, it consists of predicates only. It is as much a law of inner speech to omit subjects as it is a law of written speech to contain both subjects and predicates.

The key to this experimentally established fact is the invariable, inevitable presence in inner speech of the factors that facilitate pure predication: We know what we are thinking about – i.e., we always know the subject and the situation. Psychological contact between partners in a conversation may establish a mutual perception leading to the understanding of abbreviated speech. In inner speech, the 'mutual' perception is always there, in absolute form; therefore, a practically wordless 'communication' of even the most complicated thoughts is the rule.

The predominance of predication is a product of development. In the beginning, egocentric speech is identical in structure with social speech, but in the process of its transformation into inner speech it gradually becomes less complete and coherent as it becomes governed by an almost entirely predicative syntax. Experiments show clearly how and why the new syntax takes hold. The child talks about the things he sees or hears or does at a given moment. As a result, he tends to leave out the subject and all words connected with it, condensing his speech more and more until only predicates are left. The more differentiated the specific function of egocentric speech becomes, the more pronounced are its syntactic peculiarities – simplification and predication. Hand in hand with this change goes decreasing vocalization. When we converse with ourselves, we need even fewer words than Kitty and Levin did. Inner speech is speech almost without words.

With syntax and sound reduced to a minimum, meaning is more than ever in the forefront. Inner speech works with semantics, not phonetics. The specific semantic structure of inner speech also contributes to abbreviation. The syntax of meanings in inner speech is no less original than its grammatical syntax. Our investigation established three main semantic peculiarities of inner speech.

The first and basic one is the preponderance of the *sense* of a word over its *meaning* – a distinction we owe to Paulhan. The sense of a word, according to him, is the sum of all the psychological events aroused in our consciousness by the word. It is a dynamic, fluid, complex whole, which has several zones of unequal stability. Meaning is only one of the zones of sense, the most stable and precise zone. A word acquires its sense from the context in which it appears; in different contexts, it changes its sense. Meaning remains stable throughout the changes of sense. The dictionary meaning of a word is no more than a stone in the edifice of sense, no more than a potentiality that finds diversified realization in speech.

The last words of the previously mentioned fable by Krylov, *The Dragonfly and the Ant*, are a good illustration of the difference between sense and meaning. The words 'Go and dance!' have a definite and constant meaning, but in the context of the fable they acquire a much broader intellectual and affective sense. They mean both 'Enjoy yourself' and 'Perish'. This enrichment

of words by the sense they gain from the context is the fundamental law of the dynamics of word meanings. A word in a
context means both more and less than the same word in isolation:
more, because it acquires new content; less, because its meaning
is limited and narrowed by the context. The sense of a word, says
Paulhan, is a complex, mobile, protean phenomenon; it changes
in different minds and situations and is almost unlimited. A
word derives its sense from the sentence, which in turn gets its
sense from the paragraph, the paragraph from the book, the book
from all the works of the author.

Paulhan rendered a further service to psychology by analysing
the relation between word and sense and showing that they are
much more independent of each other than word and meaning.
It has long been known that words can change their sense. Recently
it was pointed out that sense can change words or, better, that
ideas often change their names. Just as the sense of a word is
connected with the whole word, and not with its single sounds, the
sense of a sentence is connected with the whole sentence, and not
with its individual words. Therefore, a word may sometimes be
replaced by another without any change in sense. Words and
sense are relatively independent of each other.

In inner speech, the predominance of sense over meaning, of
sentence over word, and of context over sentence is the rule.

This leads us to the other semantic peculiarities of inner
speech. Both concern word combination. One of them is rather
like agglutination – a way of combining words fairly frequent
in some languages and comparatively rare in others. German
often forms one noun out of several words or phrases. In some
primitive languages, such adhesion of words is a general rule.
When several words are merged into one word, the new word not
only expresses a rather complex idea but designates all the separate
elements contained in that idea. Because the stress is always on the
main root or idea, such languages are easy to understand. The
egocentric speech of the child displays some analogous phenomena. As egocentric speech approaches inner speech, the child uses
agglutination more and more as a way of forming compound
words to express complex ideas.

The third basic semantic peculiarity of inner speech is the
way in which senses of words combine and unite – a process

governed by different laws from those governing combinations of meanings. When we observed this singular way of uniting words in egocentric speech, we called it 'influx of sense'. The senses of different words flow into one another – literally 'influence' one another – so that the earlier ones are contained in, and modify, the later ones. Thus, a word that keeps recurring in a book or a poem sometimes absorbs all the variety of sense contained in it and becomes, in a way, equivalent to the work itself. The title of a literary work expresses its content and completes its sense to a much greater degree than does the name of a painting or of a piece of music. Titles like *Don Quixote*, *Hamlet*, and *Anna Karenina* illustrate this very clearly; the whole sense of a work is contained in one name. Another excellent example is Gogol's *Dead Souls*. Originally, the title referred to dead serfs whose names had not yet been removed from the official lists and who could still be bought and sold as if they were alive. It is in this sense that the words are used throughout the book, which is built up around this traffic in the dead. But through their intimate relationship with the work as a whole, these two words acquire a new significance, an infinitely broader sense. When we reach the end of the book, 'Dead Souls' means to us not so much the defunct serfs as all the characters in the story who are alive physically but dead spiritually.

In inner speech, the phenomenon reaches its peak. A single word is so saturated with sense that many words would be required to explain it in external speech. No wonder that egocentric speech is incomprehensible to others. Watson says that inner speech would be incomprehensible even if it could be recorded. Its opaqueness is further increased by a related phenomenon which, incidentally, Tolstoy noted in external speech: In *Childhood, Adolescence, and Youth*, he describes how between people in close psychological contact words acquire special meanings understood only by the initiated. In inner speech, the same kind of idiom develops – the kind that is difficult to translate into the language of external speech.

With this we shall conclude our survey of the peculiarities of inner speech, which we first observed in our investigation of egocentric speech. In looking for comparisons in external speech, we found that the latter already contains, potentially at least, the traits typical of inner speech; predication, decrease of vocalization, preponderance of sense over meaning, agglutination, etc., appear under certain conditions also in external speech. This, we believe, is the best confirmation of our hypothesis that inner speech originates through the differentiation of egocentric speech from the child's primary social speech.

All our observations indicate that inner speech is an autonomous speech function. We can confidently regard it as a distinct plane of verbal thought. It is evident that the transition from inner to external speech is not a simple translation from one language into another. It cannot be achieved by merely vocalizing silent speech. It is a complex, dynamic process involving the transformation of the predicative, idiomatic structure of inner speech into syntactically articulated speech intelligible to others.

VI

We can now return to the definition of inner speech that we proposed before presenting our analysis. Inner speech is not the interior aspect of external speech – it is a function in itself. It still remains speech, i.e., thought connected with words. But while in external speech thought is embodied in words, in inner speech words die as they bring forth thought. Inner speech is to a large extent thinking in pure meanings. It is a dynamic, shifting, unstable thing, fluttering between word and thought, the two more or less stable, more or less firmly delineated components of verbal thought. Its true nature and place can be understood only after examining the next plane of verbal thought, the one still more inward than inner speech.

That plane is thought itself. As we have said, every thought creates a connection, fulfills a function, solves a problem. The flow of thought is not accompanied by a simultaneous unfolding of speech. The two processes are not identical, and there is no rigid correspondence between the units of thought and speech. This is especially obvious when a thought process miscarries – when, as Dostoevski put it, a thought 'will not enter words'. Thought has its own structure, and the transition from it to speech is no easy matter. The theater faced the problem of the thought behind the words before psychology did. In teaching his system of acting, Stanislavsky required the actors to uncover the 'subtext' of their lines in a play. In Griboedov's comedy

Woe from Wit, the hero, Chatsky, says to the heroine, who maintains that she has never stopped thinking of him, 'Thrice blessed who believes. Believing warms the heart.' Stanislavsky interpreted this as 'Let us stop this talk'; but it could just as well be interpreted as 'I do not believe you. You say it to comfort me', or as 'Don't you see how you torment me? I wish I could believe you. That would be bliss.' Every sentence that we say in real life has some kind of subtext, a thought hidden behind it. In the examples we gave earlier of the lack of coincidence between grammatical and psychological subject and predicate, we did not pursue our analysis to the end. Just as one sentence may express different thoughts, one thought may be expressed in different sentences. For instance, 'The clock fell', in answer to the question 'Why did the clock stop?' could mean: 'It is not my fault that the clock is out of order; it fell.' The same thought, self-justification, could take the form of 'It is not my habit to touch other people's things. I was just dusting here', or a number of others.

Thought, unlike speech, does not consist of separate units. When I wish to communicate the thought that today I saw a barefoot boy in a blue shirt running down the street, I do not see every item separately: the boy, the shirt, its blue color, his running, the absence of shoes. I conceive of all this in one thought, but I put it into separate words. A speaker often takes several minutes to disclose one thought. In his mind the whole thought is present at once, but in speech it has to be developed successively. A thought may be compared to a cloud shedding a shower of words. Precisely because thought does not have its automatic counterpart in words, the transition from thought to word leads through meaning. In our speech, there is always the hidden thought, the subtext. Because a direct transition from thought to word is impossible, there have always been laments about the inexpressibility of thought:

How shall the heart express itself?
How shall another understand?

F. Tjutchev

Direct communication between minds is impossible, not only physically but psychologically. Communication can be achieved only in a roundabout way. Thought must pass first through meanings and then through words.

We come now to the last step in our analysis of verbal thought. Thought itself is engendered by motivation, i.e., by our desires and needs, our interests and emotions. Behind every thought there is an affective-volitional tendency, which holds the answer to the last 'why' in the analysis of thinking. A true and full understanding of another's thought is possible only when we understand its affective-volitional basis. We shall illustrate this by an example already used: the interpretation of parts in a play. Stanislavsky, in his instructions to actors, listed the motives behind the words of their parts. For example:

Text of the play	*Parallel motives*
SOPHYA	
O, Chatsky, but I am glad you've come.	Tries to hide her confusion.
CHATSKY	
You are glad, that's very nice; But gladness such as yours not easily one tells. It rather seems to me, all told, That making man and horse catch cold	Tries to make her feel guilty by teasing her. Aren't you ashamed of yourself! Tries to force her to be frank.
I've pleased myself and no one else.	
LIZA	
There, sir, and if you'd stood on the same landing here Five minutes, no, not five ago You'd heard your name clear as clear. You say, Miss! Tell him it was so.	Tries to calm him. Tries to help Sophya in a difficult situation.
SOPHYA	
And always so, no less, no more. No, as to that, I'm sure you can't reproach me.	Tries to reassure Chatsky. I am not guilty of anything!

CHATSKY

Well, let's suppose it's so.   Let us stop this conversation;
Thrice blessed who believes.   etc.
Believing warms the heart.

(A. Griboedov, *Woe from Wit*, Act I)

To understand another's speech, it is not sufficient to understand his words – we must understand his thought. But even that is not enough – we must also know its motivation. No psychological analysis of an utterance is complete until that plane is reached.

We have come to the end of our analysis; let us survey its results. Verbal thought appeared as a complex, dynamic entity, and the relation of thought and word within it as a movement through a series of planes. Our analysis followed the process from the outermost to the innermost plane. In reality, the development of verbal thought takes the opposite course: from the motive which engenders a thought to the shaping of the thought, first in inner speech, then in meanings of words, and finally in words. It would be a mistake, however, to imagine that this is the only road from thought to word. The development may stop at any point in its complicated course; an infinite variety of movements to and fro, of ways still unknown to us, is possible. A study of these manifold variations lies beyond the scope of our present task.

Our investigation followed a rather unusual path. We wished to study the inner workings of thought and speech, hidden from direct observation. Meaning and the whole inward aspect of language, the side turned toward the person, not toward the outer world, have been so far an almost unknown territory. No matter how they were interpreted, the relations between thought and word were always considered constant, established forever. Our investigation has shown that they are, on the contrary, delicate, changeable relations between processes, which arise during the development of verbal thought. We did not intend to, and could not, exhaust the subject of verbal thought. We tried only to give a general conception of the infinite complexity of this dynamic structure – a conception starting from experimentally documented facts.

To association psychology, thought and word were united by external bonds, similar to the bonds between two nonsense syllables. Gestalt psychology introduced the concept of structural bonds but, like the older theory, did not account for the specific relations between thought and word. All the other theories grouped themselves around two poles – either the behaviorist concept of thought as speech minus sound or the idealistic view, held by the Würzburg school and Bergson, that thought could be 'pure', unrelated to language, and that it was distorted by words. Tjutchev's 'A thought once uttered is a lie' could well serve as an epigraph for the latter group. Whether inclining toward pure naturalism or extreme idealism, all these theories have one trait in common – their antihistorical bias. They study thought and speech without any reference to their developmental history.

Only a historical theory of inner speech can deal with this immense and complex problem. The relation between thought and word is a living process; thought is born through words. A word devoid of thought is a dead thing, and a thought unembodied in words remains a shadow. The connection between them, however, is not a preformed and constant one. It emerges in the course of development, and itself evolves. To the Biblical 'In the beginning was the Word', Goethe makes Faust reply, 'In the beginning was the deed.' The intent here is to detract from the value of the word, but we can accept this version if we emphasize it differently: In the *beginning* was the deed. The word was not the beginning – action was there first; it is the end of development, crowning the deed.

We cannot close our survey without mentioning the perspectives that our investigation opens up. We studied the inward aspects of speech, which were as unknown to science as the other side of the moon. We showed that a generalized reflection of reality is the basic characteristic of words. This aspect of the word brings us to the threshold of a wider and deeper subject – the general problem of consciousness. Thought and language, which reflect reality in a way different from that of perception, are the key to the nature of human consciousness. Words play a central part not only in the development of thought but in the historical growth of consciousness as a whole. A word is a micro-cosm of human consciousness.

References

GOLDSTEIN, K. (1927), 'Ueber aphasie', *Abh. aus. d. Schiv. Arch. f. Neurol. u. Psychiat.*, Heft 6.

GOLDSTEIN, K. (1932), 'Die pathologischen tatsachen in ihrer bedentung fuer das problem der Sprache', *Kongr. D. Ges. Psychol.*, 12.

PIAGET, J. (1923), *Le Langage et la Pensee chez L'enfant*, Delachaux et Niestle, Neuchatel – Paris.

VYGOTSKY, L. S., and LURIA, A. R. (1929), 'The function and fate of egocentric speech', *Proceed. Ninth Intern. Congr. Psychol.*

Part Four
Cognitive Dimensions of Language: Empirical Studies

This section falls into three parts roughly corresponding to the three theoretical positions presented in Part Three.

1. The first two articles (Readings 12 and 13) demonstrate the power of language to facilitate cognitive change and to facilitate memory. Reading 14 is an unusual study of bilingual women whose responses to questions about themselves varied as a function of the language of the interview, the general topic area and the nationality of the interviewer.

2. Sinclair-de-Zwart (Reading 15) summarizes the Piagetian position on language, subordinating language to logic. She outlines her own supportive experimental work in this area.

3. The section ends with two studies of concept-formation. The first, by Vygotsky (Reading 16), establishes the directive function of the word in the formation of concepts. However, he shows that the child who has the word does not necessarily have the concept. The article by Olver and Hornsby (Reading 17) is a contemporary development of Vygotsky's position.

12 P. Greenfield, L. Reich and R. Olver

On Culture and Equivalence

Excerpt from P. Greenfield, L. Reich and R. Olver, 'On culture and equivalence, 2' in P. Greenfield, L. Reich, R. Olver, *et al*, *Studies in Cognitive Growth*, 1966, Wiley.

There has been much controversy about the place of superordinate words in conceptual thought. The Wolof language, in contrast to French (and to English), has neither the word 'color' nor the word 'shape'. It is clear that the lack of the word 'color' does not hinder color groupings from being formed. Does the absence of the general word, however, mean that the Wolofs have no general concept of color? And if not, of what consequence is this seemingly grievous deficit?

First, it is clear that the use of these general words increases with age among the children who attend school. Only 35 per cent of the Wolof first-graders employ superordinate words, in sharp contrast to 68 per cent of those Wolof sixth-graders questioned in Wolof and 81 per cent of those questioned in French. This sort of finding is in itself nothing new; the same trend has been observed before in the development of children's vocabularies (Brown, 1958). It becomes interesting only when one realizes that such a development only takes place among the unschooled Wolofs to the extent that French words are assimilated into their language, for these words do not exist in Wolof (at least in the perceptual domains relevant to the conceptual content of this experiment). Among the schooled Wolofs, moreover, this development of superordinate words means that French words such as *couleur* (color) and *forme* (form) are being introduced into a Wolof narrative.

But these results still do not answer the question of whether this lexical development (or its absence) has extralinguistic consequences. Consider, therefore, Fig. 1.

If this hierarchical organization corresponds to the type of structure generated by the subject in order to deal with the task,

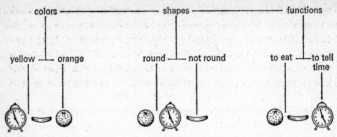

Figure 1 Possible hierarchical organization of first set of pictures[1]

then his use of the superordinate words 'color' or 'shape' should indicate that the person is at the top of the hierarchy and has access to the entire hierarchy. One would predict, then, that he would be able to supply more than one kind of attribute if pressed. For he is plainly contrasting, say, color with shape or with use. By the same reasoning his use of shape names or color names alone (e.g., 'round', 'yellow') would mean that he was operating one level lower in the hierarchy. He would be 'cut off' from the top of the hierarchy and its connections with other branches. He would therefore be less likely to operate in branches other than the one in which he was. A concept (a consciously or explicitly recognized concept) is defined as much by what it excludes as by what it includes, that is, by its contrast class. The concept of color, therefore, comes into being with the appearance of an opposing idea: and this opposing concept cannot exist on the level of specific color names: 'round' is related only to other shapes, 'yellow' only to other colors.

If this reasoning is correct, then one would expect that, if a subject ever used an abstract word like 'color' or 'shape', he would vary his choice of grouping attributes when asked to make a first and second choice of pairs for each of the three sets of pic-

1. Figure 1 illustrates one of the three sets of material referred to in the description of the task. 'The materials consisted of three sets of three pictures each. In each set it was possible to form a pair based on the color, form, or function of the objects pictured. The three sets, displayed successively, were so arrayed that no type of pair appeared twice in the same position. The children were asked to show the experimenter the two pictures out of each set of three that were most alike. They were then asked the reason for their choice.' (Greenfield et al.)

tures. But if he used only a concrete word like 'yellow', then one would expect him to form nothing but color groupings in all six tasks. The results presented in Fig. 2 do indeed indicate that there is an important association between the use of superordinate words like 'color' and 'shape' and the number of different types of attribute used for grouping. The results are presented separately

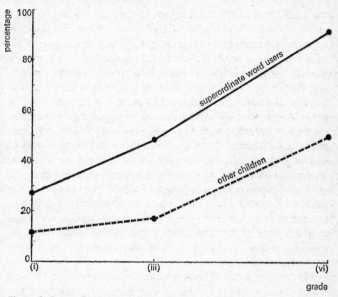

Figure 2 Percentage of Wolof school children using more than one grouping attribute

for each school group, so it is clear that this relationship holds when all other factors such as their knowledge of French and their school grade are held constant. Thus if a Wolof child uses a superordinate word, his chances of grouping by a variety of attributes are twice as great as those of a child who utilizes no superordinate vocabulary. One is reminded that when a Wolof child uses the word 'color', it is the French word that he is introducing into a Wolof linguistic context.

The relationship becomes very weak when the experiment is done in French with Wolof sixth-graders: when the children use superordinate words, 65 per cent of them use more than one type of attribute; when they do not use any of these words, 50 per cent of them use more than one attribute. The difference is comparatively small. The adverse effect on this relationship of doing the experiment in French with Wolof sixth-graders becomes especially interesting when we compare the results obtained with the French children, who also did the experiment in French. We see from Table 1 that the relationship between the use of superordinate words and the ability to shift from one kind of grouping attribute to another is stronger than that obtained not only with the Wolof school children doing the experiment in French, but also with those doing it in Wolof. If a French child uses the abstract top-of-the-hierarchy labels, he is almost certain to vary his basis of grouping at least once. The contrast between the two groups reveals that access to the pure conceptual hierarchy as diagramed is indicated by the use of abstract terms only if the linguistic terms have been thoroughly mastered in all their semantic implications. When the procedure is such that the Wolof children are obliged to speak French, their use of superordinate language seems to have a forced character and indicates little about hierarchical structure and where they are in that structure. Table 1 shows that general superordinate words more frequently imply a corresponding hierarchical structure when the French superordinates are spontaneous interjections in a Wolof context.

The reasons for color preference among the unschooled Wolofs will be discussed shortly. What needs emphasis at this point is that the basis of equivalence is not an either/or phenomenon, as so much experimentation has assumed. It is, rather, a matter of adding new bases to old and of *integrating them in a hierarchically organized structure*. Everybody is more or less limited in the range of classificatory bases available to him. It is not that one person uses color and another, shape. Rather, one can use color, the other can use shape *and* color. It is the structure of the lexicon and not simply its list of terms that is crucial.

Superordinate class words are not just a luxury for people who do not have to deal with concrete phenomena, as Brown (1958) hypothesizes. In a way quite different from that envisaged by Whorf in the lexical version of his hypothesis, we seem to have

Table 1 Percentage of Children Using and Not Using Superordinate Words in Grouping who employ One or More than One Basis for Grouping

| | Superordinate word users | | | | Other children | | | |
	Wolof in Wolof		French in French		Wolof in Wolof		French in French	
Use one attribute	24	42%	2	9%	49	80%	12	75%
More than one attribute	33	58	19	91	12	20	4	25
		100%		100%		100%		100%
Number	57		21		61		16	

found an important correspondence between linguistic and conceptual structure. It relates, however, not to words in isolation but to their depth of hierarchical embedding both in the language and in thought. This correspondence has to do not with quantitative richness of vocabulary in different domains or with 'accessibility' but with the presence or absence of words of a higher order that can be used to integrate different domains of words and objects into hierarchical structures. No matter how rich the vocabulary available to describe a given domain, it is of limited use as an instrument of thought if it is not organized into a hierarchy that can be activated as a whole.

Let us consider now the grammatical aspect of language and its relation to conceptual thought. Our focus switches from semantics to syntactics on the linguistic side, and from content to structure on the conceptual side. Remember that superordinate structure is not the same as the use of a general or superordinate word. The attribute that organizes a superordinate group may be general or specific, but it must be shared by every member of the group in question. Superordinate language structure, moreover, demands that the connection between attribute and group members be explicitly stated. Thus 'They are all the same color' would have the same structural status as 'They are all red'. In terms of this structural criterion we have seen that all the children studied in Senegal conform to the usual developmental trend except the unschooled Wolof group. At this point a set of purely grammatical criteria will be introduced in order to test connections between conceptual and grammatical organization.

On the grammatical side, three stages of symbolic reference may be distinguished. The first is the ostensive mode: mere pointing at the object of reference. The second, the labeling mode, involves a verbal tag. The simplest type of label does nothing more than symbolize the pointing operation in a word – 'this', 'here'. The next type of label is one step removed from this operation: it specifies what is being pointed at; 'yellow' and 'round' are examples of this way of labeling. The third mode is sentential placement. Here the label is integrated into a complete sentence; for example, 'This is yellow', or 'This is round'. In the present experiment these three modes were defined as follows and the definitions applied to grouping reasons:

1. *Pointing* – no verbal response.

2. *Labeling* – tag only; no verb in utterance. Either or both types of label described above could be used. For example, 'This', 'Yellow', and 'This yellow' would all fall in this category.

3. *Sentential placement* – complete sentence. Such a sentence would consist of one or both types of label described above plus a verb. 'They are long' and 'This one is round' are examples of reasons in the sentential mode.

The results of this analysis are presented on page 230. Among French monolinguals, pointing is nonexistent even among first-graders. The ostensive mode, however, occupies a definite position in the reasons of all the youngest Wolof groups, especially the unschooled, but disappears in all groups with advancing age. The other differences set the unschooled children apart from all the schoolchildren. In the unschooled groups labeling increases with age. The use of the sentential mode stays at a constantly low level, although there is some rise in the adult group. By contrast, in all the school groups, both Wolof-French bilingual and French monolingual, labeling gives way to sentential placement with age and increased schooling. The most dramatic contrast is between Wolof school children and those not in school, with virtually no overlap in the distributions of the oldest children. Some 90 per cent of the eleven- to thirteen-year-old monolinguals' reasons are simple labels; 90 per cent of the reasons formulated by the Wolof sixth-graders doing the experiment in French take the form of complete sentences.

Similarly, Deutsch (1965) finds that lower-class New York children, although weak in some usages of language, succeed perfectly well in utilizing its labeling function. And John (1963) shows that these lower-class children can label the elements in a picture as well as middle-class children, but they cannot integrate the labels into a coherent verbal description nearly so well. This is just one of a number of the parallel differences between schooled and unschooled Wolof children and between lower-class (or 'culturally deprived') and middle-class children that were noted.

These results, using purely grammatical criteria, reveal larger differences between the groups who know French and those who do not than did the first, more semantic verbal measure of grouping structure. Is there, however, any direct relation between grammatical and conceptual structure? According to theory a child can frame an explicit superordinate structure (general or itemized) in either the labeling or sentential mode. An example of a general superordinate language structure in the labeling mode would be 'These – round.' Expressed sententially, this structure would be 'These' (or 'They') are round.' An itemized superordinate in labeling form might be 'This – round; this – round.' An example of the same structure expressed in the sentential mode would be 'This' (or 'It') is round; 'This' (or 'It') is round.' Obviously, a limitless variety of nonsuperordinate structures may be expressed either as labels or as complete sentences. It is valid, then, to ask whether the use of a particular mode of reference is associated with a particular conceptual structure. The answer is a strong affirmative for both schooled and unschooled Wolof children. When a school child frames a reason in the sentential mode, the probability that he will form a superordinate structure of either type is on the average almost three times as great as when he uses simple labeling. For an unschooled child, this same probability of a superordinate structure is almost six times as great as when his reasons are sentences rather than labels.

For a school child, moreover, the probability that a superordinate structure will be in a general (rather than an itemized) form is more than four times as great when a grouping reason is expressed in the sentential mode. In the unschooled groups, the number of reasons falling into these categories is very small. If, however, all four unschooled groups are combined, the relationship does hold: superordinate reasons expressed as labels take the general form about half as often as do those expressed as complete sentences.

All these findings concerning the relations between linguistic and conceptual variables contribute important modifications to the picture of culture and equivalence that emerged from the last section. At that point, large differences in conceptual development seemed due to schooling (rather than to the degree of urbanization or to Wolof culture in general). Now, however, schooling has essentially been held constant, whereas linguistic factors have been varied. The positive results produced by this strategy lead to the hypothesis that the school is acting on grouping operations through the training embodied in the written language. This hypothesis has a good theoretical basis. The written language, as Vygotsky (1961) points out, provides an occasion in which one must deploy language out of the immediate referential context. Writing virtually forces a remoteness of reference on the language user; consequently he cannot use simple pointing as an aid, nor can he count on a labeling that depends on the present context to make clear what his label refers to. Writing, then, is a training in the use of linguistic contexts that are independent of the immediate referents. Thus the embedding of a label in a sentence structure indicates that it is less tied to its situational context and more related to its linguistic context. The implications of this fact for the manipulation of concepts are great: linguistic contexts can be turned upside-down more easily than real ones can. Indeed, the linguistic independence of context achieved by certain grammatical modes appears to favor the development of the more self-contained, superordinate structure used by the school children.

For that matter, all of the semantic and syntactic features that have been discussed in relation to concept formation – a rich and hierarchically organized vocabulary, as well as the syntactical embedding of labels – become necessary when one must communicate out of the context of immediate reference. It is precisely in this respect that written language differs from the spoken. The school itself provides an opportunity to use language out of context – even spoken language – for to a very high degree, what one talks about there are things not immediately present. Thus we make no claims that the French language is unique in being able to produce the conceptual effects described above. According to our interpretation, any written language used out of a concrete context should produce these same cognitive results.

The linguistic variables enumerated above are linked in the behavior of these subjects with an earlier accuracy in perceptual discriminations, a more diversified conceptual content in terms of classificatory bases, and a structural representation that is relatively generalized and self-contained (that is, possessing a communication value outside the situation in which it takes form). Thus far the evidence is purely correlational, however. To what extent is language a causative agent in the language–thought relations under discussion? A comparison of the performances of the Wolof sixth-graders doing the picture-grouping experiment in French with those of their classmates who were given the same experiment in Wolof should reveal what effects of school are directly related to the influence of the French language.[1]

We cannot judge whether conducting the experiment in French rather than in Wolof would promote an even earlier accuracy in color discrimination, as no younger children took the experiment in French. But we can test the effect of using French on the growth of superordinate language structures and on the diversification of content, the conceptual variables that correlate with the use of sentences and abstract words. But these conceptual features also correlate with the amount of schooling. Now we will make sure that the learning of a second (written and spoken) language is the key factor in schooling, as far as forming concepts is concerned. Does instruction in spoken and written French make the difference?

It turns out that all the trends in content (Fig. 3) and structure (Fig. 4) related to schooling [. . .] are intensified when the experiment is done in French. This generalization holds for both bush and city children. Thus color is less used by the sixth-grade children who are interrogated in French than by those of the same class and school being questioned in Wolof. Correlatively, shape and function are more frequently used when the sixth-graders speak French (in the latter case only among children in the city). As for nominal classes,[2] French appears to make their use not only increase among the city children but also appear for the very first time among the bush children. The effect of French appears even larger with respect to structure, if we look at the general type of superordinate linguistic structure (Fig. 4). (In contrast, the use of the French language is not associated with a greater frequency of itemized superordinate frames.) This difference between results when the same experiment is done in

1. The effect of inserting French words in a Wolof or French context was explored in connection with superordinate terms, but this is a somewhat different problem.

2. The child's answer falls into the nominal class, when items are grouped by using the conventional name that exists in the language, e.g. 'the apple and the orange are both fruit' [Ed].

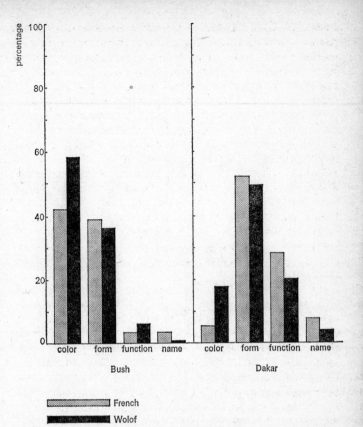

Figure 3 Percentage of four types of grouping reason used by bilingual Wolof children when tested in French and Wolof

Wolof and in French may also indicate that what is learned in one language is less than perfectly 'translatable' into another.

As for the French children, the two categories of attribute that show a developmental increase are exactly as in the United States and Mexico: functional and nominal. Let us now compare these French children with their Wolof counterparts in Dakar. These two groups of children are following identical curricula in school, and they are both from the same city. The only difference is in the depth and extent of the French language and culture

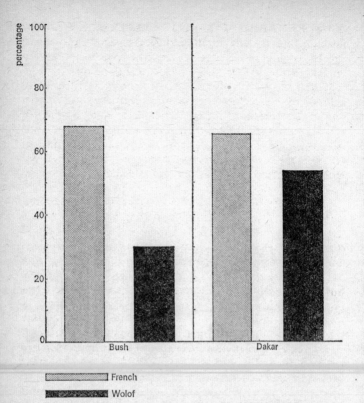

Figure 4 Percentage of grouping reasons expressed in general type of superordinate language structure by bilingual Wolof children when tested in French and Wolof

that they command. It is notable that there is no difference between the Wolof and French children in the development of functional attributes; even from a quantitative viewpoint, the final result is almost precisely the same. The French children show considerably more development of nominal equivalence, however. In the context of so much over-all similarity, this difference assumes a special significance, for the creation of a nominal class is unique in requiring a symbolic transformation that makes the leap from a critical attribute to class name. This leap is symbolic and redundant; it adds no new information about the stimuli not carried by a functional reason. It makes sense that a purely linguistic response (that is, one without referential implications) should be most susceptible to linguistic differences between groups. This point becomes even more intriguing when we consider that the most 'universal' or primary grouping attribute, color, is the one requiring the least symbolic transformation in order to be represented – namely, pointing. In fact, nothing but this action of pointing is required to communicate a color similarity. And recall that the unschooled children did point more often in our experiment. Color differs even from form in this respect, for an image is needed to simultanize the continuous tracing action necessary to represent shape.

In terms of the general type of subordinate grammatical frame, there is no difference between the sixth-grade Wolof children using French and the French children. By the sixth grade 64 per cent of the French children's reasons fall in this category, exactly the proportion observed among the sixth-grade bush children questioned in French (Fig. 4). These French children, however, form far fewer of the itemized type of frame (12 per cent of all reasons) than the Wolof children doing the experiment in French either in the bush (25 per cent of all reasons) or in Dakar (22 per cent). And their total proportion of superordinates is correspondingly less. Evidently, speaking French hinders itemized superordinates while it facilitates general ones, for sixth-grade Wolof children doing the experiment in Wolof form more of these (31 per cent of all reasons in both groups) than do any of the groups questioned in French. Thus the use of the French language *per se* (that is, when all other variables are held constant) augments the frequency of only the most abstract type of structure. Furthermore, the use (rather than the amount of knowledge) seems to be the crucial variable, for the Wolof bilinguals speaking French fare as well in this respect as do the French monolinguals.

Let us take up this same matter in terms of grammatical mode of reference. Table 2 indicates that complete sentences are formulated more readily in French than in Wolof, when there is precisely the same situational context.

Moreover, the use rather than the knowledge of French appears to be the relevant variable, for Wolof bilinguals are highly similar

Table 2 Percentage of Reasons Couched in Different Grammatical Modes

| | Monolingual Wolof | | | | Bilingual Wolof | | | | Monolingual French | |
	6–7	8–9	11–13	Adult	Gr. I	Gr. III	Gr. VI (in Wolof)	Gr. VI (in French)	Gr. I	Gr. VI
Pointing	24%	21%	0%	0	7%	2%	0%	0%	0%	0%
Labeling	64	58	90	62	86	57	31	4	33	12
Sentential	12	21	10	38	7	42	69	96	67	88
	100%	100%	100%	100%	100%	100%	100%	100%	100%	100%
No. of reasons	50	48	30	13	119	129	93	96	46	59

to French monolinguals as far as frequency of using the sentential mode is concerned. But what is the relationship between using French, grammatical mode of reference, and conceptual structure? Labeling reasons are scarce among the Wolof children questioned in French (Table 2), but it is probably meaningful that not a single one expresses a superordinate language structure. In sharp contrast, 82 per cent of the reasons expressed in the sentential mode have a superordinate structure. Taking these sentential superordinates alone, we find that 74 per cent of them are in general form – virtually the same proportion as found among the sixth-grade children questioned in Wolof when they use the sentential mode. This similarity introduces the interesting possibility that French augments the production of general superordinates by causing labels to be embedded in sentential structures. Thus the differences in the frequency of general superordinate linguistic structures between the bilingual groups using Wolof and those using French disappear, if one considers only those reasons that are couched in sentential form.

Conclusion

What has been found in this chapter supports the picture that emerged from a comparison of urban and rural children in Mexico – but it also goes beyond it. For in Senegal, we have discovered a difference between rural children and urban children which parallels that found in Mexico; and, besides, city-living Eskimos are much like urban children studied elsewhere. But though the rural-urban difference is small, it is similar in nature to a larger difference that separates children who have been to school and those who have not. The difference in both cases is most compactly described as a difference between abstractness and concreteness. We believe that the difference between the city child and the rural child derives from a differential exposure to problem solving and communication in situations that are not supported by context – as is the case with, for example, most reading and writing, the use of monetary exchange, and schooling. Rural life, it appears, is somewhat less conducive to the development of abstraction.

But what is most striking is the extension of this difference when we compare schooled and unschooled children. Schooling appears to be the single most powerful factor we have found in the stimulation of abstraction.

Our Eskimo data indicate that the 'egocentric functionalism' of Western children is not a necessary stage in the development of the idea of equivalence. Similarly, the sorting behavior of unschooled Wolof children reveals that a supposedly 'universal' stage in conceptual development, complexive grouping, is less than universal and may be produced by school learning. Complexive grouping may be the first result of the development of a semantic hierarchy of greater depth that permits more flexibility with respect to the bases used in making equivalence judgements. Complexive structure is thus probably more closely linked with the semantic or content side of grouping than with the syntactic side. In fact, neither complexes nor functional attributes are a necessary preliminary to the systematic application of a superordinate rule. What is of such great interest to us is that unschooled children, because they show so little variability in their equivalence behavior (things are always alike in terms of shared color), need not develop explicit forms of superordinate grouping. School children, newly equipped with an enriched hierarchy of possibilities for grouping, must become explicit if they are not to be confused by the changing possibilities that present themselves for forming equivalence groups.

Bush children who do not go to school rely on color attributes at every stage of development; school children, in contrast, move away from an initial reliance on color – the bush children mainly toward form, the city children toward form and function. Thus the school appears to favor the growth of a certain type of perceptual equivalence, namely, equivalence based on form. This result is analogous to the finding that the first result of schooling is to 'perceptualize' a child's approach to conservation. It must be stressed, however, that in both conservation and concept formation this perceptual development is basically a conceptual one. Likely as not, this development is also closely tied to language. By conceptual we mean that school is teaching European habits of perceptual *analysis*. An analysis into parts is plainly crucial to concepts based on the multidimensional attribute of form, whereas unitary global perception could suffice for color grouping. Similarly, the breaking up of innate shape constancies into their component parts of retinal image and angle of view is basic if one is to understand two-dimensional conventions for three-dimensional representation. And we have seen that schooling is required for recognizing objects represented in this way, although not necessarily for dealing with less analytic pictorial representations.

Because the Senegalese school is barely richer in perceptual stimuli than is the world outside, we must look elsewhere for an explanation of the effect of schooling on perceptual analysis. It has been suggested that because one of the universal design features of language is discreteness, that is, a discontinuity of material on all levels from sound to meaning, 'analysis and synthesis are literally *forced* upon anyone who would speak human language. Language, then, breaks up the natural unity of the perceptual world – or at least imposes another structure on it.' But there is more to the matter than just being a language speaker – all children are that. Where there is difference is in how language is used and what opportunities are provided for different uses. Here again, school is important. For it is the school children who have the greater opportunity to practice language in contexts that do not carry the meaning for them automatically, who are forced thereby to use sentences to the full. They are the ones who, moreover, are led by the nature of school lessons to translate their experience and actions into words and sentences that will satisfy a teacher – and thereby learn to reorganize experience and action to conform to the requirements of language. Even in conservation experiments, furthermore, children who did not show conservation were in fact responding to perceptual inequalities, but it was mainly the school children among them who could isolate particular perceptible features and describe them in language.

Now, if perceptual analysis is necessary, then language is crucial as an analytic tool. Where perceptual analysis is not necessary, as in color perception, language is much less important. This formulation is quite different from the Whorfian notion of perception that places the whole burden of explanation on lexical representation and none on the domain being represented. Thus we have seen that color categorizations may be made precisely because they do not demand any linguistic representation at all, whereas nominal classification develops last because it is totally dependent on symbolic representation and transformation. A lexicon at the lowest level of generality is therefore superfluous in determining the content domain of equivalence groupings. But it can affect the perceptual analysis of a given domain, that is, the way in which the domain is subdivided into categories. The fineness of lexical coding can in this way affect the accuracy of perceptual discriminations, at least in children, as our data on color-matching errors indicate.

Language can also act as a synthetic device, once it has broken up the world into pieces. Whereas a lexicon at a single level of generality analyses a given domain into component parts, a lexicon at higher levels synthesizes various domains into unified hierarchical structures.

Not only do linguistic representations have the properties of analysis and synthesis, they also have a potential for self-containment and isolation from context. As with analysis and synthesis, however, this property is not always exploited to the fullest in linguistic performance and therefore cannot be utilized for the symbolic manipulation of experience. It is this feature of linguistic performance that the Senegalese school seems to develop and utilize for the growth of superordinate conceptual structures that are both generalized and context-independent. One must bear in mind that both unschooled Wolofs and those who have had schooling have the linguistic *competence* to form sentences, but their *performances* with respect to this variable are quite different. What makes the difference is that the school children are trained not only in the context-free use of language, but in the written form of language, and in a second language at that – French, which probably has more 'abstract' capacity inherent in it than Wolof. At least, bilingual Wolof children perform more abstractly in French than in their native tongue.

In the end we place great stress on the role of linguistic variables in conceptual growth, at the same time rejecting almost completely Whorf's simple notions about the relation between language and reality.

Looking at cross-cultural differences and cognitive growth from another point of view, Werner (1948) remarked that: 'Development among primitive people is characterized on the one hand by precocity and, on the other, by a relatively early arrest of the process of intellectual growth.'

This is an accurate formulation with respect to the difference between the performance of school children and those who have not been to a Western-style school in the present experiments. The unschooled children early hit on stable rules of color equivalence. School children are perfectly capable of grouping according to color, but they go on to other things. Their progress is therefore sometimes marred by 'errors of growth'. In conservation behavior, too, there is this 'early arrest of the process of intellectual growth' in the unschooled children. And so the differences between those in school and those out increase with age. This has also been a persistent observation concerning the differences between 'culturally deprived' and other American children (Deutsch, 1965; John, 1963). Thus it seems that the conceptual development of lower-class American children resembles that of the unschooled Wolof children in this regard. If so, then early intellectual stabilization signifies that full cognitive skill is not being attained. In short, it appears that some environments 'push' cognitive growth *longer* than do others.

With respect to the growth of representation, what turns out to be virtually impossible for the unschooled Wolofs are cognitive accomplishments that can be carried out *only* by symbolic means, for instance, nominal equivalence and superordinate language structures. To at least some degree school alters both the ikonic and enactive modes of representation by insisting that they be placed in some confrontation with the symbolic mode. So it may be that modern technical societies demand of their members a fundamental cognitive change as their capacities change with biological growth; whereas traditional nontechnical societies demand only the perfection and elaboration of first ways of looking at the world.

References

BROWN, R. W. (1958), *Words and Things*, Free Press.
DEUTSCH, M. (1965), 'The role of social class in language development', *Amer. J. Orthopsychiat.*, vol. 35, pp. 78–88.
JOHN, V. (1963), 'The intellectual development of slum children: some preliminary findings', *Amer. J. Orthopsychiat.*, vol. 33, pp. 813–22.
VYGOTSKY, L. S. (1962), *Thought and Language*, Wiley.
WERNER, H. (1948), *Comparative Psychology of Mental Development*, Follett.

13 De Lee Lantz and V. Stefflre[1]

Language and Cognition Revisited

De Lee Lantz and V. Stefflre, 'Language and cognition revisited', *Journal of Abnormal and Social Psychology* (1964), vol. 69, pp. 172–81.

The general problem with which this study is concerned is the relation between language and nonlinguistic behavior. One position which may be taken is that all languages deal with the same 'reality' and that thought and behavior are independent of the language used by the person. Language is simply used to express what is arrived at independently. Another position is that language shapes the way we experience and conceptualize the world and that our cognitive operations are dependent on the language in which we describe things.

Studies of relationships between language and thought, or language and nonlinguistic behavior, have mainly been of two types: the first type attempts to measure the ease with which the same experiences can be described in different languages – or the ease with which different stimulations can be described in the same language – and relates these measures of codability to the accuracy of retention of the stimuli.

Lenneberg (1953) has developed a methodology for research of this type. His method employs the color continuum, but this is just one example of the type of stimuli that might be used. The words used to describe the color continuum are the designated aspect of the language to be studied. The variable of color terminology which Lenneberg chose to use was codability, which may be defined as the efficiency with which a color can be transmitted in a given language. There are various ways this can be measured. The nonlinguistic behavior to be related to codability was memory, as measured by accuracy of recognition.

A study by Brown and Lenneberg (1954) applied this method. They asked the question: does the differential way we code differ-

1. The authors wish to thank E. H. Lenneberg for his criticism and comments and M. Kahn for his helpful suggestions in preparing this manuscript.

ent areas of the color solid influence other behavior toward color (such as recognition). Codability was the language variable chosen for study. The *measure* of codability used was *intersubject agreement* on naming color chips. The higher the intersubject agreement on a name, the higher the codability for that name, as defined operationally. The cognitive variable they studied was ability to pick from an array of colors one or more colors previously shown to the subject. These two variables were found to be positively correlated. Positive relationships between these same variables, using both colors and photographs of faces, were also found by van De Geer (1960) and van De Geer and Frijda (1960). Glanzer and Clark (1962, 1963) successfully predicted accuracy of reproduction of black and white figures and binary numbers from the brevity of verbal descriptions of these stimuli given by the subjects. This brevity measure was also used by Brown and Lenneberg in developing their original index. These studies seemed to be evidence that ease in naming a stimulus may influence ease in remembering that stimulus.

However, Lenneberg (1961) noted that the conclusions of the Brown and Lenneberg (1954) study could not be generalized beyond the specific stimulus array they used. He compared recognition scores found by Burnham and Clark (1955) using a different array of colors, with naming behavior for that same array from a previous study of his own. This time he found not a positive correlation, but a negative correlation between his measure of codability and recognition. These differing results were explained on the basis of the differences in the color arrays with respect to salient anchoring points. However explained, the fact remained that this measure of codability could not predict recognition for color arrays constructed in very different ways.

The second type of study of the relationship between language and other forms of behavior attempts to predict nonverbal measures of the similarity of pairs of stimuli from properties of the language spoken by subjects from different cultures. For example, the prediction might be made that objects having the same name or requiring the same verb stem will be put into the same category. Carroll and Casagrande (1958) asked Hopi- and English-speaking subjects to decide which two of three pictures 'went together'. The hypothesis was that differences in the lexicons would lead the two groups of subjects to make different judgements. Maclay (1958) and Carroll and Casagrande also investigated grammatical categories used in Navaho and compared the way Navahos and English-speaking Americans sorted objects. The results of these studies have been ambiguous.

The current consensus among those engaged in this type of research (Carroll, 1959; Furth, 1961; Greenberg, 1959; Lenneberg, 1962) appears to be that relations between language and non-linguistic behavior are weak and equivocal. An alternative interpretation might be that we have not yet developed adequate techniques for prediction of other forms of behavior from language or verbal responses. We will describe below some alternative measures of codability and item-item similarity. These are members of a large family of possible techniques described in Stefflre (1963).

We will view memory as though it were a situation in which an individual communicates to himself through time using the brain as a channel. This communication process can be approximated by having individuals communicate with other people. Items accurately communicated interpersonally would then be predicted to be more accurately communicated intrapersonally as measured by the usual memory tests. And, pairs of items confused in interpersonal communication would tend to be confused in tests of memory.

Thus, for our measure of codability, people were presented with a stimulus array and asked to make up messages that would enable another person to pick out the stimulus it refers to – for example, 'describe this item in such a way that another person will be able to pick it out.' In this way we can measure the accuracy with which each item can be communicated by the messages composed by the subjects. This offers a direct measure of codability rather than the indirect measures such as agreement among people in selection of names (Brown and Lenneberg, 1954) or the mean number of words in the description (Glanzer and Clark, 1962). Stefflre used this direct measure of codability to predict recognition of pictures (1958) and recall of nonsense syllables (1963).

To attempt to predict confusions among color chips in the recognition task several techniques are possible. A measure of the tendency of chips to be confused in the communications task can be compared with a measure of confusions in recognition, or a measure of subjects' tendency to describe pairs of stimuli in the same way can be used as a measure of item-item similarity (Stefflre, 1958). Here we asked the subject which color chip was the most 'typical' of the description he had given for each chip.

This experiment attempts to unravel the conflicting relations found between codability and recognition in the studies of Brown and Lenneberg (1954) and Lenneberg (1961) by using a different measure of codability. We predicted that communication accuracy (as our measure of codability will be referred to) will correlate positively with recognition for both the original Brown-Lenneberg color array and the Farnsworth-Munsell color array, which, it will be recalled, yielded a negative correlation between recognition and the Brown and Lenneberg measure of codability, name agreement (Lenneberg, 1961). We also examined the Glanzer and Clark (1962) measure (brevity of descriptions) in relation to our stimulus materials. Finally, we wished to see if our measures of item-item similarity allowed us to predict the pattern of errors found in the recognition task.

Method

Subjects

College undergraduates were used. All subjects were native English speakers who had had no specialized training with color. They were screened for color blindness.

Stimulus materials

Two sets of Munsell color arrays were used: a portion of the Farnsworth-Munsell 100 Hue Test and the Munsell colors used by Brown and Lenneberg (1954). The Farnsworth-Munsell array is a circular array of colors varying only in hue and having nearly constant saturation and brightness (Farnsworth, 1949). These colors are perceptually equidistant steps apart. The array consists of Munsell color papers mounted in black plastic caps.

The Brown-Lenneberg array varies on both hue and brightness, saturation being relatively constant. It is constructed so as to sample the outer shell of the color space evenly (highest saturation). They are not perceptually equidistant steps apart. These colors were mounted on cards.

Test apparatus

The apparatus used for showing the Farnsworth-Munsell array was a modified version of the apparatus used by Burnham and Clark (1955). It consists of a wheel on which two sets of chips are mounted in concentric circles. There are twenty chips on the inner circle. We will refer to these as the 'test colors', since they are the ones on which subjects were tested in the memory task. The outer circle consists of forty-three colors – to be referred to as 'comparison colors' – including duplicates of the twenty test colors. The wheel itself is enclosed in a case with a flat black finish. When the lid of the case is closed, a handle for rotating the wheel protrudes through the center. Near the edge of the cover is a set of four sliding panels that may be opened individually or together to present to the subject's view one to four of the test chips in the inner circle. Another aperture allows the subject to see the comparison colors in the outer circle one at a time.

No special apparatus was used to present the Brown-Lenneberg colors. The twenty-four test colors were mounted on individual 3×5 cards. Mounted on a large chart were 120 comparison colors, including duplicates of the twenty-four test colors. The chart was covered by a curtain which could be pulled back to reveal the chart to the subject. Throughout all the procedures, General Electric standard daylight fluorescent lights were used.

Procedures

Codability. It was first necessary to establish codability scores for each test color in the two stimulus arrays. Codability was measured in three ways: by *communication accuracy*, *naming agreement*, and *brevity of description*. Communication accuracy is the measure we described in the introduction which we feel will more adequately predict nonlinguistic behavior than previously used measures. Naming agreement is the measure used by Brown and Lenneberg (1954), and brevity of description is the measure used by both Brown and Lenneberg and Glanzer and Clark (1962, 1963).

Communication accuracy is a measure of how accurately a color can be communicated. If one person names a color, and that name is given to another person, how accurately can he pick out that same color from an array? Communication accuracy required two groups of subjects: one group who named colors and another group who received the names and tried to find the colors the names originally referred to.

These two groups can be called, respectively, *encoders* and *decoders*. For the Farnsworth-Munsell array, the general procedure for encoding was to show each of twenty subjects (ten men and ten women) the twenty test colors one at a time in the modified Burnham-Clark-Farnsworth-Munsell apparatus. The following instructions were given:

I'm going to show you some colors, one at a time, through this opening and I'd like you to name each color using the word or words you would use to name it to a friend so that he or she could pick it out. Do it as quickly as you can, but take time to be satisfied with your answer. Before we begin, I'll show you the colors you'll be naming. [This is to give the subject a chance to see the range of colors he will be naming.] All right, we're ready to begin. Here's the first color. [The color was then shown through one of the openings.]

The next step in determining communication accuracy for the Farnsworth-Munsell colors was having another group of subjects decode the names given by the first group. Since there were twenty encoders and each named twenty colors, there was a total of 400 messages to be decoded. This was obviously too many messages to ask each subject to decode. Therefore, four messages (or names) from each encoder's total of twenty were read to each subject, making a total of eighty randomized messages for him to decode. In this way individual differences in the subjects' encoding and decoding ability would affect all colors equally. Twenty decoders were used. Every message from each encoder was decoded four times by different receivers. Therefore, each color had eighty decoded messages.

The decoding subjects were shown the eighty-five Farnsworth-Munsell colors with these instructions:

I'm going to read some color names to you, one at a time. After I say a name, look at the colors in front of you and point to the color that seems to be the color that name refers to.

The experimenter began reading the names and wrote down the

Farnsworth-Munsell number (written on the underside of the cap) of the color chosen.

By comparing the degree of accuracy with which decoders could refer back to the color the encoder had originally described, a score of communication accuracy could be obtained for each color. Communication accuracy can be scored simply by determining the number of correctly decoded messages regarding each chip or by calculating the mean error score for each chip. This latter procedure entailed recording the difference between the code number of the chip each decoder selected when read a name and the code number of the chip to which the encoder originally gave the name, dropping the sign, and then summing the differences for all the messages referring to a chip and dividing by N. This averaging procedure was possible because Farnsworth-Munsell code numbers correspond to hue steps and the steps are perceptually equidistant. These two ways of computing communication accuracy were found to correlate 0·712 with one another. Since there was a wider range of scores and fewer ties with the mean error score it was used as the measure of communication accuracy for these chips.

The procedure for establishing communication accuracy for the Brown-Lenneberg colors was essentially the same. The twenty-four test colors were shown to the subject one at a time on 3×5 cards. The naming instructions were the same as for the Farnsworth-Munsell subjects and the same kind of decoding procedure was followed. Scores for communication accuracy for the Brown-Lenneberg colors were simply the number of correct selections made by decoders. Since the colors are not equidistant and they vary on two dimensions, a mean error score could not be computed.

The second measure of codability was naming agreement. The scores for naming agreement were derived from the data from the first group of subjects, the encoders. The Brown and Lenneberg computational formula was used. The naming agreement score for a particular color was determined by the amount of intersubject agreement on naming that color. While some colors are consistently given the same name by most speakers, others are given a variety of names. From the total of twenty responses given to a color, the number of *different responses* was subtracted from the number of times the most *common response* was given. A constant of twenty was added to keep the resulting scores positive.

The third measure of codability was brevity of descriptions. The brevity score for each color chip was the mean number of words used to describe that chip.

Recognition. To be related to these measures of our linguistic variable, codability, was a nonlinguistic memory task. For both sets of stimulus materials, three different recognition conditions were used. Condition 1 consisted of showing the subject one color at a time for five seconds followed by a five-second interval, after which the subject was instructed to find the color just shown him. In Condition 2, four colors were presented simultaneously for five seconds, and after a five-second interval the subject was asked to find each of the four colors. Condition 3 presented four colors for five seconds followed by a thirty-second interval after which the subject was asked to find the colors.

The subjects using the Farnsworth-Munsell array were told:

You will be shown one [four] color[s] at a time through this opening [referring to the openings in the test wheel]. You will have five seconds to look at it, then it will be covered for five [thirty] seconds. After that time I'll give the wheel a turn and open this hole [referring to the opening above the comparison chips]. You take the wheel and find the color[s] you were just shown.

For the Brown-Lenneberg array, the recognition procedure consisted of holding one or four colors in front of the subject for five seconds. Also in front of the subjects was the randomized chart of 120 comparison colors which was covered by a draw-curtain while the test chips were being presented and during the interval following the presentation. After the interval, the curtain was drawn and the subject tried to find the colors he had just been shown.

Recognition scores were necessarily computed slightly differently for the two arrays, again because the Brown-Lenneberg colors were not amenable to a mean error score. The Farnsworth-Munsell recognition score was obtained by recording the difference between the code number of the comparison chip selected by the subject and the code number of the test chip presented. The total score for a chip was the sum of each of these individual scores divided by N. This yielded a mean error score for each chip which could be compared to the mean error score for communication accuracy for that chip.

The method used for obtaining recognition scores for the Brown-Lenneberg colors was that originally devised by Brown and Lenneberg (1954). The number of correct identifications made by each subject was found and considered to be unity. Each individual correct response was given a fractional value of unity. The score for each color was the sum of all twenty subjects' fractional scores for that color.

The Farnsworth-Munsell colors were also scored this way to determine the comparability of the mean error scores and the scores weighted to take account of a subject's ability to correctly identify colors, that is, the Brown and Lenneberg formula. There was a rank-order correlation of 0·801 between the two ways of scoring the Farnsworth-Munsell results. The mean error score was used in preference to the fractional score because it is directly comparable to the scores for other measures of the same data, which the fractional score is not.

Measure of item-item similarity. In the introduction we referred to the giving of the same name to more than one color chip as a measure of similarity. We obtained this measure by asking the subjects for the most 'typical' instance of each name they used. After the encoders had given names to the twenty test colors, they were shown the entire Farnsworth-Munsell array of eighty-five colors, or the chart of 120 Brown-Lenneberg colors. The subject was told:

I'm going to read back to you, one at a time, the names you just gave me. When I say the name, look at the colors on the table and point to the 'best' example, or the most 'typical' example of that name. You may choose the one to which you originally gave the name, but there may be another color you think is an even better example of that name. If so, point to that one.

Results
Codability and recognition

Our hypothesis was that communication accuracy is a superior measure of codability and therefore would be a better predictor of memory than the other measures of codability which have been used. Communication accuracy should therefore correlate more highly with all recognition conditions on both the Farnsworth-Munsell and the Brown-Lenneberg color arrays. It was also our expectation that communication accuracy would predict recognition for any color array, no matter how the array is constructed, whereas naming agreement probably would predict only for specific kinds of arrays, such as the Brown-Lenneberg array. The results of Spearman rank-order correlations among the variables are shown in Table 1 and intercorrelations among the codability measures are shown in Table 2. As predicted, communication accuracy was positively correlated with both sets of stimulus materials. (See Figs. 1 and 2 for a graphic illustration of the strength of this relationship.) Moreover, communication accuracy was an even better predictor of Brown-Lenneberg recognition scores than the Brown-Lenneberg measure of naming agreement.

Table 1 Correlations between Codability Measures and Recognition Conditions

Codability	Recognition condition		
	1	2	3
Farnsworth-Munsell array			
Communication accuracy	0·32	0·71***	0·66**
Naming agreement	−0·18	−0·05	−0·30
Brevity of description	−0·29	0·31	0·23
Brown-Lenneberg array			
Communication accuracy	0·51**	0·86***	0·78***
Naming agreement	−0·02	0·40*	0·32
Brevity of description	0·19	0·42*	0·33

 * $p \leqslant 0.05$.
 ** $p \leqslant 0.01$.
 *** $p \leqslant 0.001$.

While naming agreement did correlate significantly with the second recognition condition for the Brown-Lenneberg colors, it was not correlated with recognition of the Farnsworth-Munsell colors, as Lenneberg (1961) had reasoned. As one would expect communication accuracy and naming agreement correlated -0.10 (*ns*) with each other on the Farnsworth-Munsell data, and 0.43 ($p < 0.05$) on the Brown-Lenneberg data. We examined the correlation between naming agreement and Recognition Condition 2 on the Brown-Lenneberg array (the best of the naming agreement predictions) to see what would remain when communication accuracy was partialed out. The resulting partial correlation was 0.06. Thus, it is because naming agreement is related to communication accuracy for the Brown-Lenneberg array that it is able to predict, not because of anything unique to naming agreement.

Table 2 Intercorrelations between Measures of Codability

Measure	Name agreement	Brevity of description
Farnsworth-Munsell array		
Communication accuracy	-0.10	0.13
Naming agreement		0.09
Brown-Lenneberg array		
Communication accuracy	0.43	$0.45*$
Naming agreement		$0.54**$

* $p \leqslant 0.05$.
** $\leqslant 0.01$.

We also examined the relationship between Glanzer and Clark's (1962, 1963) measure of brevity of description and recognition. None of the correlations between this measure and the recognition conditions was significant for the Farnsworth-Munsell color array, nor was brevity of description found to be significantly correlated with naming agreement or communication accuracy for these colors. For the Brown-Lenneberg array, the correlation between brevity of description and recognition reached significance on Condition 2. The rather close parallel between the naming agreement and brevity of description correlations with recognition conditions for the Brown-Lenneberg colors suggests that these two codability measures are related for this array. The correlation between naming agreement and brevity of description was found to be 0·54 ($p < 0·01$). Since we know naming agreement and communication accuracy are related for this array, we would, then, also expect a relationship between brevity of description and communication accuracy. That correlation was 0·45 ($p < 0·05$). Again, a partial correlation was made between brevity of description and the Brown-Lenneberg Recognition Condition 2 with communication accuracy held constant. And, as with naming agreement, the correlation dropped to 0·07.

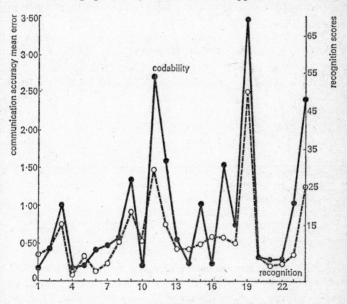

Figure 1 Relationship between codability and combined recognition scores (all three conditions) for Brown-Lenneberg colors

Thus, communication accuracy is a codability measure superior to naming agreement and brevity of description, both in strength of relationship and in ability to predict regardless of what kind of stimulus array is used. Where the latter two measures do predict, it is because, in those cases, they are related to communication accuracy.

In both stimulus arrays, the correlation between codability and recognition was greatest for the second recognition condition (four colors, five-second interval). However, although Conditions 2 and 3 both differed significantly from Condition 1 in number of errors made, they did not differ significantly from one another

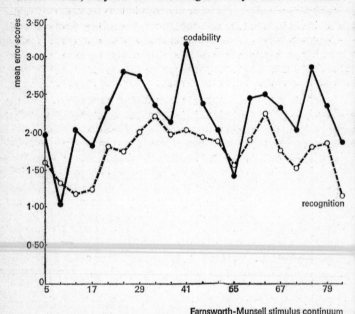

Figure 2 Relationship between codability and combined recognition scores for Farnsworth-Munsell colors

(as determined by t tests). Brown and Lenneberg discussed their lack of correlation between codability and recognition in Condition 1 (which we also found) as possibly being due to the shortness of time between presentation of the test chip and recognition. Direct visual memory can be relied on for a five-second interval, but when several colors must be remembered, or when there is a longer interval, the necessity of storing a name is increased.

There were two kinds of data on judgements of the 'typical instance' of a color. First, there were *aggregate* typical judgements for each chip, where each of the twenty encoders found the most typical example for his name for that chip. For chip number 55 of the Farnsworth-Munsell array, for example, there are typical judgements for nine names for that chip, because nine different names were given by the twenty subjects. A single typical judgement was scored by taking the difference between the number of the chip to which the name was originally given and the chip that was judged to be the best example of that name. The twenty judgements were averaged, keeping the sign, and this average was the overall typical score for that chip. For chip 67, the average of the typical judgements was $+0.925$, meaning that, on the average, the color nearly one hue step beyond number 67 was judged by the subjects to be a better example of the names elicited by 67 than 67 itself.

The relationship between the mean recognition errors and the judgements of the typical instance for that chip was examined (see Fig. 3). Errors in recognition went in the same direction as the judgement of the typical sixteen out of twenty times. A sign test for the sameness of direction was significant at the 0·01 level. But more than this, not only did recognition errors go in the direction of the typical instance, they were less extreme than the typical. That is, they assimilated toward it. There are only two exceptions to this – chips 55 and 59, where the recognition errors were slightly more extreme than the typical.

Although the results were quite marked, one might argue that these were, after all, aggregated judgements and may or may not have anything to do with what goes on in the individual. Therefore a second means of examining the relations between recognition errors and judgements of the typical was used. A group of fifteen subjects were asked individually to name the color chips, select the typical chips for those names, and then were given the recognition test as in Condition 2. The chip each subject picked as his recognition response for each of the test chips could then be compared with the chip he had picked as 'typical' for the name he had given the test chip. We then compared for each chip the number of people making errors in the

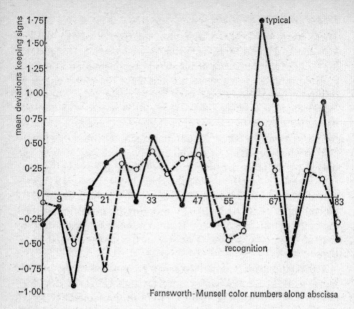

Figure 3 Relationship of combined recognition scores to judgements of the typical

expected direction – that is, toward the chip they had picked as typical – with the number making errors in the opposite direction. For five chips a majority went in the expected direction while for fifteen chips the majority went in the other direction (away from the typical). A result like this would occur less than once in twenty times through chance, but it was, interestingly enough, in the wrong direction.

Considering this paradoxical result we decided that by asking the subject to select the chips typical of his description before he attempted the recognition task we were forcing him during recognition to reconsider the adequacy of his original descriptions. That is, we were warning our subjects against the phenomena we were attempting to demonstrate and altering the ways in which stimuli were encoded in the recognition task. To test this speculation ten more subjects were run but the order of tests reversed. First these subjects were given a recognition task, then they were asked to name the color chips, and finally they were asked to select the chips typical of each of the names. This alternation in procedure led seventeen of the chips to exhibit more errors in the expected direction (toward the typical) and three chips to exhibit more in the opposite direction. This result was beyond the 0·002 level of significance, and in the expected direction.

It has been our experience that any modification in an experimental procedure that alters the way subjects describe the situation to themselves may alter the results of the experiment. The example above is simply one case in point.

Discussion

The results are clear-cut evidence that communication accuracy is a superior predictor of memory for colors than naming agreement or brevity of description. It is superior in two senses: it correlates more highly with recognition results than do the other measures, and it predicts for at least two very different stimulus arrays, which naming agreement and brevity of description do not. It thereby brings together what were formerly disparate results.

It had previously been assumed that communality in verbal response reflected ease and accuracy in communication. The fact that naming agreement and communication accuracy were not highly positively correlated demonstrates that this assumption is not justified. These measures will not correlate when the appearance of numerous names simply indicates a proliferation of vocabulary for describing the item, or when there are a number of items in the stimulus array that are all named in the same way. Naming agreement will predict recognition only when it reflects communications differences.

The nature of the context in which a color – and presumably any other sensory stimulus – is found is very important in determining what kind of verbal measure will successfully predict non verbal behavior in regard to it. For example, a color called 'blue' by 100 per cent of the subjects (high naming agreement) will almost always be correctly decoded (high communication accuracy) if it is set in a context of reds, yellows, oranges, and greens. It will also be recognized quite easily. In this case, naming agreement and communication accuracy will correlate with one another and both will predict recognition. If that same color is in a context of twenty other shades of blue, there may still be high communality in naming it 'blue', but ease of recognition would be sharply altered, as would communication accuracy. Here the communication accuracy measure reflects the effects of context on ease of recognition, while naming agreement does not. If the nonverbal measures obtained on a given item can be radically altered by context – as recognition can – then the verbal measure from which we are trying to predict should also have this property, as communication accuracy does.

Communication accuracy also predicted far better than the brevity of description measure for the type of stimulus arrays used here. For a fair test of the relative generality of the two measures, communication accuracy should be obtained on the Glanzer and Clark stimulus materials to determine if it would still predict as well or better than brevity of description.

The communication accuracy technique described here will fail to work under certain conditions. If we used subjects who each had a different native language but shared a common *lingua franca* the intrapersonal coding for each individual might be in his native language while the interpersonal communication would be in the *lingua franca*. Here communication accuracy would not predict recognition. Also, if our stimuli were of a type such that each individual had his own personal language to describe it to himself, and used a different description for interpersonal communication, the relation between codability and recognition could be sharply attenuated. The private and the public descriptions may have very different properties in terms of their adequacy in communicating specific stimulus materials and in the pattern of errors they imply.

The key problem in predicting memory from the interpersonal measures is to insure that the descriptions given by the encoding subjects are comparable to the descriptions given by the recognition subjects. The kind of incomparability described above is obvious. However, minor differences in the situation in which the verbal measures are obtained and that in which the nonverbal measures are obtained may also lead to differences in the way stimuli are described in the two situations. For example, the subjects in the recognition task in this study necessarily saw the entire array of comparison colors on their first trial. Having seen all the colors may have led them to describe the test chips to themselves differently than if they had not seen them. Therefore, we showed the subjects who named colors (the encoders) the entire array before they began their task. This procedure was followed in order to make the situation in which the verbal data were obtained as equivalent as possible to that in which the non-verbal data were obtained. It is difficult to tell what alterations in the situation may make a difference in how subjects describe even such simple stimuli as color chips. Therefore, everything possible should be done to assure comparability, for otherwise verbal measures will not predict nonverbal measures effectively. Fortunately, it is usually possible to test directly to see if the descriptions given in the encoding situation are in fact comparable to the descriptions generated covertly by the subjects in the nonverbal task.

The kind of formulation presented here of relations between language and behavior emphasizes the productivity of language – new descriptions may be formed spontaneously and function to encode stimuli effectively. For example, 'light sky blue with a tinge of pink' may communicate (either to oneself or to another) quite well, while a more commonly agreed upon name such as 'blue' may not be so effective. Any description of the relations between language and behavior or language and thought that does not take this into account and emphasizes only the role of dictionary words and/or grammatical categories will find it difficult to deal with the facts found in a particular experimental context.

Although the correlations found in this study between language and non-linguistic behavior are striking, it might be argued that they do not necessarily demonstrate any causal relations. However, Lantz (1963) was able to manipulate the relationship experimentally. She taught subjects new names for previously poorly communicated chips and in this way increased the accuracy with which they were recognized. This type of experimental procedure allows inferences to be made about causal relations.

References

BROWN, R. W., and LENNEBERG, E. H. (1954), 'A study in language and cognition', *J. abnorm. soc. Psychol.*, vol. 49, pp. 454–62.

BURNHAM, R. W., and CLARK, J. R. (1955), 'A test of hue memory', *J. appl. Psychol.*, vol. 39, pp. 164–72.

CARROLL, J. B. (1959), 'Language and thought studied across languages: a report of the "Southwest Project"', paper read at American Psychological Association, Cincinnati, September.

CARROLL, J. B., and CASSAGRANDE, J. B. (1958), 'The function of language classification in behavior', in Eleanor E. Maccoby, T. M. Newcomb, and E. L. Hartley (eds.), *Readings in Social Psychology* (3rd edn.), Holt, Reinhart & Winston, pp. 18–31.

FARNSWORTH, D. (1949), *The Farnsworth-Munsell 100 Hue Manual*, Munsell Color Company, Baltimore.

FURTH, H. (1961), 'The influence of language on the development of concept formation in deaf children', *J. abnorm. soc. Psychol.*, vol. 63, pp. 386–9.

GLANZER, M., and CLARK, W. H. (1962), 'Accuracy of perceptual recall: an analysis of organization', *J. verbal. Learn. verbal Behav.*, vol. 1, pp. 225–42.

GLANZER, M., and CLARK, W. H. (1963), 'The verbal loop hypothesis: binary numbers', *J. verbal Learn. verbal Behav.*, vol. 2, pp. 301–9.

GREENBERG, J. H. (1959), 'Current trends in linguistics', *Science*, vol. 130, pp. 1165–70.

LANTZ, DELEE, (1963), 'Color naming and color recognition: a study in the psychology of language', unpublished doctoral dissertation, Harvard University.

LENNEBERG, E. H. (1954), 'Cognition in ethnolinguistics', *Language*, vol. 29, pp. 463–71.

LENNEBERG, E. H. (1961), 'Color naming, color recognition, color discrimination: a re-appraisal', *Percept. mot. Skills*, vol. 12, pp. 375–92.

LENNEBERG, E. H. (1962), 'The relationship of language to the formation of concepts', *Synthese*, vol. 14, pp. 103–9.

MACLAY, H. (1958), 'An experimental study of language and nonlinguistic behavior', *SW. J. Anthropol.*, vol. 14, pp. 220–9.

STEFFLRE, V. (1958), 'An investigation of the role of language in E. Heidbreder's experiments on concept formation', unpublished honors thesis, Reed College.

STEFFLRE, V. (1963), 'An outline for the study of some relations between language and nonlinguistic behavior', paper read at Social Science Research Council Conference on Transcultural Studies of Cognitive Processes, Mérida, Yucatan, June.

VAN DE GEER, J. P. (1960), *Studies in Codability, no. 1: Identification and Recognition of Colors*, report no. 60, Psychological Institute, State University of Leyden, The Netherlands.

VAN DE GEER, J. P., and FRIJDA, N. H. (1960), *Studies in Codability: no. 2: Identification and Recognition of Facial Expression*, report no. E002-60, Psychological Institute, State University of Leyden, The Netherlands.

14 S. Ervin-Tripp

An Analysis of the Interaction of Language, Topic and Listener[1]

S. Ervin-Tripp, 'An analysis of the interaction of language, topic and listener', *American Anthropologist* (1964), vol. 66, pp. 94–100.

A Japanese bilingual experiment

Bilingual speech is convenient to study because the formal changes are vividly apparent. There are many forms of social relation between two language communities. American immigrants, for example, range through a wide spectrum in the diversity of function-language distributions. At one extreme might be an old storekeeper in Chinatown. He rarely needs any knowledge of English except to ask limited-response questions of his customers, or to tell the cost of an item. On the whole, he is like a tourist with request forms and a vocabulary limited to the goods or services exchanged. If he employs English in restricted settings, he may succeed in communicating with a minimum of knowledge of English grammar or phonology.

At the opposite extreme are immigrants who have married Americans and raised families here. They typically vary widely in the functional distribution of their use of English, frequently employing English for as many uses as their native language at home before. The limitations in their use of English occur in certain aspects of the code. They may have little gaps in their English vocabulary, reflecting differential exposure, for instance, to rural life in the two countries. They may have difficulties learning a new sound system after adolescence; it is clear that aptitude, personality, and perhaps willingness to lose one's identity as a foreigner vary. Japanese women, for example, often do not respect Nisei, and

1. The point of view and the sources in this article have both been enriched by discussions with Dell Hymes and John Gumperz. The study of Japanese bilinguals mentioned below was supported by the National Science Foundation. The author is especially grateful to Yaeko Nishijima Putzar and Naomi Litt Quenk for their work on this project.

may not wish to be taken for Nisei. Yet it is common to find women who have extensive mastery of the vocabulary and grammar of English, and whose English dominance is so great that they may be unable to speak their native tongue without intrusions at all levels from English.

The first step in the experimental study of Japanese-American speech in terms of the topic-audience-language correlations was an ethnographic description of their covariance, based on informant interviews. Thousands of Japanese women marry Americans every year, and come to this country to live and to raise their American offspring. In the San Francisco area, they are generally isolated socially from the American Japanese who seem un-Japanese to them, from the immigrant Japanese, who are older and of rural backgrounds, and from the temporary officials and business personnel from Japan. Usually they do not live in areas with Japanese shops. As a result of their isolation, they use Japanese in three situations: visits to Japan; jobs (for some) in Japanese restaurants; and talks with bilingual friends. The women who took part in the study usually had friends who were also 'war brides'. These were their confidantes, their recourse when worried. With these friends, in Japanese, they reminisced about Japan, discussed news from home, gossiped; Japanese was the language of social interchange and expressive monologues.

By contrast, the functions of English covered a varying range for different women. For all, it was the language for talking of goods and services, for shopping. In a few marriages, the husband was a companion and confidant, teaching a large variety of English words, teaching about American activities and values, discussing many topics. Such women had learned the subtleties of social interchange in English. In other families, the absence of the husband at sea, or his silence, left the wife with little occasion to use English at home. One woman who spoke little English at the time of her marriage reported that the couple 'spoke the language of the eyes'. It is quite clear that there was not an equivalent distribution of functions for Japanese and English for most of the women interviewed.

The women spoke English primarily with their husbands, children, and neighbors. We would expect that when they spoke English the content would reflect the objects, experiences, and points of view encountered in this country. With their Japanese friends, language shifted with topic – American food, clothing, and husbands being discussed in English, and matters Japanese, or personal concerns being discussed in Japanese. Some reported never using English with Japanese friends except when the husbands were present, a situation presumably altering the topical distribution of conversations.

Language and content

Our first hypothesis is that as language shifts, content will shift. This hypothesis was tested earlier for French and American content (Ervin, 1964; Lambert, 1963). In this case, we have the explicit hypothesis that wherever monolingual American women and Japanese women tested in Japan differ in content, the bilingual women will tend to show an analogous content shift with language, even though the situations are otherwise identical. A Japanese interviewer saw each woman twice in the same setting, and tape recorded the sessions. At the first, only Japanese was used, and at the second, only English. Verbal materials employed were word associations, sentence completions, semantic differentials, problem stories, and Thematic Apperception Tests.

Here are some illustrative examples, the speaker being the same for the Japanese and English. Where the American and Japanese monolingual comparison groups gave a particular item uniquely or more frequently than the other language group, the word is marked with (A) or (J).

Moon
(Japanese) moon-viewing (J), zebra-grass (J), full moon (J), cloud (J)
(English) sky (A), rocket (A), cloud (J)
New Year's Day
(Japanese) pine decoration (J), rice-cake (J), feast (J), kimono (J), seven-spring-herbs (J), shuttlecock (J), tangerine (J), foot-warmer (J), friends (A)
(English) new clothes, party (A), holidays (A)
Tea
(Japanese) bowl (J), saucer (A), green (J), tea-cake (J), tea-ceremony (J)

(English) teapot, kettle, tea leaf (A), party (A), green tea (J),
lemon (A), sugar (A), cookies (J)

Similar contrasts may be illustrated with sentence completions.
The informants heard (and read) the first half of the sentence.
The same woman's responses in both languages are cited below:

1. *When my wishes conflict with my family . . .*
(Japanese) it is a time of great unhappiness.
(English) I do what I want.
2. *I will probably become . . .*
(Japanese) a housewife.
(English) a teacher.
3. *Real friends should . . .*
(Japanese) help each other.
(English) be very frank.

On the last point, many women mentioned in attitude interviews
that they particularly admired the frankness of American women.

It was found that when the sentences were weighted by their
frequency in the American and Japanese monolingual comparison
groups, the bilingual women's sentences were significantly less
'Japanese' in content when the women spoke English. This change
in content could not be simulated by women who did not change
language but were instructed to give 'typically Japanese' or
'typically American' answers at the two sessions. Thus the change
in the associations and the sentence completions is an effect of
language, and not of self-instruction or set.

In the preceding experiment, everything was held constant
except language, and the effects of a specified language on content
were examined. It was expected that in the relatively abnormal
situation of a Japanese woman forced to speak English to another
Japanese woman, content typical of conversations between
Americans would more often appear. This shift presumably
would reflect English discourse with neighbors and husband
and thematic material from the English mass media.

Participant and form

In a second experiment, the receiver was changed in each session,
but the language was consistently English. The women were
interviewed either by a Caucasian American or by a Japanese

interviewer. Again, the women were in an abnormal situation when they were asked to speak English with another Japanese woman. The effects on the style of English were clear when the two situations were compared. With the Japanese listener, there was much more disruption of English syntax, more intrusion of Japanese words, and briefer speech.

A Japanese person provides an imperfect model of English, and as a listener is tolerant of and can understand Japanese intrusions. On the whole, the Japanese women are very tolerant of interpenetration of the two languages. We had found with French in the United States that those who had frequent discourse with other bilinguals had the highest incidence of borrowing of each language in the other (Ervin, 1955). Thus we can say that bilinguals who speak only with other bilinguals may be on the road to merger of the two languages, unless there are strong pressures to insulate by topic or setting.

Topic and form

In this experiment, it is possible to compare topics within each interview. In the word-associations, a stimulus word might be considered a topic. We know that some topics are more closely connected with life in the United States, others with Japan. For example, 'love', 'marriage', and 'kitchen' have American associations for these women. On the other hand, 'mushroom', 'fish', and 'New Year's Day' are strongly associated with Japanese life. When we weighted the English responses according to their frequency in the monolingual norm groups in Japan and the United States, it appeared that the war brides were closer to American women when associating to 'love', 'marriage', and 'kitchen' but closer to Japanese women for the other three topics. This was true even though, as we have seen, these 'Japanese' topics elicited less characteristically Japanese content when the language used was English, not Japanese.

In one part of the interview, the informants were asked to explain or describe, in English, a set of fourteen topics. The topics designed to be associated with English were the husband's work and leisure activities, American housekeeping, American cooking, and shopping for food and clothing here. Another set of topics were designed to be more frequent in Japanese: Japanese festivals,

Japanese New Year's Day, Japanese cooking and housekeeping, Doll Festival, and street story-tellers. The last two topics in each set were accompanied with photographs of the event to be described.

From this procedure we found that it was not the receiver alone, nor the topic alone, which affected speech but a specific combination of the two. When the informants were instructed to speak English, they had difficulty only when they spoke of Japanese topics. The combination of a Japanese receiver and a Japanese topic almost always demands the use of Japanese in a normal situation. The effect of artificially violating this rule was that the women's speech was disrupted. They borrowed more Japanese words, had more disturbed syntax, were less fluent, and had more frequent hesitation pauses. Thus a simple change in the topic and listener had a marked effect on the formal features of speech even though the most obvious formal change, a switch of code, was not allowed.

In the analysis both of content and form changes, we had assumed that a bilingual is like two monolinguals with a single nervous system. The differences in two settings or audiences of a bilingual are viewed as extensions of the differences in monolinguals. But there are limits to this simplified assumption. One is a cognitive limit. There are reasons to believe that it is very hard to maintain in one nervous system two category systems with only slight differences between them. This is true whether it be a semantic system such as color terminology (Ervin, 1961) or a phonemic system (Gumperz, 1962). Thus there are pressures constantly towards a merger of the two systems of the bilingual. Also, the very fact that a larger repertoire of alternative behavior is available to the bilingual makes him a victim of the special signs of response-competition, such as hesitation pauses and less fluency.

The second limit to this assumption lies in the very functional specialization we mentioned before. No bilingual, however fluent in two languages, has exactly equivalent experiences in both language communities. One may have been learned at home, one at school. One may have been learned in childhood, the other in adolescence. Perhaps now one is used at work and one in the family. Even in multilingual communities such as those of India and Switzerland, some specialization exists. Lowie, who grew up in a German-speaking family in the United States, reported a deliberate effort to keep an equivalent vocabulary (1945). He failed, for he could not control the difference in frequency or social context for the lexicon he acquired.

Thus, we cannot expect that a woman whose direct experience as a wife and mother was entirely in the United States would have, even when speaking Japanese, quite the same content as a woman in Japan. Her familiarity with these domains of life will be second-hand in some sense. In the same way, a woman who has never raised children in the United States will have most of the domain of meaning involving childhood much more fully developed in Japanese.

Finally, to the extent that the norms for Japanese and American monolingual behavior are current, they misrepresent the realities of contact, for these Japanese women know the Japan of five or ten years ago, not rapidly-changing contemporary Japan and its language.

Methods in sociolinguistics

If we examine the research which satisfies our definition of socio-linguistic, we find the methods used appear to be of four general types:

1. *Studies of the speech of social groups.* It has long been a practice among linguists and sociologists to study certain properties of the speech (usually the code) of predefined classes of speakers. We have, for example, studies reporting homosexual jargon (Cory, 1952, pp. 103–113) and thieves' jargon (Sutherland, 1937). Dialect atlas studies have selected speakers by geographical criteria and mapped the distribution of selected code features such as special lexicon (e.g. spider *v* frying-pan) and pronunciation (e.g. /griysiy/*v*/griyziy/). Traditionally, none of these studies takes the larger social community as a unit; speakers are selected out of context, and we may not know whether their speech varies with setting or receiver. We might expect, for instance, that 'criminals' might use different speech to judges, parole officers, patrolmen, and cell-mates, and Sutherland reports that this is the case (1937).

2. *Ethnographic studies.* A form of study discussed in detail by Hymes (1962) would employ traditional methods of observation

and interview to study when speech is used at all, and variations according to setting and participants. Naturalistic observations such as those of Barker and Wright (1954), Barker (1963), Watson and Potter (1962), Coser (1960) and Newman (1955) have ranged widely over the intercorrelational problems we have mentioned earlier. However, the drawback of such studies is that normally there is so much variation at once that we can find descriptive information about distributions but little definitive knowledge of which of the covarying features may be effective. Gump, Schoggen, and Redl (1963), for instance, compared a child's behavior in two social settings – but the settings involved different participants, different activities, and different physical surroundings. The authors point out that the child changed his forms of interaction, but it is not clear that this would have happened had his family been transported to a camp setting.

3. *Experimental studies*. Inevitably, experiments set up artificial situations. That is just their purpose, for they allow artificial constraints on normal covariance, permitting us for example to control the social composition of juries (Strodtbeck *et al.*, 1957), the size of a group (Bales and Borgatta, 1955), or the power relation of participants (Cohen, 1958) without varying any other significant features. Such studies would normally be based first on ethnographic research to explore the distribution of speech in the natural community so that extrapolation might be made to the artificial situation.

4. *Distribution of forms*. One can start with the analysis of formal alternatives and employ any of the above methods to study the determinants of the alternation. Fischer (1958), Brown and Gilman (1960), and Brown and Ford (1961) have done just this. This kind of study lends itself to a form of analysis we might call the description of equivalence patterns. For example, in some languages, the stylistic alternation which occurs when a man speaks to his superior rather than to a peer is similar to the alternation which occurs when a woman speaks to a man rather than to another woman. This is just a fragment of what is undoubtedly a wider set of corresponding alternations. If we looked at all societies in which such sets of correspondences occur, they might have common features, such as inferior ascribed status for women.

Another example is suggested by the distribution of the features of baby talk. The alternation which accompanies speech to adults versus speech to infants has some similarities to the alternations between neutral versus affectionate speech between intimates. Should this relation turn out to be universal, we might hunt for manipulable variables to test the psychological basis of the correspondence. If it is not universal, we need to know what systematic differences between societies are related; frequently such societal differences have individual analogues that can be studied (the baby talk user versus the non-baby-talk user).

These equivalence structures in verbal behavior are similar to the lexical classes which so interest cognitive theorists, for similarity in formal verbal behavior implies testable similarities in other types of behavior such as perception, memory, or emotional response.

This treatment of sociolinguistics has placed the face-to-face verbal encounter at the center of the definition. In contrast, a macroscopic approach to sociolinguistics might consider codes rather than finer formal contrasts, societal functions (such as education or law) rather than individual functions, institutionally classified settings (such as churches and mass media) rather than finer differentiations of setting in local communities, and values about language use as expressed in administrative actions and political behavior rather than merely in community norms and attitudes toward speakers of particular languages or dialects.

If one examines the generalizations in the studies we have cited, one finds that frequently they are special instances of more general social or psychological propositions. Brown and Ford (1961), for instance, noted that changes in address forms are expected to be initiated by the higher status participant; probably all respect behavior is so. Herman (1961) explicitly couched his study of multilingual code-switching in a broader framework of a theory of choice behavior.

Yet language is distinct in certain respects. Unlike other formally coded social behavior it can have semantic content. The internal imitations of external speech constitute a kind of portable society, both the voice of conscience and a categorization system, promoting socialization even of private behavior. Most of the uniquely human forms of social behavior are dependent on shared language, so that the structure of language use in society may be related to societal functioning in unique ways. If this is the case, sociolinguistics will contribute a new dimension to the social sciences rather than provide further exemplifications of the otherwise known.

References

BALES, R. F., and BORGATTA, E. F. (1955), 'A study of group size: size of group as a factor in the interaction profile', in P. Hare, E. F. Borgatta and R. F. Bales (eds.), *Small Groups*, Knopf.

BARKER, R. G. (1963), *The Stream of Behavior*, Appleton-Century-Crofts.

BARKER, R. G., and WRIGHT, H. F. (1954), *Midwest and its Children*, Evanston, Row, Peterson.

BROWN, R. W., and FORD, M. (1961), Address in American English, *J. abnorm. and soc. Psychol.*, no. 62, pp. 376–85.

BROWN, R. W., and GILMAN, A. (1960), 'The pronouns of power and solidarity', in T. A. Sebeok (ed.), *Style in Language*, Wiley.

COHEN, A. R. (1958), 'Upward communication in experimentally created hierarchies', *Hum. Rel.*, no. 11, pp. 41–53.

CORY, D. W. (1952), *The Homosexual in America*, Greenberg.

COSER, R. (1960), 'Laughter among colleagues', *Psychiatry*, no. 23, pp. 81–96.

ERVIN, S. M. (1955), 'The verbal behavior of bilinguals: the effects of adult French bilinguals': Ph.D. dissertation, microfilm abstracts, 55, 2228, University of Michigan.

ERVIN, S. M. (1961), 'Semantic shift in bilingualism', *Amer. J. Psychol.*, vol. 74, pp. 233–41.

ERVIN, S. M. (1964), 'Language and thematic apperception test content in bilinguals', *J. abnorm. and soc. Psychol.*, no. 68, pp. 500–507.

FISCHER, J. L. (1958), 'Social influences on the choice of a linguistic variant', *Word*, vol. no. 14, pp. 47–56.

GUMP, P. V., SCHOGGEN, P., and REDL, F. (1963), 'The behavior of the same child in different milieus', in R. G. Barker (ed.), *The Stream of Behavior*, Appleton-Century-Crofts.

GUMPERZ, J. J. (1962), 'Types of linguistic communities', *Anthropological Linguistics*, vol. 4, pp. 28–36.

HERMAN, S. (1961), 'Explorations in the social psychology of language choice', *Hum. Rel.*, vol. 14, pp. 149–64.

HYMES, D. (1962), 'The ethnography of speaking', in T. Gladwin and W. Sturtevant (eds.), *Anthropology and Human Behavior*, Anthropological Society of Washington, pp. 15–53.

LAMBERT, W. E. (1963), 'Psychological approaches to the study of language, pt 2: on second language learning and bilingualism', *Mod. Lang. J.*, vol. 47, pp. 114–21.

LOWIE, R. (1945), 'A case of bilingualism', *Word*, vol. 1, pp. 249–60.

NEWMAN, S. (1955), 'Vocabulary levels: Zuni sacred and slang usage', *Southwest J. Anthropology*, vol. 11, pp. 345–54.

STROTBECK, F. L., JAMES, R. M., and HAWKINS, C. (1957), 'Social status and jury deliberations', *Amer. soc. Rev.*, no. 22, pp. 713–19.

SUTHERLAND, E. (1937), *The Professional Thief*, University of Chicago Press.

WATSON, J., and POTTER, R. J. (1962), 'An analytic unit for the study of interaction', *Hum. Rels.*, vol. 15, pp. 245–63.

15 H. Sinclair-de-Zwart

Developmental Psycholinguistics

Excerpt from H. Sinclair-de-Zwart, 'Developmental psycholinguistics' in D. Elkind and J. Flavell (eds.) *Studies in Cognitive Development*, 1969, Oxford University Press, pp. 315–25.

One of the questions a Genevan psycholinguist who works with Jean Piaget hears often is: how does language figure in Piaget's theory? Does his theory of cognitive development provide a framework for the acquisition of language? Does he have an epistemology of language? It is difficult to answer these questions in a straightforward manner; the more so, since the few articles Piaget himself has written on language are almost uniquely concerned with the problem of language as a factor in development, and may seem to be written almost reluctantly (one of them starts off 'il aurait fallu me poser cette question à une epoque ou. . . .' (1963); his very early work, *Le langage et la pensée chez l'enfant* (1923) concerns far more 'la pensée' than 'le langage'. On the other hand, it is quite wrong to assert, as many authors do, that Piaget leaves language completely outside his considerations, and that, in fact, his experiments may lose some of their meaning because of this refusal to consider language as a separate, important variable.

To live with, or rather in, Piaget's theories for a number of years may have curious effects on a psycholinguist: from an initial irritation at the rather off-hand manner in which language is dealt with in many of Piaget's works and in much of his experimentation, one reaches the conviction that spread over a number of works, Piaget has in fact provided the bases for a general theory of both language-acquisition and of the role of language as a factor of development. However this may be, the following is an attempt to explain and elaborate Piaget's views on language. These views will be presented in two contexts: language viewed as a factor in cognitive development, and as a possible theory of language-acquisition.

Piaget's conception of the role of language in cognitive development

In several articles Piaget has been most explicit on this relationship between language and intellectual operations. The two main points that recur in his writings on the subject are the following:

1. The sources of intellectual operations are not to be found in language, but in the preverbal, sensorimotor period where a system of schemes is elaborated that prefigures certain aspects of the structures of classes and relations, and elementary forms of conservation and operative reversibility. In fact, the aquisition of the permanency of objects (elaborated between 6 and 18 months) constitutes a first 'invariant'. The search for an object which has disappeared is conducted in function of its successive localizations: these localizations depend on the constitution of an elementary *groupe de déplacements*, in which detours (associativity) and returns (reversibility) are coordinated.

2. The formation of representational thought is contemporaneous with the acquisition of language; both belong to a more general process, that of the constitution of the symbolic function in general. This symbolic function has several aspects; different kinds of behaviours, all appearing at about the same time in development, indicate its beginnings. The first verbal utterances are intimately linked to, and contemporaneous with, symbolic play, deferred imitation, and mental images as interiorized imitations.

The first point is elaborated in many works by Piaget and his co-workers (Inhelder in particular). Intellectual operations are actions that have become interiorized and reversible, but they are still actions. The coordination and decentrations of sensorimotor activity are not limited to this first period of life, but are found, in a different form, at work in the constitution of operational intelligence as well. And, as Piaget frequently remarks (1963, p. 72), they are also found in linguistic acts. This may account for a partial isomorphism between language and logic. It is important to bear in mind that already in the sensorimotor period object-permanency is a general acquisition. It would be a contradiction in terms to speak of one specific operation, since an operation is always part of a structured whole, of a system of operations; but in the same way, object-permanency is not to be understood as the permanency of one or of some objects (a toy, the baby's bottle) but of objects in general. Similarly, the *groupe de déplacements* does not mean that the baby can make one specific detour, or return to his starting point in one particular case: these first prefigurations of associativity and reversibility are, again, general. Thought has its roots in action; at the end of the sensori-motor period, and before the appearance of language or of the symbolic function in general, the baby has overcome his initial perceptive and motor egocentrism by a series of decentrations and coordinations. The construction of operations demands a new series of decentrations; not only from the momentary, present perceptive centration, but also from the totality of the actions of the subject.

As regards the second point, Piaget has devoted a whole work to *La formation du symbole chez l'enfant* (1946). This important work cannot be summarized in a few pages, but the main concepts bearing on the role of language in the development of thought may be expressed as follows.

At the end of the sensorimotor period the first decentrations appear in the child's dealings with his *hic-et-nunc* environment; action-schemata appear that permit the child to attain his practical aims, which are limited to the immediate present and to the manipulation of concrete objects within his reach. These spatio-temporal restrictions will slowly disappear with the development of thought. Moreover, the activity of the baby is directed toward success in his manipulations (from the cognitive point of view) and toward personal satisfaction (from the affective point of view). Later on, his activity takes on another dimension: cognitively, immediate success will no longer be the sole aim, but he will search for explanations and will reflect on his own actions; affectively, he will seek not only satisfaction, but also communication; he will want to tell other people about his discoveries, that now become *knowledge of* objects and events rather than *reactions to* objects and events.

One might be tempted to regard language, in the sense of learning to speak one's mother tongue through contact with the persons in one's environment, as the sole or main instrument that causes this transformation. Piaget, however, shows clearly that language is only a symptom and not the source of this change. Retracing the development step by step through careful observation of his own children, he demonstrates that language, despite the fact that later on it becomes most pervasive and takes on the guise of an autonomous capacity, is only part of the symbolic function. The symbolic function can be defined essentially as the capacity to represent reality through the intermediary of signifiers that are distinct from what they signify. The important term in this definition is the word *distinct*. In fact, around six months of age the baby already is capable of treating a partial perceptive datum as an indication of the presence of the whole; even if only a bit of the object is visible, it indicates the presence of the object. But such signals are directly linked to the objects, or are part of the object, whereas distinct signifiers imply a differentiation between signifier and signified, *introduced by the subject himself*. Signals (like the tracks an animal leaves in the snow, or the smell of food, or visible bits of partially hidden objects) are temporally and spatially restricted; the most distinct signifiers (words, algebraic symbols, and such) are free from such restrictions. Using a slightly different terminology, the linguist Bally said that the signal is a signifier only for whoever interprets it; and that a sign (distinct signifier) is a 'voluntary act', and also meaningful for whoever uses it.

The child who pushes a small shell along the edge of a box saying 'meow' knows full well that the shell is not a cat and the edge of the box is not a fence. And even if for the child the words 'meow' or 'cat' are at first somehow inherent in the animal, they are signifiers, and certainly not the animal itself. Piaget introduces a dichotomy in the distinct signifiers themselves:

1. Symbols, which like the shell have a link of resemblance with the object or event.

2. Signs (words), which are arbitrary.

Symbols, moreover, are usually personal; every child invents them in his play, whereas signs are social. Finally, we may add, symbols are mostly isolated, though within the context of symbolic play they may be loosely associated; signs on the other hand form systems.

According to Piaget, this capacity to represent reality by

distinct signifiers has its roots in imitation, which starts very early in the sensorimotor period (around six months of age) and which already constitutes some sort of representation by action. At the end of the sensorimotor period imitation becomes possible in the absence of the model, and evolves from a direct sensori-motor model to gesticulative evocation. First one sees action-schemes appear out of their proper context as representations (for instance, pretending to be asleep); then these representations become detached from the activity of the subject (for instance, putting a doll to sleep). Slowly these deferred imitations become interiorized, and constitute sketchy images, which the child can already use to anticipate future acts. Piaget gives several examples of these action-imitations that announce interiorization: when L. tries to open a box of matches (which is not quite shut), she first manipulates it, but without result; then she stops acting, seems to reflect on the problem and opens and shuts her mouth, several times in succession: she uses a motor-signifier to represent the problem and to find a way of solving it. After this short period of 'reflection' she pushes her finger into the small opening and pulls to open the box completely.

A wealth of such observations throws light on the development of the symbolizing capacity, which has many different aspects that are at first inextricably linked in observable behavior. Small children pass extremely swiftly from what looks like pure imitation to symbolic play and to acts of practical intelligence accompanied by words (or onomatopoaeia), but at first these different aspects cannot even be distinguished. Language as seen by Piaget is thus part of a much larger complex of processes that go on during the second year of life; it has the same roots, and in the beginning the same function as symbolic play, deferred imitation, and mental images; it does not appear *ex nihilo* (nor simply from early, prelinguistic vocalizations) but partakes of the entire cognitive development in this crucial period. It is, of course, just as closely linked to affective development; but this aspect of the question has been frequently dealt with by other authors, and the aim of this paper is restricted to the relationship between language and intellectual operations.

In summary, Piaget considers language not to be a sufficient condition for the constitution of intellectual operations, and he has said so, explicitly, in several articles (1954, 1961, 1962, 1963, 1965, Piaget and Inhelder, 1966). As to the question of whether language (in the sense of the normal acquisition of natural language by the young child) is, if not a sufficient, all the same a necessary condition for the constitution of operations, Piaget leaves the question open as regards the operations of formal logic. He notes (1963, p. 58) however, that these operations go beyond language, in the sense that neither the lattice of possible combinations nor the group of four transformations is as such present in language; they cannot even be expressed in ordinary, natural language. As regards concrete operations, Piaget considers language (again, in the limited sense) not even a necessary condition for their constitution, though he has not explicitly said so. However, he does state:

the sensorimotor schemata seem to be of a fundamental importance from their very first beginnings; these schemes continue to develop and structure thought, even verbal thought, as action progresses, up till the constitution of logico-mathematical operations, which are the authentic end-product of coordinated action-logic, when the latter can be interiorized and combined into group structures (1965).

Moreover, as regards concrete operations, Piaget quotes experiments with deaf-mute children, which clearly seem to point to the fact that the symbolic function is an obvious necessity for the constitution of these operations, but that the normal acquisition of a natural language is not. A brief summary of experimental data pertaining to the relationship between language and thought can be given and two different kinds of experiments can be distinguished.

1. The comparison of the reactions of normal children to Piaget-type tests with those of deaf-mute children on the one hand, and blind children on the other. The deaf-mutes have intact sensorimotor schemes, but have not acquired spoken language (or are only at the beginning of an 'oral' education), whereas the blind are in the inverse situation. Studies of deaf children have been made by Oléron (1957) and Furth (1966) among others. Their results concur fundamentally, and indicate that deaf children acquire the elementary logical operations with only a slight retardation as compared to normal children. The same stages of

development are found as the ones established by Piaget on a normal population. Both Oléron and Furth point out some differences in the reactions of their deaf subjects (particularly in the conservation of liquids). In the case of the conservation of liquids, however, certain difficulties in the presentation of the tests may account for these differences (e.g. in the pouring of liquids, the distinction between the quantity of liquid and the volume of the container is difficult to convey).

Furth notes an interesting difference in the comparative performance of deaf and hearing on 'logical symbol discovery' versus 'symbol use' tasks. While the deaf are inferior to the hearing on the former, they show equal ability on the use of logical symbols in a structured task. Furth points to several factors that could explain the results: among others, a different approach on the part of the deaf towards problems that call for invention, which may be due to a general lack of social contact. Oléron finds that seriation-tests are only very slightly retarded; that spatial operations are normal, and that classifications possess the same general structures and appear at the same age as with normals, but seem slightly less mobile or flexible (when classificatory criteria have to be changed). Here again, the cause may be more due to a general lack of social exchange and stimulation than to operational retardation.

These results with deaf children are all the more striking when it is considered that the same tests are only solved by blind children, on the average, four years later than by normal. The sensorial deficit of the blind has retarded the constitution of sensorimotor schemes and inhibited their coordination. The verbal acquisitions cannot compensate for this retardation, and action-learning is necessary before blind children reach an operational level comparable to that of the normal and the deaf (Hatwell, 1960).

2. A second group of experiments, directly bearing on the relationship between language and intellectual operations has been carried out in Geneva by Inhelder in collaboration with the author. These experiments have been described in detail elsewhere (Sinclair-de-Zwart, 1967), and in this paper we shall do no more than briefly indicate their technique and summarize the results. Our aims were twofold: (a) to see whether the profound modifica-

tion that occurs in the child's thinking with the constitution of the first concrete operations is paralleled by a linguistic development; (b) if the answer to (a) were in the affirmative, to determine whether a child who still lacks a certain concept or operation would show operatory progress after having undergone verbal training aiming to make him acquire expressions used by children who already possess the concept in question.

Consequently, we first chose some Piagetian tasks (conservation of liquids and seriation) that call for understanding and using certain expressions (quantitative and dimensional terms and comparatives). We explored the child's verbal capacities in this domain by first asking him to describe simple situations (which do not touch upon conservation or seriation problems: e.g. we present the child with two dolls, to one of whom we give four big marbles and to the other two small marbles, and we ask: 'Is this fair? Are both dolls happy? Why not?' Or we ask him to tell us the difference between two pencils, e.g. a short thick one and a long thin one). After this exploration of the child's use of certain expressions, we studied his comprehension, by asking him to execute orders couched in 'adult' but simple terms (e.g. 'give more plasticine to the boy than to the girl'; 'find a pencil that is shorter but thicker than this one').

After dividing our subjects into three groups according to their results on the Piagetian conservation task (total absence of conservation, intermediary stage, and conservation present), we compared their answers in the verbal task. The results can be summarized as follows:

(a) No difference was found among the three groups in the comprehension tasks; in fact, almost all subjects executed all orders correctly; only a very few young children (four years old) had some difficulties in questions of the type: 'Find a pencil that is longer but thinner.'

(b) Striking differences were found between the two extreme groups (no conservation at all and conservation acquired) as regards the description tasks.

Of the children with conservation, 70 per cent used comparatives (without adjectives) for the description of different quantities of

H. Sinclair-de-Zwart 273

plasticine, and 100 per cent did so for the description of different numbers of marbles: *le garçon a plus que la fille* (the boy has more than the girl).

Of children without conservation, 90 per cent used absolute terms (in contrast to comparatives): *le garçon a beaucoup, la fille a peu* (the boy has a lot, the girl has a little).

An interesting point was that 20 per cent already used comparatives for discrete units (marbles) whereas they did not do so for continuous quantities (plasticine); and the conservation of discrete units is acquired before that of continuous quantities.

Of the children with conservation, 100 per cent used different terms for different dimensions, using two couples of opposites (e.g. *grand/petit, gros/mince*, big/little, fat/thin).

Of children without conservation, 75 per cent used undifferentiated terms for the two dimensions, i.e. they would use at least one word to indicate two dimensions: e.g. *gros* (fat) for long and for thick, or *petit* (small) for short and for thin.

Of children with conservation, 80 per cent described two objects differing in two dimensions in two sentences, coordinating the two dimensions: *ce crayon est (plus) long mais (plus) mince, l'autre est court mais gros* (this pencil is long(er) but thin(ner), the other is short but thick).

Of children without conservation, 90 per cent either described only the one dimension, or used four separate sentences, dealing first with length, and then with thickness: *ce crayon est long, l'autre est court, ce crayon* (the first one again) *est mince, l'autre est gros.* (Percentages are approximate; slight variations occurred in different groups of items and with different materials, not described here.)

In a second series of experiments we tried to teach children without conservation the expressions used by children with conservation: comparative terms, differentiated terms and coordinated description of a difference in two dimensions. After this verbal training we again tested their operational level in the conservation task. The results of these experiments were as follows:

It was easy (in the sense that only a small number of repetitions were necessary) to teach the children without conservation the use of differentiated terms; it was more difficult (and about a quarter of the subjects did not succeed) to teach them to use the comparatives *plus* and *moins* in our situations; it was still more difficult to teach them the coordinated structure *long et (mais) mince, court et (mais) gros*.

Even for children who succeeded in learning to use these expressions, operational progress was rare (10 per cent of our subjects acquired conservation).

On the other hand, more than half the children who made no clear operational progress, changed their answers in the post-test. Instead of simply using the level of the liquid to decide that there was more to drink in one of the glasses, they now noticed and described the covarying dimensions (higher level, narrower glass); they sometimes explained that the liquid goes up higher in a narrower glass, but this did not lead them to the compensation argument and conservation.

From the first series of experiments we drew the following conclusions:

1. A distinction must be made between lexical acquisition and the acquisition of syntactical structures, the latter being more closely linked to operational level than the former. The operator-like words (e.g. more, less, as much as, none) form a class apart whose correct use is also very closely linked to operational progress. The other lexical items (e.g. long, short, thin, thick, high, low) are far less closely linked to operativity.

2. Operational structuring and linguistic structuring or rather linguistic restructuring thus parallel each other. The lexical items are already being used or at least easily learned at a pre-operational level; the coordinated structures and operator-like words are correctly 'understood' in simple situations; but the latter are only precisely and regularly used with the advent of the first operational structures. Moreover, the difficulties encountered by the child in the use of these expressions seem to be the same as those he encounters in the development of the operations themselves: lack of decentration and incapacity to coordinate.

3. Verbal training leads subjects without conservation to direct their attention to pertinent aspects of the problem (covariance of the dimensions), but it does not *ipso facto* bring about the acquisition of operations.

An additional experiment may be briefly mentioned: in interrogating a group of severely retarded children (ages 8 to 15, IQs 50 or below) we found that when we used the description patterns of children with conservation for simple orders (*donne plus à la poupee-fille, moins au garçon*), the retarded children were incapable of reacting consistently; but if we used the descriptive terms of our normal nonconservational group (e.g. *donne beaucoup à la fille, et peu au garçon*) their reactions were both correct and consistent. This result illustrated the psychological 'reality' of the different descriptive patterns used by normal children.

A second group of experiments dealt with seriation and its verbal aspects, and yielded comparable results.

These Genevan results, together with the results of the research on deaf and blind children mentioned earlier, confirm Piaget's view on the role of language in the constitution of intellectual operations: language is not the source of logic, but is on the contrary structured by logic. [. . .]

References

FURTH, H. C. (1966), *Thinking Without Language: the Psychological Implications of Deafness*, Free Press.

HATWELL, Y. (1960), *Privation Sensorielle et Intelligence*, Presses Univer, Paris.

OLÉRON, P. (1957), *Recherches sur le Developpment Mental des Sourds-muets*, Centre National de Recherche Scientifique, Paris.

PIAGET, J. (1923), *Le Langage et la Pensée chez L'Enfant*, Neuchâtel et Paris.

PIAGET, J. (1946), *La Formation du Symbole chez L'Enfant*, Delachaux et Niestlé (translated as *Play, Dreams and Imitation in Childhood*, Norton, 1951).

PIAGET, J. (1954), 'Le Langage et la pensee du point de vue genetique' in G. Revensz (ed.), *Thinking and Speaking, A Symposium*, North Holland, Amsterdam.

PIAGET, J. (1961), 'The language and thought of the child', in T. Shipley (ed.), *Classics in Psychology*, Philos. Lib., New York.

PIAGET, J. (1962), *Comments on Vygotsky's Critical Remarks*, MIT Press.

PIAGET, J. (1963), 'Language at operations intellectuelles', in *Problemes de Psycholinguistique*, Symposium de l'association de psychologie scientifique de langue français, Neuchâtel, Presses Univers, Paris.

PIAGET, J. (1965), 'Language at pensee', tome 15, *La Recue du Praticien*, vol. 17, pp. 2253–4.

PIAGET, J., and INHELDER, B. (1966), *La Psychologie de L'Enfant*, Presses Univer, Paris ('Que said-je?' series).

SINCLAIR-DE-ZWART, H. (1967), *Acquisition du Langage et Developpement de la Pensee*.

16 L. S. Vygotsky

An Experimental Study of Concept Formation

'An experimental study of concept formation', in L. S. Vygotsky, *Thought and Language* (1962), MIT Press, pp. 52–100.

I

Until recently the student of concept formation was handicapped by the lack of an experimental method that would allow him to observe the inner dynamics of the process.

The traditional methods of studying concepts fall into two groups. Typical of the first group is the so-called method of definition, with its variations. It is used to investigate the already formed concepts of the child through the verbal definition of their contents. Two important drawbacks make this method inadequate for studying the process in depth. In the first place, it deals with the finished product of concept formation, overlooking the dynamics and the development of the process itself. Rather than tapping the child's thinking, it often elicits a mere reproduction of verbal knowledge, of ready-made definitions provided from without. It may be a test of the child's knowledge and experience, or of his linguistic development, rather than a study of an intellectual process in the true sense. In the second place, this method, concentrating on the word, fails to take into account the perception and the mental elaboration of the sensory material that give birth to the concept. The sensory material and the word are both indispensable parts of concept formation. Studying the word separately puts the process on the purely verbal plane, which is uncharacteristic of child thinking. The relation of the concept to reality remains unexplored; the meaning of a given word is approached through another word, and whatever we discover through this operation is not so much a picture of the child's concepts as a record of the relationship in the child's mind between previously formed families of words.

The second group comprises methods used in the study of

abstraction. They are concerned with the psychic processes leading to concept formations. The child is required to discover some common trait in a series of discrete impressions, abstracting it from all the other traits with which it is perceptually fused. Methods of this group disregard the role played by the symbol (the word) in concept formation; a simplified setting substitutes a partial process for the complex structure of the total process.

Thus each of the two traditional methods separates the word from the perceptual material and operates with one or the other. A great step forward was made with the creation of a new method that permits the combination of both parts. The new method introduces into the experimental setting nonsense words which at first mean nothing to the subject. It also introduces artificial concepts by attaching each nonsense word to a particular combination of object attributes for which no ready concept and word exist. For instance, in Ach's experiments (1921) the word *gatsun* gradually comes to mean 'large and heavy'; the word *fal*, 'small and light'. This method can be used with both children and adults, since the solution of the problem does not presuppose previous experience or knowledge on the part of the subject. It also takes into account that a concept is not an isolated, ossified, changeless formation but an active part of the intellectual process, constantly engaged in serving communication, understanding, and problem-solving. The new method focuses the investigation on the *functional conditions of concept formation*.

Rimat (1925) conducted a carefully designed study of concept formation in adolescents, using a variant of this method. His main conclusion was that true concept formation exceeds the capacities of pre-adolescents and begins only with the onset of puberty. He writes:

We have definitely established that a sharp increase in the child's ability to form, without help, generalized objective concepts manifests itself only at the close of the twelfth year. . . . Thought in concepts, emancipated from perception, puts demands on the child that exceed his mental possibilities before the age of twelve (p. 112).

Ach's and Rimat's investigations disprove the view that concept formation is based on associative connections. Ach demonstrated that the existence of associations, however numerous and strong, between verbal symbols and objects is not in itself sufficient for concept formation. His experimental findings did not confirm the old idea that a concept develops through the maximal strengthening of associative connections involving the attributes common to a group of objects, and the weakening of associations involving the attributes in which these objects differ.

Ach's experiments showed that concept formation is a creative, not a mechanical passive, process; that a concept emerges and takes shape in the course of a complex operation aimed at the solution of some problem; and that the mere presence of external conditions favoring a mechanical linking of word and object does not suffice to produce a concept. In his view, the decisive factor in concept formation is the so-called determining tendency.

Before Ach, psychology postulated two basic tendencies governing the flow of our ideas: reproduction through association, and perseveration. The first brings back those images that had been connected in past experience with the one presently occupying the mind. The second is the tendency of every image to return and to penetrate anew into the flow of images. In his earlier investigations, Ach demonstrated that these two tendencies failed to explain purposeful, consciously directed acts of thought. He therefore assumed that such thoughts were regulated by a third tendency, the 'determining tendency', set up by the image of the goal. Ach's study of concepts showed that no new concept was ever formed without the regulating effect of the determining tendency created by the experimental task.

According to Ach's schema, concept formation does not follow the model of an associative chain in which one link calls forth the next; it is an aim-directed process, a series of operations that serve as steps toward a final goal. Memorizing words and connecting them with objects does not in itself lead to concept formation; for the process to begin, a problem must arise that cannot be solved otherwise than through the formation of new concepts.

This characterization of the process of concept formation, however, is still insufficient. The experimental task can be understood and taken over by children long before they are twelve, yet they are unable until that age to form new concepts. Ach's own study demonstrated that children differ from adolescents and adults not in the way they comprehend the aim but in the way their minds work to achieve it. Usnadze's (1929) detailed experimental study of concept formation in pre-schoolers also showed that a child at that age approaches problems just as the adult does when he operates with concepts but goes about their solution in an entirely different manner. We can only conclude that it is not the goal or the determining tendency but other factors, unexplored by these researchers, that are responsible for the essential difference between the adult's conceptual thinking and the forms of thought characteristic of the young child.

Usnadze points out that, while fully formed concepts appear relatively late, children begin early to use words and with their aid to establish mutual understanding with adults and among themselves. From this he concludes that words take over the function of concepts and may serve as means of communication long before they reach the level of concepts characteristic of fully developed thought.

We are faced, then, with the following state of affairs: A child is able to grasp a problem, and to visualize the goal it sets, at an early stage in his development; because the tasks of understanding and communication are essentially similar for the child and the adult, the child develops functional equivalents of concepts at an extremely early age, but the forms of thought that he uses in dealing with these tasks differ profoundly from the adult's in their composition, structure, and mode of operation. The main question about the process of concept formation – or about any goal-directed activity – is the question of the means by which the operation is accomplished. Work, for instance, is not sufficiently explained by saying that it is prompted by human needs. We must consider as well the use of tools, the mobilization of the appropriate means without which work could not be performed. To explain the higher forms of human behavior, we must uncover the means by which man learns to organize and direct his behavior.

All the higher psychic functions are mediated processes, and signs are the basic means used to master and direct them. The mediating sign is incorporated in their structure as an indispensable, indeed the central, part of the total process. In concept formation, that sign is the *word*, which at first plays the role of means in forming a concept and later becomes its symbol. In Ach's experiments this role of the word is not given sufficient attention. His study, while it has the merit of discrediting once and for all the mechanistic view of concept formation, did not disclose the true nature of the process – genetically, functionally, or structurally. It took the wrong turn with its purely teleological interpretation, which amounts to asserting that the goal itself creates the appropriate activity via the determining tendency – i.e., that the problem carries its own solution.

II

To study the process of concept formation in its several developmental phrases, we used the method worked out by one of our collaborators, Sakharov (1930). It might be described as the 'method of double stimulation': Two sets of stimuli are presented to the subject, one set as objects of his activity, the other as signs which can serve to organize that activity.[1]

1. Vygotsky does not describe the test in detail. The following description is taken from Hanfmann and Kasanin (1942, pp. 9–10) Ed.

The material used in the concept formation tests consists of twenty-two wooden blocks varying in color, shape, height, and size. There are five different colors, six different shapes, two heights (the tall blocks and the flat blocks), and two sizes of the horizontal surface (large and small). On the underside of each figure, which is not seen by the subject, is written one of the four nonsense words: *lag, bik, mur, cev*. Regardless of color or shape, *lag* is written on all tall large figures, *bik* on all flat large figures, *mur* on the tall small ones, and *cev* on the flat small ones. At the beginning of the experiment all blocks, well mixed as to color, size and shape, are scattered on a table in front of the subject. . . . The examiner turns up one of the blocks (the 'sample'), shows and reads its name to the subject, and asks him to pick out all the blocks which he thinks might belong to the same kind. After the subject has done so . . . the examiner turns up one of the 'wrongly' selected blocks, shows that this is a block of a different kind, and encourages the subject to continue trying. After each new attempt another of the wrongly placed blocks is turned up. As the number of the turned blocks increases, the subject by degrees obtains a basis for discovering to which characteristics of the blocks the nonsense words refer. As soon as he makes this discovery the . . . words . . . come to stand for definite kinds of objects (e.g., *lag* for large tall blocks, *bik* for large flat ones), and new concepts for which the language provides no names are thus built up. The subject is then able to complete the task of separating the four kinds of blocks indicated by the nonsense words. Thus the use of concepts has

In some important respects this procedure reverses Ach's experiments on concept formation. Ach begins by giving the subject a learning or practice period; he can handle the objects and read the nonsense words written on each before being told what the task will be. In our experiments, the problem is put to the subject from the start and remains the same throughout, but the clues to solution are introduced stepwise, with each new turning of a block. We decided on this sequence because we believe that facing the subject with the task is necessary in order to get the whole process started. The gradual introduction of the means of solution permits us to study the total process of concept formation in all its dynamic phases. The formation of the concept is followed by its transfer to other objects: the subject is induced to use the new terms in talking about objects other than the experimental blocks, and to define their meaning in a generalized fashion.

III

In the series of investigations of the process of concept formation begun in our laboratory by Sakharov and completed by us and our associates Kotelova and Pashkovskaja, more than three hundred people were studied – children, adolescents, and adults, including some with pathological disturbances of intellectual and linguistic activities.

The principal findings of our study may be summarized as follows: The development of the processes which eventually result in concept formation begins in earliest childhood, but the intellectual functions that in a specific combination form the psychological basis of the process of concept formation ripen, take shape, and develop only at puberty. Before that age, we find certain intellectual formations that perform functions similar to those of the genuine concepts to come. With regard to their com-

---

a definite functional value for the performance required by this test. Whether the subject actually uses conceptual thinking in trying to solve the problem . . . can be inferred from the nature of the groups he builds and from his procedure in building them: Nearly every step in his reasoning is reflected in his manipulations of the blocks. The first attack on the problem; the handling of the sample; the response to correction; the finding of the solution – all these stages of the experiment provide data that can serve as indicators of the subject's level of thinking.

position, structure, and operation, these functional equivalents of concepts stand in the same relationship to true concepts as the embryo to the fully formed organism. To equate the two is to ignore the lengthy developmental process between the earliest and the final stage.

Concept formation is the result of a complex activity in which all the basic intellectual functions take part. The process cannot, however, be reduced to association, attention, imagery, inference, or determining tendencies. They are all indispensable, but they are insufficient without the use of the sign, or word, as the means by which we direct our mental operations, control their course, and channel them toward the solution of the problem confronting us.

The presence of a problem that demands the formation of concepts cannot in itself be considered the cause of the process, although the tasks with which society faces the youth as he enters the cultural, professional, and civic world of adults undoubtedly are an important factor in the emergence of conceptual thinking. If the environment presents no such tasks to the adolescent, makes no new demands on him, and does not stimulate his intellect by providing a sequence of new goals, his thinking fails to reach the highest stages, or reaches them with great delay.

The cultural task *per se*, however, does not explain the developmental mechanism itself that results in concept formation. The investigator must aim to understand the intrinsic bonds between the external tasks and the developmental dynamics, and view concept formation as a function of the adolescent's total social and cultural growth, which affects not only the contents but also the method of his thinking. The new significative use of the word, its use *as a means of concept formation*, is the immediate psychological cause of the radical change in the intellectual process that occurs on the threshold of adolescence.

No new elementary function, essentially different from those already present, appears at this age, but all the existing functions are incorporated into a new structure, form a new synthesis, become parts of a new complex whole; the laws governing this whole also determine the destiny of each individual part. Learning to direct one's own mental processes with the aid of words or signs is an integral part of the process of concept formation.

The ability to regulate one's actions by using auxiliary means reaches its full development only in adolescence.

IV

Our investigation brought out that the ascent to concept formation is made in three basic phases, each divided in turn into several stages. In this and in the following six sections, we shall describe these phases and their subdivisions as they appear when studied by the method of 'double stimulation'.

The young child takes the first step toward concept formation when he puts together a number of objects in an *unorganized congeries*, or 'heap', in order to solve a problem that we adults would normally solve by forming a new concept. The heap, consisting of disparate objects grouped together without any basis reveals a diffuse, undirected extension of the meaning of the sign (artificial word) to inherently unrelated objects linked by chance in the child's perception.

At that stage, word meaning denotes nothing more to the child than a *vague syncretic conglomeration of individual objects* that have somehow or other coalesced into an image in his mind. Because of its syncretic origin, that image is highly unstable.

In perception, in thinking, and in acting, the child tends to merge the most diverse elements into one unarticulated image on the strength of some chance impression. Claparède gave the name 'syncretism' to this well-known trait of child thought. Blonski called it the 'incoherent coherence' of child thinking. We have described the phenomenon elsewhere as the result of a tendency to compensate for the paucity of well-apprehended objective relations by an overabundance of subjective connections and to mistake these subjective bonds for real bonds between things. These syncretic relationships, and the heaps of objects assembled under one word meaning, also reflect objective bonds in so far as the latter coincide with the relations between the child's perceptions or impressions. Many words, therefore, have in part the same meaning to the child and the adult, especially words referring to concrete objects in the child's habitual surroundings. The child's and the adult's meanings of a word often 'meet', as it were, in the same concrete object, and this suffices to ensure mutual understanding.

The first phase of concept formation, which we have just out-lined, subsumes three distinct stages. We were able to observe them in detail within the framework of the experimental study.

The first stage in the formation of syncretic heaps that repre-sent to the child the meaning of a given artificial word is a manifestation of the *trial-and-error* stage in the development of thinking. The group is created at random, and each object added is a mere guess or trial; it is replaced by another object when the guess is proven wrong, i.e. when the experimenter turns the object and shows that it has a different name.

During the next stage, the composition of the group is deter-mined largely by the spatial position of the experimental objects, i.e. by a purely syncretic *organization of the child's visual field*. The syncretic image or group is formed as a result of the single element's contiguity in space or in time, or of their being brought into some other more complex relationship by the child's imme-diate perception.

During the third stage of the first phase of concept formation, the syncretic image rests in a more complex base: It is composed of *elements taken from different groups or heaps that have already been formed by the child in the ways described above*. These newly combined elements have no intrinsic bonds with one another, so that the new formation has the same 'incoherent coherence' as the first heaps. The sole difference is that in trying to give meaning to a new word the child now goes through a two-step operation, but this more elaborate operation remains syncretic and results in no more order than the simple assembling of heaps.

V

The second major phase on the way to concept formation com-prises many variations of a type of thinking that we shall call *thinking in complexes*. In a complex, individual objects are united in the child's mind not only by his subjective impressions but also by *bonds actually existing between these objects*. This is a new achievement, an ascent to a much higher level.

When the child moves up to that level, he has partly outgrown his egocentrism. He no longer mistakes connections between his own impressions for connections between things – a decisive step away from syncretism toward objective thinking. Thought, in complexes, is already coherent and objective thinking, although it does not reflect objective relationships in the same way as conceptual thinking.

Remains of complex thinking persist in the language of adults. Family names are perhaps the best example of this. Any family name, 'Petrov', let us say, subsumes individuals in a manner closely resembling that of the child's complexes. The child at that stage of development thinks in family names, as it were; the universe of individual objects becomes organized for him by being grouped into separate, mutually related 'families'.

In a complex, the bonds between its components are *concrete and factual* rather than abstract and logical, just as we do not classify a person as belonging to the Petrov family because of any logical relationship between him and other bearers of the name. The question is settled for us by facts.

The factual bonds underlying complexes are discovered through direct experience. A complex therefore is first and foremost a concrete grouping of objects connected by factual bonds. Since a complex is not formed on the plane of abstract logical thinking, the bonds that create it, as well as the bonds it helps to create, lack logical unity; they may be of many different kinds. *Any factually present* connection may lead to the inclusion of a given element into a complex. That is the main difference between a complex and a concept. While a concept groups objects according to one attribute, the bonds relating the elements of a complex to the whole and to one another may be as diverse as the contacts and relationships of the elements are in reality.

In our investigation we observed five basic types of complexes, which succeed one another during this stage of development.

We call the first type of complex the *associative type*. It may be based on any bond the child notices between the sample object and some other blocks. In our experiment, the sample object, the one first given to the subject with its name visible, forms the nucleus of the group to be built. In building an associative complex, the child may add one block to the nuclear object because it is of the same color, another because it is similar to the nucleus in shape or in size, or in any other attribute that happens to strike him. Any bond between the nucleus and another object suffices to make the child include that object in the group and to designate it by the common 'family name'. The bond between the nucleus and the other object need not be a common trait, such as the same color or shape; a similarity, or a contrast, or proximity in space may also establish the bond.

To the child at that stage the word ceases to be the 'proper name' of an individual object; it becomes the family name of a group of objects related to one another in many kinds of ways, just as the relationships in human families are many and different.

VI

Complex thinking of the second type consists in combining objects or the concrete impressions they make on the child into groups that most closely resemble *collections*. Objects are placed together on the basis of some one trait in which they differ and consequently complement one another.

In our experiments the child would pick out objects differing from the sample in color, or in form, or in size, or in some other characteristic. He did not pick them at random; he chose them because they contrasted with and complemented the one attribute of the sample which he took to be the basis of grouping. The result was a collection of the colors or forms present in the experimental material, e.g. a group of blocks each of a different color.

Association by contrast, rather than by similarity, guides the child in compiling a collection. This form of thinking, however, is often combined with the associative form proper, described earlier, producing a collection based on mixed principles. The child fails to adhere throughout the process to the principle he originally accepted as the basis of collecting. He slips into the consideration of a different trait, so that the resulting group becomes a mixed collection, e.g., of both colors and shapes.

This long, persistent stage in the development of child thinking is rooted in his practical experience, in which collections of complementary things often form a set or a whole. Experience teaches the child certain forms of functional grouping: cup, saucer, and spoon; a place setting of knife, fork, spoon, and plate; the set of clothes he wears. All these are models of natural collection complexes. Even adults, when speaking of dishes or clothes, usually have in mind sets of concrete objects rather than generalized concepts.

To recapitulate, the syncretic image leading to the formation of 'heaps' is based on vague subjective bonds mistaken for actual bonds between objects; the associative complex, on similarities or other perceptually compelling ties between things; the collection complex, on relationships between objects observed in practical experience. We might say that the collection complex is a *grouping of objects on the basis of their participation in the same practical operation* – of their functional cooperation.

VII

After the collection stage of thinking in complexes, we must place the *chain complex* – a dynamic, consecutive joining of individual links into a single chain, with meaning carried over from one link to the next. For instance, if the experimental sample is a yellow triangle, the child might pick out a few triangular blocks until his attention is caught by, let us say, the blue color of a block he has just added; he switches to selecting blue blocks of any shape – angular, circular, semicircular. This in turn is sufficient to change the criterion again; oblivious of color, the child begins to choose rounded blocks. The decisive attribute keeps changing during the entire process. There is no consistency in the type of the bonds or in the manner in which a link of the chain is joined with the one that precedes it and the one that follows it. The original sample has no central significance. Each link, once included in a chain complex, is as important as the first and may become the magnet for a series of other objects.

The chain formation strikingly demonstrates the perceptually concrete, factual nature of complex thinking. An object is included because of one of its attributes enters the complex not just as the carrier of that one trait but as an individual, with *all* its attributes. The single trait is not abstracted by the child from the rest and is not given a special role, as in a concept. In complexes, the hierarchical organization is absent: All attributes are functionally equal. The sample may be disregarded altogether when a bond is formed between two other objects; these objects may have nothing in common with some of the other elements either, and yet be parts of the same chain on the strength of sharing an attribute with still another of its elements.

Therefore, the chain complex may be considered the *purest form of thinking in complexes*. Unlike the associative complex, whose elements are, after all, interconnected through one element – the nucleus of the complex – the chain complex has no nucleus; there are relations between single elements, but nothing more.

A complex does not rise above its elements as does a concept; it merges with the concrete objects that compose it. This fusion of the general and the particular, of the complex and its elements, this psychic amalgam, as Werner called it, is the distinctive characteristic of all complex thinking and of the chain complex in particular.

VIII

Because the chain complex is factually inseparable from the group of concrete objects that form it, it often acquires a vague and floating quality. The type and nature of the bonds may change from link to link almost imperceptibly. Often a remote similarity is enough to create a bond. Attributes are sometimes considered similar, not because of genuine likeness, but because of a dim impression that they have something in common. This leads to the fourth type of complex observed in our experiments. It might be called the diffuse complex.

The *diffuse complex* is marked by the fluidity of the very attribute that unites its single elements. Perceptually concrete groups of objects or images are formed by means of diffuse, indeterminate bonds. To go with a yellow triangle, for example, a child would in our experiments pick out trapezoids as well as triangles, because they made him think of triangles with their tops cut off. Trapezoids would lead to squares, squares to hexagons, hexagons to semicircles, and finally to circles. Color as the basis of selection is equally floating and changeable. Yellow objects are apt to be followed by green ones; then green may change to blue, and blue to black.

Complexes resulting from this kind of thinking are so indefinite as to be in fact limitless. Like a Biblical tribe that longed to multiply until it became countless like the stars in the sky or the sands of the sea, a diffuse complex in the child's mind is a kind of family that has limitless powers to expand by adding more and more individuals to the original group.

The child's generalizations in the nonpractical and nonperceptual areas of his thinking, which cannot be easily verified through perception or practical action, are the real-life parallel of the diffuse complexes observed in the experiments. It is well known that the child is capable of surprising transitions, of startling associations and generalizations, when his thought ventures beyond the boundaries of the small tangible world of his experience. Outside it he often constructs limitless complexes amazing in the universality of the bonds they encompass.

These limitless complexes, however, are built on the same principles as the circumscribed concrete complexes. In both, the child stays within the limits of concrete bonds between things, but in so far as the first kind of complex comprises objects outside the sphere of his practical cognition, these bonds are naturally based on dim, unreal, unstable attributes.

IX

To complete the picture of complex thinking, we must describe one more type of complex – the bridge, as it were, between complexes and the final, highest stage in the development of concept formation.

We call this type of complex the *pseudo-concept* because the generalization formed in the child's mind, although phenotypically, resembling the adult concept, is psychologically very different from the concept proper; in its essence, it is still a complex.

In the experimental setting, the child produces a pseudo-concept every time he surrounds a sample with objects that could just as well have been assembled on the basis of an abstract concept. For instance, when the sample is a yellow triangle and the child picks out all the triangles in the experimental material, he could have been guided by the general idea or concept of a triangle. Experimental analysis shows, however, that in reality the child is guided by the concrete, visible likeness and has formed only an associative complex limited to a certain kind of perceptual bond.

Although the results are identical, the process by which they are reached is not at all the same as in conceptual thinking.[2]

We must consider this type of complex in some detail. It plays a predominant role in the child's real-life thinking, and it is important as a transitional link between thinking in complexes and true concept formation.

X

Pseudo-concepts predominate over all other complexes in the preschool child's thinking for the simple reason that in real life complexes corresponding to word meanings are not *spontaneously developed* by the child: The lines along which a complex develops are predetermined by the meaning a given word already has in the language of adults.

In our experiments, the child, freed from the directing influence of familiar words, was able to develop word meanings and form

2. The following elaboration of the experimental observations is taken from the study by Hanfmann and Kasanin (1942, pp. 30–31):

In many cases the group, or groups, created by the subject have quite the same appearance as in a consistent classification, and the lack of a true conceptual foundation is not revealed until the subject is required to put in operation the ideas that underlie this grouping. This happens at the moment of correction when the examiner turns one of the wrongly selected blocks and shows that the word written on it is different from the one on the sample block, e.g. that it is not *mur*. This is one of the critical points of the experiment. . . .

Subjects who have approached the task as a classification problem respond to correction immediately in a perfectly specific way. This response is adequately expressed in the statement: 'Aha! Then it is not color' (or shape, etc.). . . . The subject removes all the blocks he had placed with the sample one, and starts looking for another possible classification.

On the other hand, the outward behavior of the subject at the beginning of the experiment may have been that of attempting a classification. He may have placed all red blocks with the sample, proceeding quite consistently . . . and declared that he thinks those red blocks are the *murs*. Now the examiner turns up one of the chosen blocks and shows that it has a different name. . . . The subject sees it removed or even obediently removes it himself, but that is all he does: he makes no attempt to remove the other red blocks from the sample *mur*. To the examiner's question if he still thinks that those blocks belong together, and are *mur*, he answers definitely, 'Yes, they still belong together because they are red.' This striking reply betrays an attitude totally incompatible with a true classification approach and proves that the groups he had formed were actually pseudo-classes.

complexes according to his own preferences. Only through the experiment can we gauge the kind and extent of his spontaneous activity in mastering the language of adults. The child's own activity in forming generalizations is by no means quenched, though it is usually hidden from view and driven into complicated channels by the influences of adult speech.

The language of the environment, with its stable, permanent meanings, points the way that the child's generalizations will take. But, constrained as it is, the child's thinking proceeds along this preordained path in the manner peculiar to his level of intellectual development. The adult cannot pass on to the child his mode of thinking. He merely supplies the ready-made meaning of a word, around which the child forms a complex – with all the structural, functional, and genetic peculiarities of thinking in complexes, even if the product of his thinking is in fact identical in its content with a generalization that could have been formed by conceptual thinking. The outward similarity between the pseudo-concept and the real concept, which makes it very difficult to 'unmask' this kind of complex, is a major obstacle in the genetic analysis of thought.

The functional equivalence of complex and concept, the coincidence, in practice, of many word meanings for the adult and the three-year-old child, the possibility of mutual understanding, and the apparent similarity of their thought processes have led to the false assumption that all the forms of adult intellectual activity are already present in embryo in child thinking and that no drastic change occurs at the age of puberty. It is easy to understand the origin of that misconception. The child learns very early a large number of words that mean the same to him and to the adult. The mutual understanding of adult and child creates the illusion that the end point in the development of word meaning coincides with the starting-point, that the concept is provided ready-made from the beginning, and that no development takes place.

The child's acquisition of the language of adults accounts, in fact, for the consonance of his complexes with their concepts – in other words, for the emergence of concept complexes, or pseudo-concepts. Our experiments, in which the child's thinking is not hemmed in by word meanings, demonstrate that if it were not for the prevalence of pseudo-concepts the child's complexes would develop along different lines from adult concepts, and verbal communication between children and adults would be impossible.

The pseudo-concept serves as the connecting link between thinking in complexes and thinking in concepts. It is dual in nature: a complex already carrying the germinating seed of a concept. Verbal intercourse with adults thus becomes a powerful factor in the development of the child's concepts. The transition from thinking in complexes to thinking in concepts passes un-noticed by the child because his pseudo-concepts already coincide in content with the adult's concepts. Thus the child begins to operate with concepts, to practice conceptual thinking, before he is clearly aware of the nature of these operations. This peculiar genetic situation is not limited to the attainment of concepts; it is the rule rather than an exception in the intellectual development of the child.

XI

We have now seen, with the clarity that only experimental analysis can give, the various stages and forms of complex thinking. This analysis permits us to uncover the very essence of the genetic process of concept formation in a schematic form, and thus gives us the key to the understanding of the process as it unfolds in real life. But an experimentally induced process of concept forma-tion never mirrors the genetic development exactly as it occurs in life. The basic forms of concrete thinking that we have enumerated appear in reality in mixed states. The morphological analysis given so far must be followed by a functional and genetic analysis. We must try to connect the forms of complex thinking discovered in the experiment with the forms of thought found in the actual development of the child and check the two series of observations against each other.

From our experiments we concluded that, at the complex stage, word meanings as perceived by the child refer to the same objects the adult has in mind, which ensures understanding be-tween child and adult, but that the child thinks the same thing in a different way, by means of different mental operations. We shall try to verify this proposition by comparing our observations with the data on the peculiarities of child thought, and of primitive thought in general, previously collected by psychological science.

If we observe what groups of objects the child links together in transferring the meanings of his first words, and how he goes about it, we discover a mixture of the two forms which we called in our experiments the associative complex and the syncretic image.

Let us borrow an illustration from Idelberger, cited by Werner (1926, p. 206). On the 251st day of his life, a child applies the word *bow-wow* to a china figurine of a girl that usually stands on the sideboard and that he likes to play with. On the 307th day, he applies *bow-wow* to a dog barking in the yard, to the pictures of his grandparents, to a toy dog, and to a clock. On the 331st day, to a fur piece with an animal's head, noticing particularly the glass eyes, and to another fur stole without a head. On the 334th day, to a rubber doll that squeaks when pressed, and on the 396th, to his father's cuff links. On the 433rd day, he utters the same word at the sight of pearl buttons on a dress and of a bath thermometer.

Werner analysed this example and concluded that the diverse things called *bow-wow* may be catalogued as follows: first, dogs and toy dogs, and small oblong objects resembling the china doll, e.g. the rubber doll and the thermometer; second, the cuff links, pearl buttons, and similar small objects. The criterial attribute is an oblong shape or a shiny surface resembling eyes.

Clearly, the child unites these concrete objects according to the principle of a complex. Such spontaneous complex formations make up the entire first chapter of the developmental history of children's words.

There is a well-known, frequently cited example of these shifts: a child's use of *quah* to designate first a duck swimming in a pond, then any liquid, including the milk in his bottle; when he happens to see a coin with an eagle on it, the coin also is called *quah*, and then any round, coinlike object. This is a typical chain complex: Each new object included has some attribute in common with another element, but the attributes undergo endless changes.

Complex formation is also responsible for the peculiar phenomenon that one word may in different situations have different or even opposite meanings as long as there is some associative link between them. Thus, a child may say *before* for both before and after, or *tomorrow* for both tomorrow and yesterday. We have here a perfect analogy with some ancient languages – Hebrew, Chinese, Latin – in which one word also sometimes indicated opposites. The Romans, for instance, had one word for high and deep. Such a marriage of opposite meanings is possible only as a result of thinking in complexes.

XII

There is another very interesting trait of primitive thought that shows us complex thinking in action and points up the difference between pseudo-concepts and concepts. This trait – which Levy-Bruhl was the first to note in primitive peoples, Storch in the insane, and Piaget in children – is usually called *participation*. The term is applied to the relationship of partial identity or close interdependence established by primitive thought between two objects or phenomena which actually have neither contiguity nor any other recognizable connection.

Lévy-Bruhl (1918) quotes von den Steinen regarding a striking case of participation observed among the Bororo of Brazil, who pride themselves on being red parrots. Von den Steinen at first did not know what to make of such a categorial assertion but finally decided that they really meant it. It was not merely a name they appropriated, or a family relationship they insisted upon: What they meant was identity of beings.

It seems to us that the phenomenon of participation has not yet received a sufficiently convincing psychological explanation, and this for two reasons: First, investigations have tended to focus on the contents of the phenomenon and to ignore the mental operations involved, i.e., to study the product rather than the process; second, no adequate attempts have been made to view the phenomenon in the context of the other bonds and relationships formed by the primitive mind. Too often the extreme, the fantastic, like the Bororo notion that they are red parrots, attracts investigation at the expense of less spectacular phenomena. Yet careful analysis shows that even those connections that do not outwardly clash with our logic are formed by the primitive mind on the principles of complex thinking.

Since children of a certain age think in pseudo-concepts, and words designate to them complexes of concrete objects, their thinking must result in participation, i.e., in bonds unacceptable to adult logic. A particular thing may be included in different complexes on the strength of its different concrete attributes and consequently may have several names; which one is used depends on the complex activated at the time. In our experiments, we frequently observed instances of this kind of participation where an object was included simultaneously in two or more complexes. Far from being an exception, participation is characteristic of complex thinking.

Primitive peoples also think in complexes, and consequently the word in their languages does not function as the carrier of a concept but as a 'family name' for groups of concrete objects belonging together, not logically, but factually. Storch (1922) has shown that the same kind of thinking is characteristic of schizophrenics, who regress from conceptual thought to a more primitive level of mentation, rich in images and symbols. He considers the use of concrete images instead of abstract concepts one of the most distinctive traits of primitive thought. Thus the child, primitive man, and the insane, much as their thought processes may differ in other important respects, all manifest participation – a symptom of primitive complex thinking and of the function of words as family names.

We therefore believe that Lévy-Bruhl's way of interpreting participation is incorrect. He approaches the Bororo statements about being red parrots from the point of view of our own logic when he assumes that to the primitive mind, too, such an assertion means identity of beings. But since words to the Bororo designate groups of objects, not concepts, their assertion has a different meaning: The word for parrot is the word for a complex that includes parrots and themselves. It does not imply identity any more than a family name shared by two related individuals implies that they are one and the same person.

XIII

The history of language clearly shows that complex thinking with all its peculiarities is the very foundation of linguistic development.

Modern linguistics distinguishes between the meaning of a

word, or an expression, and its referent, i.e. the object it designates. There may be one meaning and different referents, or different meanings and one referent. Whether we say 'the victor at Jena' or 'the loser at Waterloo', we refer to the same person, yet the meaning of the two phrases differs. There is but one category of words – proper names – whose sole function is that of reference. Using this terminology, we might say that the child's and the adult's words coincide in their referents but not in their meanings.

Identity of referent combined with divergence of meaning is also found in the history of languages. A multitude of facts support this thesis. The synonyms existing in every language are one good example. The Russian language has two words for moon, arrived at by different thought processes that are clearly reflected in their etymology. One term derives from the Latin word connoting 'caprice, inconstancy, fancy'. It was obviously meant to stress the changing form that distinguishes the moon from the other celestial bodies. The originator of the second term, which means 'measurer', had no doubt been impressed by the fact that time could be measured by lunar phases. Between languages, the same holds true. For instance, in Russian the word for tailor stems from an old word for a piece of cloth; in French and in German it means 'one who cuts'.

If we trace the history of a word in any language, we shall see, however surprising this may seem at first blush, that its meanings change just as in child thinking. In the example we have cited, *bow-wow* was applied to a series of objects totally disparate from the adult point of view. Similar transfers of meaning, indicative of complex thinking, are the rule rather than the exception in the development of a language. Russian has a term for day-and-night the word *sutki*. Originally it meant a seam, the junction of two pieces of cloth, something woven together; then it was used for any junction, e.g. of two walls of a house, and hence a corner; it began to be used metaphorically for twilight, 'where day and night meet'; then it came to mean the time from one twilight to the next, i.e., the twenty-four-hour *sutki* of the present. Such diverse things as a seam, a corner, twilight, and twenty-four hours are drawn into one complex in the course of the development of a word, in the same way as the child incorporates different things into a group on the basis of concrete imagery.

What are the laws governing the formation of word families? More often than not, new phenomena or objects are named after unessential attributes, so that the name does not truly express the nature of the thing named. Because a name is never a concept when it first emerges, it is usually both too narrow and too broad. For instance, the Russian word for cow originally meant 'horned', and the word for mouse, 'thief'. But there is much more to a cow than horns, and to a mouse than pilfering; thus their names are too narrow. On the other hand, they are too broad, since the same epithets may be applied – and actually are applied in some other languages – to a number of other creatures. The result is a ceaseless struggle within the developing language between conceptual thought and the heritage of primitive thinking in complexes. The complex-created name, based on one attribute, conflicts with the concept for which it has come to stand. In the contest between the concept and the image that gave birth to the name, the image gradually loses out; it fades from consciousness and from memory, and the original meaning of the word is eventually obliterated. Years ago all ink was black, and the Russian word for ink refers to its blackness. This does not prevent us today from speaking of red, green, or blue 'blacking' without noticing the incongruity of the combination.

Transfers of names to new objects occur through contiguity or similarity, i.e. on the basis of concrete bonds typical of thinking in complexes. Words in the making in our own era present many examples of the process by which miscellaneous things are grouped together. When we speak of 'the leg of a table', 'the elbow of a road', 'the neck of a bottle', and 'a bottleneck', we are grouping things in a complex-like fashion. In these cases the visual and functional similarities mediating the transfer are quite clear. Transfer can be determined, however, by the most varied associations, and if it has occurred in the remote past, it is impossible to reconstruct the connections without knowing exactly the historical background of the event.

The primary word is not a straightforward symbol for a concept but rather an image, a picture, a mental sketch of a concept, a short tale about it – indeed, a small work of art. In naming an object by means of such a pictorial concept, man ties it into one group with a number of other objects. In this respect the process of language creation is analogous to the process of complex formation in the intellectual development of the child.

XIV

Much can be learned about complex thinking from the speech of deaf-mute children, in whose case the main stimulus to the formation of pseudo-concepts is absent. Deprived of verbal intercourse with adults and left to determine for themselves what objects to group under a common name, they form their complexes freely, and the special characteristics of complex thinking appear in pure, clear-cut form.

In the sign language of deaf-mutes, touching a tooth may have three different meanings: 'white', 'stone', and 'tooth'. All three belong to one complex whose further elucidation requires an additional pointing or imitative gesture to indicate the object meant in each case. The two functions of a word are, so to speak, physically separated. A deaf-mute touches his tooth and then, by pointing at its surface or by making a throwing gesture, tells us to what object he refers in a given case.

To test and supplement our experimental results, we have taken some examples of complex formation from the linguistic development of children, the thinking of primitive peoples, and the development of languages as such. It should be noted, however, that even the normal adult, capable of forming and using concepts, does not consistently operate with concepts in his thinking. Apart from the primitive thought processes of dreams, the adult constantly shifts from conceptual to concrete, complexlike thinking. The transitional, pseudo-concept form of thought is not confined to child thinking; we too resort to it very often in our daily life.

XV

Our investigation led us to divide the process of concept formation into three major phases. We have described two of them, marked by the predominance of the syncretic image and of the complex, respectively, and we come now to the third phase. Like the second, it can be subdivided into several stages.

In reality, the new formations do not necessarily appear only after complex thinking has run the full course of its development. In a rudimentary shape, they can be observed long before the child begins to think in pseudo-concepts. Essentially, however, they belong in the third division of our schema of concept formation. If complex thinking is one root of concept formation, the forms we are about to describe are a second, independent root. They have a distinct genetic function, different from that of complexes, in the child's mental development.

The principal function of complexes is to establish bonds and relationships. Complex thinking begins the unification of scattered impressions; by organizing discrete elements of experience into groups, it creates a basis for later generalizations.

But the advanced concept presupposes more than unification. To form such a concept it is also necessary *to abstract, to single out* elements, and to view the abstracted elements apart from the totality of the concrete experience in which they are embedded. In genuine concept formation, it is equally important to unite and to separate: Synthesis must be combined with analysis. Complex thinking cannot do both. Its very essence is overabundance, overproduction of connections, and weakness in abstraction. To fulfill the second requirement is the function of the processes that ripen only during the third phase in the development of concept formation, though their beginnings reach back into much earlier periods.

In our experiment, the first step toward abstraction was made when the child grouped together *maximally similar* objects, e.g. objects that were small *and* round, or red *and* flat. Since the test material contains no identical objects, even the maximally similar are dissimilar in some respects. It follows that in picking out these 'best matches' the child must be paying more attention to some traits of an object than to others – giving them preferential treatment, so to speak. The attributes which, added up, make an object maximally similar to the sample become the focus of attention and are thereby, in a sense, abstracted from the attributes to which the child attends less. This first attempt at abstraction is not obvious as such, because the child abstracts a whole group of traits, without clearly distinguishing one from another; often the abstraction of such a group of attributes is based only on a vague, general impression of the objects' similarity.

Still, the global character of the child's perception has been breached. An object's attributes have been divided into two parts unequally attended to – a beginning of positive and negative abstraction. An object no longer enters a complex *in toto*, with all its attributes – some are denied admission; if the object is impoverished thereby, the attributes that caused its inclusion in the complex acquire a sharper relief in the child's thinking.

XVI

During the next stage in the development of abstraction, the grouping of objects on the basis of maximum similarity is superseded by grouping on the basis of a single attribute: e.g. only round objects or only flat ones. Although the product is undistinguishable from the product of a concept, these formations, like pseudo-concepts, are only precursors of true concepts. Following the usage introduced by Groos (1913), we shall call such formations *potential concepts*.

Potential concepts result from a species of isolating abstraction of such a primitive nature that it is present to some degree not only in very young children but even in animals. Hens can be trained to respond to one distinct attribute in different objects, such as color or shape, if it indicates accessible food; Koehler's chimpanzees, once they had learned to use a stick as a tool, used other long objects when they needed a stick and none was available.

Even in very young children, objects or situations that have some features in common evoke like responses; at the earliest preverbal stage, children clearly expect similar situations to lead to identical outcomes. Once a child has associated a word with an object, he readily applies it to a new object that impresses him as similar in some ways to the first. Potential concepts, then, may be formed either in the sphere of perceptual or in that of practical, action-bound thinking – on the basis of similar impressions in the first case and of similar functional meanings in the second. The latter are an important source of potential concepts. It is well known that until early school age functional meanings play a very important role in child thinking. When asked to explain a word, a child will tell what the object the word designates can do, or – more often – what can be done with it. Even abstract concepts are often translated into the language of concrete action: '*Reasonable* means when I am hot and don't stand in a draft.'

Potential concepts already play a part in complex thinking, in so far as abstraction occurs also in complex formation. Associative complexes, for instance, presuppose the 'abstraction' of one trait common to different units. But as long as complex thinking predominantes, the abstracted trait is unstable, has no privileged position, and easily yields its temporary dominance to other traits. In potential concepts proper, a trait once abstracted is not easily lost again among the other traits. The concrete totality of traits has been destroyed through its abstraction, and the possibility of unifying the traits on a different basis opens up. Only the mastery of abstraction, combined with advanced complex thinking, enables the child to progress to the formation of genuine concepts. A concept emerges only when the abstracted traits are synthesized anew and the resulting abstract synthesis becomes the main instrument of thought. The decisive role in this process, as our experiments have shown, is played by the word, deliberately used to direct all the part processes of advanced concept formation.[3]

XVII

In our experimental study of the intellectual processes of adolescents, we observed how the primitive syncretic and complex forms of thinking gradually subside, potential concepts are used less and less, and true concepts begin to be formed – seldom at first, then with increasing frequency. Even after the adolescent has learned to produce concepts, however, he does not abandon the more elementary forms; they continue for a long time to operate, indeed to predominate, in many areas of his thinking. Adolescence is less a period of completion than one of crisis and transition.

The transitional character of adolescent thinking becomes especially evident when we observe the actual functioning of the

3. It must be clear from this chapter that words also fulfil an important, though different, function in the various stages of thinking in complexes, Therefore, we consider complex thinking a stage in the development of *verbal* thinking, unlike many other authors who extend the term *complex* to include preverbal thinking and even the primitive mentation of animals.

newly acquired concepts. Experiments specially devised to study the adolescent's operations with concepts bring out, in the first place, a striking discrepancy between his ability to form concepts and his ability to define them.

The adolescent will form and use a concept quite correctly in a concrete situation but will find it strangely difficult to express that concept in words, and the verbal definition will, in most cases, be much narrower than might have been expected from the way he used the concept. The same discrepancy occurs also in adult thinking, even at very advanced levels. This confirms the assumption that concepts evolve in ways differing from deliberate conscious elaboration of experience in logical terms. Analysis of reality with the help of concepts precedes analysis of the concepts themselves.

The adolescent encounters another obstacle when he tries to apply a concept that he has formed in a specific situation to a new set of objects or circumstances, where the attributes synthesized in the concept appear in configurations differing from the original one. (An example would be the application to everyday objects of the new concept 'small and tall', evolved on test blocks.) Still, the adolescent is usually able to achieve such a transfer at a fairly early stage of development.

Much more difficult than the transfer itself is the task of defining a concept when it is no longer rooted in the original situation and must be formulated on a purely abstract plane, without reference to any concrete situation or impressions. In our experiments, the child or adolescent who had solved the problem of concept formation correctly very often descended to a more primitive level of thought in giving a verbal definition of the concept and began simply to enumerate the various objects to which the concept applied in the particular setting. In this case he operated with the name as with a concept but defined it as a complex – a form of thought vacillating between complex and concept, and typical of that transitional age.

The greatest difficulty of all is the application of a concept, finally grasped and formulated on the abstract level, to new concrete situations that must be viewed in these abstract terms – a kind of transfer usually mastered only toward the end of the adolescent period. The transition from the abstract to the concrete proves just as arduous for the youth as the earlier transition from the concrete to the abstract. Our experiments leave no doubt that on this point at any rate the description of concept formation given by traditional psychology, which simply reproduced the schema of formal logic, is totally unrelated to reality.

According to the classical school, concept formation is achieved by the same process as the 'family portrait' in Galton's composite photographs. These are made by taking pictures of different members of a family on the same plate, so that the 'family' traits common to several people stand out with an extraordinary vividness, while the differing personal traits of individuals are blurred by the superimposition. A similar intensification of traits shared by a number of objects is supposed to occur in concept formation; according to traditional theory, the sum of these traits *is* the concept. In reality, as some psychologists have long ago noted, and as our experiments show, the path by which adolescents arrive at concept formation never conforms to this logical schema. When the process of concept formation is seen in all its complexity, it appears as a *movement* of thought within the pyramid of concepts, constantly alternating between two directions, from the particular to the general, and from the general to the particular.

Our investigation has shown that a concept is formed, not through the interplay of associations, but through an intellectual operation in which all the elementary mental functions participate in a specific combination. This operation is guided by the use of words as the means of actively centering attention, of abstracting certain traits, synthesizing them, and symbolizing them by a sign.

The processes leading to concept formation develop along two main lines. The first is complex formation: The child unites diverse objects in groups under a common 'family name'; this process passes through various stages. The second line of development is the formation of 'potential concepts', based on singling out certain common attributes. In both, the use of the word is an integral part of the developing processes, and the word maintains its guiding function in the formation of genuine concepts, to which these processes lead.

References

ACH, N. (1921), *Ueber die Begriffsbildung*, Buchner.

GROOS, K. (1913), *Das Seelenleben der Kinder*, Reuther & Reichard.

HANFMANN, E., and KASANIN, J. (1942), 'Conceptual Thinking in schizophrenia', *Nerv. and Mental Dis. Monograph*, no. 67.

LÉVY-BRUHL, L. (1918), *Les Fonctions Mentales dans les Societes Inférieures*, Alcan.

RIMAT, F. (1925), *Intelligenzuntersuchungen Anschliescend an die Ach'sche Suchmethode*, Calvoer.

SAKHAROV, L. (1930), 'O metodakh issledovanija ponjatij', *Psikhologija*, vol. 3, no. 1.

STORCH, A. (1922), 'Das archaisch-primitive erleben und denken in der schizophrenie', *Monogr. aus. d. Gesamtgeb. de. Neurol. u Psychiat.*, vol. 32.

USNADZE, D. (1929), 'Gruppenbildungsversuche bei vorschulpflichtigen kindern', *Arch. ges. Psychol.*, vol. 73.

WERNER, H. (1926), *Einfuehrung in die Entwicklungspsychologie*, Barth.

17 R. Olver and J. Hornsby

On Equivalence

R. Olver and J. Hornsby, 'On equivalence', in J. S. Bruner, R. Olver,
N. Greenfield, *et al* (eds.), *Studies in Cognitive Growth*, 1966, Wiley,
pp. 66–85.

That children and adults group discriminately different things and
treat them as 'the same' or 'alike' is hardly debatable.[1] And
indeed, were they not naturally prone to do so, the diversity of
the environment would soon overwhelm them. Such equivalence-
making is in large measure a learned achievement; it may be
expected to change with growth and development in a manner
consistent with more general changes in cognitive development.
Elsewhere in *Studies in Cognitive Growth* a good deal is made of
how the very young child represents and 'knows' by doing, how
there is added to this primitive mode a capacity for knowing by
depicting in images, and finally how the growing child achieves
the ability to give an account of his world in the powerful medium
of language. This course of growth by which finally all three
techniques of knowing come into force – enactive, ikonic, and
symbolic representation – is reflected in the changing ways that
children have for imposing equivalence on the things of their
world.

  Enactive, ikonic, and symbolic representation might each, for
example, be expected to emphasize different features of the environment as bases for establishing equivalence. Under enactive
representation, things should be seen as alike on the basis of a
common role in some action. Equivalence with ikonic representation might more likely be accomplished by grouping items accord-

1. This chapter has grown out of two theses carried out at the Center for
Cognitive Studies. The first is a doctoral dissertation, *A Developmental
Study of Cognitive Equivalence*, and was completed by R. Olver in 1961. The
second, by Joan Rigney (Hornsby), entitled *A Developmental Study of
Cognitive Equivalence Transformations and Their Use in the Acquisition
and Processing of Information*, was submitted as an honors thesis one year
later. Both were submitted to the Department of Social Relations at Harvard.

ing to perceptual kinship or likeness. With the achievement of symbolic representation, equivalence might well be expected to be governed by such grammatical principles as synonymy, super-ordination, or syntactic substitutability. It is with such a course of growth that this chapter deals. The transitions with which we shall be concerned are interesting in their own right as a documentary on development. More interesting still is the picture of the underlying form of organization in thought that is revealed.

For example, it is not only the 'semantics' of equivalence that changes with growth – the features of the environment used as the basis of equivalence – but the 'syntax' of equivalence formation as well. Might equivalence groupings under enactive representation demonstrate the sequential properties of action sequences? Might groupings governed by ikonic representation, reflecting the domination of the perceptually vivid be based on a kind of conjunctive joining of attributes? Does the development of symbolic equivalence groupings take on the form of conventional categorization and hierarchical organization?[2]

2. Vygotsky (1962), in tracing the development of concepts from 'heaps' to complexes to 'true concepts', also remarks upon changes in the syntax of equivalence. Initially, according to his account, 'Word meaning denotes nothing more to the child than a vague syncretic conglomeration of individual objects that have somehow or other coalesced into an image in his mind' (pp. 59–60). The second major step toward 'true' concept formation is 'thinking in complexes'. Here the child groups diverse elements into a complex on the basis of perceptually concrete and factual relationships. Complexes are thus distinguished from 'heaps' in that the objects included are united not only by subjective impressions but also by 'bonds actually existing between these objects' (p. 61) and from true concepts, in that 'an object included because of one of its attributes enters the complex not just as the carrier of that one trait but as an individual, with *all* its attributes. The single trait is not abstracted by the child from the rest and is not given a special role, as in a concept. In complexes, the hierarchical organization is absent: all attributes are functionally equal' (p. 64). The final stage, that of 'true concepts', occurs when the child guides his mental operations 'by the use of words as a means of actively centering attention, of abstracting certain traits, synthesizing them, and symbolizing them by a sign' (p. 81). According to Vygotsky, this stage of genuine concepts is achieved during adolescence. The reader will see that Vygotsky has provided us with a framework with which to begin, but that we have diverged from him in several critical ways: in the separation of semantic and syntactic features of equivalence, and in a variety of other ways that become clearer in the description of experiments and results.

The studies reported here trace the development of equivalence from age six to age nineteen, from the first year of regular school work to the first year in college. The materials we have used permit the child to demonstrate both the basis on which he renders things equivalent and the syntax or structure of the groups he forms.

Experiment 1: equivalence formation with verbal materials

We gave children from age six to nineteen the task of telling us how different items are alike. We presented the words *banana* and *peach*, each typed on a small white card and spoken aloud as well, and asked the child, 'How are banana and peach alike?' We then added *potato* to the list, first asking, 'How is potato different from banana and peach?' and then, 'How are banana, peach, and potato all alike?' Next we added *meat*, asking, 'How is meat different from banana, peach, and potato?' and then, 'How are banana, peach, potato, and meat all alike?' This procedure was continued until the array consisted of: *banana, peach, potato, meat, milk, water, air, germs*. At the end of the array we included an item about which we asked only how it differed from the preceding items; for example, *stones* was presented as the final item in the banana-peach list. We presented a second array of items in the same manner: *bell, horn, telephone, radio, newspaper, book, painting, education*, and as the contrast item, *confusion*.

Note that the arrays are made up of successively more distant items, but, though the items become increasingly more diverse, they share a common characteristic. The items in the banana-peach array, for example, are all ingestible; those in the bell-horn array all carry messages, and so forth. As words are added, the task gets more difficult, and so it was intended, for we were interested in pushing our subjects to their limits. The two lists were constructed impressionistically. Could we have found a more systematic method – we tried several – it would have been better. The present lists do at least evoke responses that serve our purpose.

Sixty children formed the subjects in this investigation. The children in the youngest grades – from age six to fourteen – were enrolled in suburban public schools near Boston; the sixteen-year-olds came from a nearby suburban high school; and the oldest group (the college freshmen) were students at Harvard and Radcliffe Colleges. There were five boys and five girls in each age group, and their mean ages and IQ scores are shown in Table 1.

Children of different ages go about such a task in rather different ways. One six year old said that banana, peach, potato, and meat were alike because 'a banana is yellow, and a peach is red and yellow, or sometimes red and sometimes just yellow, and a potato is light flesh, and meat is brown.' Another responded, 'Meat and potato are most of the time together, peach and banana can be for dessert, and the banana is close to the kind of vegetable.'

Table 1 Subjects in Experiment 1 – Ages, IQs, Number of Children

Grade	Mean Age		Mean IQ	Number
1	6 years	3 months	*	10
4	9 years	6 months	122	10
6	11 years	7 months	115	10
8	13 years	5 months	122	10
10	15 years	11 months	122	10
Freshmen	18 years	7 months	*	10

* IQ data not available.

Older children, for example, the sixteen-year-olds, grouped the same items as 'They're all something to eat', or 'They're all food'. The six-year-old, consistent with his reliance on ikonic representation, seemed caught by the way things look – their color or where they are found together. The sixteen-year-old spoke of the function of the items – what they are used for. Not only did the bases for grouping differ, but the syntax as well. While the older child used a common characteristic to form a class, some property shared by all members, the six-year-old linked each item only to the next one, or stated a characteristic separately for each item in the group.

Consider more closely now on what bases the items are judged to be 'the same'. Since they all vary from one another in a number of different dimensions, a variety of different characteristics could be used as the basis of equivalence. Five main modes can be distinguished: *perceptible*, *functional*, *affective*, *nominal*, and *fiat equivalence*. For each mode we can set forth a typical language frame for characterizing the basis of equivalence.

1. *Perceptible:* The child may render the items equivalent on the basis of immediate phenomenal qualities such as color, size, shape, or on the basis of position in time or space.

Perceptible Intrinsic They are — . (X:adjective: '. . . both yellow.')
They have — . (X:noun: '. . . writing on them.')

Perceptible Extrinsic They are (preposition) — . (X:position in time or space: '. . . all in a house.')

2. *Functional:* The child may base equivalence on the use or function of the items, considering either what they do or what can be done to them.

Functional Intrinsic They — . (X:verb: '. . . make noise.')
Functional Extrinsic You — them. (X:verb: '. . . can turn them on.')

3. *Affective:* The child may render the items equivalent on the basis of the emotion they arouse or of his evaluation of them.

Affective You — them. (X:value or internal state: '. . . like them both.')
They are — . (X:adjective indicating value: '. . . very important.')

4. *Nominal:* The child may group the items by giving a name that exists ready-made in the language.

Nominal They are (or are not) — . (X:noun: '. . . both fruit.')

5. *Fiat Equivalence:* The child may merely state that the items are alike or are the same without giving any further information as to the basis of his grouping, even when he is prodded.

Fiat Equivalence 'A' is (or is not) — 'B.' (X:like, similar to, the same as, and so forth: 'They are the same thing, really.')

Six year olds do, indeed, group more often according to perceptible properties than do older children. Their protocols are laced with the colors, sizes, shapes, and places of things. More than a quarter of their groupings are of the perceptible intrinsic type; no older group forms even half that many on this basis. From age six on there is a steady increase in functionally based equivalence

– from 49 per cent of all responses at age six to 73 per cent at age nineteen (Fig. 1). Initially the turn to functional attributes as the basis of equivalence is extrinsic as we have defined it, and often it is seemingly arbitrary – the child speaks of what *he* can do *to* the objects: turn them on, roll them up into a ball, and so forth. At age nine half of the children's groupings are formed in this way. It is as if the child were taking himself as reference point in order to create a common basis for grouping an apparently diverse array.

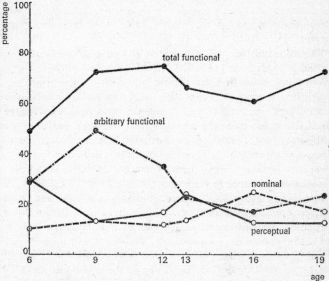

Figure 1 Percentage of groupings based on different attributes

What emerges at this point is a bit surprising. One is at first taken aback by the central role of 'functionalism' as an arm or at least an accompaniment to intellectual growth. It has about it some of the properties of enactive representation – definition by an action taken. But a closer examination suggests that this new functionalism provides a means for the child to get free of responding to the more immediate, surfacy aspects of the things around him. Indeed, functionalism in its egocentric form is what permits the child to distinguish between objects and actions taken toward them. Yet a closer look at the syntactic aspect of grouping as it expresses itself at this time in the child's life – and we shall have a closer look presently – also makes it plain that functionalism is highly associated with more mature forms of grouping. It may well be that as the child breaks away from the perceptual domination of vivid things he must fall back on a more practical way of dealing with the environment – through action, or at least vicarious action. The common uses of things are pitted against their divergent appearances, and the conflict promotes growth. Whether functionalism is made possible by the child's ability to use new grouping principles, or the other way round, must remain a moot point.

Consider further this increase in grouping according to use, even arbitrary use. The nine-year-old, for all his functionalism, forms groupings that are neither particularly appropriate nor realistic for adaptive action. Without intending a philosophical point, we may say that their functional groups are often arbitrary and that they ignore the conventional or sensible uses to which objects are put. The child at this age ignores the possible reciprocal relations between himself and the objects he is sorting and, instead, imposes functions upon them. There is, for example, a sharp increase at age nine in the use of the pronouns 'you' and 'I' in answering the questions we pose. And the use of 'you' and 'I' in framing responses declines beyond age nine as the child turns from extrinsic to intrinsic functional properties as the basis of grouping. The shift is from responses such as, 'I can crinkle up a newspaper and then it will make a noise like the bell and horn' to 'They all tell ideas in their own way.' Fig. 2 depicts the relevant data.

Consider now the structure or 'syntax' of the groupings formed by children of different ages. We can distinguish three general grouping structures: *superordinate*, *complexive*, and *thematic* (Fig. 3).

1. *Superordinate groupings* are constructed on the basis of a common feature or features characterizing the items included in a group or class. This is the classic category of Venn diagrams and the like. Any array of items has a number of common characteristics, any one or combination of which can serve as the

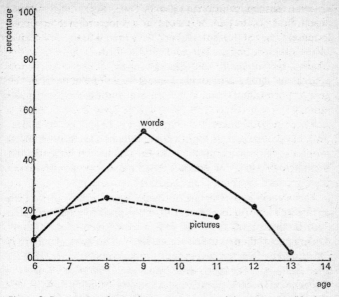

Figure 2 Percentage of grouping responses containing pronouns 'You' and 'I' - verbal and picture array

general superordinate	
itemized superordinate	
edge matching	
key ring	
association	
collection	
multiple grouping	

Figure 3 Grouping syntax diagrams

criterion for their inclusion in a group. Thus, for example, banana, peach, and potato can be placed in a superordinate grouping because, 'They all have skins,' or 'They are all food,' or because 'They all can be bought at a store,' and so forth.

General superordinate. The general superordinate construction consists of stating a common characteristic of the items in the group. For example, bell and horn are 'both things that make noise.'

Itemized superordinate. Itemization may be added to super-ordinate grouping such that, while the items have a generalized property that joins them, the basis on which each item qualifies is explicitly stated. For example, 'Bell makes noise, horn makes noise too, bell says ding-dong, horn says doo-doo.'

2. *Complexive structures* are formed by using attributes of an array so as to form local rather than universal rules for grouping and, in this sense, these are closer to Wittgenstein's[3] 'family resemblances' than to the classic category. This general pattern is illustrated by five maneuvers for forming complexes: *collections, edge matchings, key rings, associations,* and *multiple groupings.*

Collections. The collection complex consists in finding complementary or somehow contrasting or otherwise related properties that all the things have, but not in tying them together in terms of attributes that are shared. For example, 'Bell is black, horn is brown, telephone is blue, radio is red.' Or, 'Newspaper you can read, book you can read, telephone you get messages over, radio you get messages over, and a horn you can blow.'

Edge matchings. The edge-matching complex consists in forming associative links between neighboring items. A chain of items is formed by tying the items together in linked pairs. For example, 'Banana and peach are both yellow, peach and potato are round, potato and meat are served together, meat and milk both come from cows.' There is no consistency in the attribute or character-istic by which one link of the chain is joined with the one that precedes and the one that follows.

3. See Wittgenstein (1953, 1958). Wittgenstein is quite right in pointing out that such complexes as we describe have a useful status in scientific as in everyday thinking. We may at times in our discussion appear to denigrate complexive thinking, but that is not our intention. Rather, our concern is with the child's capacity to go beyond such grouping – not simply with whether he abandons or forswears complexive grouping.

Key rings. The key-ring complex consists in taking an item and linking all the others to it by choosing attributes that form relations between the central item and each of the others. For example, 'Painting – well, one thing is a newspaper has got some painting in it, a book has got some black printing, a radio and a telephone have painting on them and a horn – well, there's a little painting on it, and a bell is also the color of paints.' Or, 'Germs are in banana, peach, potato, meat, milk, water, and air.'

Associations. In the association complex the child links two items and then uses the bond between these items as a nucleus for the addition of other items. For example, 'Bell and horn are music things, when you dial a telephone it's music a little.' Or, 'Bell, horn, telephone, and radio make noises, if you fold back a newspaper, then it will crackle and make a noise.'

Multiple groupings. The multiple-grouping complex consists of the formation of several subgroupings. For example, 'A telephone is like a radio – I know that. A horn and a bell both make sounds, but I don't know about a newspaper.' The list is thus segmented into several groups, and the gap between them is not bridged.

3. *Thematic groupings* are formed on the basis of how the items fit in a sentence or a story or a thema. The construction of thematic groupings, in fact, most often depends on a sentence for tying items together. The sentence carries a story or thematic line: 'The little boy was eating a banana on the way to the store to buy some peaches and potatoes.'

We can turn now to the patterns of growth observed in the children. To begin with, there is a massive change that takes place between the sixth and nineteenth year (Fig. 4). At six, half of the groupings made by the children are complexive, half superordinate. By nine, the balance shifts to three-quarters superordinated. And by nineteen, the complexive grouping has virtually disappeared, at least among these subjects and in this culture.

Not only do the younger children use complexive groupings more often, they also fall back on them more readily when the going gets hard. Recall that the items in an array diverged increasingly from the opening pair as successive ones are added to the list. The degree of divergence is an inexact matter, but at the very least it can be said that for virtually anybody, child and adult alike, it is more difficult to form a grouping for the first four or five items in a list than for the first pair. We took advantage of this fact to compare the performance of our subjects on the first pair, trio, and quadrad of items (easier items) with performance on five, six, seven, and eight items. The results tell their own story – brave starts and weak finishes by the younger subjects, until finally the task is within reach of the older ones (Fig. 5). And when the younger children fall back on complexes with the longer lists, they tend to use the less demanding forms such as collections and edge-matchings, whereas the older ones use associations and key rings more often.

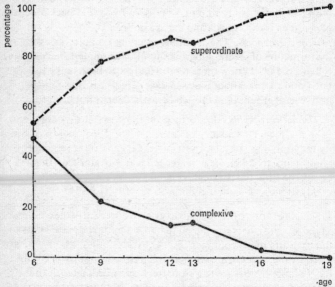

Figure 4 Percentage of grouping structures of two types

There is a striking relation between the syntax and the semantics of the groupings the children made. If the attributes used in grouping are perceptible, then the grouping is likely to be complexive. If attributes are functional, on the other hand, the chances are greater that they will be grouped superordinately.

Our excursion into the domain of grouping, using verbal

materials as stimuli, leads us to several conclusions. Perhaps the most obvious is that in tasks such as we presented our subjects, growth is reflected by a steady movement from grouping complexively to grouping by superordination. This progress is achieved at the same time that the child stops paying sole attention to the perceptible properties of the objects to be grasped and begins attending more to their functional significance.

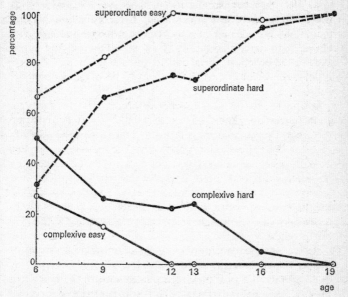

Figure 5 Percentage of groupings in easy and hard sequences that are complexive and superordinate in structure

We cannot help saying a word of caution. It is evident that the tasks we used were ones that the children were increasingly likely to see as they grew older as 'academic', to be dealt with 'intellectually', as one deals with such tasks. To a degree, their competence to deal with tasks in this way – consistently, logically, and so on – depends upon their being in the culture, whether in school or in social settings where we demand of older children that they put aside childish ways of thinking. There is a little question that our older subjects were also able to be more complexive, though they did not sense this experiment as an appropriate occasion for it. We shall have ample opportunity to explore this question later.

We have observed both the 'overshoot' of complexive thinking in the younger children and the corresponding 'overshoot' of the use of superordinates in somewhat older children. Six-year-olds who attempt to use superordinates in the 'easier' first half of the array fall back on complexes in the more difficult portion of the task. Yet by a comparable token, nine- and twelve-year-olds get lost in what we have come to call 'hyperordination'. Trying to use the superordinate rule, they mire down by grouping highly diverse items under the rubric, 'They are all things,' and fail to achieve the benefit of the simplicity of such grouping – 'hyper-ordination' is knowing the form of the behavior but not the substance.

Obviously, the two approaches to grouping are required in adult functioning, and though in our data we see one replacing the other, the replacement is probably more for public activities than for those done more subjectively. The loose-knit complex, as Wittgenstein and others have noted, is a vehicle for searching out possibilities of kinship. It is also the vehicle of poetry and fantasy. What it lacks in tidiness, it recovers in richness. So too the superordinate category: if its applicability is limited to well-formed problems, at least it is capable of precision and a workable exclusiveness.

Before drawing conclusions, we should examine a variant of the present experiment, lest we be victim of results imposed by our methods. We turn now to a related experiment much like the first, save in two respects: the first experiment used verbal materials, and it forced them in a fixed order on the children. To some extent, these procedures constrained the nature of the response made. [. . .]

In the second experiment, the stimuli were pictorial, and the subjects could deal with them in their own order. [. . .]

To summarize: the same pattern of growth emerges whether we use words or pictures as stimuli, and whether the child is given items in a fixed order or chooses his own groups *ad libitum*. Equivalence for the six-year-old reflects a basis in imagery, both in what he uses as a basis for grouping and in how he forms his groups. From age six on, linguistic structures increasingly guide what and how things will be judged alike. With the development of symbolic representation, the child is freed from dependence upon moment-to-moment variation in perceptual vividness and is able to keep the basis of equivalence invariant. A first step away from domination by the perceptually salient comes when the child, at about age nine, takes himself egocentrically as a reference point for establishing equivalence among things. He does this by imposing upon the world what *he* can do to things, producing equivalence by reference to his own actions. In time, he accommodates to more conventional definitions of how things are 'alike'.

However, it is not entirely a matter of what features of the world serve as a basis for defining how things are alike. There is also the grammar of grouping what is alike and segregating it from the rest of the world. The effort begins with loosely ordered definitions of likeness, ordered sequentially and in a fashion that makes discrimination difficult and combination awkward. Only gradually and by dint of much language development does the child work his way toward true conceptual grouping, based on the rule of the superordinate class, which opens new possibilities for relating and combining and structuring information about the world. By early adolescence the rules are mastered, and then the question remains as to how well the child learns to apply them in a variety of contexts.

We could (and perhaps should) go on at this point to an interpretation of the phenomena reported in the experiments in this chapter. It is better, perhaps, to wait until different aspects of the developments we are studying have been looked at more closely. Yet this much must be said. It is quite clear that the shift from complexive-perceptual definitions of equivalence to ones that are superordinate-functional is *not* a universal property of 'growing up'. For one thing, we shall see that the 'natural' terminus of growth depends to a very considerable extent on the pattern imposed by the culture. The techniques used in this chapter have, in modified form, been used in studies of children in Alaska, Mexico, and Senegal and it is plain that school children in Dakar or Mexico City look very much like the school children of this reading. But it is equally plain that the village child of rural Mexico and the unschooled Wolof of Senegal seem very different, much more complexive, much more perceptually oriented. Later we shall explore why this may be.

A second consideration has to do with the relation of the two systems of representation and their interaction in growth. We know from the searching studies of Wallach and Kogan (1965) that the two orientations – call them ikonic and symbolic as a shorthand – can be quite independent one of the other. That is to say, one finds children who are clearly provident both in the kinds of complex and metaphoric activities of the first mode and in the more abstract activities of the second. In others, the first suffers a kind of replacement by the second, and a different style emerges. All this is within the limits of our own culture.

The need for delaying interpretation is, then, obvious enough. All we need say here is that our middle-class children do show a pattern of growth in which 'appropriate' rational classification based on the functional properties of things 'replaces' earlier complexive grouping based on the surface properties of events. But such growth is not inevitable, not complete, and not something that invades every corner of the mind.

References

VYGOTSKY, L. S. (1962), *Thought and Language*, Wiley.
WALLACH, M. A., and KOGAN, N. (1965), *Modes of Thinking in Young Children*, Holt, Rinehart & Winston.
WITTGENSTEIN, L. (1953), *Philosophical Investigations*, Macmillan.
WITTGENSTEIN, L. (1958), *The Blue and Brown Books*, Blackwell.

Part Five Language and the Structure of Mind

It is necessary to postulate some initial structures of mind to explain aspects of human knowledge. What is at issue in the two articles that follow (Readings 18 and 19) is the degree of innateness and the nature of the structure which underlies language. The key question is: Does language acquisition unfold in a manner dictated by an initial structure or is it more directly dependent on the particular skills the child builds up in the pre-linguistic stage?

18 N. Chomsky

Linguistic Contributions to the Study of Mind: Future

'Linguistic contributions to the study of mind: future', in N. Chomsky, *Language and Mind*, 1968, Harcourt, Brace & World, pp. 58–85.

In discussing the past, I referred to two major traditions that have enriched the study of language in their separate and very different ways; and in my last lecture, I tried to give some indication of the topics that seem on the immediate horizon today, as a kind of synthesis of philosophical grammar and structural linguistics begins to take shape. Each of the major traditions of study and speculation that I have been using as a point of reference was associated with a certain characteristic approach to the problems of mind; we might say, without distortion, that each evolved as a specific branch of the psychology of its time, to which it made a distinctive contribution.

It may seem a bit paradoxical to speak of structural linguistics in this way, given its militant anti-psychologism. But the paradox is lessened when we take note of the fact that this militant anti-psychologism is no less true of much of contemporary psychology itself, particularly of those branches that until a few years ago monopolized the study of use and acquisition of language. We live, after all, in the age of 'behavioral science', not of 'the science of mind'. I do not want to read too much into a terminological innovation, but I think that there is some significance in the ease and willingness with which modern thinking about man and society accepts the designation 'behavioral science'. No sane person has ever doubted that behavior provides much of the evidence for this study – all of the evidence, if we interpret 'behavior' in a sufficiently loose sense. But the term 'behavioral science' suggests a not-so-subtle shift of emphasis toward the evidence itself and away from the deeper underlying principles and abstract mental structures that might be illuminated by the evidence of behavior. It is as if natural science were to be designated 'the science of meter readings'. What, in fact, would we expect of natural science in a culture that was satisfied to accept this designation for its activities?

Behavioral science has been much preoccupied with data and organization of data, and it has even seen itself as a kind of technology of control of behavior. Anti-mentalism in linguistics and in philosophy of language conforms to this shift of orientation. As I mentioned in my first lecture, I think that one major indirect contribution of modern structural linguistics results from its success in making explicit the assumptions of an anti-mentalistic, thoroughly operational and behaviorist approach to the phenomena of language. By extending this approach to its natural limits, it laid the groundwork for a fairly conclusive demonstration of the inadequacy of any such approach to the problems of mind.

More generally, I think that the long-range significance of the study of language lies in the fact that in this study it is possible to give a relatively sharp and clear formulation of some of the central questions of psychology and to bring a mass of evidence to bear on them. What is more, the study of language is, for the moment, unique in the combination it affords of richness of data and susceptibility to sharp formulation of basic issues.

It would, of course, be silly to try to predict the future of research, and it will be understood that I do not intend the subtitle of this lecture to be taken very seriously. Nevertheless, it is fair to suppose that the major contribution of the study of language will lie in the understanding it can provide as to the character of mental processes and the structures they form and manipulate. Therefore, instead of speculating on the likely course of research into the problems that are coming into focus today,[1] I will concentrate here on some of the issues that arise when we try to develop the study of linguistic structure as a chapter of human psychology.

1. A number of such problems might be enumerated – for example, the problem of how the intrinsic content of phonetic features determines the functioning of phonological rules, the role of universal formal conditions in restricting the choice of grammars and the empirical interpretation of such grammars, the relations of syntactic and semantic structure, the nature of universal semantics, performance models that incorporate generative grammars, and so on.

It is quite natural to expect that a concern for language will remain central to the study of human nature, as it has been in the past. Anyone concerned with the study of human nature, and human capacities must somehow come to grips with the fact that all normal humans acquire language, whereas acquisition of even its barest rudiments is quite beyond the capacities of an otherwise intelligent ape – a fact that was emphasized quite correctly, in Cartesian philosophy.[2] It is widely thought that the extensive modern studies of animal communication challenge this classical view; and it is almost universally taken for granted that there exists a problem of explaining the 'evolution' of human language from systems of animal communication. However, a careful look at recent studies of animal communication seems to me to provide little support for these assumptions. Rather, these studies simply bring out even more clearly the extent to which human language appears to be a unique phenomenon, without significant analogue in the animal world. If this is so, it is quite senseless to raise the problem of explaining the evolution of human language from more primitive systems of communication that appear at lower levels of intellectual capacity. The issue is important, and I would like to dwell on it for a moment.

The assumption that human language evolved from more

2. Modern attempts to train apes in behavior that the investigators regard as language-like confirm this incapacity, though it may be that the failures are to be attributed to the technique of operant conditioning and therefore show little about the animal's actual abilities. See, for example, the report by Ferster (1964). He attempted to teach chimpanzees to match the binary numbers 001, . . . , 111 to sets of one to seven objects. He reports that hundreds of thousands of trials were required for 95 per cent accuracy to be achieved, even in this trivial task. Of course, even at this stage the apes had not learned the principle of binary arithmetic; they would not, for example, be able to match a four-digit binary number correctly, and, presumably, they would have done just as badly in the experiment had it involved an arbitrary association of the binary numbers to sets rather than the association determined by the principle of the binary notation. Ferster overlooks this crucial point and therefore concludes, mistakenly, that he has taught the rudiments of symbolic behavior. The confusion is compounded by his definition of language as 'a set of symbolic stimuli that control behavior' and by his strange belief that the 'effectiveness' of language arises from the fact that utterances 'control almost identical performances in speaker and listener'.

primitive systems is developed in an interesting way by Popper in his recently published Arthur Compton Lecture, 'Clouds and Clocks'. He tries to show how problems of freedom of will and Cartesian dualism can be solved by the analysis of this 'evolution'. I am not concerned now with the philosophical conclusions that he draws from this analysis, but with the basic assumption that there is an evolutionary development of language from simpler systems of the sort that one discovers in other organisms. Popper argues that the evolution of language passed through several stages, in particular a 'lower stage' in which vocal gestures are used for expression of emotional state, for example, and a 'higher stage' in which articulated sound is used for expression of thought – in Popper's terms, for description and critical argument. His discussion of stages of evolution of language suggests a kind of continuity, but in fact he establishes no relation between the lower and higher stages and does not suggest a mechanism whereby transition can take place from one stage to the next. In short, he gives no argument to show that the stages belong to a single evolutionary process. In fact, it is difficult to see what links these stages at all (except for the metaphorical use of the term 'language'). There is no reason to suppose that the 'gaps' are bridgeable. There is no more of a basis for assuming an evolutionary development of 'higher' from 'lower' stages, in this case, than there is for assuming an evolutionary development from breathing to walking; the stages have no significant analogy, it appears, and seem to involve entirely different processes and principles.

A more explicit discussion of the relation between human language and animal communication systems appears in a recent discussion by the comparative ethologist Thorpe (1967). He points out that mammals other than man appear to lack the human ability to imitate sounds, and that one might therefore have expected birds (many of which have this ability to a remarkable extent) to be 'the group which ought to have been able to evolve language in the true sense, and not the mammals'. Thorpe does not suggest that human language 'evolved' in any strict sense from simpler systems, but he does argue that the characteristic properties of human language can be found in animal communication systems, although 'we cannot at the moment say

definitely that they are all present in one particular animal.'
The characteristics shared by human and animal language are
the properties of being 'purposive', 'syntactic', and 'propositional'. Language is purposive 'in that there is nearly always in
human speech a definite intention of getting something over to
somebody else, altering his behavior, his thoughts, or his general
attitude toward a situation'. Human language is 'syntactic' in
that an utterance is a performance with an internal organization,
with structure and coherence. It is 'propositional' in that it
transmits information. In this sense, then, both human language
and animal communication are purposive, syntactic, and
propositional.

All this may be true, but it establishes very little, since when we
move to the level of abstraction at which human language and
animal communication fall together, almost all other behavior
is included as well. Consider walking: Clearly, walking is purposive
behavior, in the most general sense of 'purposive'. Walking is
also 'syntactic' in the sense just defined, as, in fact, Lashley
pointed out a long time ago (1951) in his important discussion of
serial order in behavior, to which I referred in the first lecture.
Furthermore, it can certainly be informative; for example, I can
signal my interest in reaching a certain goal by the speed or
intensity with which I walk.

It is, incidentally, precisely in this manner that the examples
of animal communication that Thorpe presents are 'propositional'. He cites as an example the song of the European robin,
in which the rate of alternation of high and low pitch signals the
intention of the bird to defend its territory; the higher the rate of
alternation, the greater the intention to defend the territory. The
example is interesting, but it seems to me to show very clearly
the hopelessness of the attempt to relate human language to
animal communication. Every animal communication system
that is known (if we disregard some science fiction about dol-
phins) uses one of two basic principles: Either it consists of a
fixed, finite number of signals, each associated with a specific
range of behavior or emotional state, as is illustrated in the extensive primate studies that have been carried out by Japanese
scientists for the past several years; or it makes use of a fixed,
finite number of linguistic dimensions, each of which is associated

with a particular nonlinguistic dimension in such a way that selection of a point along the linguistic dimension determines and signals a certain point along the associated nonlinguistic dimension. The latter is the principle realized in Thorpe's bird-song example. Rate of alternation of high and low pitch is a linguistic dimension correlated with the nonlinguistic dimension of intention to defend a territory. The bird signals its intention to defend a territory by selecting a correlated point along the linguistic dimension of pitch alternation – I use the word 'select' loosely, of course. The linguistic dimension is abstract, but the principle is clear. A communication system of the second type has an indefinitely large range of potential signals, as does human language. The mechanism and principle, however, are entirely different from those employed by human language to express indefinitely many new thoughts, intentions, feelings, and so on. It is not correct to speak of a 'deficiency' of the animal system, in terms of range of potential signals; rather the opposite, since the animal system admits in principle of continuous variation along the linguistic dimension (insofar as it makes sense to speak of 'continuity' in such a case), whereas human language is discrete. Hence, the issue is not one of 'more' or 'less', but rather of an entirely different principle of organization. When I make some arbitrary statement in a human language, say, that 'the rise of supranational corporations poses new dangers for human freedom', I am not selecting a point along some linguistic dimension that signals a corresponding point along an associated non-linguistic dimension, nor am I selecting a signal from a finite behavioral repertoire, innate or learned.

Furthermore, it is wrong to think of human use of language as characteristically informative, in fact or in intention. Human language can be used to inform or mislead, to clarify one's own thoughts or to display one's cleverness, or simply for play. If I speak with no concern for modifying your behavior or thoughts, I am not using language any less than if I say exactly the same things *with* such intention. If we hope to understand human language and the psychological capacities on which it rests, we must first ask what it is, not how or for what purpose it is used. When we ask what human language is, we find no striking similarity to animal communication systems. There is nothing useful to be said about behavior or thought at the level of abstraction at which animal and human communication fall together. The examples of animal communication that have been examined to date do share many of the properties of human gestural systems, and it might be reasonable to explore the possibility of direct connection in this case. But human language, it appears, is based on entirely different principles. This, I think, is an important point, often overlooked by those who approach human language as a natural, biological phenomenon; in particular, it seems rather pointless, for these reasons, to speculate about the evolution of human language from simpler systems – perhaps as absurd as it would be to speculate about the 'evolution' of atoms from clouds of elementary particles.

As far as we know, possession of human language is associated with a specific type of mental organization, not simply a higher degree of intelligence. There seems to be no substance to the view that human language is simply a more complex instance of something to be found elsewhere in the animal world. This poses a problem for the biologist, since, if true, it is an example of true 'emergence' – the appearance of a qualitatively different phenomenon at a specific stage of complexity of organization. Recognition of this fact, though formulated in entirely different terms, is what motivated much of the classical study of language by those whose primary concern was the nature of mind. And it seems to me that today there is no better or more promising way to explore the essential and distinctive properties of human intelligence than through the detailed investigation of the structure of this unique human possession. A reasonable guess, then, is that if empirically adequate generative grammars can be constructed and the universal principles that govern their structure and organization determined, then this will be an important contribution to human psychology, in ways to which I will turn directly, in detail.

In the course of these lectures I have mentioned some of the classical ideas regarding language structure and contemporary efforts to deepen and extend them. It seems clear that we must regard linguistic competence – knowledge of a language – as an abstract system underlying behavior, a system constituted by rules that interact to determine the form and intrinsic meaning of a potentially infinite number of sentences. Such a system – a generative grammar – provides an explication of the Humboldtian idea of 'form of language', which in an obscure but suggestive remark in his great posthumous work, *Über die Verschiedenheit des Menschlichen Sprachbaues*, Humboldt defines as 'that constant and unvarying system of processes underlying the mental act of raising articulated structurally organized signals to an expression of thought.' Such a grammar defines a language in the Humboldtian sense, namely as 'a recursively generated system, where the laws of generation are fixed and invariant, but the scope and the specific manner in which they are applied remain entirely unspecified.'

In each grammar there are particular, idiosyncratic elements, selection of which determines one specific human language; and there are general universal elements, conditions on the form and organization of any human language, that form the subject matter for the study of 'universal grammar'. Among the principles of universal grammar are those I discussed in the preceding lecture – for example, the principles that distinguish deep and surface structure and that constrain the class of transformational operations that relate them. Notice, incidentally, that the existence of definite principles of universal grammar makes possible the rise of the new field of mathematical linguistics, a field that submits to abstract study the class of generative systems meeting the conditions set forth in universal grammar. This inquiry aims to elaborate the formal properties of any possible human language. The field is in its infancy; it is only in the last decade that the possibility of such an enterprise has been envisioned. It has some promising initial results, and it suggests one possible direction for future research that might prove to be of great importance. Thus, mathematical linguistics seems for the moment to be in a uniquely favorable position, among mathematical approaches in the social and psychological sciences, to develop not simply as a theory of data, but as the study of highly abstract principles and structures that determine the character of human mental processes. In this case, the mental processes in question are those involved in the organization of one specific domain of human knowledge, namely knowledge of language.

The theory of generative grammar, both particular and universal, points to a conceptual lacuna in psychological theory that

I believe is worth mentioning. Psychology conceived as 'behavioral science' has been concerned with behavior and acquisition or control of behavior. It has no concept corresponding to 'competence', in the sense in which competence is characterized by a generative grammar. The theory of learning has limited itself to a narrow and surely inadequate concept of what is learned – namely a system of stimulus-response connections, a network of associations, a repertoire of behavioral items, a habit hierarchy, or a system of dispositions to respond in a particular way under specifiable stimulus conditions.[3] Insofar as behavioral psychology has been applied to education or therapy, it has correspondingly limited itself to this concept of 'what is learned'. But a generative grammar cannot be characterized in these terms. What is necessary, in addition to the concept of behavior and learning, is a concept of what is learned – a notion of competence – that lies beyond the conceptual limits of behaviorist psychological theory. Like much of modern linguistics and modern philosophy of language, behaviorist psychology has quite consciously accepted methodological restrictions that do not permit the study of systems of the necessary complexity and abstractedness.[4] One important future contribution of the study of language to general psychology may

3. This limitation is revealed, for example, in such statements as this from Wiest (1967): 'An empirical demonstration . . . that a child has learned the rules of grammar would be his exhibiting the verbal performance called "uttering the rules of grammar". That this performance is not usually acquired without special training is attested to by many grammar school teachers. One may even speak quite grammatically without having literally learned the rules of grammar.' Wiest's inability to conceive of another sense in which the child may be said to have learned the rules of grammar testifies to the conceptual gap we are discussing. Since he refuses to consider the question of *what* is learned, and to clarify this notion before asking *how* it is learned, he can only conceive of 'grammar' as the 'behavioral regularities in the understanding and production of speech' – a characterization that is perfectly empty, as it stands, there being no 'behavioral regularities' associated with (let alone 'in') the understanding and production of speech. One cannot quarrel with the desire of some investigators to study 'the acquisition and maintenance of *actual occurrences of verbal behavior*' (*ibid.*). It remains to be demonstrated that this study has something to do with the study of language. As of now, I see no indication that this claim can be substantiated.
4. See my paper in Morgenbesser, Suppes, and White (in press), for a discussion of the work on Quine and Wittgenstein from this point of view.

be to focus attention on this conceptual gap and to demonstrate how it may be filled by the elaboration of a system of underlying competence in one domain of human intelligence.

There is an obvious sense in which any aspect of psychology is based ultimately on the observation of behavior. But it is not at all obvious that the study of learning should proceed directly to the investigation of factors that control behavior or of conditions under which a 'behavioral repertoire' is established. It is first necessary to determine the significant characteristics of this behavioral repertoire, the principles on which it is organized. A meaningful study of learning can proceed only after this preliminary task has been carried out and has led to a reasonably well-confirmed theory of underlying competence – in the case of language, to the formulation of the generative grammar that underlies the observed use of language. Such a study will concern itself with the relation between the data available to the organism and the competence that it acquires; only to the extent that the abstraction to competence has been successful – in the case of language, to the extent that the postulated grammar is 'descriptively adequate' – can the investigation of learning hope to achieve meaningful results. If, in some domain, the organization of the behavioral repertoire is quite trivial and elementary, then there will be little harm in avoiding the intermediate stage of theory construction, in which we attempt to characterize accurately the competence that is acquired. But one cannot count on this being the case, and in the study of language it surely is not the case. With a richer and more adequate characterization of 'what is learned' – of the underlying competence that constitutes the 'final state' of the organism being studied – it may be possible to approach the task of constructing a theory of learning that will be much less restricted in scope than modern behavioral psychology has proved to be. Surely it is pointless to accept methodological strictures that preclude such an approach to problems of learning.

Are there other areas of human competence where one might hope to develop a fruitful theory, analogous to generative grammar? Although this is a very important question, there is very little that can be said about it today. One might, for example, consider the problem of how a person comes to acquire a certain concept of three-dimensional space, or an implicit 'theory of human action', in similar terms. Such a study would begin with the attempt to characterize the implicit theory that underlies actual performance and would then turn to the question of how this theory develops under the given conditions of time and access to data – that is, in what way the resulting system of beliefs is determined by the interplay of available data, 'heuristic procedures,' and the innate schematism that restricts and conditions the form of the aquired system. At the moment, this is nothing more than a sketch of a program of research.

There have been some attempts to study the structure of other, language-like systems – the study of kinship systems and folk taxonomies comes to mind, for example. But so far, at least, nothing has been discovered that is even roughly comparable to language in these domains. No one, to my knowledge, has devoted more thought to this problem than Lévi-Strauss. For example, his recent book on the categories of primitive mentality (Lévi-Strauss, 1967) is a serious and thoughtful attempt to come to grips with this problem. Nevertheless, I do not see what conclusions can be reached from a study of his materials beyond the fact that the savage mind attempts to impose some organization on the physical world – that humans classify, if they perform any mental acts at all. Specifically, Lévi-Strauss's well-known critique of totemism seems to reduce to little more than this conclusion.

Lévi-Strauss models his investigations quite consciously on structural linguistics, particularly on the work of Troubetzkoy and Jakobson. He repeatedly and quite correctly emphasizes that one cannot simply apply procedures analogous to those of phonemic analysis to subsystems of society and culture. Rather, he is concerned with structures 'where they may be found . . . in the kinship system, political ideology, mythology, ritual, art', and so on, (Lévi-Strauss, 1963) and he wishes to examine the formal properties of these structures in their own terms. But several reservations are necessary when structural linguistics is used as a model in this way. For one thing, the structure of a phonological system is of very little interest as a formal object; there is nothing of significance to be said, from a formal point of view, about a set of forty-odd elements cross-classified in terms of eight or ten features. The significance of structuralist phonology, as developed by Troubetzkoy, Jakobson, and others, lies not in the formal properties of phonemic systems but in the fact that a fairly small number of features that can be specified in absolute, language-independent terms appear to provide the basis for the organization of all phonological systems. The achievement of structuralist phonology was to show that the phonological rules of a great variety of languages apply to classes of elements that can be simply characterized in terms of these features; that historical change affects such classes in a uniform way; and that the organization of features plays a basic role in the use and acquisition of language. This was a discovery of the greatest importance, and it provides the groundwork for much of contemporary linguistics. But if we abstract away from the specific, universal set of features and the rule systems in which they function, little of any significance remains.

Furthermore, to a greater and greater extent, current work in phonology is demonstrating that the real richness of phonological systems lies not in the structural patterns of phonemes but rather in the intricate systems of rules by which these patterns are formed, modified, and elaborated.[5] The structural patterns that arise at various stages of derivation are a kind of epiphenomenon. The system of phonological rules makes use of the universal features in a fundamental way,[6] but it is the properties of the systems of rules, it seems to me, that really shed light on the specific nature of the organization of language. For example, there appear to be very general conditions, such as the principle of cyclic ordering (discussed in the preceding lecture) and others that are still more abstract, that govern the application of these rules, and there are many interesting and unsolved questions as to how the choice of rules is determined by intrinsic, universal relations among features. Furthermore, the idea of a mathematical investigation of language structures, to which Lévi-Strauss occasionally alludes, becomes meaningful only when one considers systems of rules with infinite generative capacity. There is nothing to be said about the abstract structure of the various patterns that appear at various stages of derivation. If this is

5. See discussion in the preceding lecture [this is the third of a series] and the references cited there.

6. The study of universal features is itself in considerable flux. See Chomsky and Halle (1968), chapter 7, for recent discussion.

correct, then one cannot expect structuralist phonology, in itself, to provide a useful model for investigation of other cultural and social systems.

In general, the problem of extending concepts of linguistic structure to other cognitive systems seems to me, for the moment, in not too promising a state, although it is no doubt too early for pessimism.

Before turning to the general implications of the study of linguistic competence and, more specifically, to the conclusions of universal grammar, it is well to make sure of the status of these conclusions in the light of current knowledge of the possible diversity of language. In my first lecture, I quoted the remarks of Dwight Whitney about what he referred to as 'the infinite diversity of human speech,' the boundless variety that, he maintained, undermines the claims of philosophical grammar to psychological relevance.

Philosophical grammarians had typically maintained that languages vary little in their deep structures, though there may be wide variability in surface manifestations. Thus there is, in this view, an underlying structure of grammatical relations and categories, and certain aspects of human thought and mentality are essentially invariant across languages, although languages may differ as to whether they express the grammatical relations formally by inflection or word order, for example. Furthermore, an investigation of their work indicates that the underlying recursive principles that generate deep structure were assumed to be restricted in certain ways – for example, by the condition that new structures are formed only by the insertion of new 'propositional content', new structures that themselves correspond to actual simple sentences, in fixed positions in already formed structures. Similarly, the grammatical transformations that form surface structures through reordering, ellipsis, and other formal operations must themselves meet certain fixed general conditions, such as those discussed in the preceding lecture. In short, the theories of philosophical grammar, and the more recent elaborations of these theories, make the assumption that languages will differ very little, despite considerable diversity in superficial realization, when we discover their deeper structures and unearth their fundamental mechanisms and principles.

It is interesting to observe that this assumption persisted even through the period of German romanticism, which was, of course, much preoccupied with the diversity of cultures and with the many rich possibilities for human intellectual development. Thus, Wilhelm von Humboldt, who is now best remembered for his ideas concerning the variety of languages and the association of diverse language structures with divergent 'world-views', nevertheless held firmly that underlying any human language we will find a system that is universal, that simply expresses man's unique intellectual attributes. For this reason, it was possible for him to maintain the rationalist view that language is not really learned – certainly not taught – but rather develops 'from within', in an essentially predetermined way, when the appropriate environmental conditions exist. One cannot really teach a first language, he argued, but can only 'provide the thread along which it will develop of its own accord,' by processes more like maturation than learning. This Platonistic element in Humboldt's thought is a pervasive one; for Humboldt, it was as natural to propose an essentially Platonistic theory of 'learning' as it was for Rousseau to found his critique of repressive social institutions on a conception of human freedom that derives from strictly Cartesian assumptions regarding the limitations of mechanical explanation. And in general it seems appropriate to construe both the psychology and the linguistics of the romantic period as in large part a natural outgrowth of rationalist conceptions.[7]

The issue raised by Whitney against Humboldt and philosophical grammar in general is of great significance with respect to the implications of linguistics for general human psychology. Evidently, these implications can be truly far-reaching only if the rationalist view is essentially correct, in which case the structure of language can truly serve as a 'mirror of mind', in both its particular and its universal aspects. It is widely believed that modern anthropology has established the falsity of the assump-

7. This is put forth as the 'Boas Tradition'. American linguistics, Joos maintains, 'got its decisive direction when it was decided that an indigenous language could be described without any preexistent scheme of what a language must be ...' (1966, p. 1). Of course this could not literally be true – the procedures of analysis themselves express a hypothesis concerning the possible diversity of language. But there is, nevertheless, much justice in Joos's characterization.

tions of the rationalist universal grammarians by demonstrating through empirical study that languages may, in fact, exhibit the widest diversity. Whitney's claims regarding the diversity of languages are reiterated throughout the modern period; Martin Joos, for example, is simply expressing the conventional wisdom when he takes the basic conclusion of modern anthropological linguistics to be that 'languages can differ without limit as to either extent or direction' (Joos, 1966).[8]

The belief that anthropological linguistics has demolished the assumptions of universal grammar seems to me to be quite false in two important respects. First, it misinterprets the views of classical rationalist grammar, which held that languages are similar only at the deeper level, the level at which grammatical relations are expressed and at which the processes that provide for the creative aspect of language use are to be found. Second, this belief seriously misinterprets the findings of anthropological linguistics, which has, in fact, restricted itself almost completely to fairly superficial aspects of language structure.

To say this is not to criticize anthropological linguistics, a field that is faced with compelling problems of its own – in particular, the problem of obtaining at least some record of the rapidly vanishing languages of the primitive world. Nevertheless, it is important to bear in mind this fundamental limitation on its achievements in considering the light it can shed on the theses of universal grammar. Anthropological studies (like structural linguistic studies in general) do not attempt to reveal the underlying core of generative processes in language – that is, the processes that determine the deeper levels of structure and that constitute the systematic means for creating ever novel sentence types. Therefore, they obviously cannot have any real bearing on the classical assumption that these underlying generative processes vary only slightly from language to language. In fact, what evidence is now available suggests that if universal grammar has serious defects, as indeed it does from a modern point of view, then these defects lie in the failure to recognize the abstract nature of linguistic structure and to impose sufficiently strong and restrictive conditions on the form of any human language. And a characteristic feature of current work in linguistics is its concern for

8. For some discussion of these matters, see my book (1966).

linguistic universals of a sort that can only be detected through a detailed investigation of particular languages, universals governing properties of language that are simply not accessible to investigation within the restricted framework that has been adopted, often for very good reasons, within anthropological linguistics.

I think that if we contemplate the classical problem of psychology, that of accounting for human knowledge, we cannot avoid being struck by the enormous disparity between knowledge and experience – in the case of language, between the generative grammar that expresses the linguistic competence of the native speaker and the meager and degenerate data on the basis of which he has constructed this grammar for himself. In principle the theory of learning should deal with this problem; but in fact it bypasses the problem, because of the conceptual gap that I mentioned earlier. The problem cannot even be formulated in any sensible way until we develop the concept of competence, alongside the concepts of learning and behavior, and apply this concept in some domain. The fact is that this concept has so far been extensively developed and applied only in the study of human language. It is only in this domain that we have at least the first steps toward an account of competence, namely the fragmentary generative grammars that have been constructed for particular languages. As the study of language progresses, we can expect with some confidence that these grammars will be extended in scope and depth, although it will hardly come as a surprise if the first proposals are found to be mistaken in fundamental ways.

Insofar as we have a tentative first approximation to a generative grammar for some language, we can for the first time formulate in a useful way the problem of origin of knowledge. In other words, we can ask the question, What initial structure must be attributed to the mind that enables it to construct such a grammar from the data of sense? Some of the empirical conditions that must be met by any such assumption about innate structure are moderately clear. Thus, it appears to be a species-specific capacity that is essentially independent of intelligence, and we can make a fairly good estimate of the amount of data that is necessary for the task to be successfully accomplished. We know that the grammars that are in fact constructed vary only slightly among speakers of the same language, despite wide variations not only in intelligence but also in the conditions under which language is acquired. As participants in a certain culture, we are naturally aware of the great differences in ability to use language, in knowledge of vocabulary, and so on that result from differences in native ability and from differences in conditions of acquisition; we naturally pay much less attention to the similarities and to common knowledge, which we take for granted. But if we manage to establish the requisite psychic distance, if we actually compare the generative grammars that must be postulated for different speakers of the same language, we find that the similarities that we take for granted are quite marked and that the divergences are few and marginal. What is more, it seems that dialects that are superficially quite remote, even barely intelligible on first contact, share a vast central core of common rules and processes and differ very slightly in underlying structures, which seem to remain invariant through long historical eras. Furthermore, we discover a substantial system of principles that do not vary even among languages that are, as far as we know, entirely unrelated.

The central problems in this domain are empirical ones that are, in principle at least, quite straightforward, difficult as they may be to solve in a satisfactory way. We must postulate an innate structure that is rich enough to account for the disparity between experience and knowledge, one that can account for the construction of the empirically justified generative grammars within the given limitations of time and access to data. At the same time, this postulated innate mental structure must not be so rich and restrictive as to exclude certain known languages. There is, in other words, an upper bound and a lower bound on the degree and exact character of the complexity that can be postulated as innate mental structure. The factual situation is obscure enough to leave room for much difference of opinion over the true nature of this innate mental structure that makes acquisition of language possible. However, there seems to me to be no doubt that this is an empirical issue, one that can be resolved by proceeding along the lines that I have just roughly outlined.

My own estimate of the situation is that the real problem for tomorrow is that of discovering an assumption regarding innate structure that is sufficiently rich, not that of finding one that is simple or elementary enough to be 'plausible'. There is, as far as I can see, no reasonable notion of 'plausibility', no *a priori* insight into what innate structures are permissible, that can guide the search for a 'sufficiently elementary assumption'. It would be mere dogmatism to maintain without argument or evidence that the mind is simpler in its innate structure than other biological systems, just as it would be mere dogmatism to insist that the mind's organization must necessarily follow certain set principles, determined in advance of investigation and maintained in defiance of any empirical findings. I think that the study of problems of mind has been very definitely hampered by a kind of apriorism with which these problems are generally approached. In particular, the empiricist assumptions that have dominated the study of acquisition of knowledge for many years seem to me to have been adopted quite without warrant and to have no special status among the many possibilities that one might imagine as to how the mind functions.

In this connection, it is illuminating to follow the debate that has arisen since the views I have just sketched were advanced a few years ago as a program of research – I should say, since this position was resurrected, because to a significant extent it is the traditional rationalist approach, now amplified and sharpened and made far more explicit in terms of the tentative conclusions that have been reached in the recent study of linguistic competence. Two outstanding American philosophers, Goodman and Putnam, have made recent contributions to this discussion – both misconceived, in my opinion, but instructive in the misconceptions that they reveal.[9]

Goodman's treatment of the question suffers first from an historical misunderstanding and second from a failure to formulate correctly the exact nature of the problem of acquisition of knowledge. His historical misunderstanding has to do with the issue between Locke and whomever Locke thought he was

9. See Goodman (1967) and Putnam (1967). Together with a paper of mine, these were presented at the Innate Ideas Symposium of the American Philosophical Association and the Boston Colloquium for the Philosophy of Science in December 1966. The three essays also appear in Cohen and Wartofsky (1968), pp. 81–107. A more extensive discussion of the papers of Putnam and Goodman, along with a number of others, appears in my contribution to the symposium (Chomsky, 1970).

criticizing in his discussion of innate ideas. According to Goodman, 'Locke made . . . acutely clear' that the doctrine of innate ideas is 'false or meaningless'. In fact, however, Locke's critique had little relevance to any familiar doctrine of the seventeenth century. The arguments that Locke gave were considered and dealt with in quite a satisfactory way in the earliest seventeenth-century discussions of innate ideas, for example those of Lord Herbert and Descartes, both of whom took for granted that the system of innate ideas and principles would not function unless appropriate stimulation took place. For this reason, Locke's arguments, none of which took cognizance of this condition, are without force;[10] for some reason, he avoided the issues that had been discussed in the preceding half-century. Furthermore, as Leibnitz observed, Locke's willingness to make use of a principle of 'reflection' makes it almost impossible to distinguish his approach from that of the rationalists, except for his failure to take even those steps suggested by his predecessors toward specifying the character of this principle.

But, historical issues aside, I think that Goodman misconstrues the substantive problem as well. He argues that first-language learning poses no real problem, because prior to first-language learning the child has already acquired the rudiments of a symbolic system in his ordinary dealings with the environment. Hence, first-language learning is analogous to second-language learning in that the fundamental step has already been taken, and details can be elaborated within an already existing framework. This argument might have some force if it were possible to show that the specific properties of grammar – say, the distinction of deep and surface structure, the specific properties of grammatical transformations, the principles of rule ordering, and so on – were present in some form in these already acquired prelinguistic 'symbolic

10. This observation is a commonplace. See, for example, the commentary by Fraser (1959) in his edition of Locke. As Fraser notes, Descartes' position is one 'which Locke's argument always fails to reach. . . . Locke assails [the hypothesis of innate ideas] . . . in its crudest form, in which it is countenanced by no eminent advocate.' Goodman is free to use the term 'innate idea' in conformity with Locke's misinterpretation of the doctrine if he wishes, but not to charge 'sophistry', as he does, when others examine and develop rationalist doctrine in the form in which it was actually presented.

systems'. But since there is not the slightest reason to believe that this is so, the argument collapses. It is based on an equivocation similar to that discussed earlier in connection with the argument that language evolved from animal communication. In that case, as we observed, the argument turned on a metaphorical use of the term 'language'. In Goodman's case, the argument is based entirely on a vague use of the term 'symbolic system', and it collapses as soon as we attempt to give this term a precise meaning. If it were possible to show that these prelinguistic symbolic systems share certain significant properties with natural language, we could then argue that these properties of natural language are acquired by analogy. Of course, we would then face the problem of explaining how the prelinguistic symbolic systems developed these properties. But since no one has succeeded in showing that the fundamental properties of natural language – those discussed in the second lecture in this series, for example – appear in prelinguistic symbolic systems or any others, the latter problem does not arise.

According to Goodman, the reason why the problem of second-language learning is different from that of first-language learning is that 'once one language is available,' it 'can be used for giving explanation and instruction.' He then goes on to argue that 'acquisition of an initial language is acquisition of a secondary symbolic system' and is quite on a par with normal second-language acquisition. The primary symbolic systems to which he refers are 'rudimentary prelinguistic symbolic systems in which gestures and sensory and perceptual occurrences of all sorts function as signs.' But evidently these prelinguistic symbolic systems cannot be 'used for giving explanation and instruction' in the way a first language can be used in second-language instruction. Therefore, even on his own grounds, Goodman's argument is incoherent.

Goodman maintains that 'the claim we are discussing cannot be experimentally tested even when we have an acknowledged example of a "bad" language' and that 'the claim has not even been formulated to the extent of citation of a single general property of "bad" languages.' The first of these conclusions is correct, in his sense of 'experimental test', namely a test in which we 'take an infant at birth, isolate it from all the influences of our language-bound culture, and attempt to inculcate it with one of the "bad" artificial languages'. Obviously this is not feasible. But there is no reason why we should be dismayed by the impossibility of carrying out such a test as this. There are many other ways – for example, those discussed in the second lecture in this series and the references cited there – in which evidence can be obtained concerning the properties of grammars and conclusions regarding the general properties of such grammars can be put to empirical test. Any such conclusion immediately specifies, correctly or incorrectly, certain properties of 'bad' languages. Since there are dozens of papers and books that attempt to formulate such properties, his second claim, that not 'a single general property of "bad" languages' has been formulated, is rather surprising. One might try to show that these attempts are misguided or questionable, but one can hardly maintain seriously that they do not exist. Any formulation of a principle of universal grammar makes a strong empirical claim, which can be falsified by finding counter-instances in some human language, along the lines of the discussion in lecture 2. In linguistics, as in any other field, it is only in such indirect ways as this that one can hope to find evidence bearing on nontrivial hypotheses. Direct experimental tests of the sort that Goodman mentions are rarely possible, a matter that may be unfortunate but is nevertheless characteristic of most research.

At one point Goodman remarks, correctly, that even though 'for certain remarkable facts I have no alternative explanation ... that alone does not dictate acceptance of whatever theory may be offered; for the theory might be worse than none. Inability to explain a fact does not condemn me to accept an intrinsically repugnant and incomprehensible theory'. But now consider the theory of innate ideas that Goodman regards as 'intrinsically repugnant and incomprehensible'. Notice, first, that the theory is obviously not 'incomprehensible', on his terms. Thus he appears to be willing, in this article, to accept the view that in some sense the mature mind contains ideas; it is obviously not 'incomprehensible', then, that some of these ideas are 'implanted in the mind as original equipment', to use his phraseology. And if we turn to the actual doctrine as developed in rationalist philosophy, rather than Locke's caricature, the theory becomes even more obviously comprehensible. There is nothing incomprehensible in the view that stimulation provides the occasion for the mind to apply certain innate interpretive principles, certain concepts that proceed from 'the power of understanding' itself, from the faculty of thinking rather than from external objects directly. To take an example from Descartes (*Reply to Objections*, book 5):

When first in infancy we see a triangular figure depicted on paper, this figure cannot show us how a real triangle ought to be conceived, in the way in which geometricians consider it, because the true triangle is contained in this figure, just as the statue of Mercury is contained in a rough block of wood. But because we already possess within us the idea of a true triangle, and it can be more easily conceived by our mind than the more complex figure of the triangle drawn on paper, we, therefore, when we see the composite figure, apprehend not it itself, but rather the authentic triangle (Haldane and Ross, 1955).[11]

In this sense the idea of a triangle is innate. Surely the notion is comprehensible; there would be no difficulty, for example, in programing a computer to react to stimuli along these lines (though this would not satisfy Descartes, for other reasons). Similarly, there is no difficulty in principle in programing a computer with a schematism that sharply restricts the form of a generative grammar, with an evaluation procedure for grammars of the given form, with a technique for determining whether given data is compatible with a grammar of the given form, with a fixed substructure of entities (such as distinctive features), rules, and principles, and so on – in short, with a universal grammar of the sort that has been proposed in recent years. For reasons that I have already mentioned, I believe that these proposals can be properly regarded as a further development of classical rationalist doctrine, as an elaboration of some of its main ideas regarding language and mind. Of course, such a theory will be 'repugnant' to one who accepts empiricist doctrine and regards it as immune to question or challenge. It seems to me that this is the heart of the matter.

Putnam's paper (see footnote 9) deals more directly with the points at issue, but it seems to me that his arguments are also

11. The citation, and the preceding remarks, appear in my contribution to the Innate Ideas Symposium of December 1966 (see footnote 9).

inconclusive, because of certain incorrect assumptions that he makes about the nature of the acquired grammars. Putnam assumes that on the level of phonetics the only property proposed in universal grammar is that a language has 'a short list of phonemes'. This, he argues, is not a similarity among languages that requires elaborate explanatory hypotheses. The conclusion is correct; the assumption is quite wrong. In fact, as I have now pointed out several times, very strong empirical hypotheses have been proposed regarding the specific choice of universal features, conditions on the form and organization of phonological rules, conditions on rule application, and so on. If these proposals are correct or near correct, then 'similarities among languages' at the level of sound structure are indeed remarkable and cannot be accounted for simply by assumptions about memory capacity, as Putnam suggests.

Above the level of sound structure, Putnam assumes that the only significant properties of language are that they have proper names, that the grammar contains a phrase structure component, and that there are rules 'abbreviating' sentences generated by the phrase structure component. He argues that the nature of the phrase structure component is determined by the existence of proper names; that the existence of a phrase structure component is explained by the fact that 'all the natural measures of complexity of an algorithm – size of the machine table, length of computations, time, and space required for the computation – lead to the . . . result' that phrase structure systems provide the 'algorithms which are "simplest" for virtually any computing system,' hence also 'for naturally evolved "computing systems"'; and that there is nothing surprising in the fact that languages contain rules of abbreviation.

Each of the three conclusions involves a false assumption. From the fact that a phrase structure system contains proper names one can conclude almost nothing about its other categories. In fact, there is much dispute at the moment about the general properties of the underlying phrase structure system for natural languages; the dispute is not in the least resolved by the existence of proper names.

As to the second point, it is simply untrue that all measures of complexity and speed of computation lead to phrase structure rules as the 'simplest possible algorithm'. The only existing results that are even indirectly relevant show that context-free phrase structure grammars (a reasonable model for rules generating deep structures, when we exclude the lexical items and the distributional conditions they meet) receive an automata-theoretic interpretation as nondeterministic pushdown storage automata, but the latter is hardly a 'natural' notion from the point of view of 'simplicity of algorithms' and so forth. In fact, it can be argued that the somewhat similar but not formally related concept of real-time deterministic automation is far more 'natural' in terms of time and space conditions on computation.[12]

However, it is pointless to pursue this topic, because what is at stake is not the 'simplicity' of phrase structure grammars but rather of transformational grammars with a phrase structure component that plays a role in generating deep structures. And there is absolutely no mathematical concept of 'ease of computation' or 'simplicity of algorithm' that even vaguely suggests that such systems may have some advantage over the kinds of automata that have been seriously investigated from this point of view – for example, finite state automata, linear bounded automata, and so on. The basic concept of 'structure-dependent operation' has never even been considered in a strictly mathematical context. The source of this confusion is a misconception on Putnam's part as to the nature of grammatical transformations. They are not rules that 'abbreviate' sentences; rather, they are operations that form surface structures from underlying deep structures, in such ways as are illustrated in the preceding lecture and the references there cited. Hence, to show that transformational grammars are the 'simplest possible' one would have to demonstrate that the 'optimal' computing system would take a string of symbols as input and determine its surface structure, its underlying deep structure, and the sequence of transformational operations that relates them. Nothing of the sort has been shown; in fact, the question has never even been raised.

12. For some discussion of these matters, see my article, 1963. For a more extensive discussion of the automatatheoretic framework, see Nelson (1968). A detailed presentation of properties of context-free grammars is given in Ginsburg (1966). There have been a number of studies of speed of computation, simplicity of algorithms, and so on, but none of them has any bearing on the issue under discussion.

Putnam argues that even if significant uniformities among languages were to be discovered, there would be a simpler explanation than the hypothesis of an innate universal grammar, namely their common origin. But this proposal involves a serious misunderstanding of the problem at issue. The grammar of a language must be discovered by the child from the data presented to him. As noted earlier, the empirical problem is to find a hypothesis about initial structure rich enough to account for the fact that a specific grammar is constructed by the child, but not so rich as to be falsified by the known diversity of language. Questions of common origin are of potential relevance to this empirical issue in only one respect: If the existing languages are not a 'fair sample' of the 'possible languages', we may be led mistakenly to propose too narrow a schema for universal grammar. However, as I mentioned earlier, the empirical problem that we face today is that no one has been able to devise an initial hypothesis rich enough to account for the acquisition by the child of the grammar that we are, apparently, led to attribute to him when we try to account for his ability to use the language in the normal way. The assumption of common origin contributes nothing to explaining how this achievement is possible. In short, the language is 'reinvented' each time it is learned, and the empirical problem to be faced by the theory of learning is how this invention of grammar can take place.

Putnam does face this problem and suggests that there might be 'general multipurpose learning strategies' that account for this achievement. It is, of course, an empirical question whether the properties of the 'language faculty' are specific to language or are merely a particular case of much more general mental faculties (or learning strategies). This is a problem that has been discussed earlier in this lecture, inconclusively and in a slightly different context. Putnam takes for granted that it is only general 'learning strategies' that are innate but suggests no grounds for this empirical assumption. As I have argued earlier, a nondogmatic approach to this problem can be pursued, without reliance on unargued assumptions of this sort – that is, through the investigation of specific areas of human competence, such as language, followed by the attempt to devise a hypothesis that will account for the development of this competence. If we discover through such investigation that the same 'learning strategies' are sufficient to account for the development of competence in various domains, we will have reason to believe that Putnam's assumption is correct. If we discover that the postulated innate structures differ from case to case, the only rational conclusion would be that a model of mind must involve separate 'faculties', with unique or partially unique properties. I cannot see how anyone can resolutely insist on one or the other conclusion in the light of the evidence now available to us. But one thing is quite clear: Putnam has no justification for his final conclusion, that 'invoking "Innateness" only postpones the problem of learning; it does not solve it.' Invoking an innate representation of universal grammar does solve the problem of learning, if it is true that this is the basis for language acquisition, as it well may be. If, on the other hand, there are general learning strategies that account for the acquisition of grammatical knowledge, then postulation of an innate universal grammar will not 'postpone' the problem of learning, but will rather offer an incorrect solution to this problem. The issue is an empirical one of truth or falsity, not a methodological one of states of investigation.[13]

To summarize, it seems to me that neither Goodman nor Putnam offers a serious counter-argument to the proposals concerning innate mental structure that have been advanced (tentatively, of course, as befits empirical hypotheses) or suggests a plausible alternative approach, with empirical content, to the problem of acquisition of knowledge.

Assuming the rough accuracy of conclusions that seem tenable today, it is reasonable to suppose that a generative grammar is a system of many hundreds of rules of several different types, organized in accordance with certain fixed principles of ordering and applicability and containing a certain fixed substructure, which, along with the general principles of organization, is common to all languages. There is no *a priori* 'naturalness' to

13. It is surprising to see that Putnam refers disparagingly to 'vague talk of "classes of hypotheses" – and "weighting functions"' in the course of his discussion of 'general learning strategies'. For the moment, the latter is a mere phrase without any describable content. On the other hand, there is a substantial literature detailing the properties of the classes of hypotheses and weighting functions to which Putnam refers. Hence, the shoe seems to be on the other foot in this case.

such a system, any more than there is to the detailed structure of the visual cortex. No one who has given any serious thought to the problem of formalizing inductive processes or 'heuristic methods' is likely to set much store by the hope that such a system as a generative grammar can be constructed by methods of any generality.

To my knowledge, the only substantive proposal to deal with the problem of acquisition of knowledge of language is the rationalist conception that I have outlined. To repeat: Suppose that we assign to the mind, as an innate property, the general theory of language that we have called 'universal grammar'. This theory encompasses the principles that I discussed in the preceding lecture and many others of the same sort, and it specifies a certain subsystem of rules that provides a skeletal structure for any language and a variety of conditions, formal and substantive, that any further elaboration of the grammar must meet. The theory of universal grammar, then, provides a schema to which any particular grammar must conform. Suppose, furthermore, that we can make this schema sufficiently restrictive so that very few possible grammars conforming to the schema will be consistent with the meager and degenerate data actually available to the language learner. His task, then, is to search among the possible grammars and select one that is not definitely rejected by the data available to him. What faces the language learner, under these assumptions, is not the impossible task of inventing a highly abstract and intricately structured theory on the basis of degenerate data, but rather the much more manageable task of determining whether these data belong to one or another of a fairly restricted set of potential languages.

The tasks of the psychologist, then, divide into several subtasks. The first is to discover the innate schema that characterizes the class of potential languages – that defines the 'essence' of human language. This subtask falls to that branch of human psychology known as linguistics; it is the problem of traditional universal grammar, of contemporary linguistic theory. The second subtask is the detailed study of the actual character of the stimulation and the organism-environment interaction that sets the innate cognitive mechanisms into operation. This is a study now being undertaken by a few psychologists, and it is particularly active right here in Berkeley. It has already led to interesting and suggestive conclusions. One might hope that such study will reveal a succession of maturational stages leading finally to a full generative grammar.[14]

A third task is that of determining just what it means for a hypothesis about the generative grammar of a language to be 'consistent' with the data of sense. Notice that it is a great oversimplification to suppose that a child must discover a generative grammar that accounts for all the linguistic data that has been presented to him and that 'projects' such data to an infinite range of potential sound-meaning relations. In addition to achieving this, he must also differentiate the data of sense into those utterances that give direct evidence as to the character of the underlying grammar and those that must be rejected by the hypothesis he selects as ill-formed, deviant, fragmentary, and so on. Clearly, everyone succeeds in carrying out this task of differentiation – we all know, within tolerable limits of consistency, which sentences are well formed and literally interpretable, and which must be interpreted as metaphorical, fragmentary, and deviant along many possible dimensions. I doubt that it has been fully appreciated to what extent this complicates the problem of accounting for language acquisition. Formally speaking, the learner must select a hypothesis regarding the language to which he is exposed that rejects a good part of the data on which this hypothesis must rest. Again, it is reasonable to suppose this is possible only if the range of tenable hypotheses is quite limited – if the innate schema of universal grammar is highly restrictive.

14. It is not unlikely that detailed investigation of this sort will show that the conception of universal grammar as an innate schematism is only valid as a first approximation; that, in fact, an innate schematism of a more general sort permits the formulation of tentative 'grammars' which themselves determine how later evidence is to be interpreted, leading to the postulation of richer grammars, and so on. I have so far been discussing language acquisition on the obviously false assumption that it is an instantaneous process. There are many interesting questions that arise when we consider how the process extends in time. For some discussion relating to problems of phonology, see my paper in Levin (Chomsky, in press). Notice also that it is unnecessary to suppose, even in the first approximation, that 'very few possible grammars conforming to the schema' will be available to the language learner. It is enough to suppose that the possible grammars consistent with the data will be 'scattered' in terms of an evaluation procedure.

The third subtask, then, is to study what we might think of as the problem of 'confirmation' – in this context, the problem of what relation must hold between a potential grammar and a set of data for this grammar to be confirmed as the actual theory of the language in question.

I have been describing the problem of acquisition of knowledge of language in terms that are more familiar in an epistemological than a psychological context, but I think that this is quite appropriate. Formally speaking, acquisition of 'common-sense knowledge' – knowledge of a language, for example – is not unlike theory construction of the most abstract sort. Speculating about the future development of the subject, it seems to me not unlikely, for the reasons I have mentioned, that learning theory will progress by establishing the innately determined set of possible hypotheses, determining the conditions of interaction that lead the mind to put forth hypotheses from this set, and fixing the conditions under which such a hypothesis is confirmed – and, perhaps, under which much of the data is rejected as irrelevant for one reason or another.

Such a way of describing the situation should not be too surprising to those familiar with the history of psychology at Berkeley, where, after all, Tolman has given his name to the psychology building; but I want to stress that the hypotheses I am discussing are qualitatively different in complexity and intricacy from anything that was considered in the classical discussions of learning. As I have now emphasized several times, there seems to be little useful analogy between the theory of grammar that a person has internalized and that provides the basis for his normal, creative use of language, and any other cognitive system that has so far been isolated and described; similarly, there is little useful analogy between the schema of universal grammar that we must, I believe, assign to the mind as an innate character, and any other known system of mental organization. It is quite possible that the lack of analogy testifies to our ignorance of other aspects of mental function, rather than to the absolute uniqueness of linguistic structure; but the fact is that we have, for the moment, no objective reason for supposing this to be true.

The way in which I have been describing acquisition of knowledge of language calls to mind a very interesting and rather neglected lecture given by Peirce more than fifty years ago, in which he developed some rather similar notions about acquisition of knowledge in general (Peirce, 1957). Peirce argued that the general limits of human intelligence are much more narrow than might be suggested by romantic assumptions about the limitless perfectibility of man (or, for that matter, than are suggested by his own 'pragmaticist' conceptions of the course of scientific progress in his better-known philosophical studies). He held that innate limitations on admissible hypotheses are a precondition for successful theory construction, and that the 'guessing instinct' that provides hypotheses makes use of inductive procedures only for 'corrective action'. Peirce maintained in this lecture that the history of early science shows that something approximating a correct theory was discovered with remarkable ease and rapidity, on the basis of highly inadequate data, as soon as certain problems were faced; he noted 'how few were the guesses that men of surpassing genius had to make before they rightly guessed the laws of nature.' And, he asked, 'How was it that man was ever led to entertain that true theory? You cannot say that it happened by chance, because the chances are too overwhelmingly against the single true theory in the twenty or thirty thousand years during which man has been a thinking animal, ever having come into any man's head.' *A fortiori*, the chances are even more overwhelmingly against the true theory of each language ever having come into the head of every four-year-old child. Continuing with Peirce: 'Man's mind has a natural adaptation to imagining correct theories of some kinds. . . . If man had not the gift of a mind adapted to his requirements, he could not have acquired any knowledge.' Correspondingly, in our present case, it seems that knowledge of a language – a grammar – can be acquired only by an organism that is 'preset' with a severe restriction on the form of grammar. This innate restriction is a precondition, in the Kantian sense, for linguistic experience, and it appears to be the critical factor in determining the course and result of language learning. The child cannot know at birth which language he is to learn, but he must know that its grammar must be of a predetermined form that excludes many imaginable languages. Having selected a permissible hypothesis, he can use inductive evidence for corrective action, confirming or disconfirming his choice. Once the hypothesis is sufficiently well confirmed, the child knows the language defined by this hypothesis; consequently, his knowledge extends enormously beyond his experience and, in fact, leads him to characterize much of the data of experience as defective and deviant.

Peirce regarded inductive processes as rather marginal to the acquisition of knowledge; in his words, 'Induction has no originality in it, but only tests a suggestion already made.' To understand how knowledge is acquired, in the rationalist view that Peirce outlined, we must penetrate the mysteries of what he called 'abduction', and we must discover that which 'gives a rule to abduction and so puts a limit upon admissible hypotheses.' Peirce maintained that the search for principles of abduction leads us to the study of innate ideas, which provide the instinctive structure of human intelligence. But Peirce was no dualist in the Cartesian sense; he argued (not very persuasively, in my opinion) that there is a significant analogy between human intelligence, with its abductive restrictions, and animal instinct. Thus, he maintained that man discovered certain true theories only because his 'instincts must have involved from the beginning certain tendencies to think truly' about certain specific matters; similarly, 'You cannot seriously think that every little chicken that is hatched, has to rummage through all possible theories until it lights upon the good idea of picking up something and eating it. On the contrary, you think that the chicken has an innate idea of doing this; that is to say, that it can think of this, but has no faculty of thinking anything else. . . . But if you are going to think every poor chicken endowed with an innate tendency towards a positive truth, why should you think to man alone this gift is denied?'

No one took up Peirce's challenge to develop a theory of abduction, to determine those principles that limit the admissible hypotheses or present them in a certain order. Even today, this remains a task for the future. It is a task that need not be undertaken if empiricist psychological doctrine can be substantiated; therefore, it is of great importance to subject this doctrine to rational analysis, as has been done, in part, in the study of language. I would like to repeat that it was the great merit of structural linguistics, as of Hullian learning theory in its early stages and of several other modern developments, to have given precise form to certain empiricist assumptions.[15] Where this step has been taken, the inadequacy of the postulated mechanisms has been clearly demonstrated, and, in the case of language at least, we can even begin to see just why any methods of this sort must fail – for example, because they cannot, in principle, provide for the properties of deep structures and the abstract operations of formal grammar. Speculating about the future, I think it is not unlikely that the dogmatic character of the general empiricist framework and its inadequacy to human and animal

15. In contrast, the account of language acquisition presented by Skinner (1957), seems to me either devoid of content or clearly wrong, depending on whether one interprets it metaphorically or literally (see my review of this book in *Language*, vol. 35, no. 1, 1959, pp. 26–58). It is quite appropriate when a theory is disproven in a strong form to replace it by a weaker variant. However, not infrequently this step leads to vacuity. The popularity of Skinner's concept of 'reinforcement', after the virtual collapse of Hullian theory, seems to me a case in point (note that the Skinnerian concepts can be well defined and can lead to interesting results, in a particular experimental situation – what is at issue is the Skinnerian 'extrapolation' to a wider class of cases).

Another example appears in Salzinger (1967, pp. 35–54). Salzinger argues that George Miller is not justified in criticizing learning theory for its inability to explain linguistic productivity – that is, the ability of a speaker to determine, of a sequence of words that he has never heard, whether or not it is a well-formed sentence and what it means. The defect can be overcome, he argues, by making use of the notion of 'response class'. True, it cannot be that each response is reinforced, but the class of acceptable sentences constitutes a response class, like the set of bar-presses in a particular Skinnerian experiment. Unfortunately, this is empty verbiage until the condition that defines membership in this class is established. If the condition involves the notion 'generation by a given grammar', then we are back where we started.

Salzinger also misconstrues the attempts to provide an experimental test that will distinguish grammatical from ungrammatical strings. He states that such tests have failed to confirm such a division and therefore concludes, apparently, that the distinction does not exist. Obviously, the failure indicates nothing more than that the tests were ineffective. One can invent innumerable tests that would fail to provide some given classification. Surely the classification itself is not in question. Thus, Salzinger would agree, quite apart from any experimental test that might be devised, that the sentences of this footnote share an important property that does not hold of the set of strings of words formed by reading each of these sentences, word by word, from right to left.

intelligence will gradually become more evident as specific realizations, such as taxonomic linguistics, behaviorist learning theory, and the perceptron models,[16] heuristic methods, and 'general problem solvers' of the early enthusiasts of 'artificial intelligence', are successively rejected on empirical grounds when they are made precise and on grounds of vacuity when they are left vague. And – assuming this projection to be accurate – it will then be possible to undertake a general study of the limits and capacities of human intelligence, to develop a Peircean logic of abduction.

Modern psychology is not devoid of such initiatives. The contemporary study of generative grammar and its universal substructure and governing principles is one such manifestation. Closely related is the study of the biological bases of human language, an investigation to which Eric Lenneberg has made substantial contributions (Lenneberg, 1967). It is tempting to see a parallel development in the very important work of Piaget and others interested in 'genetic epistemology', but I am not sure that this is accurate. It is not clear to me, for example, what Piaget takes to be the basis for the transition from one of the stages that he discusses to the next, higher stage. There is, furthermore, a possibility, suggested by recent work of Mehler and Bever, that the deservedly well-known results on conservation, in particular, may not demonstrate successive stages of intellectual development in the sense discussed by Piaget and his co-workers, but something rather different. If the preliminary results of Mehler and Bever (1967) are correct, then it would follow that the 'final stage', in which conservation is properly understood, was already realized at a very early period of development. Later, the child develops a heuristic technique that is largely adequate but that fails under the conditions of the conservation experiment. Still later, he adjusts this technique successfully and once again makes the correct judgements in the conservation experiment. If this analysis is correct, then what we are observing is not a succession of stages of intellectual development, in Piaget's sense, but rather slow progress in bringing heuristic techniques into line with general concepts that have always been present. These are

16. For a discussion of such systems and their limitations, see Minsky and Papert, (1967).

interesting alternatives; either way, the results may bear in important ways on the topics we are considering.

Still more clearly to the point, I think, are the developments in comparative ethology over the past thirty years, and certain current work in experimental and physiological psychology. One can cite many examples: for example, in the latter category, the work of Bower suggesting an innate basis for the perceptual constancies; studies in the Wisconsin primate laboratory on complex innate releasing mechanisms in rhesus monkeys; the work of Hubel, Barlow, and others on highly specific analysing mechanisms in the lower cortical centers of mammals; and a number of comparable studies of lower organisms (for example, the beautiful work of Lettvin and his associates on frog vision). There is now good evidence from such investigations that perception of line, angle, motion, and other complex properties of the physical world is based on innate organization of the neural system.

In some cases at least, these built-in structures will degenerate unless appropriate stimulation takes place at an early stage in life, but although such experience is necessary to permit the innate mechanisms to function, there is no reason to believe that it has more than a marginal effect on determining *how* they function to organize experience. Furthermore, there is nothing to suggest that what has so far been discovered is anywhere near the limit of complexity of innate structures. The basic techniques for exploring the neural mechanisms are only a few years old, and it is impossible to predict what order of specificity and complexity will be demonstrated when they come to be extensively applied. For the present, it seems that most complex organisms have highly specific forms of sensory and perceptual organization that are associated with the *Umwelt* and the manner of life of the organism. There is little reason to doubt that what is true of lower organisms is true of humans as well. Particularly in the case of language, it is natural to expect a close relation between innate properties of the mind and features of linguistic structure; for language, after all, has no existence apart from its mental representation. Whatever properties it has must be those that are given to it by the innate mental processes of the organism that has invented it and that invents it anew with each succeeding generation, along with whatever properties are associated with the conditions of its use. Once again, it seems that language should be, for this reason, a most illuminating probe with which to explore the organization of mental processes.

Turning to comparative ethology, it is interesting to note that one of its earliest motivations was the hope that through the 'investigation of the *a priori*, of the innate working hypotheses present in subhuman organisms,' it would be possible to shed light on the a priori forms of human thought. This formulation of intent is quoted from an early and little-known paper by Lorenz (1941). Lorenz goes on to express views very much like those Peirce had expressed a generation earlier. He maintains:

One familiar with the innate modes of reaction of subhuman organisms can readily hypothesize that the *a priori* is due to hereditary differentiations of the central nervous system which have become characteristic of the species, producing hereditary dispositions to think in certain forms. . . . Most certainly Hume was wrong when he wanted to derive all that is *a priori* from that which the senses supply to experience, just as wrong as Wundt or Helmholtz who simply explain it as an abstraction from preceding experience. Adaptation of the *a priori* to the real world has no more originated from 'experience' than adaptation of the fin of the fish to the properties of water. Just as the form of the fin is given a priori, prior to any individual negotiation of the young fish with the water, and just as it is this form that makes possible this negotiation, so it is also the case with our forms of perception and categories in their relationship to our negotiation with the real external world through experience. In the case of animals, we find limitations specific to the forms of experience possible for them. We believe we can demonstrate the closest functional and probably genetic relationship between these animal *a priori*'s and our human *a priori*. Contrary to Hume, we believe, just as did Kant, that a 'pure' science of innate forms of human thought, independent of all experience, is possible.

Peirce, to my knowledge, is original and unique in stressing the problem of studying the rules that limit the class of possible theories. Of course, his concept of abduction, like Lorenz's biological *a priori*, has a strongly Kantian flavor, and all derive from the rationalist psychology that concerned itself with the forms, the limits, and the principles that provide 'the sinews and connections' for human thought, that underlie 'that infinite amount of knowledge of which we are not always conscious,' of which Leibnitz spoke. It is therefore quite natural that we should link these developments to the revival of philosophical grammar, which grew from the same soil as an attempt, quite fruitful and legitimate, to explore one basic facet of human intelligence.

In recent discussion, models and observations derived from ethology have frequently been cited as providing biological support, or at least analogue, to new approaches to the study of human intelligence. I cite these comments of Lorenz's mainly in order to show that this reference does not distort the outlook of at least some of the founders of this new domain of comparative psychology.

One word of caution is necessary in referring to Lorenz, now that he has been discovered by Ardrey and Alsop and popularized as a prophet of doom. It seems to me that Lorenz' views on human aggression have been extended to near-absurdity by some of his expositors. It is no doubt true that there are innate tendencies in the human psychic constitution that lead to aggressiveness under specific social and cultural conditions. But there is little reason to suppose that these tendencies are so dominant as to leave us forever tottering on the brink of a Hobbesian war of all against all – as, incidentally, Lorenz at least is fully aware, if I read him rightly. Skepticism is certainly in order when a doctrine of man's 'inherent aggressiveness' comes to the surface in a society that glorifies competitiveness, in a civilization that has been distinguished by the brutality of the attack that it has mounted against less fortunate peoples. It is fair to ask to what extent the enthusiasm for this curious view of man's nature is attributable to fact and logic and to what extent it merely reflects the limited extent to which the general cultural level has advanced since the days when Clive and the Portuguese explorers taught the meaning of true savagery to the inferior races that stood in their way.

In any event, I would not want what I am saying to be confused with other, entirely different attempts to revive a theory of human instinct. What seems to me important in ethology is its attempt to explore the innate properties that determine how knowledge is acquired and the character of this knowledge. Returning to this theme, we must consider a further question: How did the human mind come to acquire the innate structure that we are led to attribute to it? Not too surprisingly, Lorenz takes the position that this is simply a matter of natural selection. Peirce offers a rather different speculation, arguing that 'nature fecundates the mind of man with ideas which, when these ideas grow up, will resemble their father, Nature.' Man is 'provided with certain natural beliefs that are true' because 'certain uniformities . . . prevail throughout the universe, and the reasoning mind is [it]self a product of this universe. These same laws are thus, by logical necessity, incorporated in his own being.' Here, it seems clear that Peirce's argument is entirely without force and that it offers little improvement over the preestablished harmony that it was presumably intended to replace. The fact that the mind is a product of natural laws does not imply that it is equipped to understand these laws or to arrive at them by 'abduction'. There would be no difficulty in designing a device (say, programing a computer) that is a product of natural law, but that, given data, will arrive at any arbitrary absurd theory to 'explain' these data.

In fact, the processes by which the human mind achieved its present stage of complexity and its particular form of innate organization are a total mystery, as much so as the analogous questions about the physical or mental organization of any other complex organism. It is perfectly safe to attribute this development to 'natural selection', so long as we realize that there is no substance to this assertion, that it amounts to nothing more than a belief that there is some naturalistic explanation for these phenomena. The problem of accounting for evolutionary development is, in some ways, rather like that of explaining successful abduction. The laws that determine possible successful mutation and the nature of complex organisms are as unknown as the laws that determine the choice of hypotheses.[17] With no knowledge of the laws that determine the organization and structure of complex biological systems, it is just as senseless to ask what the 'probability' is for the human mind to have reached its present

17. It has been argued on statistical grounds – through comparison of the known rate of mutation with the astronomical number of imaginable modifications of chromosomes and their parts – that such laws must exist and must vastly restrict the realizable possibilities. See the papers by Eden, Schützenberger, and Gavadan (Wistar Symposium 1967).

N. Chomsky 359

state as it is to inquire into the 'probability' that a particular physical theory will be devised. And, as we have noted, it is idle to speculate about laws of learning until we have some indication of what kind of knowledge is attainable – in the case of language, some indication of the constraints on the set of potential grammars.

In studying the evolution of mind, we cannot guess to what extent there are physically possible alternatives to, say, transformational generative grammar, for an organism meeting certain other physical conditions characteristic of humans. Conceivably, there are none – or very few – in which case talk about evolution of the language capacity is beside the point. The vacuity of such speculation, however, has no bearing one way or another on those aspects of the problem of mind that can be sensibly pursued. It seems to me that these aspects are, for the moment, the problems illustrated in the case of language by the study of the nature, the use, and the acquisition of linguistic competence.

There is one final issue that deserves a word of comment. I have been using mentalistic terminology quite freely, but entirely without prejudice as to the question of what may be the physical realization of the abstract mechanisms postulated to account for the phenomena of behavior or the acquisition of knowledge. We are not constrained, as was Descartes, to postulate a second substance when we deal with phenomena that are not expressible in terms of matter in motion, in his sense. Nor is there much point in pursuing the question of psycho-physical parallelism, in this connection. It is an interesting question whether the functioning and evolution of human mentality can be accommodated within the framework of physical explanation, as presently conceived, or whether there are new principles, now unknown, that must be invoked, perhaps principles that emerge only at higher levels of organization that can now be submitted to physical investigation. We can, however, be fairly sure that there will be a physical explanation for the phenomena in question, if they can be explained at all, for an uninteresting terminological reason, namely that the concept of 'physical explanation' will no doubt be extended to incorporate whatever is discovered in this domain, exactly as it was extended to accommodate gravitational and electromagnetic force, massless particles, and numerous other entities and processes that would have offended the common sense of earlier generations. But it seems clear that this issue need not delay the study of the topics that are now open to investigation, and it seems futile to speculate about matters so remote from present understanding.

I have tried to suggest that the study of language may very well, as was traditionally supposed, provide a remarkably favorable perspective for the study of human mental processes. The creative aspect of language use, when investigated with care and respect for the facts, shows that current notions of habit and generalization, as determinants of behavior or knowledge, are quite inadequate. The abstractness of linguistic structure reinforces this conclusion, and it suggests further that in both perception and learning the mind plays an active role in determining the character of the acquired knowledge. The empirical study of linguistic universals has led to the formulation of highly restrictive and, I believe, quite plausible hypotheses concerning the possible variety of human languages, hypotheses that contribute to the attempt to develop a theory of acquisition of knowledge that gives due place to intrinsic mental activity. It seems to me, then, that the study of language should occupy a central place in general psychology.

Surely the classical questions of language and mind receive no final solution, or even the hint of a final solution, from the work that is being actively pursued today. Nevertheless, these problems can be formulated in new ways and seen in a new light. For the first time in many years, it seems to me, there is some real opportunity for substantial progress in the study of the contribution of the mind to perception and the innate basis for acquisition of knowledge. Still, in many respects, we have not made the first approach to a real answer to the classical problems. For example, the central problems relating to the creative aspect of language use remain as inaccessible as they have always been. And the study of universal semantics, surely crucial to the full investigation of language structure, has barely advanced since the medieval period. Many other critical areas might be mentioned where progress has been slow or nonexistent. Real progress has been made in the study of the mechanisms of language, the formal principles that make possible the creative aspect of language use and that determine the phonetic form and semantic content of utterances. Our understanding of these mechanisms, though only fragmentary, does seem to me to have real implications for the study of human psychology. By pursuing the kinds of research that now seem feasible and by focusing attention on certain problems that are now accessible to study, we may be able to spell out in some detail the elaborate and abstract computations that determine, in part, the nature of percepts and the character of the knowledge that we can acquire – the highly specific ways of interpreting phenomena that are, in large measure, beyond our consciousness and control and that may be unique to man.

References

CHOMSKY, N. (1970), 'Linguistics and philosophy', in S. Hook (ed.), *Philosophy and Language*.

CHOMSKY, N. (in press), 'Phonology and reading', in H. Levin (ed.), *Basic Studies on Reading*.

CHOMSKY, N. (1963), 'Formal properties of grammars', in R. D. Luce, R. Bush and E. Galanter (eds.), *Handbook of Mathematical Psychology*, Wiley.

CHOMSKY, N. (1966), *Cartesian Linguistics*, Harper & Row.

CHOMSKY, N., and HALLE, M. (1968), *The Sound Pattern of English*, Harper & Row.

COHEN, R. S., and WARTOFSKY, M. W. (eds.) (1968), *Boston Studies in the Philosophy of Science*, vol. 3, Humanities, New York.

FERSTER, C. B. (1964), 'Arithmetic behavior in chimpanzees', *Scientific American*, May, pp. 98–106.

FRASER, A. C. (ed.) (1959), *Locke's Essay Concerning Human Understanding*, Dover.

GOODMAN, N. (1967), 'The epistemological argument', *Synthèse*, vol. 17, no. 1, pp. 2–28.

GINSBURG, S. (1966), *The Mathematical Theory of Context – Free Languages*, McGraw-Hill.

HALDANE, E. S., and ROSS, G. R. T. (eds.) (1955), *Descartes, Philosophical Works*, Dover.

JOOS, M. (1966), *Readings in Linguistics*, (4th edn), University of Chicago Press.

LASHLEY, K. S. (1951), 'The problem of serial order in behavior', in L. A. Jeffress (ed.), *Cerebral Mechanisms in Behavior*, pp. 112–36, Wiley.

LENNEBERG, E. H. (1967), *Biological Foundations of Language*, Wiley.

LÉVI-STRAUSS, C. (1963), *Structural Anthropology*, Basic Books.

LÉVI-STRAUSS, C. (1967), *The Savage Mind*, University of Chicago Press.

LORENZ, K. (1941), 'Kants Lehre vom aprioriechen in Lighte generwartiger Biologie', *Blätter fur Deutsche Philosophie*, vol. 15, pp. 94–125.

MEHLER, J., and BEVER, T. G. (1967), 'Cognitive capacities of young children', *Science*, vol. 158, no. 3797.

MINSKY, M., and PAPERT, S. (1967), *Perceptions and Pattern Recognition*, Artificial Intelligence Memo, no. 140, MAC-M-358, Project MAC, Cambridge, Massachusetts.

MORGENBESSER, S., SUPPES, P., and WHITE, M. (in press), *Essays in Honor of Ernest Nagel*, St Martin's.

NELSON, R. J. (1968), *Introduction to Automata*, Wiley.

PEIRCE, C. S. (1957), 'The logic of abduction', in V. Thomas (ed.), *Peirce's Essays in the Philosophy of Science*, Liberal Arts Press.

POPPER, K. (n.d.), 'Clouds and clocks', Arthur Comton Lecture.

PUTNAM, H. (1967), 'The innateness hypothesis and explanatory models in linguistics', *Synthese*, vol. 17, no. 1, pp. 2–28.

SALZINGER, K. (1967), 'The problem of response class in verbal behavior', in K. Salzinger and S. Salzinger (eds.), *Research in Verbal Behavior and Some Neurophysiological Implications*, Academic Press.

SKINNER, B. F. (1957), *Verbal Behaviour*, Appelton-Century-Crofts.

THORPE, W. H. (1967), 'Animal vocalization and communication', in F. L. Darley (ed.), *Brain Mechanisms Underlying Speech and Language*, Grune and Stratton.

WIEST, W. M. (1967), 'Recent criticisms of behaviorism and learning', *Psychol. Bull.*, vol. 67, no. 3, pp. 214–25.

WISTAR SYMPOSIUM (1967), papers in *Mathematical Challenges to the Neo-Darwinian Interpretation of Evolution*, monograph no. 5, June.

19 H. Sinclair-de-Zwart

A Possible Theory of Language Acquisition within the General Framework of Piaget's Developmental Theory

Excerpt from H. Sinclair-de-Zwart, 'A possible theory of language acquisition within the general framework of Piaget's developmental theory', in D. Elkind and J. Flavell (eds.) *Studies in Cognitive Development*, 1969, Oxford University Press, pp. 326–36.

No theory of language acquisition has been explicitly proposed by Piaget. We can, however, speculate on the general form that such a theory might take. The problem is complex for several reasons.

In the first place, language, in Piaget's terms (Piaget and Inhelder 1966, p. 69) is 'a ready-made system that is elaborated by society and that contains, for persons that learn it before they contribute to its enrichment, a wealth of cognitive instruments (relations, classifications, and so on) at the service of thought.' The knowing person expresses his 'knowledge' in this code. As such, language takes the place of symbolization in the relationship knower-symbolization-known. But this code is itself an object of knowing; as such it takes the place of the 'known' in the knower-known relationship. Piaget stresses mainly the first aspect; most psycholinguists pay attention only to the second.

A second difficulty lies in the fact that language, though it is a system of signs (in terms of the distinction between signals on the one hand and symbols and signs on the other) that can be used for rational discourse and communication, it need not only be used as such. In fact, linguistic forms can be used as signals 'to be reacted to' rather than 'to be understood': trivial examples are animal training and verbal conditioning; they can be used as symbols, as in rituals and certain kinds of literature.

Consequently, a theory of the acquisition of language would have to be based on a theory of the developmental changes in the knower-symbolization-known relationship: in other words, on genetic epistemology. On the other hand, it would also have to be based on a theory of the formal properties of language, in other words, on linguistic theory. To understand *how* something is acquired, we first have to know *what* is acquired.

Modern linguistics (since de Saussure) has been concerned with the establishment of systems of elements and procedures for making inventories of elements (segmentation, substitution, association, classification, and so on). For this reason, Chomsky (1964) calls this type of theory taxonomic linguistics.

Taxonomic linguistics was combined with associationist learning theory to produce theories of language-acquisition that left honest observers of young children mystified and that failed completely to account for the fundamental fact of language: the ability to produce and to understand an indefinite number of sentences that have not been previously heard. The comparative ease and rapidity with which young children learn their mother-tongue remained completely mysterious as long as both the learning organism and the verbal behavior to be learned were thought to be as amorphous in structure as associationist theory supposed them to be. Thanks to Chomsky's nontaxonomic theory of language, which aims at a system of rules rather than at a system of elements, our insight into the structural properties of natural languages has so far deepened that it becomes possible to begin to envisage a theory of language acquisition which would be in accordance with the linguistic facts, with the known facts about children's verbal behavior and with the theory of cognitive development in general. Chomsky's theories are most often referred to as 'transformational linguistics' or 'generative grammar', highlighting two important aspects of his conception of language.

While no attempt is made to summarize Chomsky's far-reaching theory, it seems necessary to underline certain points that have often led to confusion.

A generative grammar is an explicit description of the internalized rules of a language as they must have been mastered by an idealized speaker-hearer. It is adequate insofar as it corresponds to the intuition of the native speaker. However, it is *not* a model of performance; first, the speaker-hearer may not be aware of (or even capable of becoming aware of) the grammatical rules; and secondly, and more profoundly, the grammar assigns a structural description to a sentence, but the derivation of this sentence as made explicit by the grammar does not tell us how a speaker actually (and psychologically) proceeds to produce the utterance.

A generative grammar is said to be descriptively adequate if it meets the criterion of corresponding to the competence of the native speaker. It is said to attain explanatory adequacy if it is linked to a theory of language that deals with the form of human language as such (and not only of the particular language). In this case it contains an account of linguistic universals. It is the universal grammar that deals with the creative aspect of language. General linguistic theory would ultimately provide a theory of the fundamental form of possible human languages and of the strategies necessary for selecting a particular grammar. In this sense, general linguistics belongs to epistemology; in this sense, also, it would give an explanatory model of language acquisition.

A generative grammar contains a system of rules that have three components – syntactical, phonological and semantic. The syntactical rules account for the creative aspect of language. The phonological and semantic components are purely interpretive. The syntactical component consists of a base, which generates deep structures according to certain rules. The basic strings of elements form a highly restricted set; within this set there is a subset of 'kernel' sentences. These kernel sentences (exemplified by simple affirmative-active sentences) have played an important role in psycholinguistic experimentation, though often in a confused way. The rules of the base are a very special class of those that are studied in recursive function theory, and may be mostly universal, and thus not part of particular grammars. In addition to the base, the syntactical component contains a transformational subcomponent. These transformational rules are concerned with generating a sentence – with its surface structure – from the base. Elementary transformational rules are drawn from a base set of substitutions, deletions, and adjunctions.

This, necessarily superficial, account of transformational linguistics, points to its deep concern with the creative aspect and epistemology of language. Because of this epistemological position, a psycholinguist who accepts Chomsky's theories of generative grammars for particular languages, cannot at the same time simply reject his, be it tentative, model of language acquisition.

His model is still in the nature of a hypothesis; and though many of his fundamental discoveries about language seem to stem from the fact that he considers the problem from the viewpoint of a language acquisition device, not all assumed properties of the device would appear to be necessary to the theory as a whole. The following is a brief discussion of Chomsky's (and his followers') hypotheses about the device and of the points on which a Piagetian psychologist would raise objections.

Katz (1966; following Chomsky, 1957, 1965) who uses the model of a language acquisition device that has as its output the internalized linguistic rules and as its input speech (and, he adds, other relevant data from senses), shows conclusively that such an input is far too impoverished to produce the rules if the device were to be constructed according to empiricist, associationist hypotheses. Up to this point, a Piagetian psychologist cannot but agree. Subsequently, however, Katz develops the rationalist hypothesis that 'the language acquisition device contains as innate structure each of the principles stated within the theory of language.' Once again, we encounter the epistemological dilemma of structuralism without development or geneticism without structure. But is the choice really restricted to these two extremes? And is it necessary, in order to enrich the internal structure of the learning organism, to postulate innate linguistic structures?

Chomsky's own treatment of the rationalist hypothesis seems at the same time more cautious, more supple and more far-reaching than that given by Katz. Chomsky poses the problem as follows:

A theory of linguistic structure that aims for explanatory adequacy incorporates an account of linguistic universals, and it attributes tacit knowledge of these universals to the child. It proposes, then, that the child approaches the data with the presumption that they are drawn from a language of a certain well-defined type, his problem being to determine which of the (humanly) possible languages is that of the community in which he is placed. Language learning would be impossible unless this were the case. The important question is: What are the initial assumptions concerning the nature of the language that the child brings to language learning, and how detailed and specific is the innate schema (the general definition of 'grammar') that gradually becomes more explicit and differentiated as the child learns the language?

For the present we cannot come at all close to making a hypothesis about innate schemata that is rich, detailed and specific enough to account for the fact of language acquisition (1965, p. 27).

And

A consideration of the character of the grammar that is acquired, the degenerate quality and narrowly limited extent of the available data, the striking uniformity of the resulting grammars, and their independence of intelligence, motivation and emotional state, over wide ranges of variation, leave little hope that much of the structure of language can be learned by an organism initially uninformed as to its general character. . . . The real problem is that of developing a hypothesis about initial structure that is sufficiently rich to account for acquisition of language, yet not so rich as to be inconsistent with the known diversity of language (1965, p. 58).

From the point of view of developmental psychology, three criticisms can be made:

1. This view of language acquisition fails to take into account the knower-symbolization-known relationship indicated above; it only considers language as the object of knowledge in the knower-known relationship.

2. It assumes tacitly that from the moment the child starts to understand language and to talk, he somehow considers language as a system of signs (as opposed to signals and symbols).

3. No account at all is taken of the structural richness of the learning organism as demonstrated by the acquisitions during the preverbal sensorimotor period.

In other words, there would be agreement on the nature of the output, i.e. the internalized grammar, and also on the need for postulating a structural richness within the acquisition device. But there would be disagreement on the degree of innateness of the structure of the device and on the nature of the input, which would be much richer and more structured than merely speech-samples of a limited and degenerate quality plus (unspecified) 'other data from senses'.

Much of the need for postulating specific, innate linguistic structures seems to vanish if one considers language acquisition within the total cognitive development and, in particular, within the frame of the symbolic function. This manner of considering language acquisition would moreover be compatible with two facts that seem to be difficult to explain within the theory of innate structures: firstly the time lag between the first manifestations of practical intelligence during the sensorimotor period and the first verbal productions and secondly the particular character of these first verbal productions.

Concomitant with the development of the symbolic function, the child changes from an organism that reacts to objects and events as signals to a being that 'knows' objects and events and expresses this 'knowledge' by means of signifiers. His knowing, however, is always 'acting upon', and the first use of signifiers is only possible in function of the internal richness of coordinated action-schemes. His first verbal productions recognizable as 'words' are far from being signs in the sense of belonging to a fully structured system. They resemble far more symbols, which can be loosely associated but are essentially isolated representations of schemes. They share the characteristic of symbols in that they are inextricably entwined in the complex of objects, actions the subject can perform on objects, and symbolic representation of the objects. In Piaget's terms (1946, p. 235), the first words 'retain the imitative character of the symbol, either as onomatopoaeia (imitation of the object) or as imitation of words used in adult language, but extracted from this language and imitated in isolation. Especially, they retain the disconcerting mobility of symbols, in contrast to the fixity of signs.' And (1946, p. 236) 'The first language consists almost solely in orders and expression of desire. Denomination is not the simple attribution of a name, but the expression of a possible action.' Examples abound in all recordings of child language; here are two of Piaget's examples:

J. around 1;6 knows better and better how to take advantage of adults to get what she wants; her grandfather is especially docile in this respect. The term *panana* ('grand-père') is used not only to indicate her grandfather, but also to express, even in his absence, her desires; she points to what she wishes to have and adds *panana*. She even says *panana* to express a wish to be amused when she is bored (1946, p. 213).

T. at 1;5 uses the term *a plus* ('il n'y en a plus', or something similar, but, of course, *a plus* should not be taken to represent two separate words) to indicate a departure, then to indicate the throwing of an object onto the floor, then it is applied to an object that falls over (without disappearing) for instance when he is playing with building blocks. A little later *a plus* means 'remoteness' (anything out of reach), and the game of handing over an object for somebody to throw it back to him. Finally, at 1;7 *a plus* takes on the meaning of 'to start over again' (1946, p. 232).

The transition from what Piaget calls *jugements d'action* to *jugements de constatation* takes place soon after: 'words' then no longer simply translate sensorimotor action, but describe past actions and events (though usually in the immediate past). At this point begins the slow transition from symbols to real signs, which furnish a re-representation; and at this point the first concatenations of words begin to appear.

Both these facts, the relatively late start of the first verbal productions, and their particular character, seem difficult to reconcile with the theory of innate linguistic structures. The time-lag might conceivably be explained by an allusion to imprinting and critical periods: Katz (1966, p. 276), speaking about the fact that the effortless way in which children appear to acquire a language terminates at about puberty, says, 'thus this ability of the child's is much like the abilities of various animals described as imprinting with respect to the existence of a "critical" period'. The peculiar character of the first productions, coupled with the fact that these do not yet show real concatenations of words, might lead a staunch adherent of the theory of innate structures to refuse these verbal schemes the status of linguistic productions. This seems, however, completely unjustified psychologically; whatever their nature, they most certainly prepare the way for further verbal acquisition, and moreover they already have some of the traits of signs: they show a certain detachment from the subject's own actions and a desire to communicate by way of sound-complexes which the other person also uses.

It seems more in accordance with the facts, though less simple, to suppose that the coordination of sensorimotor schemes, which are actively built up during the first eighteen months of life, starting from hereditary reflexes, is a necessary condition for language acquisition to become possible, which, like all manifestations of the symbolic function, takes place within a context of imitation. It is true that Chomsky remarks (1965, p. 33), 'It would not be at all surprising to find that normal language learning requires use of language in real-life situations, in some way.' However, according to him, this would not affect the *manner* in which the acquisition of syntax proceeds. In our view, however, the way in which sensorimotor schemes, coordinated into practical groups, become transformed into operations would determine the manner in which the linguistic structures are acquired. Though it is not possible to make hypotheses about this mechanism detailed enough to account for language acquisition, this approach to the problem seems nearer to the psychological truth. The Genevan research on the parallelism of language-acquisition and operational development of which a few examples have been given, indicates that this hypothesis is at least not in contradiction with the admittedly very few and limited results obtained so far.

One other experiment, which is still far from being completed, also gives some results that seem to run counter to the innate-structure hypothesis. Briefly, the technique is as follows. We give the child a collection of toys, dolls, cars, animals, sponges, sticks, cups, and so on, and we ask him 'to act' with these objects a sentence we pronounce, after an introductory period during which the child gives names to the dolls, tells us something about the toys, and such. The sentences used are simple active and passive affirmative ones. We use different kinds of verbs, and 'reversible' as well as 'irreversible' sentences (reversible: 'Peter washes John' or 'the red marble pushes the blue marble'; irreversible: Peter washes his car'). Inversely, we perform an act with some of the toys and we ask the children to tell us what happened. We also try to elicit passive sentences by asking the child to start his sentence with the noun indicating the object of the action performed (We let Peter wash his car and we ask 'Now tell us what happened; but I would like you to start this way: the car . . .'). Finally we perform the action and at the same time we pronounce the passive sentence; then we ask whether what we said was correct, and we ask the child to repeat it.

To mention only one of the types of behavior that appear in this experiment, and which we are still far from being able to interpret conclusively, at about four and a half years old several subjects decode a passive sentence into a reciprocal act: 'Peter is washed by Mary' is acted so that Peter and Mary both take a sponge and wash each other; 'the red marble is pushed by the blue marble' is acted by taking a marble in each hand and making them hit each other, whereas the corresponding active sentence is acted by taking the blue marble in one hand, leaving the red marble on the table and hitting the latter with the blue one. In the items where we try to elicit passive sentences, the children also produce sentences in this way: '*Pierre et Marie se lavent*', '*La bille rouge et la bille bleu roulent ensemble*'. We also find passive sentences decoded according to active word-order: 'Peter is washed by Mary' is acted as 'Peter washes Mary'. In these items some children also say that what we ask them is impossible: 'you can't start with Peter, it's Mary who washes.' It is the reciprocities that intrigue us most; and it seems that they cannot be accounted for by a triggering of innate structures.

Epistemologically, the difference between Piaget and Chomsky seems important, but the two are certainly much nearer to each other than either is to a defender of the empiricist point of view. Moreover, their difference may be less marked than it appears. For instance, Chomsky (1965, p. 202) warns us that what he is describing as the process of acquisition is an idealization in which only the moment of the acquisition of correct grammar is considered. He adds:

It might very well be true that a series of successively more detailed and highly structured schemata (corresponding to maturational stages, but perhaps in part themselves determined in form by earlier steps of language acquisition) are applied to the data at successive stages of language acquisition.

This seems to indicate that his position is much less extreme than is often thought. However, without knowing more precisely what is meant by 'schemata' and 'maturational stages' it is difficult to interpret remarks such as these.

It is clear that we are in great need of experimental results. As far as experiments go, approaches starting from either Piaget's or Chomsky's theories would have several points in common. They would share the emphasis put on the creative aspect of language.

They would share also the wish to make a clear distinction between performance and competence. Where Chomsky (1964, p. 39) only seems to stress the fact that performance is bound to appear far poorer than an investigation (if this were possible) of real competence would show the latter to be, the Piagetian psycholinguist would add that there is also the opposite danger, namely, that performance can easily induce an overrating of competence. He would assume that the verbal productions of the child may contain prestructures and pseudostructures, just as there are preconcepts and pseudoconservations; the prestructures would be isolated instances of certain syntactic structures, strongly content-bound and context-bound; pseudostructures would be strongly imitation-bound. The prestructures are both important and understandable within a developmental, interactionist theory; they would be hard to explain within the rationalist theory. The main difference between the two approaches corresponds to the fundamental epistemological difference that has been stressed all along in this paper: the Piagetian psycholinguist would always try to study language as part of the symbolic function, within the frame of the total cognitive activity of child rather than as an autonomous 'object of knowing'.

References

CHOMSKY, N. (1957), *Syntactic Structures*, Mouton, The Hague.

CHOMSKY, N. (1964), *Current Issues in Linguistic Theory*, Mouton, The Hague.

CHOMSKY, N. (1965), *Aspects of the Theory of Syntax*, Cambridge, Mass: MIT Press.

KATZ, J. J. (1966), *The Philosophy of Language*, Harper & Row.

PIAGET, J. (1946), 'La Formation du Symbole chez L'Enfant', Delachaux et Niestlé (translated as *Play, Dreams and Initiation in Childhood*, Norton, 1951).

PIAGET, J. (1946), 'La Formation du Symbole chez L'Enfant', Delachaux et Niestlé (translated as *Play, Dreams and Imitation in Childhood*, Norton, 1951).

PIAGET, J., and INHELDER, B. (1966), *La Psychologie de L'Enfant*, Presses Univer, Paris ('Que sais-je?' series).

Further Reading

General

R. Brown, *Words and Things*, Free Press (1958).

J. B. Carroll (ed.), *Language, Thought, and Reality: Selected Writings of Benjamin L. Whorf*, M I T Press (1956).

J. P. De Cecco (ed.), *The Psychology of Language, Thought, and Instruction*, Holt, Rinehart & Winston (1967).

J. R. Hayes (ed.), *Cognition and the Development of Language*, Wiley (1970).

E. Lenneberg, *Biological Foundations of Language*, Wiley (1967).

G. Miller, and D. McNeill, 'Psycholinguistics', in G. Lindzey and E. Aronson (eds.), *The Handbook of Social Psychology*, vol. 3, (2nd edn), Addison Wesley (1969).

J. Piaget, *The Language and Thought of the Child*, Harcourt, Brace & World (1926).

S. Saporta (ed.), *Psycholinguistics: A Book of Readings*, Holt, Rinehart & Winston (1961).

L. S. Vygotsky, *Thought and Language*, M I T Press (1962).

Part One

H. Furth, *Thought without Language*, MacMillan Co. (1965).

D. Premack, 'The Education of Sarah', *New Society*, pp. 268–70, 29 October (1970).

Part Two

R. Brown, and U. Bellugi, 'Three processes in the child's acquisition of syntax', in E. Lenneberg, (ed.), *New Directions in the Study of Language*, M I T Press (1964).

S. Ervin, 'Imitation and structural change in children's language', in E. Lenneberg (ed.), *New Directions in the Study of Language*, M I T Press (1964).

A. R. Luria, 'The directive function of speech in development and dissolution', *Word*, vol. 15, no. 3, pp. 341–352 (1959).

D. McNeill, 'Developmental psycholinguistics', in F. Smith and G. A. Miller (eds.), *The Genesis of Language*, MIT Press (1966).

Part Three

M. Black, 'Linguistic relativity and the views of Benjamin Lee Whorf', *Philosophical Review*, vol. 68 (1959).

H. Hoijer, 'Cultural implications of some Navaho linguistic categories', *Language*, vol. 27 (1951).

H. Hoijer, 'Language in culture', *American Anthropologist*, Memoir no. 79, pp.1–279 (1954).

E. Lenneberg, and J. M. Roberts, 'The language of experience: a study in methodology', *International Journal of American Linguistics*, Memoir no. 13 (and in S. Saporta, (ed.) (1961), *Psycholinguistics*, Holt, Rinehart & Winston) (1956).

E. Lenneberg, 'The relation of language to the formation of concepts', *Synthese*, vol. 14, pp. 103–9 (1962).

J. Piaget, *Play, Dreams and Imitation in Childhood*, Norton & Co. (1962).

J. Piaget, 'Language and intellectual operations', in H. Furth, (ed.), *Piaget and Knowledge*, Prentice-Hall (1969).

W. V. O. Quine, *Word and Object*, ch. 2, MIT Press (1960).

Part Four

N. H. Frijda, and J. P. Van de Geer, 'Coding and recognition; experiments with facial expressions', *Acta Psychologica*, vol. 18 (1961).

J. J. Goodnow, 'Problems in research on culture and thought', in D. Elkind, and J. H. Flavell (eds.), *Studies in Cognitive Development*, Oxford University Press (1969).

H. Maclay, 'An experimental study of language and non-linguistic behaviour', *SW. J. Anthrop.*, vol. 14, pp. 220–29 (1958).

Part Five

N. Chomsky, *Aspects of a Theory of Syntax*, MIT Press (1965).

N. Chomsky, 'Recent contributions to the theory of innate ideas', *Synthèse*, vol. 17, no. 1, pp. 2–11 (1967).

N. Goodman, 'The epistemological argument', *Synthèse*, vol. 17, no. 1, pp. 23–28 (1967).

H. Putnam, 'The "Innateness Hypothesis" and explanatory models in linguistics', *Synthèse*, vol. 17, no. 1, pp. 12–22 (1967).

Acknowledgements

Permission to reproduce the Readings in this volume is acknowledged to the following sources:

1 R. A. Gardner and *Science*
3 H. G. Furth and the American Psychological Association
4 Society for Research in Child Development
5 M. Donaldson, R. Wales and John Wiley & Sons, Inc.
6 Appleton–Century–Crofts
7 University of Utah Press
8 Harcourt, Brace & World, Inc.
9 E. H. Lenneberg and the Linguistic Society of America
10 Random House, Inc. and University of London Press
11 MIT Press
12 John Wiley & Sons, Inc.
13 De Lee Lantz and the American Psychological Society
14 S. Ervin-Trip and the American Anthropological Association
15 Oxford University Press
16 MIT Press
17 John Wiley & Sons Inc.
18 Harcourt, Brace & World, Inc.
19 Oxford University Press

Author Index

Subject Index

Concept — *continued*
  formation
    and abstraction, 300–302,
      312–14, 317
    associative complexes, 285–7,
      294, 300, 314
    in children, 279 ff.
    in chimpanzee, 37–8
    collections, 287–8, 314
    complexive grouping, 232,
      285–300
    congeries or 'heaps', 284
    in deaf and hearing children,
      51–3, 61, 67, 272
    diffuse complexes, 289–90
    edge-matching and chain
      complexes, 11, 288–9, 294, 314
    key-rings, 315–6
    method of abstraction, 277–8
    method of verbal definition,
      277, 303
    partial identity, 296
    pseudo-concept, 290–3
    thematic groupings, 315
    words as means to concept
      formation, 11, 12, 13, 56–7,
      185, 235, 278, 280–81, 283,
      292, 302, 304
  group and contrast
    simultaneously, 218, 300
Concrete attitude in the deaf,
  44–6; *see also* Deafness
Concrete operational period *see*
  Logical operations *and*
  Thinking
Conservation
  and the development of
    language, 273–6
  and equivalence, 85; *see also*
    Equivalence
  and perceptual analysis, 232
Context
  and comparative adjectives, 99

  see also Relational terms
  functional appropriateness and
    grammaticality, 106, 187–8
  and sociological determinants of
    communication, 225, 231, 232
  and word 'sense', 12, 205–6

Deafness
  and communication accuracy,
    58, 59, 61, 64, 65, 67–74
    see also Communication
    accuracy
  and concept formation *see*
    Concept formation, in deaf
    and hearing children
  conceptual abilities without
    language, 7, 11, 15, 50–51,
    272, 299
  conceptual classification in
    and concrete and abstract
      principles, 46–8
    of objects, 43–7
    and perceptual dominance, 46–8
  and language experience, 48, 50
  and logical operations, 175, 271
    see also Logical operations
Deep structure
  and negation, 109
    see also Negation
  semantically derived, 106
  and surface structure, 330, 335,
    366
  and transformations, 330, 335
    see also Generative grammar *and*
    Innate ideas
Determining tendency in concept
  formation, 279
Distinctive features
  of phonological systems, 333–4
  of syntactic systems, 329 ff.
    see also Generative grammar
    and Syntactic structure
    and Innate ideas

as a generative system, 329 ff.,
365–7
see also Generative grammar
and Innate ideas
and semantics in development,
111–19
see also Word meaning

Thematic Apperception Test, 257
Thinking
in concrete operational period,
11, 170, 173–6
in formal operational period,
170, 174
magical thought in Hopi, 138–41
primacy over language, 8, 9, 173,
176, 276, 341–2
see also Language, primacy
over thought
and representation, 171, 268–70
see also Representation
in sensorimotor period, 7, 10,
170–73, 175, 176, 180, 267,
270, 368
and symbolic function *see*
Symbol, development of
symbolic function
and words *see* Word meaning *and*
Concept formation
Topical emphasis *see* Context,
functional, appropriateness
and grammaticality
Egocentric speech *and*
Inner speech
Transformations
in grammar *see* Deep structure
in logic *see* Logical operations
Translatability
and the reality of psychological
differences, 9, 10, 127, 159–62
see also Language, linguistic

differences and psychological
reality
in sign languages, 21
see also Sign language and
understanding the cultural and
metaphoric context, 150–51,
155, 161
see also Context, and
sociological determinants of
communication
Trobriand language, 150 ff.

Universals *see* Innate ideas

Verbal thought *see* Inner speech
Vicki, 19, 24, 28
Vocalization in chimpanzee, 19
see also Sign language

Washoe, 17, 18, 21 ff.
see also Sign language
Weigl Sorting Test, 44, 48
see also Concept, conceptual
classification tests
Wolof, Senegal, 217 ff.
Word meaning
and associationism, 181–3
and complexive thinking, 297–8
see also Concept formation
contrasted with verbal code, 163
development of, 11, 181–5
and Gestalt psychology, 184–5
public meaning contrasted with
'sense', 12, 205–8
role of word meanings in thought
see Concept formation
Writing and contextual constraint,
225
see also Inner speech, and
written speech
Würzburg school, 183, 185, 212